The Celestial Ship of the North

THE CELESTIAL SHIP OF THE NORTH

WITH SYMBOLICAL ILLUSTRATIONS AND A GLOSSARY

E. Valentia Straiton

ISBN 1-56459-265-0

I GRATEFULLY DEDICATE MY BOOK

to my friend S. E. D., who has ever been ready to enrich my resources with the treasures of her priceless wisdom and has inspired me to rise above the bondage of materialism into that paradise of promise, the happy fields of Aah-en-Ru. My great desire is that all who read this book may be similarly inspired to look above and to love the Great Cosmic Mother and her children, the Luminaries, the stately Planets and the brilliant Stars.

THE CELESTIAL SHIP OF THE NORTH

FOREWORD

Age after age the Great Architect of the Universe has sent his messengers in many lands to make plain to man that the laws under which life spiritual and temporal evolves have been the same from the foundation of the world and are but the reactions of the planet earth to the stimuli of the moon, stars, suns and super-suns of the heavens. And amongst these the Mighty Ruler, "Ship of the North," was ever pre-eminent in its primal energising.

The relation between the heavens and earth has been the same fundamentally in all ages. Out of knowledge of this ancient bond has been born the only true religion or "binding back" to causation.

Heavenly forces play upon earth and visibly impress their operative laws. The sun governs earth's motion. The moon sways earth's tides. The pole-star exerts a law-giving, orbit-directing influence upon earth's polar axis. And the signs of the zodiac through which the Sun takes his royal course year after year and in one of which earth dwells every age, being at present in Pisces and proceeding thence into Aquarius, were called the "living creatures" because of their lively magisterial modification of all forces playing through the sun upon earth. Of old other celestial governors of earth were known and their forces differentiated and reverenced.

Reverence in its highest essence is an eternal and non-personal attribute of the soul and withers slowly but fatally in the face of the reiterated assertion of a personal exegetic dogma divorced from Nature's laws. To continue in spiritual growth man must worship his Maker alone, that First Cause of which all other causes are but relegations or emanations.

Astrology and astronomy, esoteric and exoteric knowledge of the heavenly bodies or entities, have lain at the generating heart of every great religion that has waxed and waned upon earth in accordance with cyclic celestial law.

Out of the past the author has brought path-finding clues to this First Cause which reveals Itself.

These pages are a contribution to that painstaking, scientific, selfless research which shall in the coming years identify behind the allegory, symbology and ritual of many faiths the same everlasting truth, which perceived will unite all races and creeds in reverence of creature for Creator, the one eternal religion or "binding back" to Causation.

S. E. D.

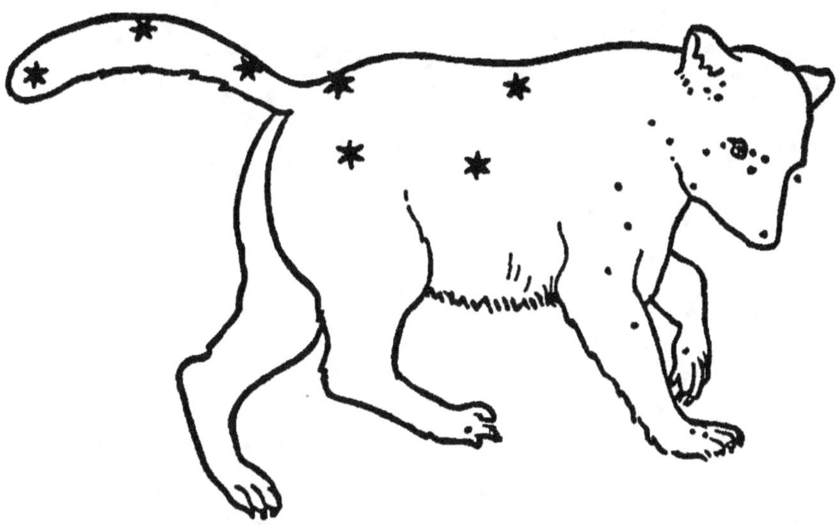

"Every one of these Stars that are in Heaven, do not make the like, or an equal course; who is it that hath prescribed unto every one, the manner and the greatness of their course?

"This Bear that turns round about its own self; and carries the whole World with her, who possessed and made such an Instrument.

"Who hath set the Bounds of the Sea? Who hath established the Earth? For there is somebody, O Tat, that is the Maker and Lord of these things.

"For it is impossible, O Son, that either place, or number, or measure, should be observed without a Maker.

"For no order can be made by disorder or disproportion."

Hermes Trismegistus.

CONTENTS

INTRODUCTION
Book One

The Dawn of Divine Conception

Page

ILLUSTRATIONS
Book One

BOOK ONE
Dawn of Divine Conception

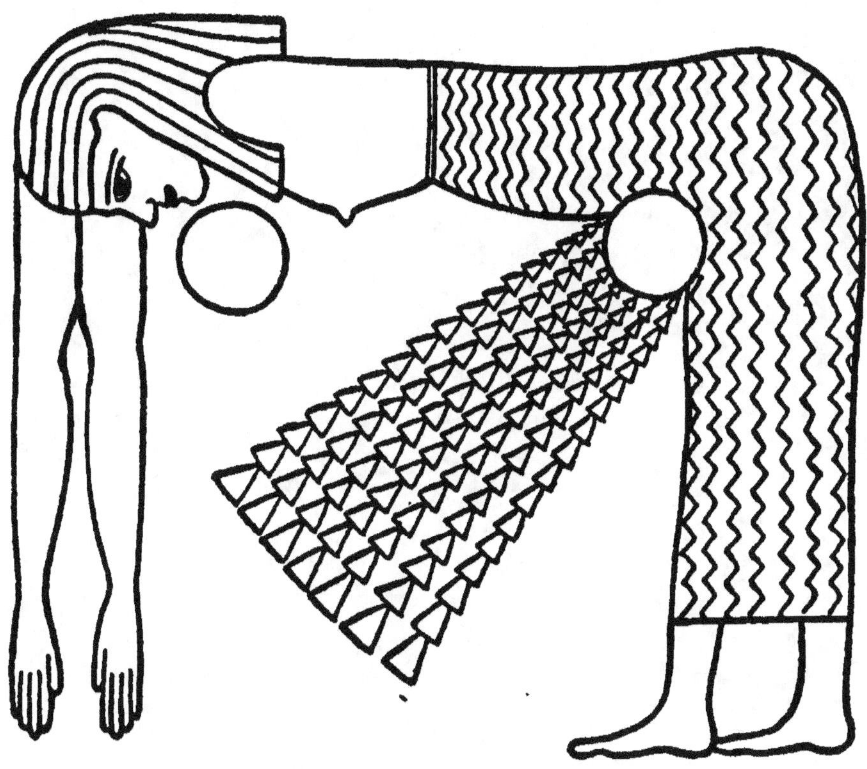

THE VIRGIN MOTHER

"Depicted on the walls of the secret and sealed Shrine in the Temple of Denderah is this picture of Hathor, known to the Egyptians as the Virgin Mother or the Mother of God, to whom the Temple was dedicated. Her name Hat-hor implying that she was the "Habitation of the Holy Light" or the incarnate Horus, shewn by the rays of divine splendor streaming from her.

"The secret and sealed Shrine was entered once a year by the high-priest, on the night of midsummer and an image of the Holy Mother was conveyed by a procession of priests up a secret stairway to the roof where communion with her divine father Ra was held, while within the Temple a festival to Hathor was celebrated." From "The Book of the Master," by Marsham Adams.

CHAPTER I

THE MOTHER MYSTERY

The most ancient peoples believed that God gave Revelation, and was the One Supreme, the Eternal, the Infinite, pervading all places and exalted in a super-celestial place of Divine Light, that He was spiritual in essence, self-existent, uncreated, yet was made manifest to all as the most tender love and truth, which they received in their lives on earth with happiness and joy. Born of this Supreme One was She of celestial loveliness and purity, Divine in nature, whom they called the Spirit of God, the Dove[1], the Virgin Spirit, the Logos which is the Word of God, the earliest first Mother, whose name came to represent the essence of all that was beautiful and pure, and of most divine love. She was, in the Talmud, "The Spirit of God that hovered over the water like a dove, which spreads her wings over her young." She was the Shekinah, a mystic word often variously typified as a Lotus, a Rose, an Egg, and by symbols that were oval, as a Cup, a Boat or a Moon.

"God when He meditates on Divine Beauty, is said to be one; but when He creates to be Bi-Une. The Syrians symbolized this communion by their image of Ad-Ad, the Sun-Father, shooting down his splendid rays toward the Earth, while she sent forth rays of splendor upward that met and mingled with His beam."[2]

She was also the Argha, a most ancient form of the

---

[1]Wine has a mystical relation to the Dove, which is the Holy Spirit, in a passive sense, the Creator being the active power. Wine and the Holy Spirit are of one root in primitive language. "Truth, her essence, is spiritually called Wine, and sometimes Blood, for Wine is the Blood of the Grape." These symbols all play a remarkable part in both the Old and the New Testament.

[2]Kenealy—The Book of God.

"Ship," the Ark that floated over the celestial waters of the Abyss, the Great Matrix of the Universe, that place of spiritual birth and re-birth and emergence into Immortality. Argha also means a Cup, a Vessel in which flowers and fruit are offered to Deity, the Cup that must always be curved like a ship.

This Argha was the primordial Mother of all, and was called the "Holy Spirit," the Ark that held the germs of all nature, that brooded over the Great Abyss, the Ship of the North, or Ship of Life, that bore the germs of all being over the vast ocean of the Infinite. She was the Immaculate of Supreme Heaven, in which God was the ruling Force. "When God has been called the Holy Spirit, the implication has been incorrect, the Holy Spirit was only His Regent or representation, the second Great Being of the Universe, the Anima Mundi, the Great Mother of Nature."

The Navi-formed Argha of the mysteries typified the Holy Spirit, the Great Mother of all existence. The High Priests of the Arabians make the Holy Spirit symbolized as a Cup or Ship, a necessary part of their religion. In the "Vision of Hermas"[1] the Holy Spirit was called "The Old Woman who was the first of all creation."

The basic belief of all ancient cults is that Spirit is from God, and that Souls come from the Holy Spirit, the great Soul of the world, ever productive and having the attributes of the Supreme. "The Spirit of God hath made me, and the breath of the Almighty hath given me life."—Job xxxiii, 4.

Again the Holy Spirit was Virgo, the Virgin of the Zodiac, who bore the Immaculate Son. She was the great nurse of all existence; she was Wisdom; she was the Power of God, more beautiful than the Sun, and when "compared with the

---

[1] This Hermean work was an elementary Scripture used in the church, as Eusebius says, "before the Christ had been completely carnalized by the Sarkolatrae." This work was always held in very great reverence by Irenaeus, Clement of Alexandria, and other great thinkers, who considered it a divinely inspired work. Hermas was surnamed "The Shepherd."

light she is found before it." She was the Mother of the Gods; She was Issa, the Virgin of God; she was the Sea, the mystical Rose, the Cup with wings. To typify her transcendent beauty, she was called the Rainbow, having the seven colors or the seven stars in One. At Sais she was bespangled with stars, and there she gave her mystic message: "I am all that is; I am all that hath been; I am all that will forever be: and my veil no mortal hath drawn aside. The fruit that I brought forth was the Sun."

She was called by the Sanconiathans, "The air shining with ethereal light."

She has been imaged as intensely black, her bosom bare, crowned with a golden pyramid, about which twined an immense serpent. Night and Darkness belong as symbols to very great antiquity. A superabundance of darkness metaphysically is Light. "Darkness adopted illumination in order to make itself visible."[1]

Out from the boundless Abyss of Darkness, acted upon by divine power, came the Holy Light. Paracelsus called the Sidereal Light the Astral Light, the reflection of the Great Immaculate Mother, to whom the name of the Astral Light had been given;[2]—a name never given to the father, or the fatherless son of the Immaculate Mother, who was placed on the physical plane, as the lowest of the manifestations.

This Holy Spirit, the Great Mother,[3] is symbolized by a great Tree whose branches spread over the entire world, and reach above the heavens. A more beautiful symbol can hardly be conceived. This Tree "has three roots, widely remote from each other. The first is among the Gods; the second among the Giants (the blessed spirits); the third embraces hell (region of all who are not among the heavenly blessed). Under the roots is the fountain of carnal

---

[1] Fludd, Robert.

[2] Astral Light—Light derived from the stars; a light only perceived psychically.

[3] The Mexicans worshipped the Holy Spirit under the name Chuacohuatl, the Serpent woman; and as Tonacacihua, the woman of flesh.

desires, whence flow the infernal rivers, and the roots are gnawed upon by the mighty serpent, Midhager (Conscience warring with carnal desires) ; under this, reaching towards the land of the Giants, is the Fountain of Wisdom and Knowledge."[1]

At a very much later period in the mysteries, Apuleius presents a portrait of the supreme goddess mother, as she was unveiled to the Initiates—"the Mother-earth, flower crowned, with her bounteous-bosomed body full of fruit. The Mother-heaven in her black mantle, lustrous with moon and stars ; a radiant reality of the divinest dreaming, unveiled in human form ; a visible revelation of the bringer-forth."[2]

In addition to these there are many beautiful revelations of the Mother, earliest known thought of the Creator and His first Creation, who, being direct from God, was the medium through which life was given to the world.

The Sons of God were offspring of this Mother, and the ancient world overflows with memories and symbols of these sons or Celestial Messengers, who were called the Messiahs, emanations from the Holy Spirit of God. The Messiahs were all incarnations of the Sun. They were all concealed, buried, and arose from the dead thereby typifying the setting and the rising of the Sun. Their "Incarnation was symbolized as a Golden Serpent coming out of the ark." The Serpent was a symbol of Immortality and Wisdom. The Ark was the Holy of Holies.

The religion of the ancient peoples seems to have been one throughout the entire world ; a great brotherhood, a universal faith. Strange has been the impulse of priests and theologians, to deviate from the ancient holiness which was so solemn and majestic in primeval days, and to instruct the masses in false doctrines.

The Garden of Eden, or Paradise, was the place of birth of Man, and of Time. The Holy Spirit *was* a Garden, the

---

[1]Kenealy—The Book of God, p. 324.
[2]Massey, Gerald, The Natural Genesis, Vol. ii, p. 79.

Garden of Paradise, the female principle under its venerated symbol. In this garden, which was also called Meru, grew all the delicious fruits, flowers and vines, and among them the "Golden Apple" of primitive times. This Garden was placed at the North, the Egyptians called it Sais, and Proclus remarks, "It partakes of a peculiar emanation from God." This is the Garden of Eden, the North Pole itself, the North that was called Sacred, the home of the constellation of the Great Bear, "The Genitrix," whose Seven Stars were the Sailors, who watched over and ever will watch over the celestial sea—"beautiful for situation, the joy of the whole earth, *is* Mount Zion, *on* the side of the North." —Psalm lxviii, 2.

The Abyss, in Egypt is a name of the North, and the original mother of this Abyss, which was Space, was called Typhon, the Mother of Beginnings, the Mother of the Fields of Heaven, the Mother of Revolutions (time cycles),[1] as well as the Mother of Gods and Men. She was later made goddess of the constellation of the Great Bear, Mother-Goddess, and her first son was called Sut, the Dog-Star in the south. It is here, in the mythical allegory born amongst the stars, that we find the origin of the Immaculate Conception. This Mother was called "The Old Woman," because she was the first of all creation, and the world had been made for her. From this early beginning developed the so-called Typhonian Religion, which, with its types, is the oldest of all.

We read that from one Mother the Universe was born. This was the Mother Typhon, a primordial figure of Power. A very ancient form of Typhon was the Water Horse, the "Bearer of the Waters" which was the Hippopotamus. This animal has four toes on each of its four feet, and there-

---

[1] This Mother of Revolutions was called the Producer and Re-producer of souls, or gods, who were the self-born who came from the cycles, created by the revolutions of the stars of the Great Bear. They were later known as spirits of the gods, and in another phase as the planetary spirits. Helios, the Sun-God, was born in the cycles of the Sun—the Light-born.

fore was considered a type of the four corners of the earth. The earliest types were always feminine, and were represented as animals or having the properties of animals. Jehovah, who at first was considered female, was also represented as a type of animal, and by the Rabbins was known by the mystical name of four letters—J H V H—their Tetragrammaton. The portrayal of a woman, arching over the earth and resting on her hands and feet, represents the four corners, or the four cardinal points. The Zodiac was given as a human female figure, and upon this the Astrological Chart was founded. Atum (the first Adam) is called in the "Book of the Dead," "The Mother Goddess of Time." All beginnings were founded on the feminine.

The constellation of the Great Bear was known as the Typhonian Thigh, the "Thigh of the North," the birthplace of the beginnings among the stars. In our Bible we read "The days come, saith the Lord, that it shall no more be said, the Lord liveth, that brought up the children of Israel out of the land of Egypt; but the Lord liveth, that brought up the children of Israel *from the land of the North.*"— Jeremiah xvi, 14-15.

The original Mother Typhon, "Lady of the Heavens," was Mother of the male child known as Sut who grew up to be her consort, and who eventually became his own father, in the character of the generator. "The oldest permutation known in Theogony became apparent at this point, which is that of the son becoming his own father and the mother being generated by the son."[1] It is in this Typhonian Religion that we first find the worship of the Virgin Mother, and the fatherless child, which later found a home in Rome. "But she came to be portrayed as a male virgin or maleless, to indicate the begetting or creating power on the way towards the final fatherhood." It was Manu who said the male-virgin gave birth to the Light. All mythical allegories of the heavens state that from herself the Mother came first.

____
[1] Blavatsky, H. P.

At a far later period when solar time (i. e. time told by the Sun) took the place of the early Sabean time (time told by the stars), the self-creator was made in the image of the male. Forms of worship of this very early religion are somewhat obscure, but it did not in any way constitute a mystery of immodesty, for it is known that originally it was pure and beautiful relating to the mystery of life itself. Nothing impure had ever been connected with it. All that was claimed to be obscene and anathematized as unclean, was due to other and later interpretations. It represented the naked nature of primal beginnings, the primitive physiological conceptions of a creative force. There was nothing gross in it, but much that was of absorbing interest. This religion finally passed into Judea, making its home in Jerusalem. "The branding of the Sut-Typhonians as the fatherless ones, religiously speaking, came through worship of the mother and child, who became the harlot of Revelation, and the bastard of the Osirians."[1]

Sut, son of Typhon, was the name given to the first male ever recognized or known, and though his manifestations were many, his beginning was as Sut, the Dog-Star, as we know it, in the south. He ended by becoming the Alpha and Omega of the Book of Revelation. Al-Shadai, Adonis, Baal and others were all personifications of this early son of the first Mother, and originally belonged to her cult, which is the same as that of the Church of Rome today—the worship of the Mother and the Child.

By a little searching many secrets of the ancient cult are recognizable as explanations given for the so-called orthodox forms of the religion of today. The Mother and Son worshipped by modern Christians, hark back to Typhon in the Egypt above and her son Sut. This Virgin Mother and the Child of heavenly conception were ages old before they became Semitic. They were also worshipped by the Hekshus, called the Shepherd Kings, of pre-monumental Egypt,

____
[1] Blavatsky, H. P.

who were the rulers for thirteen thousand years before the time of their first king, Menes. The Shus-en-Har, or Hekshus, were known as the followers of the great Egyptian God, Horus, with whom mythologically the Israelites were connected.

When superseded the Sut-Typhonians were denounced by those who had come to worship a Father and Son instead of the Mother and Son. Of the good Typhon it was said, however, "Hers is a figure so ancient that it belongs to a typology which preceded eschatology and mythology, and of an order set in heaven for use and not for worship, type of Time, and Force, and not for Beauty."

Primitive man knew nothing of the one God of a later religion. In all earlier cults, God meant the Absolute, pervading all places, in and of all, yet none might share His surpassing celestial majesty. God was not a solitary figure, a Silence. "He was surrounded by other gods of light, beauty, purity and divineness, immortal in their essence for it emanated from the Most High,"[1] but all were encompassed by His love, a source of all. The second Spirit of God, the second great power that began to exist when God developed beauty out of Himself was the Mother, the Mother first and foremost everywhere preceding any knowledge of that One God. She was Nature, the Spirit of God, the Virgin Spirit of ineffable loveliness, and as such received worship.[2]

Serpent worship, Tree worship and Water worship were all feminine. The Serpent sloughed periodically as the feminine type, and the bearing Tree with its fruit was feminine and Water was feminine and the source of life, the Mother. Motherhood antedated by aeons of time any knowledge of a

---

[1]Kenealy—The Book of God.

[2]The Egyptians symbolically named God the "Ancient Darkness." Of this Darkness H. P. Blavatsky writes, "Darkness is the root of Light, Light is matter, Darkness pure Spirit, Darkness metaphysically is absolute Light. Light is merely a mass of shadows as it can never be eternal, and is simply an illusion, or Maya."

The Hindu Initiates whose vision was sublime, recognized God as "The One who is All" which we are apt to veil in the present era.

fatherhood that could have been identified as such, and even among the original seven gods (later planets) there was no mention of fatherhood.

In that far off beginning everything was Sabean, i. e. belonging to the stars. It was only later when Sabean (Star) and then Lunar (Moon) periods had made way for the Solar (Sun) periods that a male element appears, and introduces the male and female as separate deities, for in the beginning all was considered in double aspect as male-female, Bi-Une. When at the advent of the solar period the worship of the fatherhood in heaven became established, then, time was reckoned by the Sun instead of as formerly by the Stars and the Moon. Atum in Egypt, Hea in Assyria and Abraham in Israel became the Father of the Gods, and the Child of the Mother became known as the Son of the Father. This individualization of the Father, whom the people then enthroned above the ancient Mother, was acclaimed with great rejoicings. Finally the Child of both became a substitute for the Mother and the Father of a later period of theology.

The seventh day, Saturday, was always the day of Sut, Saturn, but when Sut of Sabean origin was turned into a solar God, his day became Sunday, the day of the Sun.[1] In this solar form he became known as Sebek-Ra, the Lamb of the thirteenth dynasty. This occurred when, at the equinox, the Sun entered the Zodiacal sign Aries symbolized as the Ram or Lamb, and, He, who was in his Sabean origin the leader of the Typhonian Seven of the constellation of the Great Bear, was continued as the Lamb of the Seven Stars of the Book of Revelation.

The starting place was always in the North, where the ancients noted that the revolving of the constellations around the Pole Star took place. One of these early constellations was called Cassiopia, the "Lady of the Seat." She can be

---

[1]The secular church was founded by Constantine, who set aside the day of the Sun—Sunday—for the worship of Jesus.

seen sitting in a chair in the pictorial charts of the heavens. She was Queen of Ethiopia, our Biblical Kush, and this ancestral seat in the north, as a point of beginning, suggests Ethiopia as the first mystical birthplace. In the Hebrew writings Ethiopia, Kush and Zaba are convertible terms for the same country, the Egypt beyond Egypt, and combine with the "Za-be-ans from the Wilderness."—Ez., xxiii, 42. Kush and Ethiopia are both names of the North, where the constellation called The Thigh, the Matrix of the World, is found.

At first, when the elementary Powers ruled lawlessly and destructively, we learn that there was Chaos, and from out of this chaotic dissolution in space, Creation brought with it the beginnings of mythology, and ushered in the first period of Fixed Time. The Seven Stars of the Constellation at the Pole, came to convey the idea of this First Time. They were called "The Beginningless Lights," and were held most sacred by the priests, and many of the observations and the information given in the sacred mysteries concerning these "Lights" have fortunately been so carefully preserved that no type has ever been completely lost, and all can still be studied in their pristine purity.

Knowledge of celestial time was attributed to Typhon, Goddess Mother of the Great Bear, and to her son Sut, the Dog-Star. When she made her first circle around the North Pole, at the rising of the Dog-Star, in the south, the first year or cycle of time was accomplished, of which Sut was made the announcer.[1] Only an upper and lower heaven were given at this period, it was before the four corners or cardinal points had been represented, and before the equinoxes and solstices had been established. This fulfilment of the first year of Time remains fixed in the planisphere forever; and regardless of all changes, this origin

---

[1]Every race, tribe, and cult of olden time has had its traditions of the early Seven Stars, and everywhere can be found myths of "The woman and her dog"—Typhon and the Dog-Star, and the divisions of Light and Darkness.

has never been entirely lost or superseded. It was found in the heaven above and reflected in the earth below, and will remain as witness of the early Sabean time which began with the old mother Typhon and her son, Sut.

Although the roots of religion seem almost hidden in a remote past, many proofs are extant of its having been developed from Mythology, never Mythology from Religion. The conception of a concealed deity lies at the foundation of all religions, which explains perhaps the endeavors to make religion come before mythology. The origin was with the Mother, who preceded the Father and who had produced the first Seven Great Stars of the Bear as early Forces born out of space or chaos, called Creative Forces by all ancient peoples. These by the Christians were termed "The Virtues of God;" in the Greek and Roman churches they were the Seven Archangels, which belong also to the Parsee scriptures. They had under their care and protection men, animals, fire, metal, earth, water and plants. The original Seven have a common origin in Egypt, Akkadia, India, Britain, and New Zealand.

Jacob Boehme says of the Feminine producer and of these Powers or Forces, which he calls "Fountain Spirits," that "We find especial properties in nature whereby this only Mother works all things—desire, bitterness, anguish, fire, light, sound, and substantiality; whatever the six forms are spiritually, that the seventh is essentially. These are the seven forms of the Mother of all being from whence all that is in the world is generated." And again in his Theosophy he says, "The Creator hath, in the body of this world, generated himself as it were *creaturely* in his qualifying or Fountain Spirits, and all the stars are nothing else but God's powers and the whole body of the world consisteth in the seven qualifying or fountain spirits. Therefore man's life hath such a beginning and rising up as was that of the planets and the stars. . . . But that there are so many stars, of manifold effects and operations, is from the infiniteness that is in the efficiency of the Seven Spirits of God in one another, which generate themselves infinitely. . . . Man's property lieth in sundry *degrees* according to the inward and outward heavens, viz.: according to Divine manifestation, through the seven powers of nature."

These were the mystical Seven, first found in the Seven large Stars of the constellation of the Great Bear, and representing the first Great Mother in her likeness as Mother of the first elementary Forces and of Time. When the Solar period was established these became the seven souls of Ra, the Egyptian Sun.

These Creative Forces, or Powers, were always known as gods, and the higher gods of antiquity were always sons of the Mother before they became sons of a Father. Sut, Horus, Shu, and others never had a Father. In their origins they were male-female, as were all the ancient gods. Zeus was often called the Beautiful Virgin, Venus has been found bearded, the original Apollo was bi-sexual, Horus is given in both sexes, Osiris and Isis are found to interchange. In the vision of St. John in the Book of Revelation is found the Logos, now connected with Jesus Hermaphrodite, and portrayed with female breasts. Jehovah was originally female.

On a Babylonian tablet Venus is depicted as a male at sunrise and a female at sunset. To the Peruvians Venus was a morning star called "The Youth with the Curling Locks." Philo tells us that Astarte placed on her head a Bull's horn as a symbol of her lordship or male-female nature. In Sanscrit writings it was said that the Bull was eaten as food but that the Cow was too sacred as she was the Mother of Life. These were types of the early Mother.

The gods, divinities, and personages of mythology were universal. They were made sacred and divine because they were never human, though their attributes were often based upon human experiences, due to the knowledge of the ancient scholars, so conversant with life here below and so versed in astronomical knowledge. They taught their myths and allegories whithersoever they went. These did not spring up independently in various places in the world. Their unity in mythology is conclusively proven. The further one searches into the great past the more profound grows his wonder.

"Origen observes, 'If the Law of Moses had contained nothing which was to be understood as having a secret meaning, the prophet would not have said, 'Open thou mine eyes and I will behold wondrous things out of thy law'," (Psalm cxix, 18), whereas he knew that there was a veil of ignorance lying upon the heart of those who read and do not understand the figurative meanings," and he tells Celsus that the Egyptians veiled their knowledge of things in fable and allegory—'The learned may penetrate into the significance of all Oriental mysteries, but the vulgar can only see the exterior symbol. It is allowed, by all who have any knowledge of the Scriptures, that everything is conveyed enigmatically'."[1]

The Egyptian Khepsh, or Kush, became the Hebrew Chavvach, personified throughout Inner Africa as "The Old Mother," who, whether as Typhon, Khepsh, Kefa, or the Hebrew Chavvach, was the early Kamite Eve, the Eve of the Biblical Genesis, typifying the Birthplace of Existence, whether human or divine, i. e. celestial, tradition says that this earliest Kamite Eve, called Adam's second wife, was the cause of mankind losing Paradise, but creations in primordial myths have naught to do with human creations, but became humanized at a later period.

The Egyptian Kefa, as the first mother, meant "Mystery," and can be identified as our Eve. She was the serpent woman, goddess of gestation, and in Egypt had a serpent placed upon her head. The oldest subject matter in the world is found in the Book of Genesis. Misconceptions have

----

[1]Massey, Gerald—A Book of the Beginnings, Vol. ii, p. 184.

arisen solely through wrong conception regarding the very ancient wisdom of this first book of the Bible.

In the beginnings of mythology, the elements of Fire, Earth, Air and Water were first typified, before there was any formation of the world; later they became the establishers of Time and Order.   All creations were first Stellar, then Lunar, and last Solar, and as such are found everywhere in ancient tradition.   There were three primary heavens in the Babylonian astronomy, the heaven of fire, of aether and the planetary heaven.   These answer to the star stations, the lunar station and the solar station.

The very ancient form of Typhon, called the "Bearer of the Waters," was the Hippopotamus wearing a crocodile's tail (anciently the crocodile or the dragon interchanged as the Constellation Draco, adjoining that of the Great Bear). This was the old Typhon who became outcast in a later theology, but as Kefa she was made the Seven-fold Watcher, whose "Seven Eyes (stars) went to and fro through all the earth."   As she was Goddess of Time, they called her child, Seb-Kronus, a second condition of Time (Kronus, Time). As Sut he was the first announcer of Time, but as Seb-Kronus he became a repeater of Time in dual aspect called the Sun and Sirius (or Saturn).   The earliest type of Sirius was not the dog but an Inner African Giraffe,[1] called the Ser which was a figure of Sut-Typhon, counterpart of Sirius.   From Ser we have Sirius just as from Sut we have

---

[1]The Giraffe, which is pictured in the heavens as the Constellation Camelo Pardalis, lies close to the Pole Star and is a peculiarly made animal, which became a type of great interest to the deep-thinking and far-seeing Egyptian.   Its head and body resemble a horse, the neck and shoulders a camel.   Its ears are like those of an ox, and its tail like that of an ass.   The legs seem to be in imitation of an antelope's, while the color markings seem to have been borrowed from the panther.   He appears to be all out of proportion, with his short body and long neck and legs, and lacks beauty and grace in the sloping body and height. The head is very beautiful, the eyes very brilliant yet with a softened beauty. They are spiritual eyes.   He never utters a sound, not even in the agonies of death.   His native land odor has been compared with that of a hive of heather honey; both hearing and sight are highly developed.   Naturalists claim that the name Giraffe is a corruption of the Arabic Serafe meaning "Lovable," which so truly fits this animal.   It has no vocal organs.

Sothis (Sirius). This animal can see both ways without turning its head or its eyes, which made it the primary type of a steadfast watcher, begotten as were other types through primitive man's closeness to external nature.

Sut, as the first child of the mother of Time, when called Seb or Sevekh-Kronus, was named the Dragon of the Seven Stars of the Lesser Bear (Ursa Minor), the manifestor of the Seven which encircled the Pole with her, when forming the first primary circle. Records and cycles of time had depended upon these starry turners, until they were found to be "unfaithful," not keeping the true time. Sevekh, who was the earlier Sut, became the planet Saturn, and one of his names was Sut-Nub. Nub means golden. When he became famous as the ruler of the Golden Age of the Greeks, he was christened Sut-Nub.

The Seven Stars of the Great Bear were also called the "Bringers Forth;" i. e., of perennial time and creations, creators of the first form taken in space. "Thus Time, and Space were figured as a circle by placing a boundary around that which was boundless." In ancient times the body of this constellation was nearer the North Pole, and as the tail moved around the North Pole it was said strongly to resemble a Pointer, like the hand of a clock—a Time Teller. "Typhon in the north and Sut in the south were likened to the two hands of a clock, the Bear being the pointer hand, and Sut the Dog-Star the hour hand. Pythagoras calls the two bears the two hands of the Genitrix."

The Chinese named this constellation "A Bushel," which was a measure of time. In the writing of Hoh-Kwantsze we are told that the Chinese determined their seasons and months of the year by the revolutions of the Great Bear,— "When the tail of the Bear points to the East (at nightfall) it is Spring to all the world; when the tail of the Bear points to the South, it is Summer all over the world; when the tail of the Bear points to the West, it is Autumn to all the world; when the tail of the Bear points to the North, it

is Winter to all the world." The tail is also called the
Handle.

From the hidden Sun of the Solar régime and through
the knowledge of the evolutionist came the cycles of Time.
The Egyptian God Taht, the Moon God, later the planet
Mercury, and Seb, the Star-God, later the planet Jupiter,
were said to be born as Time-keepers or Watchers in the
heaven.   They were types of gods and angels but when history began these types were transformed into demons.   In
the early beginnings types and symbols were necessities of
daily usage in the life of primitive man.

The element of Fire, the fire that vivifies, was called Heh,
a Serpent.   The goddess Hea was the earlier Kefa, Chav-
vah, Hovah, or Eve.   Hovah is the feminine side of Jehovah.   The Akkadian Hea was a God of Wisdom, the repository of all wisdom.   These all meet in the first-mother
Typhon, and among her many types was that of a serpent.   Heh as an element of Fire typified the Sun in its
motion without visible means, like the gliding of the serpent.
Breathing, or heaving as the motion of the serpent, became
a type of visibility.   Kefa, Hefa (Eve), became the Great
Serpent of Life, the Serpent Woman, Goddess of Gestation.

The Serpent Fire of the occultists is said to lie at the base
of the spine coiled like a serpent.   The Lord said unto
Moses, "Make thee a Seraph," which means a Fiery Serpent.   Serf signifies a Flame, and Ref is the serpent of
Life.

The mythology of Israel begins, as we see, with the cult
of Hovah, who was Eve, the Typhonian Mother of Sut,
also called Seth.   The serpent type belongs to an early representation of the Mother, and followed the time when she was
known by the type of the Hippopotamus, and coincides with
the change in Israel from the worship of the North, and the
stars, to that instituted by Moses in the Wilderness.
"And the manna fed to the children of the Wilderness is

emblematic of feminine reckoning and rule, and the angels' food supplied by the Genitrix from the *Gynoceum* above to the children below." "Man did eat angels' food," (Psalm lxxviii, 25), which was the Bread of the Mighty, meaning that celestial knowledge which originated at this northern point in the heavens.

The serpent became one of the special symbols of this oldest of mothers. The Two Great Truths of the Egyptians were said to be written with the Serpent; they were also given in the two characters of the Gestator of the sign Pisces and the Virgin of the Zodiacal sign Virgo, typical of gestation and maternity. She was the Tree of Life as well as the Serpent of Life.

The two northern constellations of the Bears, called the Primal Pair, became humanized as the parents of our race, and were placed in the Garden of Eden, called the Mount, in which stood the Tree, or the Pole. The Fall was introduced when the earlier stars as timekeepers were found not to be keeping correct time, so they were called Laggards. The imperfect creations preceded the perfect. The earlier attempts at time-reckoning by the stars had failed.

The ancient traditions and allegories of the Egyptians and the Chaldeans with their rootage in the far past were continued by the Gnostics. They identified the early Seven Stars of the Great Bear by name and nature, as the Seven Daemons who always opposed and resisted the human race, because, as they claimed, the father of the Seven had been cast down to a lower world, not meaning the earth. This was portrayed in the Bible as the fall of Adam the mortal on earth, but its origin was purely astronomical.

Error and darkness had their beginning together. It is said in the Apocrypha, "Their beginning was with sinners." The true doctrine of the Fall belongs to the hidden wisdom, known only to teachers who have kept its meaning unsullied; and the books of the Hidden Wisdom tell us that "to be allied to Wisdom is immortality." "By means of her, I shall obtain immortality, and leave behind me an everlasting memorial to them that come after me." (Wisdom of Solomon, Chap. viii, 17.)

In the Divine Pymander it is said, "This is the Mystery that to this day is hidden, and kept secret; for Nature being mingled with Man brought forth a Wonder most wonderful; for he having the Nature of the Harmony of the Seven, from him whom I told thee, the Fire and the Spirit, Nature continued not, but forthwith brought forth seven Men, all Males and Females, and sublime, or on high, according to the Natures of the Seven Governors." And these were the Seven that finally became planetary, but primarily were the Seven Stars of the constellation of the Great Bear.

The Egyptian books, the Hindu Puranas, the Chaldean and the Assyrian scriptures all speak of seven primitive men or Adams. The Jews got their Adam from Chaldea. Ad, in Sanscrit, is "The First." The Assyrian Father is Ak-Ad, or Father Creator, and Ad-Ad meant the "Only One." Adam stands really for the first primitive race.

In the Gnostic ideas of the Creation man was formed by "A certain company of angels as a mere wriggling worm; the worm becomes winged, a living spirit." Their Adam was Adam the "Red," or the Sun. In Genesis we are told "Male and female created he them." The Mohammedan tradition affirms that the body of Adam was at first a figure of clay that was forty years in drying, and then the Creator endowed it with breath. (Koran ch. lv.) Many are the traditions of a first Adam or that which his name symbolized.

The Biblical account of the war in heaven is explained astronomically, when Typhon and Sut, or the Northern constellation of The Bear and the glowing Dog-Star in the south proved false in their time reckoning, causing their own degradation, their downfall. This was also brought about by the change in the earth's axis, which had gradually pointed to a star other than the one around which it had been revolving. It was the Egyptian Osirians who cast out and condemned the ancient Typhon, and who changed the Star-god into Sevek-Ra the Sun-god.   They then placed upon his head a pair of horns, and he became the Ram or Lamb symbolized in the Zodiacal sign, Aries, and when the Sun passed into this sign, Aries became typical of the change from one Pole Star to another.   This casting out of the old Mother took place when theology turned many of these ancient myths into religious history.   Religious chaos resulted and the past was almost lost in obscurity.   But strange to relate, followers of the ancient Typhonian cult of the first Immaculate Conception are spread over the world today, though many of them are in ignorance of the foundation of their religious belief.

It is well never to lose sight of the fact that in the heaven-world all is pure and beautiful in its symbolism; nothing is material, for all exists through God, whose rays are the Light now piercing through the veil of His creations. There are many who do not realize the beauty to be found in the old symbols, which have been so cleverly falsified and maligned.

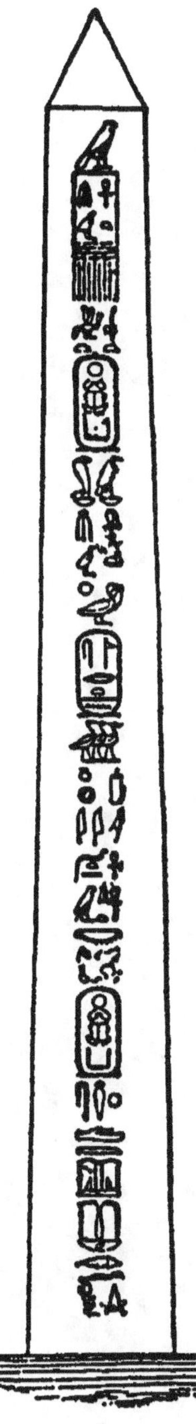

Obelisk at Heliopolis

Obelisks were usually placed in front of Temples, Pyramids or Tombs. They were engraved with mystical symbolical characters and apparently raised in commemoration of the gods or the departed. These solid shafts of stone have been variously called "A Finger of the God," the "Altars of the Gods," but more generally "a Ray or Shaft of the Sun," emblem of Light. This obelisk was placed in front of the Temple of the Sun at Heliopolis over 5,000 years ago. Many others are known to be far older. Anciently they were set on either side of the door leading to the dwelling place of the dead. The character of the Obelisk has been changed to suit the Christian idea. It is surmounted with a cross, and placed in our present day temples or churches, and in our church yards.

CHAPTER II

THE LAND OF LIGHT

Kinship between Egypt and India is very closely marked, so that debate arises as to which country can rightfully claim the oldest astronomical knowledge.

In support of the Indian theory, it is said that the so-called Eastern Ethiopians, a matured people, who colonized the Egyptian territory, which was the home of the Kushite, or Hamitic, race, came from southern India. The lower part of Egypt had been formerly a gulf of the sea, but the sediment of thousands of years, brought down by the river Nile and deposited there, made lower Egypt in no uncertain way an offshoot of Ethiopia. It was called the Land of Ham, or Kam.

Herodotus wrote, "I am of the opinion that the Egyptians commenced their existence with the country called the Delta, but that they always were, since men have been; and that, as the soil gradually increased, many of them remained in their former homes, and many came lower down. For ancient Thebes was called Egypt, and the inhabitants considered themselves the most ancient of mankind."

Egypt lies near the center of the land surface of the world. Piazzi Smith tells us that the base of her great Pyramid lies near to the heart of all the world. "There is a Hermean fragment that pictures the earth as a prostrate woman, her arms stretched forth towards the heavens, and her feet pointing in the direction of the northern constellation of the Great Bear; her body represents the geographical divisions, while Egypt is typified as the heart of all."[1]

---

[1] Stobeous.

Tradition also claims that Ethiopia was the home of the Egyptians, that the founders of Egypt came from Meru, a word which signifies the inhabitants of the "Mount at the North," "the Birthplace," "the Outlet." In Hebrew writings, Zaba, land of the Zabeans, Ethiopia and Kush, are names of the same country—the "Egypt beyond Egypt." "Zaba, the first-born son of Kush," is mentioned with Kush and Mitzraim. The inhabitants of Meru were the "Zabeans from the wilderness." It is to be remembered that there is a "wilderness" above, in the heavens, as well as a wilderness below, on earth.

The name "Kam" means "to create," and also "black;" hence Kam signifies the home of the black race, the Ethiopians. Mythologically, this race came from Khepsh, the constellation in the northern heavens called "The Thigh," signifying Typhon, Mother of the human race to the people who looked to the North, as the ideal place for primitive parentage and birthplace of the world.

Kam, the Ham of the Hebrews, was known as the country of the "coming forth." Research brings to light in the Hebrew writings much mythological astrology evolved from a study of the heavens, which afterward was given to the world as history and religion. Later sophistries garbled and falsified that ancient learning, which, primitive and simple, had been founded on the laws of nature itself. Its very simplicity was unfathomable to later theorists. The knowledge of astronomy and the perfection which this science attained in ancient times seems beyond modern comprehension. Near the city of Benares, in India, there are astronomical instruments cut out of the solid rock of a mountain. In former times these were used for making observations.

Semitic origins show etymologically their Kamitic derivation. The "K" of Kam was transformed into the "S" of Sam, which was the root of the word Semite. The Semites were known later as the Sumarians. The Sumarians followed the Kamites when the race of Kam left its primitive or nomadic habitat. The earliest "Wise men" were known to have come from the south, not from the east, and to have formulated the language of the earlier settlers, or squatters, when they settled in Sumaria on their journey northward.

Both Kam and Sam signify "black." The Semites were Kamites in a later phase of development.

Since Kamite names are the earliest known, it seems probable that Egypt is the missing link between the Inner African origins and the rest of the world. As her myths are incalculably old, much substantiality can be given to the theory that Egypt was the place of Beginnings. No country on earth is like her, or situated so favorably for the study of the stars; bounded at thirty degrees north latitude by the sea; and traversed by a river which overflows its banks three months of every year, and is dry during nine months, typical of the period of gestation. Egypt is reborn annually as her waters add layer after layer to her soil, she literally comes from herself like her great goddess Isis. In Egyptian mythology, typology, and symbology the celestial is primordial and continually contains the clue to the terrestrial; the earthly is ever but the image of the heavenly. Egypt has no Genesis, no Exodus, her rootage cannot be traced back to any line. Her offspring is civilization.

"Divinest foresight could have found no fitter cradle for the youthful race, no more quickening birthplace for the early mind of man, no mouthpiece more adapted, for utterance to the whole world.....fruitful and fertile for man and beast, Life was easy there from the first."[1]

In Egypt the migratory instinct was fostered from most remote times. Her colonies were scattered over the world, and the four racial colors, black, red, yellow, and white— all blending into the Egyptian types, are depicted on her

---

[1]Massey, Gerald—A Book of the Beginnings, Vol. i, p. 21.

monuments.[1] The antiquity of Egypt is traced by both occultists and antiquarians for hundreds of thousands of years. In the Egyptian "Book of the Dead" can be found indications of a greater knowledge of the heavens than the astronomy of today can touch.

"Egypt below" was but a replica of "Egypt above." Her myths and fables, founded on her astronomes, have been so misunderstood by many interpreters, so torn to bits in attempts to make history out of myths, that their identity is at times barely recognizable. Her ancient Truths, traced back to their Sabean origins, find their verification in "the Egypt that never dies." Primitive human customs were interpreted and preserved in her mythology of the heavens, and were carved deep in the hieroglyphic symbols of her imperishable monuments, all held sacred and divine, as coming direct from God. This mythology was later called the Word of God. Door after door opens in an endless vista to those who are earnestly seeking the sacred truths known of old.

The Egyptian "Book of the Dead," which is traced back to 4260 B. C., years before the writing of the New Testament, has its foundation in the lore of the heavens, and in poetical imagery follows the path of the Sun through the different signs of the Zodiac. Many phrases, many headings of the chapters of the New Testament are similar to those in the "Book of the Dead." Egypt originated calendars, the incorporation of stars into groups and constellations and first recorded solar motions.

"But the greatest proof that the people of Egypt were the first to give names to the stars, and to arrange them

---

"[1]A pictorial representation is found on the tomb of Seti First of four races of people arranged in groups of four men each. These are the Nahsi (negroes); the Hemu, men of a light brown hue, with blue eyes, the hair in a bag; the Tamahu, who are as fair as Europeans; and the Rut, who are Egyptian." See Massey, Gerald—A Book of the Beginnings, Vol. i, p. 27.

The color of the skin does not depend on climatic conditions; these modify but do not create.

into zones, by the circle of the spheres, is the name by which that country itself has been known. It was called "Aegyptian" from its being overflowed while the Sun was in the sign of the Goat....This name is compounded of "AEgis, a Goat; and OB, the swelling of the River; and *Tan, a Country;* which makes, when put together, AEgiptan; i. e., a country overflowed by the Goat; which agrees with the original fact. But besides being called *Egypt,* and *Aman,* it was called *Mizeraim;* from which distinguishing epithet we may conclude it was a country whose people first gave the names to the Stars. . . . It was the custom with the ancients to call those brilliant points in the heavens, which we call Stars, by the name of *fires.* . . . Thus, then, this country was acknowledged to be the first that studied the stars, by its being called *Mazeroth,* or *Mizeraim.* It has been sufficiently proved, by the union of the *Tropics* with the circle formed by their Zenith, to be 40,000 years ago; or thereabouts."[1]

The constellation of "The Thigh," which we know as the Great Bear, was the primordial birthplace in the North, the oldest known, and though mythical and type of the ancient Mother Typhon, has become historical. The star Mitzar, which can be seen in the tail of the Great Bear, had been definitely identified as the Mitzraim of celestial Egypt, before it was given as a name to the land of Egypt in Africa. Thus Mitzar, Mitzraim, Mazaroth and Mes-ru are the witnesses above.

There is a fragment of ancient lore given in the Hebrew scriptures which asserts that the line of Mitzraim comes from Ham, or Kam, joined with Kush. Thus Mitzraim is the son of Ham (Kam) of the black race, and the black race was the first on earth, just as it was in prototype in the heavens. Mazaroth, in its Sabean origin, meant the stars, the "Fires of Heaven," while Mes-ru is the equivalent of the Hebrew Mitzr, plural Mitzraim. Mest is the birthplace,

---

[1]Mackey, S. A.—Mythological Astronomy.

and Ru the door, gate, mouth, or opening, thus Metz-ru is the outlet from the birthplace, found in the constellation of the Great Bear or "The Thigh," and called the "matrix of the world."

In Africa the days and nights are of equal length. A river Euphrates is there, sacred and revered as the Nile that runs through the land of Kush (Kam) the Paradise of mythology, the Garden of Eden on earth. "A rabbinical geographer of the Fifteenth Century says it is declared by the knowing ones (the Gnostics) that Paradise is situated under the middle line of the world where the days are of equal length."[1]

"If equatorial Africa be the human birthplace, it is there we may expect to find the earliest localization of the paradise and Eden of mythology, in the country from which issues the river that runs through all the land of Kush.... Moreover there is an African river Euphrates or Eufrates, the chief river in Whydah (Hwida) which is still revered as the sacred stream, and a procession in honor of it is made annually."[2]

Some of the early black settlers of India were Egyptian in type. Black Buddhas are found there whose images are cast in the negro mould. In H. P. Blavatsky's book, "Caves and Jungles of Hindustan," on page 134 an account is given of some subterranean temples of India, not far from Chandova, known as Enkay-Tenkay, in which are numerous idols ascribed to early Buddhists. "They all, from the tiniest to the hugest, are *Negroes,* with flat noses, thick lips, forty-five degrees of the facial angle, and curly hair!.... This unexpected African type, unheard of in India, upsets the antiquarians entirely. This is why the archaeologists avoid mentioning these caves." It is the immense past of the Egyptian that accounts for the persistence of type. Diana of Ephesus is of negroid type, and is a representation

---

[1]Sepher Hamunoth, f. 65, C. i. Stehelin, Vol. ii, p. 4.
[2]Massey, Gerald—A Book of the Beginnings, Vol. ii, p. 602.

of the Great Mother. The Sphinx of Egypt, whose age is so great as not to be discoverable, has the same flat nose and full thick lips as the negro.

Many such instances point to the prime antiquity of Egypt, and to the conclusion that Egypt may indeed have been the cradle of the human race. It is undoubtedly the place where primitive typology is to be sought and studied, and is the point where history and mythological astronomy converge most closely.

The negroes were thought to be sons of the mythical Ham (Kam), a Hebrew derivative of the Egyptian god called Sevekh Kronus, a second phase of the son of the first mother, who, when he became planetary, was Saturn, whose color is black. Astrologically the planet Saturn is of the greatest importance to the negro race today, because it indicates a bridging over to a new condition and into an entirely new development which has to do with Africa, where Saturn has always been peculiarly potent. Astrologically the polarity of Saturn must be repolarized in Africa by the negro race. Saturn can never reach its highest expression in the new cycle except in its bridging periods, and also through the negro race, that primitive people belonging to an immense past, with only a few remnants of correlative races remaining.

The early races being dark, a certain stigma has been placed upon them, and even to the present time, they are thought by some not only to be born without souls, but past redemption and to be excluded from the heaven of the Christians because they belong to a period previous to the entrance of the Solar reckoning of time, before the Fatherhood had been inaugurated.

This is a peculiarly provincial and grotesque opinion about the earlier races to entertain at the present time.

A study of negro horoscopes will be of great interest, as Saturn will be found to play a part in the new cycle, by evolving the dregs of the old. Saturn has been a planetary god, but will now become a planetary wet nurse. Saturn is a great Ender and a great Hanger-on.

Ancient priests of Egypt prophesied through astral motion. All prophecy is based on astrology. Egypt is passing through a period of rebirth or resurrection, as it were, today, and as her ancient astrological knowledge comes more and more to light, it emphasizes the fact that history has been evolved from this ancient mythical astrology, whose foundations were formed by natural phenomena belonging to the symbolic and sacred writings evolved from the heavens. These facts found in the heavens, which were astrological, had absolute verification on earth long before history and religion existed; and an avalanche of mistinterpretations subsequently is due to theology. The supernatural had very little in common with primitive man, who lived close to nature, looking above and below for his natural facts, which he found in phenomena.

Egypt is and has always been looked upon as a land of mystery and Light. Out of her great past that looms through the mists, her ancient carvings, her hieroglyphs, her history grow more and more beautiful, and the farther back in time one goes in his research, the more he finds of stimulating material for thought, by which is revealed the wisdom of those who held a lifelong communion with nature, and who left a heritage of nature myths, which have been permitted gradually to slip away, through the mere apathy or unnecessary ignorance of the people of today.

The mysteries of Egypt were never borrowed, but came direct from the heavens.[1] Their "Book of God" was built on the knowledge that "The first law of nature is uniformity

[1]The primordial hieroglyphic ideograph, upon which later written characters, signs, etc., were founded, was the constellation of the Great Bear. The Chinese taught that the origin of writing was traceable to the markings on the back of the tortoise, which was the Typhon symbol of that country. The Egyptian and Akkadian hieroglyphics were developed from figures all primarily taken from natural objects, which, as time went on, took on symbolical meanings, and the pictorial writing forming the basis of the cuneiform characters is unmistakably only a species of the hieroglyphics.

in diversity, and the second, the analogy.—As above so below."[1] Egypt had a marvelous past previous to the recording of the most ancient classics. It may well be called the "wonder country" of the world. There is an Arab proverb, "Let us know the first, although the followers do better."

In the second volume of the Secret Doctrine, page 432, Maspero is quoted as saying, "It is to this *prehistoric* race that belongs the honor...of having formed the principal cities of Egypt and established the most important sanctuaries," while Lenormant also cites Egypt as "the country of the great prehistoric sanctuaries, seats of the sacerdotal dominion, which played the most important part in the origin of civilization." "Egypt has kept her records of a past so great that 6,000 years ago certain parts of a book were discovered as antiquities of which tradition had been lost."[2]

It is conceded by archaelogists that the further they pierce into Egypt's night of time the more wonderful and finer become the arts in which her people excelled. Writing was known and used during the time of Menes. It has been proven that the wonderfully decorated Greek vases are copies from the Egyptian, visible on the walls of palaces and tombs of the time of Amenhept First, when Grecian art was unknown. Beer was known as a beverage 2100 years B. C. The introduction of gold between two pieces of glass existed; also perfect imitations of precious stones. Music for healing nervous disorders was used in their temples. They created the lyre of twelve strings. On the walls of a palace at Thebes Amenhept is seen playing chess with the queen. The antiquity of the game of chess goes back to the Garden of Eden, or the North Pole. Originally it was played by four people, representing the first four quarters of the world. Iron was known 20,000 years ago. Egypt was the cradle of chemistry. Alchemy was practiced in those days, and was part of prehistoric magic. Linen bands wrapped about

---

[1]Blavatsky, H. P.
[2]Deveria, M.

their mummies have been found a thousand yards in length without a break. The mystery of the circulation of the blood, of dyes, of enamels, are but a fragment of their knowledge. Egypt is indeed "old and grey in her ancient wisdom."

"In the oldest times within the memory of man we know only of *one* advanced culture, of only *one* mode of writing, and of only one literary development, viz.: those of Egypt; and we know of only *one* contemporary people who could have had knowledge of this culture, appropriated its results, and conveyed them to other nations—this was the Kushite, the masters of the Erythraean Sea to its furthest limits. It was by them that Babylonia was colonized and fertilized with Egyptian culture. . . . The astronomy of Babylonia is only a development of that of Egypt.....its architecture (that is to say, its temples as well as its pyramids and obelisks) is an imperfect imitation of Egyptian originals; and so with the other arts. At every step we meet in Babylonia with the traces of the Egyptian models. . . ."[1]

A most accurate record of the movements of the stars and planets, with their positions, was kept by the priests of Egypt, extending over an incredible number of years, and their predictions, based on the eclipses of the Sun and Moon, have been faithfully recorded. In Egypt the only fixed and definite period was astronomical, in her symbology the celestial was primordial and continually contains the clue to the terrestrial; the earthly being the image of the heavenly. It was through the astrological cycles that the ancients learned the meaning of the "Dynasties of the Gods."

Five hundred years before the reign of Menes, "Herodotus was shown, by the priests of Egypt, statues of their human Kings, and Pontiffs—*piromis* (arch-prophets, or Maha-Choans of the temples), *born one from the other,* who had reigned before Menes, their first *human* King. These statues were enormous colossi in wood, three hundred and

---

[1] Lepsius, Professor—Introduction to "Nubian Grammar."

forty-five in number, *each of which had his name, his history and his annals.* And they assured Herodotus that no historian could ever understand or write an account of these superhuman Kings, unless he had studied and learned the history *of the three dynasties* that preceded the human— namely, the DYNASTIES OF THE GODS, that of demi- gods, and of the Heroes, or giants (Giants or Titans)."[1]

Similarity is found in every tradition of these divine races. "All the classics support Herodotus in the knowledge of the Three Divine Dynasties preceding the coming of the human race."[2] It is also noted by De Rougé, "In the Turin Papyrus. Most remarkable of all, Champollion, struck with amazement, found that he had under his own eyes the whole truth. . . . It was the remains of a list of Dynasties embracing the furthest mythoic times, or the 'REIGN OF THE GODS AND HEROES'."

Herodotus claims that chronological observations were made by the Egyptian Priests during a period of fifty-two thousand (52,000) years. To cite Pandoros, "It is before the time of Menes that *the reign of the seven Gods who ruled the world, took place.* . . . It was during this period that those benefactors of humanity descended on earth and taught men to calculate the course of the Sun, Moon and Stars by the twelve signs of the Ecliptic." Creuzer writes, It is "From the spheres of the stars, wherein dwell the Gods of Light, that wisdom descends to the inferior spheres. . . . In the system of the ancient Priests, all things without exception— gods, the genii, manes (souls), the whole world, are con- jointly developed in Space and Duration. . . . The Pyramid may be considered as a symbol of the magnificent hierarchy of Spirits."

Modern writers are prone to deny these ancient annals of the Divine Dynasties, but the world is beginning to awaken to the necessity of recognizing the truths found in ancient

---

[1]Blavatsky, H. P.—The Secret Doctrine, Vol. ii, p. 369.
[2]Bailly.

traditions, and feeling the need of sweeping away the cobwebs that have been allowed to accumulate and hide them. Many of the great truths remain, awaiting that revelation which will banish much of the skepticism and doubt at present surrounding them.

It is through tradition that we first learn of Menes, and there is much evidence that he existed as king, and was the connecting link between the ancient Dynasties and the people of the Monumental Period of Egyptian history. Astrologically, his era must have been about four thousand five hundred and sixty B. C.[1] Astrological cycles give foundations for these divine Dynasties, while papyri and other written evidences coincide with this celestial chronology. The Bull and Mena of Egypt are traced to the time when the spring Equinox was in the zodiacal sign Taurus, the Bull. The name Mena is also identified with the Bull, Men-Apis, as the celestial birthplace of the Sun, or Heliopolis. This "Bull of Menes" and the Bull of Osiris, are the same which coincided with the myth of Osiris, represented as the death of the Sun taking place in the sign Scorpio, which is opposite to that of Taurus, the Bull. Scorpio is the sign of night, darkness, death, while Taurus is the sign of physical generation, Life. The Egyptians placed the crocodile in this sign of darkness, Scorpio, when the crocodile's symbolical meaning had been transformed into an evil thing or condition. This occurred at the time of the degradation of the ancient Mother, Typhon—when the male was elevated above the female.

It was at this time that history emerged from mythology, and the Pharaohs assumed the titles of Divinities, to whom temples were built. It was not the human king that was worshipped, but through the human that which was thought divine.

---

[1]Menes' date is variously given as 5869 B. C. (Champollion); 5004 B. C. (Mariette); 4455 B. C. (Brugsch); 3893 B. C. (Lieblein); 5510 B. C. (Petrie); 3892 (Lepsius); 3623 (Bunsen).

The Egyptians, at the period when Menes reigned, had all the knowledge and wisdom of the Atlanteans, whose sacred records had been carefully preserved by their priests. It was from these marvelous records that they got their extraordinary understanding of the heavens.

Since Menes belongs to a period so far back in the range of time, we only catch glimpses of him through the mists that reflect the rainbow glory of Old Egypt. Sceptical or pessimistic delvers in the ancient cults are eager to pronounce his existence fabulous, while earnest, open-minded seekers and evolutionists are convinced that he actually lived. Esotericism traces from Menes starting points of the greatest value in many different countries.

The Thirteenth Dynasty of Egypt was that of Sebek, and this God was symbolized as Sebek-Ra by the Pharaohs. Sebek, a Star-god, was the crocodile-headed God of Darkness and also typified the Dragon. Tradition says that Sebek devoured Mena, which is a purely astrological symbolism relating to the Precession, carrying us back from Taurus, the Bull, to the sign Aries, the Ram, and introducing him in a new Solar character as Sebek-Ra, the Ram-headed God of the sign Aries, the Ram, who at this point was given his horns. Sebek-Ra was the Solar form of Sut, the Star-god. His Shrine was at Ombos, and he was an older form of Seb-Kronus (Time) and earlier identified with Sut. Because of the changing of Time he manifested as the Sun-god, and became the Lamb of Sacrifice at the approach of the Piscene Manifestation. Sebek-Ra can also be seen "wearing the head of a Ram on an erect Serpent," and became a type of Shu, who in his ancient character is also seen with two horns. Shu in his latest character is the planet Mars, ruler of the Zodiacal house of the Ram. The Ram-headed in the Harris Papyrus is shown manufacturing men on the Potter's Wheel.

The Egyptians picture a serpent standing upon two legs, symbolizing a High Initiate, or Hierophant. Sometimes he wears a disc with the Ram's horn upon his head.   Similarly Moses is given with the Ram's horns upon his head, shewing him to be an Egyptian Initiate.

When Sebek-Ra became the young Sun-god, he was The Lamb, of those who called themselves "Sebek-hepts."   Hept means peace, rest, plenty, etc., as well as the number seven. The Sebekhepts of the 13th, 14th, 15th and 16th Dynasties were the Shus-en-Hars, or Hek-Shus, who were worshippers of the child and his mother as Sut-Typhon.   Sebek as the son of Typhon became her consort, thus representing one of the first Trinities.

From earliest times, whatever sign the Equinoctial colure was in, that sign represented the place of the manifestation of the Sun above (or below) the horizon, so when Taurus, the Bull, receded to Aries the Ram of Sebek-Ra, it brought about a change of the birthplace in heaven.

The Egyptians expressed the place of birth, or re-birth of the Sun, and its burial below, by saying, "The tomb of one life was ever the womb of another."   They built their cities accordingly, as places of Resurrection.

When the Vernal Equinox receded from the sign Aries, the Lamb, into Pisces, the Fishes, and when the Sun-gods were born under this sign the Gnostics, or early Christians, who were versed in ancient wisdom typified the Sun-gods as fishes.

Sacrificial types had existed under all the different signs into which the Vernal Equinox entered during the Precessional Cycles, and thus the Lamb became the sacrificial type under the sign Aries.   Before that, when the colure was in the sign Taurus, the Bull, there was the sacrifice of the Bull, and before that, when in the sign Gemini, the Twins, twins are known to have been sacrificed as offerings to the Gods.   Every type corresponded in Solar Astronomical time.   Through knowledge of these sequences of the great Precessional periods of the world proofs are found of the era of Menes, and the Divine Dynasties.

About twenty-eight thousand years ago, the Vernal colure was in the sign of the Fishes, the zodiacal Pisces, and about two thousand years ago occurred a period closely allied to it. The Precession of the Equinoxes takes approximately 26,000 years to pass through the twelve signs of the Zodiac—hence the Piscene Manifestation of two thousand years ago. Since then a lunar dark period has intervened, out of which the world is now emerging into one of great light, as the Sun enters the new precessional cycle of the zodiacal sign Aquarius, the "Light-Bearer." This Light will manifest fully ere Aquarius recedes into the sign Capricorn, the Sea-goat.

The Fish symbol, adopted so frequently in early Christian portraiture, did not originate in the Piscene period of two thousand years ago, for the end of a Great Cycle renews itself in the beginning of a new Great Cycle, although it is not always clearly defined. The Fish symbol belonged to the Vernal Equinox of 28,000 years ago, and was that of a Messiah Son, who was born in the sign of the Fishes, and whose Mother Goddess wore a fish on her head. There were other Fish-Goddesses, who were given a fish tail— imagery that belonged to that ancient time. And when the watery sign of the fishes receded into another sign, fish became an abomination, as fish out of water might presumably be. Fish now belongs to the Lenten season, when it is used as food, and is given an important place in the diet on Fridays, which is the day of the planet Venus, astrologically in its elevation in the sign Pisces, the Fishes.

All ancient myths, legends, and allegories were created by men who dealt with Nature, and who were profoundly spiritual. This cannot be repeated too often. It is through ignorant misinterpretation of mythology that history became transformed into divine revelations and allegories, falsely construed into so-called historic truths, and that the heavenly or celestial births of the Sun-gods were irreverently perverted. But Truth, however long obscured, invariably comes to light. And through their mythical significance eternal truths will be forever traceable to their pure primordial origins, for they belong to the Stars—those silent, faithful watchers in the heavens.

VULTURES

In the temple at Karnak these Vultures armed with sacred and divine emblems are carved above the naves of the hypo-style halls and on the under sides of the lintels of the immense doors through which the king must pass on his way to the sanctuary. They are the Vultures of the goddesses Nekheb and Uati.

The Vultures symbolized the Mother and as a talisman were worn to attract motherly love and protection.

CHAPTER IIJ

"IT IS IN THE MYTHICAL WE HAVE THE TRUE"

Renouf, the Roman Catholic Egyptologist, says in the Hibbert lectures, "We know that mythology is the disease that springs up at a peculiar stage of human culture." Professor Max Muller teaches and scatters broadcast the same idea—that mythology is a disease of language, and further says that "The ancient symbolism was a result of something like a primitive aberration." To this Gerald Massey, the greatest of all Egyptologists, makes answer: "They can conceive the early man in their own likeness, and look upon him as perversely prone to self-mystification, or as Fontanelle has it 'subject to beholding things that are not there' ... My reply is, 'Tis but a dream of the metaphysical theorist that mythology is a disease of language, or of anything else except his own brain. The origin and meaning of mythology have been missed altogether by these solarites and weather-mongers. . . Mythology was a primitive mode of *thinking* the early thought. It was founded on natural facts, and is still verifiable in phenomena. There is nothing insane or irrational in it, when considered in the light of evolution, and when its mode of expression by sign language is thoroughly understood. The insanity lies in mistaking it for human history and Divine revelation. Mythology is the repository of man's most ancient science, and what concerns us chiefly is this . . . when truly interpreted once more, it is destined to be the death of those false theologies to which it has given birth."

In his "Luniolatry, Ancient and Modern," Gerald Massey states: "In modern phraseology a statement is sometimes said to be mythical in proportion to its being untrue; but the ancient mythology was not a system or mode of falsifying in that sense.   Its fables were the means of conveying facts; they were neither forgeries nor fictions." Fortunately primitive man was not a metaphysician; he was spared the "darkness of subjectivity," which has been called the modern disease, and which seems to exclude the understanding of primitive man.

The beginnings of the mythology of the Akkadians and of the Egyptians are definite and identical. The ancient method of conveying facts was by mythology—a plain simple mode of expression, and in no way occult. By placing oneself in touch with this simple understanding of nature, at least a faint gleam may be had of the mysteries of the now shadowy past. In that past, diademed by the stars of heaven, sacred because celestial, began the Generations of the Heavens, with the separation of the upper from the lower, or, the separation of Light from Darkness. All falsities found in the interpretation of the myths are due to their having become literalized.

The gesture or sign language, supplementing sounds, was an outcome of the image-making faculty of primitive man. It revealed his ideas, sensations, and experiences. It was thought, visualized, a reflected mental expression before the development of words, and became permanent in typology. The earliest method of representing things, conditions, or Gods was through types, or typology. Kings and prominent personages were worshipped or glorified under various types, or symbols, which conveyed the idea of certain powers. Thus the lion was the personification of strength and vigilance; the eagle was the "Golden Bird that soared aloft fearlessly in the flame of the Sun;" the serpent was the "Image of Eternity;" the lightning held the sting of Death; and the Sun was "emblem of Life and Light."

Primitive thought dealt with things known and recognized, and in expressing it, the people dealt with simple things, which later were introduced into the mysteries. The type to them symbolized what had not yet been given a name. In this way, the cat became the symbol of the Moon, because it saw in the dark, and its eyes were luminous at night. But when in course of time it became known that the Moon was the reflection of Solar Light, the cat's eye became the type of the Sun, because it reflected the Solar Light, as the eye gives back its image in its mirror. "In its form as the goddess Pasht, it keeps watch for the Sun with its paw holding down and bruising the head of the serpent of darkness, which was called the Sun's enemy. The eye of the cat was also very symbolical as a timekeeper. The Egyptians say that the male cat changes the shape of the pupil of its eye according to the course of the Sun. In the morning, at the rising of the Sun-god, they are dilated ; in the middle of the day they become round, and about sunset appear less brilliant."[1]

A statue of a god in the City of the Sun was in the form of a cat. When a transformation of the solar god was made into a cat, the "Book of the Dead" said, "He makes the likeness of Seb," and Seb was god of Time. A timepiece made in the form of a cat is still in use by the Chinese, who employ the eye of a cat, according to the size of its pupil, to determine time.

We find in the Egyptian mythology of the heavens definite creations, their formation often being in accordance with the character of the cycle and the division of the circle. In the "Book of Enoch" are the words, "I behold the secrets of Heaven and of Paradise, according to its divisions." The first division was that of the Celestial Waters, from which the seventy-two duo-decans of the Zodiac were finally evolved. Mythical Astrology was purely Egyptian, originating from a primal source whose chief types came from the constellations and stars. Hindu, Arabian, Chaldean and Greek systems agree on this point. Ancient countries were very close to each other in the knowledge and wisdom found in the

---

[1] Hor Apollo.

heavens, as well as in many other ways. There was a time when temples of astrological knowledge were scattered all over the world—in Europe, in Asia, in Africa, and in America. This was a time when the myth of the Sun and the Dragon was sacred, and belonged to a symbolical worship.

As types the Dragon and the Serpent were interchangeable, but distinguishable. The Serpent, astronomically connected with the Sun and spiritually with Wisdom, has been found portrayed in the planisphere, scribbled or carved on rocks, in caves, or on monuments all over the world. The Serpent symbol was the most spiritual of all. It stood for physical regeneration and immortality. It should be remembered that Moses was an Egyptian Initiate, and knew the Wisdom of the Serpent.

A mythical and symbolical method of reasoning appears far back in the distant vistas of time, before the words or language of any people were known. Early beginnings were found in the heavens. Knowledge of the Kamite Serpent of Millions of Years was one of the first concepts. This was the seven-headed primordial Serpent of Darkness, whose seven heads were the Seven Constellations in the North, discovered as the makers of a circle as they turned around the Pole which was anterior to the myths and symbols founded on the Constellation Draco, the Dragon or Serpent, with its seven heads, or seven stars, which belonged to the Constellation of the Little Bear, and was joined to Draco in early reckonings.

This same Constellation Draco was also called the Crocodile, which figures so largely in all mythological astrology, and as the Crocodile was a type of Sunset and Sunrise. The tip of its tail as Sunset was called Kam (black), while its two eyes represented the Sunrise. This conforms to the natural fact, as the crocodile comes out of the darkness at sunrise, lies on the sands during the daytime, and at night, when it disappears in the water, the last seen of it is the tip of its tail, which thus became the ideograph of darkness.

This is the same Dragon, or Crocodile which was placed in the mountains of the West or at Sunset in the Akkadian myth, and because of its great jaws, was said to swallow the Lights, the Sun, Moon and Stars. The Constellation Hydra—called the Dragon of the Waters, below—and the Constellation Draco of the waters, above—representing "Overwhelming Darkness"—were interchangeable. "Out of the darkness leapt the lightning bolt, and in the deep waters lurked another subtle foe of life. Thus the jaws and fangs and sting of death were assigned to the devil of darkness, who gradually assumed the character of man's mortal enemy, that brought death to the world."[1]   It is difficult to realize that the Constellation Draco, or the Serpent belonging to the myths of the past became personified as the devil of theology.

The Scarab, or Beetle, was held very sacred, and seemingly born of itself, and from itself, was given the title of "The Only Begotten."   In the month of June, or Mesore, at the rising of the river Nile, this creature rolls its egg into a little ball which it stows away, to await birth.   Mesore means also re-birth, and was the name given to the Zodiacal sign Cancer, which marked the month of transformation, re-birth, and new beginning.   A lunar symbol was created from the Beetle or Scarab, as it was said to deposit its seed and then leave it for twenty-eight days (typical of the mystical Moon of nature) and on the twenty-ninth day the little seed-ball opened and life was renewed.   On this day the Moon came to the conjunction of the Sun, and then reappeared, resurrected into a new life.   So the beetle below transformed into a new life just as the Moon above coming to conjunction with the Sun in the chart of a native, was said mystically to give re-birth to the Christos within.

The sacred Beetle and the Crocodile because of their connection with the inundation were considered most important in Egypt.   "They were prognosticators of the height of the

---

[1]Massey, Gerald.

coming waters of the Nile; wherever their eggs were laid, would be the utmost limit to which the waters would rise that year. For, not being able to lay their eggs in the water, and being afraid to lay them far from it, they have so exact a knowledge of futurity that though they enjoy the benefit of the approaching stream at their laying and hatching, they preserve their eggs dry and untouched by the water."[1]

The Serpent was the type of renewal, and an emblem of immortality. Among South African races there was a belief that the spirits of dead ancestors came in the shape of serpents. The ancestral spirit, that preceded the individual later ancestors, became an ideograph of the serpent that transformed and renewed itself.

The caterpillar and the serpent became types of the stealthy crawling which was a necessity to early man. The Tadpole was an ideograph of Millions by reason of the fecundity of the frog. In England at one time when children were wanted a frog was swallowed by the woman.

The Sow was a very sacred symbol, and type of the Great Mother because she represented the multimammalian mother, the many-breasted nourisher and Giver of Life. She was also a destroyer of snakes, which run away from her. The Ibis was also a great destroyer of snakes, and was therefore held in honor. For a person to destroy a snake was a crime punishable by death in Egypt. The Ibis was given to Taht, the Moon-god, who was the Egyptian god of medicine, because of her internal purging and cleansing of herself. So very fastidious was this bird that it would never go near unwholesome water. The priests watched the Ibis to see from which pool of water or river it would drink in order that they might take thence the water to be used for their sacred ceremonies and lustrations. Taht as the great Hermes was supposed to watch over the Egyptians in the form of an Ibis and to teach them the occult sciences.

-----

[1] Plutarch—Of Isis and Osiris.

Primitive peoples believed in and held in great reverence divination by birds. The Christians hold the Dove sacred today as a symbol of the Holy Ghost, the Holy Spirit. The Turtle Dove was a symbol of Spirit, of Fire. Our North American Indians, the Hurons, believed the souls of their dead friends became Turtle Doves. Hor Apollo tells us that the Vulture was a symbol of the Mother. There being no male Vulture, the female became impregnated by the wind, which was called the Holy Ghost. This bird was a symbol of the primal Virgin Mother. The white Vulture, found in the heavens as the Constellation Aquila, the Eagle, is one of the paranatellons of the sign Scorpio, and was connected with the myth of Prometheus. The Vulture denoted Foreknowledge. "The Vulture indicated the place of the Sun or Solar Fire, in the abyss of the inferior hemisphere, the Fire that Prometheus was fabled to have snatched from heaven."

The mouse was especially reverenced for its blindness, as it typified the Darkness, and became the subject of many a curious tale. In Germany it was considered a symbol of the human soul. In Egypt the mouse was a type of the early god Horus, as a first condition of soul. Blood as a second condition was given to the Hawk, symbol of breath.[1] The Hawk was said to drink only blood, never water, for the soul was sustained by blood. Blood and breath were considered the primary elements or souls of life. The mouse came to represent the soul of flesh, or the mother soul. When the future life of Horus was being gestated, he was shut up in the Meshkin, or Holy Shrine, place of annihilation or transformation, and was symbolized by the Red Mouse. "The Mouse typified the mystery of shutting up the red source of

---

[1]In Germany where both rats and mice were thought to represent the human soul, there is the story of a little red mouse creeping out of the mouth of a sleeping child. It being difficult to arouse her, she was taken to another place. On the return of the little red mouse, not being able to find the child, he disappeared and with his disappearance the child died.—(Told by Baring Gould in *Curious Myths*, Vol. ii, p. 159.)

life, the flesh-maker, which was looked upon as the first factor in biology."[1]

A superstition existed among Mexican women to the effect that when the Moon was in eclipse there was danger that a woman's coming child might be turned into a Mouse. Astrologically the Moon in eclipse is fatal to gestation.

In Egypt the Hawk was reverenced as the personification of Light, and the Mouse, because of its blindness, represented the Darkness preceding light. In England the little blind Shrew Mouse was sacrificed for purposes of healing. The little animal was placed alive in a hole made in a tree and the ailment for which it had been sacrificed was said to disappear with the remains of the mouse. To denote "Disappearance" a mouse was used. Horus disappeared in the "Shut-In" place, the "Hidden Shrine," that his transformationtion might take place. The little shrew or blind Mouse was adopted as a symbol of the Hidden Shrine, which was always the place of re-birth of the Solar God. The Sun disappeared into the Hidden Shrine in the West—the dark, to be born anew on the horizon of the East as the child of Light, called the Sun of the Resurrection. The resurrection is astronomical and Kronian, and occurs at the end of all cycles.

In early mythical astrology the constellation of the Great Bear as Mother Nature was represented in various ways and by different symbolical names, among which are Rerit, the Sow, the Plough, the Sword, Khepsh, the Ass, the Aan. All typified the great Mother Typhon, called the "Almighty One" of the North, though later denounced by the solarites as an abomination, because she was too slow in her revolutions. They therefore called her "Sluggish Animal of Satan." As Rerit, the Hebrew Lilith, she was Adam's first wife, though it was Eve, his second wife, according to the Hebrew version, who was said to have caused the fall from Paradise by listening to the Serpent.

The Welsh, like the Egyptians, had their orders of Priests

[1]Massey, Gerald—The Natural Genesis, Vol. i, p. 48.

known as Diviners. The Welsh bards called their Diviners "SYW" and the Egyptian Priests called theirs "Shaau," both terms being identified with the Sow. The British Keridwen took the character of HWCH, also meaning a Sow, and HWCH was a magician, similar to the Greek Hecate. It was thought that pigs see the wind, and so they were made to represent the divining faculty. The Plough was named from this animal, the Sow, which ploughs the ground with its snout, while the constellation in the heavens makes the circuit of the Pole by ploughing through the stars and creating the furrows of heaven.

The Sow was a primordial keeper of time, and has remained as a timekeeping sacrifice once a year in many parts of the world. In ancient times they had Sow-days. In Egypt once a year a sow was sacrificed to the Moon and Isis. We hear of owners of herds of swine sacrificing one of their herd on a certain day every year, and there is still the custom of sacrificing pigs or sows at Easter and Christmas.

Leprosy is mystically said to be the result of drinking the Sow's milk, i. e., the Sow, meaning Lilith, or the Forbidden Fruit.

The Sword as the Flaming Sword, that turned every way, was the Sword of the Four Corners, or the Cardinal points of the world, and as the Crooked Sword or Sickle was a symbol of the planet Saturn, called the Scythe of Time. In Egyptian it was called Khepsh, one of the names of the constellation of the Great Bear. In the Denderah planisphere it was symbolized by the leg of a Hippopotamus indicating The Thigh, the original birthplace in heaven. When Saturn was represented as a God, a crown was placed upon his head, endowing him with majesty, and making him a Judge of the Court of Justice, held at the time of Reaping, the Harvest time, the Golden Age, of Justice. Saturn has remained a symbol of Justice down to the present day.

Khepsh, as the Constellation, making the circle of the Pole, created the Garden of Eden, with the Pole at the

center as the Tree of Life.   This Eden was made the home
of the Biblical Adam and Eve, who in ancient mythology were
represented by the Constellations of the two Bears. Adam
became one with Sevekh, the manifestor of the seven stars
of the Little Bear, and Eve became one with Kefa, the manifestor of the Seven Stars of the Greater Bear of early Sabean
days.   These two were the outcast gods of these constellations, but were later re-created as human beings.   The Fall
was from the Sabean Star to the Lunar Moon time, to a
lower heaven, called Adamah in Genesis and not to earth.

The Ass in ancient mythology was a symbol of great
importance.   The Ass originally typified the deity of the
Dog-Star, then known as Sut, son of the Typhonian Mother,
who had the honor of rearing this first child in heaven.   The
Ass, having long ears, became the "Hearer," and was known
as the "Utterer," and the "Sayer of Great Words."   The
"Book of the Dead" says, "The Great Words are spoken by
the Ass."   It was said mystically that the Ass once carried
immortality into heaven, but sold it to the Serpent.

"The Rabbins say that Moses, when in the presence of the
burning bush, was bidden to put off his shoes because they
were made of the hide of the Ass."   This is of course symbolical.   In Egyptian, the Hebrew Jah, Iao or Ieu, mean an
Ass, type of the Sabean Sut, who was the earliest El, son or
Sun.   An ideograph of an Ass's head was the equivalent of
a period of time and of a cycle.

Moses brought from Egypt to the Israelites a Solar God
Jah-Adonai, which provides a reason for his "taking off" his
shoes in the presence of the Sun-god, Jehovah, who was the
Sabean, Sut.   The Ass was also an ideographic hieroglyph of
the number Thirty, symbol of a luni-solar month, its numerical value bearing relation to the month of thirty days, which
was divided into the three weeks of ten days each in the year
of twelve months.   Twenty-eight days of the Moon period
belonged to Sut-Typhon.   When later thirty days were
allowed to the Moon, the period was called Sut's resurrection,

and then by the changing of the Sabean and Lunar periods to Solar reckoning, Saturday, which was Sut's day, was converted into Sunday, the day of the Sun.   This number thirty signifying thirty years of a celestial period, was assigned to the planet Saturn.   The triple phase of the Moon of thirty days connoted by 3×10 was represented as the three-legged Ass, found in Persian Scriptures, from which many myths of the trinities were created which later became histories.

The Ass as a lunar symbol belonged to the night side of myths and manifested great strength in the struggle with Darkness, the enemy of Light.   We find the Ass bearing the Sun, which she carries between her two ears, also hauling it along with ropes, pictured as vines.   In the Twelfth Century she was made to assume the name Iu, the original Sut, the Star-god, who became the Sun-god, and bears a very close relation to the Hebrew deity Jehovah.

The Ass, when type of the full Moon, was the Mother. The waning Moon was the impubescent son, and as the New Moon was the youth, the "Lord of Light," who became the Solar Sun-god, or Messiah, re-born from the Moon.   In the ancient myth the Great Mother, typified as the Ass, carried the "Messiah" of the mysteries, the coming "New Light." In ancient trinities a Messianic child was always the Light of the Moon, whose Father was the hidden source in the underworld and whose Mother was the Moon who brought him forth.

Our word Head is the Egyptian Hut, and the winged Hut was a symbol of the Sun.   A horse's head was typical of Hut and the Constellation Pegasus.   The Sun about 5,000 years ago entered this sign at the Winter Solstice, and when it began to mount was called the Winged Horse.   "Uttara-Bhadrapada is the twenty-seventh lunar mansion in the Hindu Asterisms, partly in Pegasus.   This was the point at which the Sun began to mount, hence the Winged Horse."

Hut was the good demon overcoming the powers of darkness, and became a substitute for the Ass of Typhon.   In the

Hebrew myth we find the Ass, used instead of the horse to carry the young hero Shiloh. The Jews are charged with preserving the symbol of the Ass Head until a late period. Sut as the Messiah was identified in Rome as the Egyptian IU. The Jews were certainly Suttites from the very beginning, and even after 200 B. C. they are known to have worshipped the Golden Head of an Ass. Zechariah's death and dumbness were due to his vision in the temple which he had entered to make offering of incense, and in which he saw a man *standing in the form of an Ass*. Epiphanius writes that this was the cause of his death, for when Zechariah came out of the temple and through surprise would have disclosed what he had seen his mouth was stopped. When he had it in his mind to say to the people—"Woe unto you, whom do you worship," he who had appeared to him in the temple took away his power of speech. Afterwards, when he had recovered his speech, he declared what he had seen to the Jews, and they slew him. "They (the Gnostics) add to this, that on this very account the high priest was commanded by the law-giver (Moses) to carry little bells, that whensoever he went into the temple to sacrifice, he *whom they worshipped*, hearing the noise of the bells, might have time enough to hide himself, and not be caught in that ugly shape and figure."

The Cynocephalus, characterized as the Egyptian Dog-headed Ape, was one of the earliest known of the sacred animals, and because of its relation to the heavens, is of unusual interest.   It also belongs to the original Seven Sacred Stars of the mystic Seven of the Constellation the Great Bear, and to the Lunar god Taht, who was the deity of "Utterance" as well as "The Oracle of the Gods."   The Cynocephalus was honored in many temples in connection with the Moon which it resembled in its feminine periodicity, and became a reckoner of time under the name of Aan, and as the Kaf-Monkey its ideograph is found amongst the hieroglyphs of the Egyptian temples. Aan was a representation of the Moon in the northern heavens, a lunar feminine type of the Great Mother from which all proceeded, and was a Giant type of Soul. Kaf was a type of the star-god Shu (Mars), who was one of the earlier determiners of Time, and was also a type of one of the first elementaries, the Wind, Air or Breath, and of Conception.   Later the Cynocephalus became the Genii of Wind of the four corners.   There are legends, and many of them, of men being turned into monkeys as the result of great hurricanes that had taken place.   There is an African superstition that men are changed into monkeys after death.

The Cynocephalus had a close symbolical connection with the conjunction of the Sun and Moon,[1] for it is said that during the dark quarter of the Moon, which is loss of light, this animal goes blind, and neither eats nor sleeps, but that when the New Moon appears, it stands erect, with its paws uplifted, and is depicted with a diadem upon its head, as it sings praises for the coming of the Light.   It was from this cry, at the coming of the Light, this soul-given cry of rejoicing, that the sounds given in the scale of music were evolved. Of this Darwin writes, "It is a remarkable fact that an Ape, one of the Gibbons, produces an exact[2] octave of musical sounds, ascending and descending the scale of half tones."

The Ape, being an imitator, was used as a symbol of the Transformer.   In consequence of this, the Ape was confused with the spirits of the dead, although it bore no relation to those invisible spirits of the air, whose aeolian melodies were played by the wind, giving rise to the magic harps.   From these spirit melodies the Eastern peoples deduced architectural forms.

---

[1] In Champollion's "Panthéon Egyptien" plates or disks are to be seen painted in brilliant colors in which the Cynocephalus wore blue at the head and red at the tail, symbols of the dual lunation.   The disk at the tail signified the Aan, as the waning Moon.   Aesculapius had *The Dog* for companion (dogs were offered him), so had the Cynocephalus of Hermes.   Sirius was the Fire Dog of the summer solstice, which rose heliacally with the Sun.   All meet as one in the Dog-Star, the Sabean Sut (Saturn), later the planet Mercury.

[2] And the monkey "alone of brute mammals may be said to sing."—(Prof. Owen, "Descent of Man—Origin of the Scale in Africa.")

Spirits were known as Breaths. Vowels as we know them are Breaths, and the correct utterance of the vowels belonged to the mysteries of Egypt as well as of India. Chanting of the vowels by the Priests of the temples was a very ancient form of religious service. They were chanted with solemnity often with great secrecy and were thought most sacred. These "Breathing Utterances" were chanted by the Egyptian priests as a hymn addressed to Serapis. These vowels were the seven primary sounds, from which all others were evolved and were finally ascribed to the planets. "These seven tones in the musical scale are given as Si, to the Moon; Ut applies to Mercury; Re, to Venus; Mi, to the Sun; Fa, to Mars; Sol, to Jupiter; and La to Saturn when making the Music of the Spheres, and seven is also the number of the Moon, whose changes occur every seven days."[1]

Chnuphis, identical with the Ophite Serpent, is portrayed raising itself aloft, with seven rays darting from its crown, every ray tipped with a vowel. These rays also represent the seven days of the week, and the planets. It is said of this seven-lettered God that he was the true and perfect Serpent, Jehovah, and that the chanting of his name was for the seeker and inquirer of the sacred wisdom. Vowels were symbolical of the life principle, and when a name contained all the vowels it was especially connected with Divinity, the Giver of all Life. The Agathodaemon, endowed with knowledge of good and evil, was the symbol of divine wisdom and was the Christos of the Gnostics, and became the Spiritual Sun of Enlightenment and Wisdom.

In the Pistis Sophia Jesus asks, "Do you seek after these mysteries? No mystery is more excellent than the seven vowels, for they shall bring your soul into the Light of Lights. Nothing, therefore, is more excellent than the mysteries which ye seek after, *saving only the mystery of*

---

[1] Dupuis—Tom 1, p. 75, authority.

the seven vowels and their forty-nine Powers, and the number thereof."

The Mantrams of India attain their full power in sound. "The most potent and effective magic agent, and the first of the keys which open the door of communication between mortals and the Immortals." Anyone who hears these Mantrams intoned will realize their awe-inspiring sacredness, which must bring a stirring of the heart, and a great spiritual quickening even to the unbeliever.

The seven vowels were consecrated to the seven principal planets, and every planet in its revolution represented a sound, the seven together forming a wondrous harmony. "It is on number seven that Pythagoras composed his doctrine on the Harmony and Music of the Spheres, calling 'a tone' the distance of the Moon from the Earth; from the Moon to Mercury half a tone, from thence to Venus the same; from Venus to the Sun $1\frac{1}{2}$ tones; from the Sun to Mars a tone; from thence to Jupiter $\frac{1}{2}$ a tone; from Jupiter to Saturn $\frac{1}{2}$ a tone; and thence to the Zodiac a tone; thus making seven tones— the diapason harmony. All the melody of nature is in those seven tones, and therefore is called 'the Voice of Nature'."[1]

Although there are countless varieties of musical instruments, all are reducible to three types. Prehistoric music passed through three developments—the Drum, the Pipe, and the Lyre; "Rhythm, Melody and Harmony."

The name Mes, meaning Mass, has as its hieroglyph a cake of earth. A cake, product of the water, was called Mesi, which was eaten as Bread belonging to the Mass, and this finally became the wafer, used in religious ceremonies today. This Mes, or Mass, produced from the mud which had become caked from being massed in water, was used in ancient Egypt, and virtually under the same name, and was made typical of primeval land. Mes was also a name of the Abyss. The reeds growing in the marshes and along the

---

[1]Blavatsky, H. P.—The Secret Doctrine, Vol. ii, p. 601.

water channels of the river Nile were the Egyptian plants Byblos and Papyrus, from which we have the words Bible and Paper.

The color Green was very sacred as a symbol of re-birth, type of immortality, and resurrection from the earth.   These types, a few of which have been given, will unlock many doors to understanding of primeval man's outlook on life. He reverenced that great mystery Birth and his unquestioning belief in re-birth as he looked to the constellation of the Great Bear, the northern heavens, as that point of commencement typified to him the first Great Mother of all time. Philo, the most illustrious of his race, an Initiate of the Mysteries, said, "It is in the mythical we have the true," and not in the literal version where so much is false.   The mis-reading of mythology, upon which theology is founded, has resulted in obscured, beclouded, chaotic, ubiquitous confusion filled with religious falsehoods.

Research points to Egypt as the source of primitive astronomical beginnings.   Her early namings were often mystical, but divine in meaning because celestial.   They were transformed into the physiological.   Many imperishable proofs are found in her "myths and fossils of language, which constituted the geology of prehistoric times," says Gerald Massey, greatest of Egyptologists, who claimed that the common center of primeval unity is found in Africa, womb of the human race, with Egypt as its outlet into the world.

The above illustration shows one of the head-dresses worn by the Egyptian gods and goddesses. The two tall feathers crowning the solar disk, symbolized upper and lower heaven. Two feathers also denoted the Two Truths of Light and Shade and were symbolical of Breath and Spirit.

CHAPTER IV

DUALITIES

The true inner meaning of certain ancient myths has been obscured by the lapse of time, and by reason of later retouchings which have worked undeniable harm. But the original myths are always reliable, and will withstand the tests of ages, they were not born from civilization, nor from the mind of man, but were the reaction of human cognition to divine impulse. Mythology commenced with the measuring and distinguishing of periods. The Egyptians were worshippers of Nature; the Greeks reveled in Beauty; the Romans demanded Law; and the Northern races reverenced Courage. Greek interpretations profusely set forth their ideals of beauty, which caused Philo to complain, saying, "They brought a mist upon learning making the discovery of truth almost impossible." Plato becomes misleading when he calls Time "the moving image of eternity," for the "foundation of the image is in planetary and stellar motion." He also, "in the foundations of the visible, tries to establish all that was invisible." "The decadence of mythology is to be found in the Greek poetizing, the Hebrew euphemerizing, and the Vedic vagueness, where in India the myths have been vaporized" is the discerning judgment of Gerald Massey, and, as he says, "Poets play with shadows but mythology was the primitive way of conveying facts."

Ancient mysteries, the oral "dark sayings of old," were whispered lip to ear in the adyta because they contained the wisdom sacredly guarded from the ignorant. When theology succeeded myth these became the Sayings—Logia of the exoteric church. Myth—Mythos and Mythology—derived from the Greek Mythos meant and were equivalent to Logos.

The earliest manifested Logos was female everywhere. She was the Holy Spirit, the first word God spoke, His message to man, His revelation. The Sayings, or Logia, in Egypt were later assigned to Taht the Moon-god, the Sayer or Utterer of Divine Words, who was reckoner and registrar of truth in the hall of Double Truth and Double Justice. A study of ancient typology shows that it laid stress upon duality, the "Two Truths" of all life.

The dual aspect of life, the Law of Opposites, lies at the root of all Egyptian thought. The beginning was simply the Oneness[1] that opened in giving birth. The act of opening brought about duality. The Constellation of the Great Bear, which appears under so many types and names, was the matrix of the North, the opener, the Female. From Darkness came the Light, from the Circle came the Cross. Nowhere is duality more beautifully expressed than in Egyptian mythology or mythical astrology, for primitive man looked for inspiration and truth to the heavens. Nothing was so mystical in Egypt that it could not be traced to its origin, for everything there was typical.

An old Jewish tradition says that man was born of both sexes. In the beginning all ancient Gods were bi-sexual, and from the early Oneness, or the Mother, emerged the Child. Sex was originally denoted in the gesture or sign language. Following this came duality in the image, which can be found in the Sphinx, the Centaur, and many others. One of the Pharaohs was known to wear the tail of a lioness behind, so that he might thus express duality, added power.

Africa is the land of equal day and night which in her Astrological Mythology were divided into day and dark, the North and South, or Life and Death. Water and Breath were known as the regulators of all life and existence. Water was the Mother Source that brought about all crea-

---

"[1]All veritable Beginning in typology, mythology, numbers and language can be traced to the Opening of a Oneness, which divides and becomes dual in its manifestation."—Massey, Gerald—The Natural Genesis, Vol. i, p. 137.

tion. Breath and Soul were synonymous. Biologically the mystical Water of Life was Blood—Breath—fire. Water and Breath, as Blood and Fire, were symbolic of the male and the female. Adam[1] was called the "Blood of the World," or the feminine Source. Blood was called the Adamic Soul which was the mystical Water or Matter of Life, the Red Earth of mythology. Adam is Red. The Virgin Earth is Red, from which we have the name Adam, who in Egypt was Atum. Red Earth was primordial matter. The Red Sea was the Egyptian Red Lake of primordial matter. In the Semitic languages Blood was simply Blood, Wine is called the blood of the grape, but the first wine in its mystical meaning was the "Blood of the Tree of Life," and the Great Mother was imaged as the Tree. The Greek Ouranus is derived from the Egyptian Urnas, representing the Celestial Waters. "The Waters of Ouranus or Urnas is the celestial water of life, i. e., Blood. Ur is the water or oil for anointing, really blood."

The dew of life and the dew of heaven, breath and spirit, are dew condensed from breath. Rock crystal was supposed to be formed from dew, and was accounted sacred. The heavens were said to be formed by the rising of the vapor from the Abyss of Darkness, the celestial water and breath.

The duality of upper and lower heaven is indicated as Breath or the constellation Scorpio and as Water in that of the Crocodile. The Scorpion is a sign of number 6, as well as Scorpio (Serk), meaning to breathe. The Scorpion is said to have 6 eyes. Breath and the number six are identical in the Zodiacal sign Taurus, the ruler of which, Venus, is number six. Taurus and Scorpio polarize each other in the Zodiac. A passage in the "Book of the Dead" reads, "I am like the Sun in the Gates—I give the breath of life to

---

[1] There is a symbolical relationship between the two Adams of the Bible, one the man of Red earth and the other the heavenly man, or earth and heaven. The humanizing of Adam through the Fall was the descent of the soul into matter in one interpretation, or heaven brought down to earth, but originally it was due to the stars that "came not in their proper season."

Osiris. I have come like the Sun through the Gate of the Sun-goers, otherwise called the Scorpion." Scorpio is the eighth gate in the Zodiac, the gate of darkness, opening into life everlasting.

Our American Quiché have the duality of wind (breath) and water. In their myth of the Four Ancestors, which were four forms of spirit or breath, they represented the four elements as male—breath, air, fire, and water—said to be created by the air in motion. Their four wives, mothers of the human race, were forms of water, as Beautiful Water, Falling Water, Water of Serpents and Water of Birds.

In the New Testament there are the two baptisms, one by water and one by fire, or as Justin says, "Fire kindled in the River Jordan."

In the duality of Light and Shade, or light and its negation, dark, are found the two primaries in which all colors blend.

There are the two solstices, north and south. Two stars or constellations are connected with this division and are known as the "Lawgivers" of the Zodiac, Kepheus in the north and Regulus in the south. The sign Libra, or the scales, when placed at the equinoctial level as a connecting link between the two heavens, is also an emblem of the Two Truths, and of the spiritual birth from above and the physical birth from below.

The Chinese have two primal principles called Yang and Yin, male and female, or father heaven and mother earth. They were originally known as Light and Shadow. They also had their two waters or rivers in the valley of Han, which is the Egyptian Aan, the Fish. It was in this valley that the mythical "Yellow Emperor" of China received the ancient Dragon Writings from the river Ho, and the Tortoise Writings from the river Lo. These two waters can be found in the planisphere as the double stream of Aquarius.[1] One of the myths speaks of a mist which hung over

---

[1]An ancient name of the birthplace is found in this double stream of Aquarius.

the river for three days and nights, and when it lifted the
Emperor saw a great Fish, to which he made sacrifice, and
as it swam out to sea, he discovered and secured the mysterious map writings. This Fish was probably the royal
star Fomalhaut. Fomalhaut means the Mouth of a Fish,
and is found in Pisces Australis, a paranatellon of Aquarius.

Among the primitive types of the old Great Mother are
found the Fish, the Crocodile, and the Water-cow, all of
which were said to "bring forth writing from the mouth,"
i. e., The Word, the Logos.

In a Maori myth the center of the heaven, was a point of
commencement, hence their custom of dividing a fish found
stranded on the beach. It must be divided through the
middle of the backbone and distributed to their chiefs.
This divided fish harks back to the one fish of the ancient
birthplace of the primordial division, which has come down
to us as the two fishes of the Zodiacal Pisces.

When the Solar Zodiac was formed, Pisces became the
Solar birthplace, as the outlet from the Abyss. Semiramis
was a fish-tailed goddess who brought forth her child from
the water. The child Vishnu issues from the mouth of a
fish holding in his hand The Word, rescued from the waters.
Rama in Egyptian means both Fish and Throat, hence the
issuing of the Word, the Logos, which in celestial allegory
means From Above. Rama was a name of the river Tiber,
the birthplace of the twins Romulus and Remus, and the
Mitre worn by the Pope of Rome represents the Fish's
Mouth.

The Tree, Serpent, and Water are basic sources whence
spring many myths. To several races they represented the
supreme type of Deity. In a Russian fable a Flying Serpent
brings two great heroes to the borders of a lake, into which
they throw the fresh green branch of a Tree. As it touches
the water it bursts into flames and is quickly consumed.
Going to another lake they throw into it an old or decayed
branch of a tree, which contacting the water immediately

becomes a mass of beautiful blossoms. When the people murmured against the bitter waters of Marah, Moses "cried unto the Lord; and the Lord showed him a Tree, which when he had cast into the waters, the waters were made sweet."—Exodus xv, 23-25.

Earliest emanations were from the Abyss, the primordial place of birth and re-birth, of which the fish became a dual type. Fish is a symbol of Breath, or Spirit, and Water. It lives and breathes in the water. Birth from the water was symbolized when the Egyptian goddess Neith was created, seven thousand years ago, under the type of a fish, and gave birth to her child Horus, whom she netted or fished from the water. Neith and Net are synonymous, and a fish was placed on her head symbolizing birth from the water. Neith Isis, as the Immaculate Virgin, is one of the oldest goddesses known. As "Isis she symbolized personified Nature and as Neith, primordial Matter and infinite space."

The double waters were said to issue from a mount called "The Rock of the Horizon," "The Two Topped Mountain Divine." This Mount or Rock first marked the Solstices and later the Equinoxes. Shu (Mars) was god of Solstices. He was the Smiter or Divider of the Rock from which the waters flowed, creating the division of the heavens. Shu typified Fire, also a Lamp and a Light.

The Gnostics had two baptismal rites recognized by them as physical and spiritual—exoteric or esoteric. "Generators of Years" was one of the names for the Two Pools, "The Pool of Natron and the Pool of Salt" in one of which the Sun was said to be re-born by day and the Moon was renewed by night. The Two Waters were often typified as the Pool of the Sun and the Pool of the Moon. Hebrews and Mohammedans also had their Pool of the Sun and their Pool of the Moon. "The fertilization of the world was from the Two Waters."

The Holy Mysteries of the Eleusinian Gnosis were read to the candidates for initiation from two large tablets of stone that fitted closely together and were called the Petroma. They represented Truth in a dual or double aspect. Petru in Egyptian means to interpret, to reveal, or explain. Similarly the Ten Commandments of the Old Testament were written on two tablets of stone, which are reverently read in the Christian churches, and are being interpreted as were the mysteries of old from the ancient Book of Stone called the Petroma, The Book of Truth, the Two Leaves of Truth.

The two serpents of the beginning were the Constellations, Draco in the North and Hydra in the South, both encircling the Poles. "Hydra is the Serpent of wet, of moisture, the first element of life; The Dragon of the North, the winged Dragon, the fiery Dragon,[1] the original of all the dragons of flame and drakes of fire, was the symbol of the second element of life, the breath, heat or fire that vivifies."[2]

The Head and the Tail of the Dragon represent the ascending and descending nodes of the Moon. These are points or degrees in the Zodiac occupied by the Moon when she crosses the Ecliptic. As she passes from South to North latitude she is portrayed as the dragon's head, and as the dragon's tail when she passes in the opposite direction. Eclipses usually take place in the neighborhood of the head or tail of the dragon.

Duality is found in the imagery of the two Bears, the Great Bear and the Lesser Bear of the planisphere; similarly in the two dogs, Canis major and Canis minor; the two Lions as Lion-gods; the two Fishes; the two Mothers as Virgo the Virgin and Pisces the Gestator; the Twins of Gemini, who in Egypt were the two Lion-gods. There were also the Ass and its foal; the Dragon of the North and the Dragon of the South; the double Anubis, or Sut in his dual form. Sut-Horus and Sut-Nub are a double manifestation of the Light and the Darkness of the horizon when portrayed with two

---

[1]This was the dragon that fulminates fire for protection.
[2]Massey, Gerald—The Natural Genesis, Vol. i, p. 346.

heads of birds. One is the Black Vulture of night, the other is the Golden Hawk of solar time.

In Egypt there were two golden harvests. The wilderness was made to blossom and bear fruits by the inundation of their River Nile, whose waters when first coming down were of a crude green color, and very unwholesome. The color gradually changed to red, due to the oxide of iron in the water, and when the Sun's rays spread over the river, the waters had the appearance of blood, which became typical. Red as Blood, represented to primitive man the Mother Source. Water as a first element, the Water of Life, was recognized in a mystical sense as Blood, hence the Mother Source of Life, a universal belief. Matter as the Red Earth was mystically found in mud as a source of beginning. The Sacred Lotus grew from roots in the mud but blossomed in the light. This was the perfect flower symbolizing the duality of life, as the breather in and out of the water. Isis is supposed to have conceived through smelling this flower. The Lotus was a flower of breath and reproduction, a type or image of primal Cause.

The primitive idea of the origin of good and evil as opposite principles, has evolved in our later day duality into God and the Devil. Thus does the Eternal Law of Opposites find a crude modern expression. All primitive myths originated in the darkness. The earliest reckonings came from the Night. Night was the great mystery of the mysteries. Darkness as the enemy of Light, later the enemy of man, was evolved from that strange old Dragon of the Dark which took its first form in Space, Darkness visible opponent of the Light. From this Dragon of the Dark myriads of fables have arisen, culminating in that curious composite of superstition, the Christian Devil, a real miracle of miracles!

WATCHING OVER EDEN

The serpent encircling the tree is keeping an eternal watch over Eden. He is the guardian of treasures, starry jewels and all precious things. The tree typifies the celestial mount or pole. Mount or pole interchanges with the tree, and the serpent, later called the Tempter instead of the Protector of the Tree of Knowledge.

CHAPTER V

THE GARDEN OF "THE BEAUTIFUL"

Eden (or Ghedon as a root word) means periodicity, or a definite time, and is feminine. It was created by the first turn of the Seven Stars which formed the Constellation of the Great Mother in the polar heaven, and these Seven were the archangels which became identical with the stars that sang together in the dawn of creation, when all the sons of Elohim shouted together for joy. Job xxxvii, 7.

Eden has another name, Gen-Eden, which means Paradise, a "Garden of Delight," a "Region of Supreme Loveliness." It also means to encompass, to surround, to clasp, to enclose. It was a circle of space, a cycle of time, a ring. As Paridhistha, it is situated on the horizon. Eden by whatever name it may be called is a symbol of the Seven Stars and their circle around the pole. It was the Paradise or Highlands of early Sanscrit-speaking people. Its etymological meaning in Greek signified voluptuousness. It was their Olympus. It was also the early Mount Meru, the abode of the gods, and must have been the Paradise of Mohammed, full of Houris. It was never the property of the Jew. The tale of the lost Paradise restoration has been attributed to the Hebrews but they had stolen it from the Persians. One day its significance as an imperishable symbol of the Mother heaven will again be recognized.

The original Eden meant Wisdom, and a place of bliss like Nirvana. This makes reference to the fact that man has power to evolve his own divine nature, since he holds within himself the Eden in which grows the Tree of Knowledge of Good and Evil, and man is the Knower thereof. "The Garden of Eden on the Euphrates became the garden of the

Astrologers and the Magi."   "China, 2000 B. C., had such a primitive garden in Central Asia, inhabited by the 'Dragons of Wisdom'," the Wise Ones.   The Japanese also had their Garden of Eden "on the Plateau of Pamir between the highest peaks of the Himalayan ranges," a culminating point of Central Asia, where four rivers flowed from a common source called *The Lake of the Dragons.*[1]   The Light descended at these places in the past.

The Jewish Eden was copied from the Chaldean, and its temptations were of a very great antiquity.   In past ages, there had been a Sacerdotal College having Priests called Aliem, the Hierophants of which were initiated into the knowledge of the Good and Evil of the world.   They taught the sons of men to become as one of them.   Thus in Genesis it is written, "Behold the man is to become one of us, to know good and evil," and there were Priests or Lords of the Garden of Eden who wore their "coats of skin."

The antiquity of the allegory of Genesis is indicated by the fact that the Fall of Man into generation took place in Mesozoic days, the Reptile Age, which is explained in the Zohar, which says that the serpent (Satan) which seduced Eve was a kind of Flying Camel.   In an old Zoroastrian manuscript there is an account of a huge serpent with a camel's neck, which in the Avesta is represented after the Fall as having lost "its nature and its name."

The banyan tree of India, so sacred to the Hindus (because Vishnu during one of his incarnations reposed under its mighty shade and there taught human philosophy and science) is called the Tree of Life and the Tree of Knowledge.   Under this tree their teachers impart the first lessons of immortality, and initiate their students into the mysteries of life and death.

In China today the teacher of the doctrine of Buddha is living in a temple of Buddha, on top of a mountain between China and Thibet, and there produces his greatest religious

---

[1]Blavatsky, H. P.—See The Secret Doctrine, Vol. ii, pp. 203, 204.

miracles under a tree called the Tree of Knowledge and Tree of Life.   These miracles take place every three years, when great throngs of Chinese Buddhists make a pilgrimage to this place.

The early Adepts, initiated at the fount of knowledge, who understood the mystery of life and death, have been accused by materially minded posterity of having been guilty of sin and of having been tempted by the serpent.   Strange interpretations have been developed out of the mystery of the Garden of Eden, its tree and its serpent.   The serpent was the symbol of Divine Wisdom which represented the Lord as the Logos speaking words of divine creative wisdom, that his hearers also might become creators of this wisdom in turn. A symbol of sacred knowledge in antiquity was a Tree, ever guarded by a serpent, the serpent or dragon of wisdom.   The serpent of Hercules was said to guard the golden apple that hung from the Pole, the Tree of Life, in the midst of the garden of the Hesperides.   The serpent that guarded the golden fruit in the garden of the Hesperides and the serpent of the Garden of Eden, which enfolded with its coils that mysterious tree, are the same.

Likewise Mount Meru with its beautiful tree, the abode of the Gods was guarded by the serpent guarding the North Pole, whose secret still defies the greatest explorers and scientists of the day. . We have also the myth of Juno giving to Jupiter on her marriage with him a Tree with Golden Fruit.   Is it not the same tree, the Tree of Knowledge enfolded in the coils of the serpent, which was given to Eve in the Garden of Eden, and from which she offered the apple to Adam?   What has changed this Serpent of Wisdom into the devil of the Christians?   The creative power in man is a gift of divine wisdom and not the result of sin.   It is far better to place the so-called curse of the Garden of Eden where it belongs.   "The Cross itself is an evolution from the Tree and Serpent, and thus became the salvation of mankind."   It was divine at first and later humanized. "To the Eastern Occultist the *Tree* of Knowledge in the paradise of man's own heart, becomes the Tree of Life Eternal, and has naught to do with man's animal senses."[1]   "The universal essence is first figured as a Tree of Life, union with the Tree of Life is said to be 'The consummation of vision and the perfection of the mystical'."

The original Pillar of heaven as applied to the North was the pivoting point or Pole. This was the Mount, with its alluring garden, that surrounded the world. In Ezekiel, chapter xxviii, 13-14, the Lord is speaking, saying "Thou hast been in Eden, the Garden of God; every precious stone *was* thy covering. . . . Thou wast upon the Holy Mountain of God, thou hast walked up and down in the midst of the precious stones of fire." These are the Stars, the Pillar, the Tree and the Pole that belong to the Garden of Eden.

Within the Temples of Egypt, Babylon and China the heavens are depicted upon the ceilings as "A Dome of Stars" the Mount that surrounded the world.

There is also the beautiful Asvattha, Tree of Life, of the Bhagavad-Gita, whose roots are generated in Heaven, representing the Supreme Being, and whose luxuriant branches spread out over the terrestrial world. Those who can reach above its branches need never reincarnate and return to experience the suffering of the world. But when this tree reached the Garden of Genesis it became changed beyond imagination, its pristine purity was soiled, and it has ever since been the herald of perverted truth and called a Curse.

The passing of aeons of time has given many names and forms to all symbols which were originally cosmic and astronomical. The Tree might always have been kept green, nurtured by the Water of Life, and the Dragon always have been divine, had they not been forced out of their Sidereal Home. The primal pair in Paradise were Typhon, goddess of the Great Bear (Ursa Major) and Sut, her son, as manifestor of the Little Bear (Ursa Minor), the two constella-

---

[1]Blavatsky, H. P.—The Secret Doctrine, Vol. ii, p. 587.

tions revolving around the pole of the Tree. There is a Kamite legend of Isis and Osiris living together in Paradise in peace and happiness until Osiris became possessed with the desire for the drink of immortality, in the search for which he fell. Osiris is the reputed discoverer of the vine, which is seen in the decans of Virgo, and Isis, Virgin of this sign, was the discoverer of wheat, branches of which she carries in her hand. Wheat is the symbol of seed, and generation of life is from the seed. The vine, or the grape, was an emblem of wisdom and knowledge. The wheat has been thought by both Rabbins and Musselmen to have been the forbidden fruit eaten by Adam. We are told that "Adam at the moment when he tasted wheat, received the seed for the propagation of mankind. From the grain which he ate sprang up a tree; life in me and in thee is its fruit."[1] The first seed belonged to the Great Mother.

The Iriquois have their legend of the lost heaven or Paradise, and of the woman who dwelt there, to whom they sent a messenger borne on the wings of a bird, who watched and waited until she came to the tree in the garden, to draw water from the well, and then tempted her to fall from grace. It is not unlike the Christian legend of Mary being watched at the well by the Angel Gabriel. In the Iriquois legend it is said that when the woman fell from heaven she was caught on the back of a tortoise, on which was placed a quantity of soil brought from the bottom of the sea by a fish, and that there she gave birth to twins, sisters, found in many myths. Ignorance leads to profination, and ridicule born of misunderstanding to untruth, conditions that inflame and energize the fiery wheels of animal instincts found in the Zodiac, the Wheel of Re-birth. The undercurrent of our world of humanity is setting toward a goal reflecting the stars above. The dogmatism that can see nothing but cobwebs in ancient philosophy and antagonizes the seeker of archaic truths, will have to do battle with the Law of Compensation.

---

[1] Shea and Troyer—Dabistan, Vol. ii, p. 338.

To sum up the entire story of the Garden of Eden, Sharp writing on Egypt says, "The whole history of the fall of man is of Egyptian origin. The temptation of the woman by the serpent, and of man by the woman, the sacred tree of knowledge, the cherubs guarding with flaming swords at the door of the garden, the warfare declared between the woman and the serpent, may all be seen upon the Egyptian sculptured monuments."

There were said to be four Rivers of Eden which proceeded from a central river. The River Pison flows around the land of Gold and Light, dispensing and receiving. The River Gihon flows around the land of Ethiopia, or Darkness, land of the most primitive races. Hiddekel runs eastward to Assyria, a stream of Power—"The stream rising and flowing back to ancient or interior ages, guiding to Assyria the land of perfection and peace." The fourth river Euphrates means the weaving together. It is fundamental power, and is joy and delight—"The Voice of Heaven." It was anciently called the "Soul of the Land."

Again we have the four rivers proceeding from a central river, as 1 plus 4 equals 5. 1 equals the Monad, the Source. 4 Signature of the Earth. But 5 equals 2 plus 3. 2 Duad, Antagonism, Light versus Darkness. 3 Light Triumphant, Divinity in triple aspect. 2 plus 3, Duad permeated by and ruled over by Superior Force. "As above, so below" is always to be remembered. Thus a correspondence is found between the four fixed stars and the mundane registration of the Cardinal Cross.

There are also the Cosmic Rivers of the Human Will or Physical Generation, with the Tree of Life at the center, and all flowing from one source as they go forth to water the Paradise of the heavens, or the heaven in one's heart. In the stars we find many mystic meanings. Do not turn aside from the mystical, nor from legends, for they are

most beautiful, and were of Celestial origin created for all
Eternity.

It was foretold that wherever a river-head could be located,
even with channels that no longer existed in usefulness, provided there were four waterways, suggesting that it had once
"run on all fours," a Biblical Eden would be discovered,
whether in Asia, Africa, Europe or America.   There is an
ancient legendary prophecy that the Lost Paradise with its
Tree of Life will reappear upon a mount, from whose summit there will spring four rivers that will reach to the four
quarters of the world.   There was an ancient hymn to the
Goddess Ishtar extolling her as the Queen of the Four Rivers
which carries us back to the ancient Mother.

The cross is of immense antiquity, and was first celestial.
The Tree of Paradise was called the Tree of the Cross, and
was placed at the Mount of the Four Corners in the Garden
of Eden, which was formed by the stars encircling the pole.
Here the great Serpent, as the constellation Draco, kept his
sacred watch, "the Cross *was* an evolution from 'The Tree
and the Serpent' and thus *became the salvation of mankind*.   By this it would become the very first fundamental
symbol of Creative cause, applying to geometry, to numbers, to astronomy, to measure and to animal reproduction."[1]

The cross that is so sacred to the Christians is supposed
to date from the Crucifixion, about two thousand years ago.
For many years the cross stood for the Christ, but not the
humanized Christ of whom we have learned from the theologians, but for the Christ that in those days of antiquity was a
personification of the Supreme Spirit, the Higher Self.
Only in the Catacombs of Rome during the early centuries
of the Christian era, has the ageless celestial Christ of the
polar cross been humanized, and set up as an alleged starting
point for a new religion.   The earliest human figure on a
cross appeared during that period and roused many question-
ings and much skepticism concerning the truths and realities

---

[1]Blavatsky, H. P.—The Secret Doctrine, Vol. ii, p. 216.

of the Christ of the new religion, since the many and various symbols used needed explanation and harked back to an allegorical Christ.   This questioning and unrest among the people disturbed the Church very much, for previously the symbol on the cross was a Lamb.   Consequently during the reign of Justinian II, fearing lest the reality of a personal Christ be lost, the Council of Trullo decided that for the future the figure of a personal Jesus should be portrayed upon the crucifix in place of the Lamb.   "He shall be represented in his human form, instead of the lamb, as in former times."

No portrait of Jesus had been extant at any time to prove either his humanity, or his divinity.   Therefore, he had been represented in many ways, even as a type of the so-called pagan gods.   It was very necessary to retain and not lose the symbol.   "Therefore, it was proclaimed that the symbol of the Lamb was to be superseded by the human form, as the Christ our Lord."   The Lamb had been mentioned as the type of sacrifice belonging to the Zodiacal sign Aries, symbolized by the Lamb or the Ram.   Adrian, Pontiff of Rome in the Eighth Century, proclaimed that the "Lamb of God must not be depicted upon the cross as the chief object, but there is no hindrance to the painting of a Lamb on the reverse or inferior portion of the cross where Christ hath been duly portrayed as a man."[1]

Over and over again one finds this imagery belonging to ancient times twisted and turned into a later historical and theological form.   The cross was that of Life, never that of Death, and was an image of Immortality.   In many countries it represented the four foundations of the world, the four corners, emblems of reproduction, duration; and type of the Eternal.

The Tree of Life and the Cross were identical also with that Mount Meru of the Four Corners that originated at the Pole, with its seven steps, our Paradise.   There is a legend

---

[1] Cited by Didron, Icon. Chret, pp. 338–339.

that tells us that "Seth obtained a shoot from the Tree of Life, and placed it on Adam's grave at Golgotha, where it sprang up as the Cross of Christ, and the spot where it was reburied was discovered by Helena."   Another legend tells us that when Adam was sick unto death he sent his son Seth to the Gate of Paradise to pray for a little oil from the Tree of Life as a cure.   But the Tree had vanished with the lost Eden."   This was the seven-branched tree, replaced by the Cross of the Four Corners, or a tree of twelve branches.

In another version Adam asks his son to tell the prophets and the patriarchs what the angel Michael had told him when he was praying at the gate of Paradise for a little oil to anoint his father's head and heal his pain.   The answer was that he had been told that he was not to entreat God for "The oil of mercy, because in no way could he obtain this oil until the Last Day and Times."

It is said by Esdras of those who are to be saved, "They shall have the tree of life for an ointment of sweet savor." Esdras, II, 12.   "The Tree of Life and knowledge is represented as being restored in the shape of the cross, and the solar god who entered Amenti once a year is now depicted as doing the same thing at the end of the great cycle, as it is written in the *'First Book of the Seventy'* in a certain sacred volume said to have been preserved by the Jews."[1]

These sayings all belong to the allegories of the heavens and that immaculate birthplace in the North, and to the great cyclic periods produced by the Precession of the Equinoxes.

The Rod of Moses was fabled to have been a shoot from the Tree of Life.   Likewise in a Christian tradition it is said that the cross of Calvary was composed of four kinds of wood—the palm, the cedar, the olive and the cypress.   This was surely the cross that represented the four corners or the four points of the Cardinal Cross of the world.   The mystical or mythological cross never consisted of four different kinds

---

[1] Massey, Gerald—The Natural Genesis, Vol. ii, pp. 382, 383.

of wood, yet many and varied are the traditions belonging to all countries of the world concerning a certain wood held most sacred, from which the cross might have been made. It was said to be the Elder, which suggests the ancient mother Typhon, "it is yet believed in England, and in other northern countries, that the wood of the *true* cross was elderwood . . . the elder was one of the trees of life in the north and a type of the old Mother. The elder is one of the wine trees, a producer of the inspiring juice, and its leaves and flowers are still held to be very healing. Also there was a sacred festival at which the Romans annually paraded a kind of crucifixion consisting of a dog stretched out alive upon a cross of elderwood. The exhibition was made between the temples of Juventus and Summanus."[1]

In King's "Gnostics," on page 91, there is shown a most curious picture of a crucifixion found on the Palatine walls of Rome, for stretched on the cross is a dog with the ears of an ass. This was paraded in one of the Gnostics annual festivals, and was thought to be the work of a pious Gnostic, but has been termed the "Blasphemous Crucifixion." The dog was a type of the Egyptian Sut—as Anup he was the Golden Jackal, and depicted on the cross or at the Crossing. Sut, as we know, was the first son of the ancient mother, who was represented as the great star in the South, Sirius, or the Dog-Star, and who as the starry announcer had three different types—the dog, the jackal, and the ass. He was the guide of the crossings in pre-solar and pre-Christian myths, when known as Sut-Nahsi or Sut-Nubti, he was the negro god, continued in Egypt as Sut-Har of the Sun and Sirius cycle, a Sabean-Solar combination found in other mythologies where a Star-god of fire became a Sun-god.

Sut as Anubis was the Egyptian embalmer and preserver of the dead; in Greece he was the Hound of Hermes, who guided souls to the River Styx. He also guided the sun and the souls (the stars) through the underworld, or night,

---

[1]Massey, Gerald—The Natural Genesis, Vol. i. p. 434.

and became the "Preparer of the Way," Guide of the passage through the dark as the Star of Sunset. He became guide of the resurrection, the deliverer, the Saviour, as he reached the Sunrise of the horizon. In planetary form the Dog-Star is Mercury. Statues of the god Mercury as a protector from harm were erected, and were in the shape of the cross. In Inner Africa, as the jackal, Mercury was called the god of thieving, and later became the Mercury of the Romans. By "thief" is meant the dark encroaching on the light. Both the jackal and the dog-headed ape were types of the thief of light, just as the fox and the jackal were the Typhonian types of the Dark Power, which was the thief of the light of the Moon. These two were also the prophesiers, their bark usually predicting calamity of some kind. The Golden Jackal as the messenger, Mercury, was the prophet of the Dog-Star, and of sunrise and sunset. The coyote, the prairie dog of the North American Indians, was thought by them to have brought the rood-diggers of California into the world. On the fifth day of their most solemn religious ceremony, the Iriquois Indians sacrificed a white dog by burning, to establish communication with the Most High God. The Lenni Lenape Indians honored the wolf as the animal that released mankind from the dark abode underground. The Dog-Star "Fiery Flaming Sentinel of the Fiery Hosts of Space," son of the Immaculate Mother—Goddess, can be traced by means of monuments and allegory to the Lamb, the type of Fulfilment.

There are pictures extant of the Lamb standing on a mountain, out of which four rivers seem to be flowing, symbolizing the four quarters of the world. Didron writes of a monument of the Eleventh Century portraying the four streams called Gyon, Phishon, Tygris and Eufrates, symbolized as men, each carrying an urn of one of the streams. Their type and head-dress show them to be members of the Mithraic cult. To this cult the Ram of Aries belonged which the Persians always called the Lamb., and we are told by Dupuis, that the Persians celebrated a feast relative to the cross just before the Sun entered the sign Aries, the Lamb, when the Southern Cross, the cross that remains in heaven for all time, shone most brilliantly at night as a beautiful type of the Vernal Equinox.

In Christian Iconography the cross is connected with the Lamb, representing the equinoctial colure in the sign of Aries, the Ram.   This crossing, as all other Zodiacal crossings, represented a cycle of 2160 years, and was called the Christ sacrifice of that cycle.   The Lamb or Ram type also belongs to India, where the Spirit or God of Fire was symbolized as the Cross of Fire ridden by the Lamb, and was their solar sign of reproducing power.   The Hindu Agni is the Agnus Dei of the Christians.

The Egyptian god Sebek-Ra, who wore the horns of the Ram or Lamb, is identical with the Lamb that was imaged on the cross for seven or eight centuries, and which bore the sins of the world or took them away, and was later converted into a human figure.   With the ending of this cycle of Aries came the beginning of that of the Fishes, or the Zodiacal sign Pisces, when the child was portrayed as a fish. This cycle of the Fishes was ushered in a little over two thousand years ago.

In the Hermean Zodiac a Fish-goddess is to be seen holding a dove in her hand.   The Fish, the Dove, the Cross and the monogram K R are all found in the Typology of the Catacombs of Rome, where "the concealed burial-place of the ancient religion, visibly becomes the birthplace of the new, and it is there we can see the types in the process of transformation."[1]

The cross is composed of Chi and Ro, which reads Chr. Chr was accepted as an abbreviated name for Christ, or conveyed that meaning, but was not of Christian origin.   Forty years before the Christian Era it was found on the coins of the Ptolemies and also on those of Herod.   Chi and

---

[1]Massey, Gerald—The Natural Genesis, Vol. i, p. 454.

Ro are the circle and the cross. The Ru is an oval, found on the top of the Ankh Cross, which we find as the symbol of the planet Venus. In Egyptian Chr or Kher or Kheru signifies a Word, a Voice, and later became the solar Logos. Ker is a circle and identified with the Ark, Kr and Ark are symbols of the cross and the circle. The ark was the circle made by the Constellation of the Great Bear, that primary circle made in heaven and earth, and is inseparable from the cross, which was the symbol and type of the first four corners of the world.[1] Ru or Kr is a circle or a course of time, and in various other languages has the meaning of a course. In Greek it became an abbreviation of Kronus. K R is the root of the name Kronus, Course, Circle, Cross, and Christ. Chrestos (Greek) was the early Gnostic name for Christ. Justin Martyr claims the early Christians were called Chrestians.

To the Gnostics, who were the early Christians, Christ as the "Word of God" was never accepted as a man of flesh; manifestation of the spirit was through the illumination of the mind, it was the purification of the Spirit. "No man hath seen God at any time; the only begotten Son, which is in the bosom of the Father, he hath declared *him.*—John i, 18. "*Even* the Son of man which is in heaven."—John iii, 13.

To them Christos meant the impersonal principle, the Atma within every man's soul, not Jesus. The Fall, Incarnation, Atonement, and Resurrection were never accepted literally by them. In the British Museum is an old Coptic MS. in which Christos is frequently referred to and this word is found to have been constantly replaced by that of Jesus. Chrest is stolen or borrowed from the pagans, and meant to them "'A disciple on probation,' a candidate for hierophantship; who, when he had attained it, through initiation, long trials and suffering, and had been anointed (rubbed with oil),

---

[1] A cross is the symbol of the old god Anu of the Assyrian myth, and Annu is the Egyptian place of the crossing and equinox; also of Anit (Neith), who brings forth the child at the crossing.

was changed to *Chrestos*—the 'purified' . . . the Chrestos, the 'man of Sorrow,' became Christos himself." The finding of the Christ within had taken place. Krishna, the Avatar, was sought for among the shepherds who had concealed him, and thousands of their newly-born babies were slain during the search. His conception, birth and childhood is the prototype of the story in the New Testament.[1]

The first Cross was celestial and Sabean, created by the revolution of the constellation of the Great Bear, and its pattern was found in the Ankh Cross of the Egyptians, their symbol of Eternal Life and Continuity. It was from this revolution that the origin of time, the cardinal points of the world, and the cross of the four quarters were derived. It was followed by the Solar God, who made his circle and crossing in the Equinoxes and Solstices. A type is also found in the Swastika, which has a nail in each of its four corners, and which is symbolized in the human figure extended with nails in hands and feet. The figure of the cube unfolded forms the figure of the cross. The cross was originally a symbol of life, but finally came to symbolize death and the blood sacrifice. Besides this fourfold cross there is the sixfold, many churches being builded on the sixfold cross of the four quarters, the Zenith, and Nadir.

In Ecclesiastical heraldry the single cross belongs to the Bishops, the double cross to the Cardinals and Archbishops, while the sixfold belongs to the Pope. The sixfold cross was known ages before the Christian era. It was the cross of the completed solar circle. In a feminine form it was the triple cross, the S S S of the Sistrum and a form of the 6 6 6 of the Book of Revelation, known as the Beast. The double triangle, known in India under the sign of Vishnu, with its apex pointing upwards, was always masculine, and with the apex pointing downwards was feminine and a form of the number 6. The circle in its primacy, as the circle in heaven as well as on earth, is the Ru, the female sign which is insep-

---

[1] See "The Key to Theosophy," H. P. Blavatsky.

arable from the cross.   In the human aspect of its typology there must always be the male-female, therefore there could never be a cross without the circle, for otherwise there could be no reproduction.

Nails were emblems of reproduction and generation for both male and female, and are found on the hands and feet on cuneiform figures, symbolizing a second life.   They also represent a phase of pubescence, gestation and resurrection. Nails are found on the chests of mummies in Egypt as a symbol of pubescence, potency and virility, and they signify "to rise again."   The number of nails used depended upon the type of cross.

In the original crucifixion there is no cross.   In the ancient cult of the Avatar Krishna the crucified one *was* the cross, and was typical of the Tree of Life.   The stigmata are seen on his hands and feet, and represent the Transfiguration, the passing from one life to another, the re-birth into a higher spiritual existence.

The crucified Vishnu is seen extended into space, with nail marks on hands and feet as tokens of his divinity and emblem of his virility, which was so powerful as to cause him to be re-born after his crucifixion.   On that wonderful Tree of Life, not Death, no wood is seen, no inscription, no nimbus, thus proving that the crucifixion of Vishnu was entirely pre-Christian.

Nails are also seen on the hands and feet of Buddha, and on Maya, just as they are seen on the arms of the Swastika cross, that "Cross of the four quarters, foundation of the world.   The Cross that can be traced back to the very depths of the unfathomable Archaic ages."

In Egypt, at the Vernal Equinox, when the Sun and the Moon were reunited at Easter time, the child Horus was born.   In mediaeval times pictures of the crucifixion were accompanied by representations of the Sun and the Moon, symbols of re-birth.   The woman arrayed with the Sun and Moon under her feet, is the Mother Moon at the Vernal

Equinox, who brings forth her child at Easter, as related in the Book of Revelation.

The position of the Sun and Moon at Easter is responsible for the two traditions of the Crucifixion (the Passover or the Crossing) occurring one on the 14th, the other on the 15th of the Egyptian month Nisan, as well as for the two celebrations of the Resurrection of Christ, which survived until a late period in Rome. There are two diverse statements concerning the Resurrection in the New Testament, one in St. Luke and the other in the Book of Acts, further explained through the Mythos by Gerald Massey:

"In Luke the risen Christ is "carried up into Heaven" on the third day following the crucifixion. In the Acts he is not "taken up" into Heaven until the fortieth day, or after forty days! Such serious discrepancies as these are forever irreconcilable as history, but they are found to contain the very facts that reconstitute the Mythos.

"The resurrection of Osiris at the Autumn equinox was lunar; at the vernal equinox it was solar. After he was betrayed to his death, when the sun was in the sign Scorpio, he rose again on the third day as Lord of Light in the moon, or as Horus, the child of the mother-moon. The solar resurrection was at the vernal equinox when the sun entered the first of the upper signs and Orion rose. This time it was in the character of the second Horus, the adult of 30 years; and this second resurrection followed the forty days of mourning for the suffering God which were celebrated in the Mysteries, and survive in a Christianized form as our Lent. And just as the myth of the double Horus in the two characters of the child of 12 years, and the adult Horus of 30 years, has been continued in the Gospels to furnish the two phases in the life of Jesus, so have the two different resurrections with their correct dates been applied to the Christ made historical.

"Thus interpreted by means of the Mythos these two versions of one alleged fact tend to corroborate my explanation already made that the two different dates for the crucifixion given in the otherwise irreconcilable accounts belong to the luni-solar reckoning in the same luni-solar myth.   In Egyptian the signs of a half moon and fourteen days are identical; and in the dark half of the moon Osiris was torn into fourteen parts.   Therefore, the 14th of the lunar month was the day of full moon.   Whereas in the soli-lunar month of thirty days the 15th was the middle of the month.   Now the crucifixion or the crossing at Easter was and still is determined by the day of full moon.   This will be on the 14th of the month of twenty-eight days in the reckoning by the moon only, but on the 15th of the month according to the soli-lunar reckoning.   Both reckonings were extant in two different cults and both were separately continued by the Eastern and Western Churches for the one day of the crucifixion.   Both cannot be historically correct, but they *are* both astronomically true.   Both could be made to meet at a given point in the total combination which was determined by the conjunction of the sun and moon at the equinox as *the* day of full moon.   But the two different dates for the mid-month remained, and these are represented by the traditions of two different dates for the crucifixion. Both the lunar and the solar dates could be utilized by the Mythos, in which there were two crucifixions and two resurrections, though these will not bear witness for the single fact of the historical crucifixion.   As we have seen, the two ascensions of Osiris on the third day and at the end of forty days, have been preserved, and are repeated as historical transactions.   Two different Crosses were also continued in the Christian Iconography as the cross of Autumn and of Easter; and although we may not be able to show two crucifixions in the Canonical Gospels, nevertheless the total matter of the Mythos is there.   When Jesus was led up into the wilderness to be tempted of the devil, and to suffer during forty days, we have the parallel to the struggle between Osiris and Sut, which was celebrated during the forty days of mourning in the mysteries. Moreover, there were two days of death or crucifixion kept in Rome until the present century, when the dead Christ used to be laid out and exhibited on the Thursday before Good Friday; and two days of resurrection were also celebrated in the two Sabbaths on Saturday and Sunday. As the Apostolic Constitutions show, both of these days were continued for the two weekly holidays of the Christians, Saturday being the day of rising again on the 7th day of the week in the lunar cult; Sunday, the Sabbath of the 8th day, according to the solar resurrection. Such are the fundamental facts; and, to my thinking, they are of sufficient force to cleave the Canonical history right in two, each half being then claimed by the Mythos. Here, as elsewhere, the Mythos does explain the fact, but only by abolishing the history. From beginning to end the ascertainable facts are astronomical, and interpretable solely by means of the Gnostic explanation of the Egyptian Mythos, which always denied, because it disproved, the alleged human history."

The mummy, type of preservation, was called by the Egyptians the Karast or Christ, and the perfection to which these people had brought the embalming of their dead indicates that it must have originated in a very remote past. The embalmed corpse of their dead was type of the Karast, and was intended as the image of their own resurrection, the spiritualized other self, which was the Eternal. It was created through a great desire to make the other self permanent, which accounts for the marvelous way in which the mummy was prepared. It has been found carefully wrapped in woven bands of linen one thousand yards in length without a seam. It was the seamless robe of their primitive Karast which was the type of the mystical Christ, the everlasting spirit within. The mummy was never intended for a physical resurrection, as their doctrine of the hereafter was one of Transformation. They believed in the continuity and immortality of the Spirit, and not in a bodily resurrection. It was the Transformed, who would arise from the dead at the re-birth of the spirit in the heaven world. This Mummy-Christ type of the Spirit was placed in the tomb, which they always called their "Good Dwelling." Great ingenuity was shown in their endeavor to retain a general likeness of the dead, as the other self, the True Self, the Spirit which was its own ancestor. This was the origin of their Ancestor Worship.

The Assyrian Mammit, which was called Shebti, the double of the dead, was also of Egyptian origin, and was spoken of "As a shape of Salvation, descending from the midst of the Heavenly Abyss." It was a preservative figure of divine attributes, which was placed in the hands of the dying, and was thought to be the "one Deity that never failed." Two images were sometimes placed with the dead in the tomb, one the Shebti, double of the dead, ready for transformation; the other the Ka, the spiritual. higher and immortal self.

Man was thought to be composed of various bodies. The Ka was an ethereal projection or double of the person, and a perfect likeness. The Ba, the soul, was portrayed as a bird, while the Khoo, "The Luminous," was the spark of divine fire. The Ka, the immortal self, remained with the body, but the Ba and the Khoo left it to follow the gods, though they kept continually returning. Body, soul and spirit seem to have been represented.

The Shebti, symbol of a second life, "was made of red clay, which denoted the flesh, and glazed with a vitreous varnish that was blue, the color sacred to the soul. This is the complexion of the deceased who has been spiritualized. The soul is likewise painted blue in the act of leaving its red body behind. This color is the symbol of human immortality. Blue is also the robe of wisdom whose bands are purple lace."[1] The embalming of the dead with red clay or red earth, which represented flesh, is of most ancient ori-

---

[1]Massey, Gerald—The Natural Genesis, Vol. ii, p. 124.

gin.   Red was the sacred color.   Sometimes a material other than earth, but of a red color was used for the embalming of the dead, a process which did not belong to Egypt alone.   In Africa the red earth was used in various ways as a covering for the body of the living as a protection from the intense heat of the Inner African sun.   This method finally developed into the preservation of the dead.   In many instances bones of the dead were unearthed and coated with it.   In the Book of the Dead we read, "I have made the dress which Ptah has woven out of clay."   "Ptah was the re-clother of the deceased in flesh, i. e., the red clay which represented flesh, and the clay dress of Ptah was initiated by this primitive way of embalming bones, a rite performed among the Maoris, the Australian aborigines, Mound Builders of Britain and the North American Indians.

The Constellation of Orion was known as the Mummy Constellation, which arose six thousand years ago.   It represented the re-arisen Horus, and was called the Star of the East.   It was the Mammit, type of Karast, image of the "Eternal when he transformed in the underworld and obtained a Soul in the stars of heaven as he arose on the horizon as or in the constellation of Orion."   Karast also means to anoint, to embalm or make a mummy.   It is that which was placed in the tomb for the re-birth of the spirit.   "His soul does not enter or is not thrust back into his mummy forever," says the "Book of the Dead."   This was that other self to whom they gave worship.[1]

Even today in the heart of Africa the dying are prepared for the tomb with the greatest reverence, for the tomb is to them typical of the womb, hence the greatest care is exercised to keep the likeness of the dead as nearly perfect

---

[1] When the vernal equinox was in the sign Taurus, Orion became the image of the re-arisen Horus, his "Glorified Body," and then it was said "to shine in the stars of the constellation Orion, on the bosom of the upper heaven."— (Book of Sen-Sen I, Records, Vol. iv, p. 121.)   In the ritual the re-arisen mummy says, "I am the great constellation Orion dwelling in the solar birthplace in the midst of the spirits."

as possible, and similar to the foetal embryo. The head
is drawn to the knees, which touch the chest, and the legs
are folded to the thighs. Many other nations prepare their
dead in the same way. In Africa a net is often used about
the body to draw it into a living shape. It is the oldest form
of burial known, and belongs to the Palaeolithic age, going
back some 50,000 years.

All ancient tombs were images of the maternal birthplace,
and their earliest form was always feminine. This mother-
mould was adopted by the ancients because of their reverence towards the mystery of birth, and their desire to reproduce. In whatever light they looked upon their Christ,
whether astronomical or mythical, he was not of the flesh,
though of both sexes, male-female, a Supreme Spirit.

All these primitive beliefs speak more eloquently of divine
truths than does anything evolved by the so-called learning
attained by man in later, darker ages. Modern teaching and
theology are devoid of the profound reverence which the
ancients had for the mystery of birth and rebirth. Primitive
phallic worship was as pure and spotless as the seamless
mummy band, robe of their Christ. Unrecognized and
unthought of by the majority of Christians, phallic emblems
and worship survive today in the symbolism of the churches
and their surrounding tombs, which symbolism was instituted
and founded upon the primitive worship of reproduction.

In Egypt, when a net was placed on the outside of the
mummy in its preparation, it was the symbol of the goddess
Neith. This was the net with which she rescued the young
Horus from the water. Interwoven with it were what were
called the "Beads of Isis," sign of reproduction and gestation, toward which they felt innate veneration. "Neith
was 'Lady of the Waters,' from whose divine personality
gushed the stream of life, and who gave to every mummy
the draught for which he thirsted," like the parched lands
thirsting for the waters of the River Nile. The scarab was
also woven in the network, symbol of the regeneration of

the mummy in the tomb, or reproduction as a primal truth.[1]

During Egyptian feasts a mummy image was carried about and presented to each person with this remark: "Look upon this, then drink, and rejoice, for thou shalt be as this."[2] This was done to remind them of immortality and the rebirth of happiness, belonging to the mystery of transformation.

One of the Quiché myths tells of four old Men, Spirits or Gods, who when dying left in their place a Bundle which could never be opened or unfolded, as it had been made seamless.   This Bundle was known as the "Enveloped Majesty" and was held sacred as a memorial to the Fathers.   These four "Old Men," after giving counsel to those they were leaving behind, sang an ancient sweet song called KAMUCU, meaning "WE SEE."   The myth says that they sang the song at the mythical sunrise of the world "when all the stars sang together and all the sons of God shouted for joy" as they shone rejoicing in the primeval dawn.   The Bundle bears a certain resemblance to the mummy of Egypt.   In the myth the four are combined into one.   In many instances fourfold gods or spirits are compounded into one.   Ezekiel, the Book of Revelation, Brahme, and Tat are examples of this and belong to the typology of the four corners.   The dropping of a garment in passing meant the leaving of the body behind.   The bundle represented the god or spirit which had departed, and reminds one of the mummy type of Egypt.

Green was a type of the Eternal, and a green stone was a symbol of reproduction.   A green stone, as well as a green axe, were worn by both the living and the dead.   The color green had the same significance with the Aztecs, the Chinese,

---

[1]Herodotus.

[2]The Tie was a hieroglyphic sign of reproduction, and also a sign of the covenant, carried by the Great and enceinte Mother as her emblem.   It was an ideograph of periodicity, of feminine pubescence, "The first Ankh-tie was put on at puberty by the leaf-wearers, some of them still clothe themselves with a leaf-girdle today."

The collar called Mena or Menka was the ring of the wet nurse.   It was made with nine or ten beads, symbolical of the nine or ten months of gestation, and sign of the covenant.

the Neolithic men, and with the Egyptians.   Axes were made
from the polished emerald, felspar, jade or jasper.   The axe
was type of founding by opening the ground, and making the
passage for the dead on its way towards the image of its resurrection.   "Axes of green stone were also buried in the
ancient mounds of Japan, and an emerald was made the base
or heart of the Aztec mummy."

The Swastika Cross was placed on the breasts of defunct
mystics, and has been found on the heart of statues of
Buddha.   "It is a *SEAL* placed also on the hearts of living
Initiates, burnt into the flesh, forever, with some"[1]—because
they must keep certain Truths inviolate, intact, and in eternal silence until an appointed time, although this symbol is
degraded today, it can never lose its mysterious power.

The earliest *Stigma* ever branded on the human body was
a totemic token of puberty, and was the origin of the cross
used as a brand cut into the flesh, or tatooed on the
thigh at the time when the crossing from boyhood into manhood was being accomplished.   This tattooing was also
typical of parenthood in either men or women.   Primitive
people knew well the life histories of the animals which they
so freely make use of as Totems.   From earliest times animals, birds, insects and reptiles were adopted as a symbolic
means of expression.   The zoological system of typology will
endure forever as it appropriately symbolized the stars and
the constellations.

The origin of Totemism and heraldry is found in Egypt,
where entymológical symbolism was used by tribes, clans or
groups of people for purposes of identification.   The earliest
ideographs, even extended to the individual man whom we
find denoted by his individual star.   Primitive people are
known to clothe themselves in figures of birds and animals,
which they wear in their primitive dances, imitating the
call of the bird or the cry of the animal which they personify,
every tribe being distinguished by its appropriate animal

---

[1]Blavatsky, H. P.—The Secret Division, Vol. ii, p. 586.

Totem sign. Totemism began ages before a male or individual fatherhood as progenitor was known. Descent came from the mother's side and she was first pictured as an animal, and that animal was the type of the entire group or clan. The Totem representing the ancestor's name did not originate until ages thereafter. These groups and clans became symbolized in the Constellations, the Star groups, thus linking their souls with the stars. Amongst the Arab tribes many used a certain star as Totem, whilst others adopted the constellations, and in certain countries shooting stars were supposed to be the souls of the departed. Star Totems became star deities, and the Totemic archetypes in heaven may be found in every likeness on earth. The twelve signs of the Zodiac are Totemic and are symbolized as animals. Today we follow that ancient method for the ruling planet of the horoscope is the "Individual Guiding Star" anciently a Totemic type.

The Cross and the Circle in our planetary symbolism are indivisible. In Mercury there is the half circle, the circle, and the cross; Jupiter gives us the cross and the crescent; Mars is the cross on the circle; Venus has the cross below the circle; Saturn has the semicircle and the cross. The square was always the symbol of the earth, and the circle that of heaven. The fourth finger wears the circle of the wedding ring because the thumb touching the fourth finger makes the circle which denotes fatherhood. The cross as a sign denoting the four corners or quarters is found everywhere. The cross of the Christians is perhaps the sole exception, since it became to the Christians type of the Eternal Region, finally found by them in the Zodiacal sign Pisces which solar birthplace became chief of all corners.

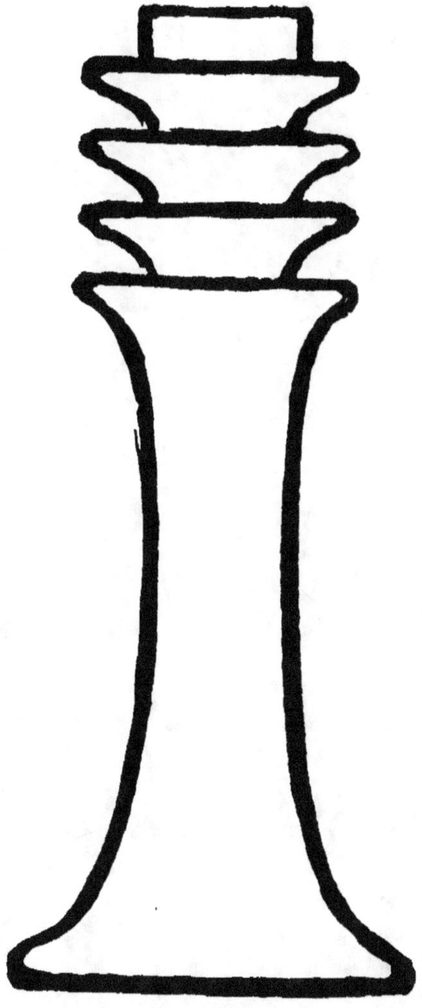

THE TAT CROSS

The Tat Cross or Pillar was a special type of the Moon-god Taht, who was the establisher of the four quarters of the Moon, as well as of Ptah the Sun-god when he established the four quarters of the solar Zodiac. It is the equivalent of the Mount of the Four Corners and was ever a sacred emblem.

CHAPTER VI

THE SACRED FOUR

The Great Mother was called the "Keeper of the Four Corners"—the primal four corners which were universal in ancient mythologies, and formed by her as she turned around the pole with her Seven Stars. From this primal circle great mysticism has evolved. The first seven elementaries, born from the Abyss, became the spirits or stars presided over by this Great Mother. Of the seven, Fire, Earth, Air and Water were and will be for all time the four sacred elements, symbolized in the four corners or the four quarters of the universe. In earliest symbolism these elements were represented as animals. Fire was portrayed as a bird, Earth a beast, Air an ape and Water a fish. Water became recognized as an element of life, and as the feminine source was the first element to be humanized and became symbolized by the Great Mother.

Originally the heavens were said to rest on four corners. These four corners typified the square and this square with the four cardinal points was an original way of registering the circle. In a first and feminine form, heaven was said to stand on four legs, as it were, over the earth, or resting on the four corners. Didron gives a figure of the square supplementing the circle in the halo of the saints (Figure 5, 26).

In Egypt the Phoenix, Bird of Fire, was said to have the star Sirius at the heart of it, and as it outshone the sunrise the South was made to represent the quarter of Fire." The crocodile, represented the earth, and the west, from which the earth was said to have emerged from the inundation. The ape, as a symbol of breath and air, represented the east, and the hippopotamus, representing water, was given to the birthplace in the north. The Genii of the early circle of the four quarters were one female and three males. With the three males, the god Har, or Ra (fire), was hawk-headed; the god Sut (earth) was ass-headed; the god Shu (air) was ape-headed, and Uati (water) the Mother, the female, was represented as human-headed. With the division into the four quarters Uati, the hippopotamus, was portrayed with the nose of an ape, the feet of a lion, and the hindquarters of a crocodile, all of very great significance to one who understands the types.

The four elements, forces, and powers were looked upon in primeval times with fear, which suggested one of the earliest religious thoughts. In connection with the god Ra, who presided over Fire, Fear was represented by devouring flames, with the god Sut, who presided over the Earth, by the terrors of the earthquake; with Shu, god of the Air, by the hurricane; with Uati, goddess of the Water, fear was represented by drowning, being swallowed by water. The death-giving heat in Egypt or Inner Africa was an early symbol of fire, from which the historical or theological Hell was evolved.

The Mexicans had four ages or aeons ruled over by the Sun, for which they made the Sun a synonym. They called the past ages so many destroyed Suns. These four great periods had all ended with a cataclysm, symbolical of the elements that had represented the age, for example, the Sun age was by fire, conflagration; the Earth age by earthquake and famine; the Air age by hurricane; and the Water period by the universal deluge.

These elements were all later personified as Gods, Genii, and Winds, progeny of the Great Mother, the "Bearer of the Waters," or the enceinte mother. She was the primordial ark, and long before boats were built was called the Ship of Life or the Ship of the North. And this primitive ark or ship contained within herself the causation of all the Fours, which still cling to the cardinal points and the cross.

The ark was later represented as the coffin of Osiris, with the four Genii standing and keeping guard at the corners. They were Ra, Sut, Shu and Uati, the four great spirits of the seven stars of the Great Bear, and of the four, Shu, was the Angel Gabriel, who in a Mohammedan legend is called the chief of the four great Genii, or the favored one of the angels, being the Spirit of Truth. He is the angel who appeared to Mohammed in his great trance. In the legends of the middle ages, the Angel Gabriel was called the second of the great spirits that stood before the throne of God. Gabriel was Shu, god of breath, a divine type of power. And as the planet Mars Shu was known as the god of generation and was given the Feather of Truth.

The typical four of India receiving the greatest honors were the Cow, the Ape, the Eagle and the Serpent. They were called the greatest of the Totemic types.

The Assyrian four Genii are represented by a lion with a man's head, (fire); by a bull with a human face, (earth); by the Uster, Aquarius, in human likeness, (air); and the Nettig or Scorpion with the head of an eagle, (water). The elementary spirits, or Genii, who are found stationed at the four corners, in whatever type, represent the four elements—Fire, Earth, Air and Water. The Mandans placed four tortoises at the corners of the earth and they were said to spout forth water.

The heraldic emblems of China are the Stag, the Phoenix, the Tortoise and the Dragon. In Egypt the Phoenix represents the south, the Tortoise west, the Dragon north, and the Stag east. The Aztecs have the four great ages of Fire, Earth, Air and Water. The Druids have the Square, the Circle, the Triangle, and the Crescent, signifying the elements. These four symbols are found in the nimbus, in the portrayals of the Christian saints, as a Glory of God. The nimbus truly belongs to the Holy Spirit, the Regent of God.

When the four corners became established, a place of

importance was given to the Spring Equinox, when the con·junction of the Sun and Moon took place, a conjunction which always signified the birth of a new Sun, Child, or Christos, just as the conjunction of the Sun and the Moon astrologically gives birth to the Christos within. A yearly festival was always held in honor of the birth of the Sun-god, or Saviour God, giving a representation of his suffering, burial, and resurrection into the new life, typifying renewal, regeneration, and a new birth of nature. This conjunction or crossing also represented the Rock of the Horizon, on which the gods were wont to find refuge from the waters.

The most important word or glyph of ancient times, set in heaven, and used figuratively, was the serpent, relating in celestial correspondence to time, seasons, and the four elements all being represented by serpents—Heh, represented Fire; Bata, Earth; Nef, Breath; and Hydra, Water. A four-headed and four-winged serpent in Egypt symbolized the four corners of the earth, and their serpent, Apta, a name signifying "The Corner or end of the World," was covered with four mystic figures, which represented the four cardinal points. Hapu means "Corner or Secret Places," and the serpent Hapu was represented with four heads. Four serpents, in various forms and conditions, were used in many countries as foundations for temples, within which, designated by a serpent were corners and places for worship.

The four corners that turned four ways were called the Sword of Flyfut, the weapon of Thor. This was a form of the four-footed cross, type of the four corners, as was the Swastica or the God Agni of the Hindus, or the Agnus Dei of the Christians.

Later the four corners were superseded by the form of the mount that would rise in some mysterious way and fill the entire world as a throne for the Solar God. For the elementaries of the beginning, emanating from the Abyss, Darkness, or the Great Mother, had become in the Solar myth the "Servants of the Solar God" Light, the Egyptian

Ra, whose mother had been the ancient Typhon. This change was typical of the struggle between Darkness and Light, "When the Lioness spends her fiery fury against the Wicked, the Scorpion stings *on behalf* of Gods and men." It is then the scorpion, kin of the serpent, which holds within itself the sting of the world.

In Jacob Boehme's "Threefold Life of Man," Chapter 2, he writes of the first elements in creative nature: "The first four forms in themselves are the anger and the wrath of God in the eternal nature; and they are in themselves nothing else, but such a source or property as standeth in the darkness, and is not material, but an originality of the Spirit, without which there would be nothing. For the four forms are the cause of all things."

These elements, originally emanating from the Great Mother, were called Primordial Forces, and became combined in a single Deity. Later the worship of this one God arose, whose name was "I am that I am," and whose symbol was the disk of the Sun, standing for Light, Truth and all-sustaining Power.

This one God belongs wholly to religion, and was not an initial creation. "No one God that is not a bi-une being, a twin form of the 'double primitive essence,' mother-mould of the producer, was primordial." If there is one god, an only one, as father of a beginning, endowed with all the powers of deity, it is the Egyptian Amen-Ra, the *hidden Sun*, whose creation came in the later solar period. The earlier gods—Ptah, Seb, Shu, Osiris and Sut never had a father. Taht, the lunar god, and Seb, the Star-god, were said to be born of time, and there is an inscription belonging to the Temple El-Karjeh referring to Amen-Ra as the "self-produced," "he has not come out of a womb he has come out of cycles." (Records of the Past.) The earlier gods were all evolved from space and from the forces known as Fire, Earth, Air and Water, before the world was made or creation had become an established fact. We learn from

Berosus that "in the beginning all was darkness and Water; and therein were generated monstrous animals with strange and peculiar forms. . . . A woman ruleth all." The conception of a Triune God has come down to us today through the vista of ages, and through its adoption by the Roman Catholic Church, it is today believed in with blind unquestioning faith.

The four types were given as symbols of one God. The four elementals of Egypt and those of the four corners became the souls of the solar god, Ra. Four rams, animals with wings, and the four Assyrian bulls with human heads, were types of the later solar god. There was the four-headed Brahma, portrayal of the body of the Hindu Creator, and signifying the four types or characters of the elemental castes. All denote the four elements that were compounded into One God, and made One.

Irenaeus assumes that for mystic reasons the Gospels needed to be four in number, due to the origin of the Four Quarters and the Spirits, Angels or Keepers of the Corners. "The books of the Egyptian Horoscopus were four in number. The first treated of the system of the fixed stars; the second and third of the solar and lunar conjunctions (eclipses and the ends of periods being called deluges and destructions); the fourth was the book of the risings or resurrections of the sun, moon and stars, and eschatologically, of the souls of men. Similarly four books of magic were assigned to Taht or Hermes. We are told in the magical texts that

'These are the titles of the four books:

  (1) *The old book;*
  (2) *The book to destroy men;*
  (3) *The great book;*
  (4) *The book to be as a God.'*

"No better identification or apter illustration of the four books of the 'Magical Texts' could be given than *the Book of Adam* for (1) the Old Book; *the Deluge* for (2) the 'Book to destroy Men;' *the Law* for (3) the Great Book; and the *Book which renews man and bears him into the kingdom of heaven* for (4) the 'Book to be as a God'." While to quote from Egyptian Texts, *"There are four mansions of life at Abtu (the abode of the four corners); each is built four stories high. There are four mansions of life. Osiris is master thereof. The four outer walls are of stone. Its foundation is sand, its exterior is jasper, one is placed to the south, another to the north, another to the west, another to the east. It is very hidden, unknown, invisible, nothing save the solar disk sees it. It escapes men that go there. The sun's librarians, the treasure-scribes, are within. . . . The writer of his divine books is Taht, who vivifies it* (the house) *each day; its excellency is neither seen nor heard. 'O thou daily hidden one'* is written in front of the house, and in the chapter to open the fate of this house it is said, *'I have opened heaven, I have opened earth, I enter'."*[1]

From the earliest Sabean reckoning by the constellation of the Great Bear down to the latest periodicity given for the Sun, the Four Corners and the ancient Sabean cycle still remain in our solar Zodiac with the four quarters marked out by the signs of the Lion, the Bird, the Waterer, and the Bull.

In all lands in all languages are found endless myths of the early Four, which belong to the circle discovered to have been made by the constellation of the Great Bear revolving around the Pole. These myths are sacred and elevating in thought, though often crudely expressed by primitive peoples who were giving their impressions and conceptions of the Spirits, Angels and Winds, which were to carry their messages of love and reverence into the Great Beyond.

The history of the world from beginning to end is found in the stars and recorded in the Zodiac by a universal symbolism, the key to which has always been and always will be with the Initiates, who have ever known and held sacred the

---

[1]Massey, Gerald—The Natural Genesis, Vol. ii, pp. 475–476.

unchangeable Laws of God. Man's first insight into life itself came through study of the stars, whereby the heavens revealed to him their sacred truths, inspiring him, when he began to realize God, the Eternal, the Absolute, to seek out the revelation of a higher destiny. Aspiration and longing were in the heart of primitive man. Thomas Carlyle realized this when he wrote these dynamic lines: "The great antique heart how like a child in its simplicity, like a man in its solemnity and depth; heaven lies over him wherever he goes or stands on earth, making all the earth a mystic temple to him, the earth's business all a kind of worship. Glimpses of bright creatures flash in the common sunlight; angels yet hover doing God's message among men." Knowledge of the Central Spiritual Sun, and the manifestation of Light appearing at certain periods of world change, came through primitive man's early piety and reverence. May the soul of man be reawakened, through knowledge of the stars and astrology as a sublime science, for "Knowledge is Recollection," and eternal memory of the precious gems of the golden age of the mythical and mystic is within man.

Moreover there are records extant on ancient monuments and temples whose starry symbolism is readily deciphered by the Initiates to whom we owe so much. We are told also that there are in existence today secret inexhaustible volumes of sacred books belonging to an immense antiquity.[1] As a matter of fact, scientific knowledge is but the development of occult knowledge, yet wherever Science identifies and formulates one of these old occult Truths, to the scientist it ceases to be occult.

---

[1] In all corners of the world people had retained a knowledge of sacred Books, which had disappeared or were mysteriously hidden. The Vatican can tell of these, but the Vatican is ever silent. All divine and holy traditions speak of these hidden Books, the Secret writing. These traditions are prevalent among all nations, and refer to the books being in a lost language.

Very priceless this Wisdom, which is within the reach of all, much of which can be found in the Apocalypse, and which was originally given to the Priests and to their followers thousands of years before the Old Testament was written. It was the Wisdom from that great Book of God, of the Sun, of the Moon, and of the Stars.

There are signs, evidently ideographic, found on hatches of the Palaeolithic period, according to Lubeck. And when our Red Indian tribes petitioned the President of the United States to grant them possession of four small lakes, the petition was written on a tiny piece of fabric barely covered with a few animals and birds. Scientists cannot decipher the different methods the American savages have of writing, nor their early hieroglyphic ciphers which are preserved today and known in occultism as Senzar. The American Indian has knowledge as profound as the hierophants of the early days of the world, yet there are those who claim that the ideographs of the Indians, as well as the written characters of the Chinese, are "an attempt of the early races of mankind to express untutored thoughts."

A tradition is extant among the Cheyenne Indian tribe that "Two or three thousand years ago in the Cheyenne tribe, a boy was born, who from babyhood possessed great intellectual powers. He not only had supernatural powers, but he was a prophet from the beginning of his life. This boy grew to manhood and lived to be four hundred years old." His name was Motzyruff. "He went to a high mountain and as he went near it a door opened for him to enter into the earth, and he entered. Inside of the mountain he communicated with the Great Medicine. There were several other men there who represented other nations and were there to learn from the Great Medicine. These men consisted of several red-skinned men, one black skinned man, who was dressed in Indian fashion, and one white skinned man who had long hair on his chin. All wore long hair on their heads. . . . After four years Motzyruff returned to his people as a man of supernatural powers, a messenger and prophet from the Great Medicine."[1]

This is evidently the Cheyenne tradition of the King of the World. Throughout Asia today the Messiah, whose

---

[1]"Cheyenne Indian Ceremonial Organization of the Cheyenne Sun Dance." —Smithsonian Publications.

coming is confidently expected, is known as the King of the World. A possible reference to this Super-Being occurs in the history of the Cheyenne Indians of the United States and bears witness to tutored thoughts of ancient wisdom on our continent prior to the white man's advent.

Cardan says "He that goes about to destroy art is far worse than he that is unskilled in it, for his mind is full of malice and idleness as well as ignorance." Egotistical super-ficial knowledge has held back many men's souls from finding the ancient eternal laws of the heavens. To the astronomical priesthood of ancient days we owe many of the sublime allegories which are our precious inheritance, and which have become the foundations of many theological systems. Sacred mysteries and their symbolism are the same today as when primordial man created them out of the traceries of the heavens. For this reason they will remain as unchangeable as the Laws of Heaven. We also owe to the astrologers the principles embodied in many myths and symbols of the Cross, the Cardinal Cross, and the number Four, which are the foundations of life.

Cosmic Forces are represented by the Cardinal Cross, the four points of the compass—North, East, South, West—each having a distinct occult force at the beginning of all great cycles. These occult properties are found in the winds of North, East, South and West, and in the four principal stars creating a first Zodiac of four signs in the making of the twelve.

The "sky is mystically spoken of as the Temple, and the eternal consciousness of God. Its altar is the Sun, whose four arms or rays typify the four corners or the cardinal cross of the universe," which have become the four fixed signs of the Zodiac, and as the four powerful sacred animal signs are both cosmical and spiritual. They represent the basic elements resembling our human principles. The sign Leo represents Fire or Spirit; Taurus, Earth or Body; Aquarius, Air, or Mind; and Scorpio represents Water likened to the Soul. Leo as the Lion, is the strength of the lower nature, and is the Serpent Force which, if directed upward, overcomes. Taurus, the Bull, is always the symbol of Creative Force. Aquarius, the Man, is the Light-bearer, or Light-bringer. Scorpio the Scorpion is often transmuted with Aquila, the Eagle, a southern para-natellon of Scorpio, which rises at the same time with Scorpio, they are closely linked in symbolism. Scorpio is "the 'Monster of Darkness,' who stings to death, and yet preserves and reproduces," symbolizing not only generation but regeneration. As the latter it is Aquila, the Eagle, the bird of the Sun which has conquered the dark side of Scorpio (that adversary that can drag man down lower than the beasts), but when transmuted is the Eagle of Light, which can exalt above the gods.

Certain fixed stars belong to every one of these signs of the Zodiac. Regulus, a star in the heart of the Lion, belongs to Leo; Aldabaran, a star in the eye of the Bull, belongs to Taurus, Fomalhaut, the eye of the Southern Fish, belongs to Aquarius; and Antares belonging to the heart of the Scorpion—to Scorpio. These four are known as the consecrated animals of the Zodiac, while the signs themselves represent the basic fundamental elements of life, Fire, Earth, Air and Water.

The Four can be traced back to the circle of Seven Stars, which together with the four quarters,[1] the four Gods, and the four constellations, marked the four cardinal points and the solstices and equinoxes, and gave us spring, summer, autumn and winter. The four fixed Signs are found as the national symbols of the Chinese, by whom the Lion is called the "Black Warrior," Taurus the "Azure Dragon," Scorpio the "White Tiger," and Aquarius the "Red Bird." These colors were prominent in the heraldry of the famous Yellow Emperor, who is supposed to have reigned about the year

---

[1]The four corners were a type of the Eternal, and in Egypt, four times, was a synonym of Forever.

2697 B. C. An ancient teacher is made to say of him, "Cherish that which is within you, and shut off that which is without; for such knowledge is a curse. Then will I place you upon that abode of Great Light which is the source of the Positive Power, and escort you through the gate of Profound Mystery which is the source of Negative Power. The Powers are the controllers of heaven and earth, and each contains the other."

The four fixed signs are also compounded in the Sphinx, of whom Denon writes, "The Sphinxes (of Egypt) have been wantonly mutilated, with few exceptions, which barbarism, *wearied with destroying has* spared; and on examining which it is easy to distinguish, that some of them had a woman's head, others that of a lion, a ram, a bull, etc. The avenue which leads from Cornac to Lugsoar, or Luxor, was of this latter description; and this space which is nearly half a league in extent, contains a constant succession of these chimerical figures to the right and left." This was the Egyptian manner of preserving their register of time through the Zodiacal signs, giving several revolutions to the equinoctial points. These so-called monsters were not gods, and were not worshipped as something divine, as many deluded modern interpreters in their anathemas against the ancients seek to make the modern world believe. They were registers of time and were preserved with veneration.

The Sphinx may possibly represent the passage of the Sun through the signs Leo and Virgo at the time of the overflow of the river Nile. The Virgin's head on the body of the lion was the passing of one great Age or Cycle to another. The word Sphinx, derived from the Hebrew, means "a woman disguised." We are all familiar with the Great Sphinx, which is the woman disguised. But as Mr. Mackay says, "The Act which put the Virgin's head upon the Lion's body, was 2100 years in passing . . . and as the stars of Leo were seen in that constellation, from whence they received the bounty of the Virgin after a lapse of 2000 years; the twofold figure pointing out the same division of the Zodiac, was as truly a superabundance."

The four horses of the Book of Revelation correspond to the four rivers of Eden and represent the Zodiacal constellations Virgo, Libra, Scorpio and Sagittarius as the struggles of the four lower planes of existence. The yellow horse is Virgo, the "Virgin at the gate," who is given power to overcome the passional side of life. The red horse is Scorpio, ridden by Mars, who gives battle to the lower desires. The black horse is Libra, the balance between, ready to bring harmony and justice. The white horse is Sagittarius, the Archer, who is the conquerer. White is a symbol of the purified magnetic force of Light which revibrates and conquers the lower mind, so that man can arouse the serpent coil, or Solar Force, from its sleep of ages. Then man becomes a true Son of God, the Central Spiritual Sun, the One God whom we are bidden to worship and no other, as revealed in the Book of Revelation.

Ezekiel says, "The glory of the Lord comes from the way of the East," the rising of the Sun, and Jeremiah, Isaiah and David assure us that all evil comes from the North and the West, while the Roman Catholics credit epidemics, wars, calamities to the invisible forces emanating from the North and West.

A grievous misconception has arisen among the Christians regarding the regents or angels guarding these points, which according to their way of thinking are either virtues or devils. The four cardinal points symbolized are allegorically in the square forms of the Tabernacle, Obelisk, Temple or Pyramid and in all sacred square buildings. Josephus takes care to explain that the pillars of the Tabernacle, described in Numbers, "were the same as those raised in Tyre to the four elements, which were placed on four angles and faced the four cardinal points; adding that the angles of the pedestals had equally the four figures of the Zodiac on them representing the same orientation."

In all sacred buildings that have escaped the ravages of time, whether in the Indian temples carved out of rock, or in the Zoroastrian caves, or as the square of the obelisk or temple, these four points as primitive elements were the basis of religion, and were symbolical of the celestial signs of the Zodiac, and with their regents, angels, or ruling planets, were typically the protectors of mankind.

Ezekiel in his vision saw four living creatures, having in their higher symbolism, four faces and four wings; faces of a man (Aquarius); a Lion (Leo); an Ox (Taurus); and an Eagle (Scorpio). Other symbolical names such as "Winged Globes," "Fiery Wheels,"[1] were also given them. Ezekiel very plainly describes the four Cosmic Angels as the four celestial signs of the Zodiac, "I looked and behold a whirlwind came out of the north, a great cloud, and a fire infolding itself? . . . Also out of the midst thereof *came* the likeness of four living creatures . . . they had the likeness of a man, and every one had four faces and every one had four wings . . . they had the face of a man, and the face of a lion . . . the face of an ox . . . and the face of an eagle. . . . Now as I beheld the living creatures, behold one wheel upon the earth by the living creatures with his four faces . . . and their appearance and their work *was* as it were a wheel in the middle of a wheel . . . for the spirit of the living creature *was* in the wheel . . . their appearance *was* like burning coals of fire, etc."—Ezekiel, Chapter I.

The four living creatures with these faces, are used in

---

[1] "The Seraphim were the fiery serpents of heaven, and are found in a passage describing Mount Meru as the exalted mass of glory, the venerable haunt of the gods and heavenly choristers . . . not reached by sinful men . . . because guarded by Serpents. These were called the Avengers, and the Winged Wheels."—Blavatsky, H. P.—The Secret Doctrine.

The chariot of Ezekiel was called the Merkabah and like the Sun was an emblem of solar worship. The doctrine of the Merkaba was a great mystery, belonging to the hidden wisdom of the Kabala. In 1 Chronicles, Chap. xxvii, 18, we read of "Gold for the pattern of the chariot of the cherubim, that opened out *their wings*, and covered the ark of the covenant." The ark was the Cosmic Mother, the Ship of the North, the earliest chariot or boat of the gods known.

the Roman Catholic New Testament to preface the Gospels and represent the Evangelists. With Zodiacal imagery, "the face of the Eagle (Scorpio) is the symbol of Cosmic Spirit and is given to St. John; the face of the ox, bull, (Taurus) is the symbol of Cosmic Strength and is given to St. Luke; the face of the lion (Leo) is the symbol of Cosmic Fire and is given to St. Mark; and the face of the man (Aquarius) synthesizes the three into the symbol of Cosmic Spirituality and is given to St. Matthew." Similarly the Ophites made use of the symbolic Dragon (Raphael), Lion (Michael), Bull (Uriel) and Eagle (Gabriel)[1] to represent the four lower principles as well as the four elements. These Four Ophite Archangels, Raphael, Michael, Uriel and Gabriel, all have their names ending with the name of the Deity, the El or Al of the Hebrews, and are the Genii who presided over the fixed stars. Nearly all anthropomorphic ideas and concepts of deity are composed of four letters, Adad,, Assyrian; Amun, Egyptian; JHVH, Hebrew; Deus, Latin; Allh, Arabian; Taht, Egyptian; and many others.

In Ezekiel we find the four living creatures having "a physical as well as a spiritual correspondence to the four constellations that form the suite and cortége of the Solar God. Ezekiel was a slave in Babylon when he had his marvelous visions, which were truly astrological in intention. The stars he describes as tiny lamps, and begins by saying "The heavens here opened and I saw a vision of God," meaning the Sun. The Sun in its travels through the Zodiac is described as the spirit of God moving up and down among the living creatures. Some of the constellations are called beasts, and the one with "eyes before and eyes behind" read-

---

[1]"Gabriel is one of the seven planetary Gods, who are attendants on the Sun circling about his Golden Throne, wherefore they are called in Christian mythology, 'The Seven Angels of the Presence.' His name, which means 'Strong Man of God,' identifies him with Mars (Aries) who occupies Scorpio as his zodiacal house, and is primarily the God of Generation."—Pryse, James, "Tidings of St. Luke," p. 689.

ily suggests the constellation Taurus, with the brilliant stars in each of the horns of the Bull. The circles, as S. A. Mackey asserts, were the Equator and the Ecliptic, and the tropics, two Parallels of Declination, having a wheel within a wheel, resembling the movements of the Ecliptic as it moves up from the earth along with the constellations, the living creatures. As they were lifted up "they turned not as they went." Being turned up to the north indicated the coming of the age of Sorrow and Trouble which would fall to nations when "the wheels mounted up to the North until they had passed the Poles as far on the other side." These first chapters of Ezekiel are considered very precious heritages of antiquity explaining the ancient science of astronomy. The visions of Ezekiel and St. John give us knowledge of the pericyclosical motion of the Poles (the Precession). To understand this motion and the Wheels of Ezekiel, the Ecliptic, the Equator, the Tropics, the Zodiac, along with their living creatures, and the Zodiacal constellations "who turned not as they went" but went withersoever the spirit (the Sun) was to go, is to perceive the immutable law "As above, so below."

The four Beasts of Ezekiel and of Revelation are similar to the Assyrian Sphinxes. They are also found on the walls of almost all Hindu Pagodas.

The Evangelists have near them one of these animals. They are grouped together in Solomon's Triangle, are in the pentacle of Ezekiel, and are found in the four Cherubs or Sphinxes of the sacred arch. Hence the early Christians adopted them, and the Roman Catholics still represent these animals of the Zodiac in their pictures of the Evangelists of the Four Gospels. Irenaeus, Bishop of Lyons, insisted upon the necessity of having Four Gospels, reasoning that there could not be less than four, as there were four zones in the world, and four principal winds coming from the four corners of the earth.

"There were four Angels standing at the four corners of

the earth, holding back the four Winds of the earth, so that no Wind should blow over the Earth or the Sea or upon any Tree." Revelation vii, 1.

And in the ninth chapter of the Book of Revelation a voice speaks saying, "Set at liberty the four Angels who are prisoners near the great River Euphrates." The Four Spirits in the Book of Enoch are the four great angels—Michael, Raphael, Gabriel and Phanuel, described as the four Winds or Spirits of the four quarters. "The first wind is called the eastern, because it is the first. The second is called the south, because the Most High there descends, and frequently there descends *he who* is blessed forever. The western wind has the name of diminution, because there all the luminaries of heaven are diminished, and descend. The fourth wind, which is named the north, is divided into three parts; one of which is for the habitation of man; another for seas of water, with valleys, woods, rivers, shady places, and snow; and the third part *contains* paradise," which is the Garden, which at a later period was placed in the East. Angels, Spirits and Winds are all interchangeable.

Tradition tells us of a grotto in Central Asia wherein light enters from four openings, placed crosswise at the four cardinal points. Every light is of a different color, red, blue, orange-gold and red, and they converge around a pillar of white marble, capped in the center with a globe supposed to represent our earth. It is named the Grotto of Zarathustra.

Four is the divine number of the Hebrews, a type of their deity, their J H V H or Jehovah, in which are hidden great truths. The Kabalists used this number to hide their secret doctrine concerning the Divine Essence of the creative God. The four fundamental elemental elements are said to be inhabited by beings called Elementals. The Salamanders inhabit the fire, the Gnomes the earth, the Sylphs the air, and the Nymphs the water.

On Egyptian monuments four different colors were

employed to represent the different races. The four corners of Mount Meru, or the North Pole, have different colors representing the four points of the compass. White was used for the east and yellow for the south; black the west and red the north. The Mayas had a different arrangement of the colors, coinciding with the Ages that were named from them. Yellow as gold was given to the east; white as silver to the north; red as copper, or brass, to the south, while black as iron was given to the west. The combining of the metals with the four quarters is found in many of the old cults. Thus in his dream Belshazzar saw clay mixed with the iron at the roots of the tree. And "when Zarathust desired immortality he beheld the root of a tree, on which were four branches, one Golden, one of Silver, one of Steel, and one mixed with Iron."[1]

On almost all ancient ruined monuments, towers and temples, the four-armed cross is found. It was traced on the forehead of the Neophyte with water and oil—"The Father's name written on the forehead." The intersection of the Equator with Ecliptic forms the Cross and symbolizes the Crucified. The cross has also been called the Tree of Life, the mystery of the dual nature.

There are also the higher quaternaries of Space and Time. In space there is length, breadth, thickness and the within; for Time, there is past, present, future and ineffable time neither past, present nor future, but including all time in every instant of time. And there are the four planes of consciousness—physical, astral, mental and spiritual. Zechariah saw four chariots. One was red; one, black; one, white; and one, grizzled. Ezekiel saw four living creatures, having four faces and four wings—faces of a man, a lion, an ox, and an eagle. St. John saw four creatures—a lion, a young ox, a man, and a flying eagle.

How easily can divinity be brought close to us! Look up to the starry heavens above and also to the starry sphere

---

[1] Bahman Yast—Ch. i, p. 2.

within, for as above, so below, or within. The Law of Compensation was accurately known to the ancients. From the higher they looked to the lower. They knew that positive energy meeting its magnetic opposite would polarize its activities, and that polarity or sympathetic attraction was a proof of the universe. Out of the darkness of the past age, astrology will rise Phoenix-like uplifting its ancient truth. "Time destroys the speculations of man, but it confirms the judgment of nature." (Cicero.) Theology today, combined with materialism, has tried to destroy many of the marvelous philosophical and astrological conceptions of the past, but new weapons are being forged out of the old, and we who love those ancient days with their celestial symbolism will rejoice in the forthcoming period.

From very far away has come the message, "There is somewhat in us that loveth the mystical things, and so we tell not all, but the love which seeketh and is not wearied." Seek and you will surely find, seek with love in your heart, and the beautiful treasures of heaven are yours.

"The trees are two date-palms in fruit, and three myrrh-trees (odoriferous sycamore), the foliage of the latter being indicated by a line bounding the tops of the branches."

The mystical Sycamore or Fig Tree was a chief type of the Tree of Life or of Knowledge, the "Tree that Told." It imaged the Mother as the Giver of Life. In the above illustration the Sycamore Tree with its enclosing line, oval in shape, maintains the ancient symbol. The Mother of the Gods of ancient Egypt was hidden in a Sycamore Tree. Christians from many lands worship a Sycamore Tree in the gardens at Helipolis where tradition states that Mary, Joseph and the child sought shelter. "Religious traditions never die, but reappear in new dress from time to time."

CHAPTER VII

THE TREE

There is a tradition that the first great tree of earth was hung with clusters of beautiful stars or constellations, and that certain human beings climbing ever higher and higher reached the uppermost branches. There were others who stayed below, and thus the trunk of the tree was divided in two, those human beings in the branches remaining above in the heavens, while those below had their roots in the earth. The vault of heaven was upheld by the first tree, which putting forth two branches, produced the four quarters.

The Tree in the beginning was single, feminine, the Mother, the nourisher of life. When the heavens divided, there were two branches. Then there were four, the four quarters or the four cardinal points of the world, and then it became seven-branched, and these were the seven constellations revolving around the Pole, or the Seven Stars of the Great Bear. Then came the tree with its twelve branches, and variable fruits for every month, representing the twelve signs of the Zodiac, and finally this celestial Tree is depicted. with seventy-two branches, the duo-decans of the Zodiac, and known as the Kabalistic Tree. "By means of the Tree space was first penetrated, identified, divided and configurated." The twelve-branched Tree of the Book of Revelation is the Bearer, celestial type of the Zodiac. The Chinese Tree of heaven and earth has twelve branches, signifying their twelve hours, which are our twenty-four. The thirty-six Crossings of the Syrians were the decans of .the twelve Zodiacal signs, originally known as the thirty-six Crossing Stars. The Zodiac is completed with three hundred and sixty degrees. The square of ninety degrees is one-fourth of the circle, creating the four corners, which is the Cross within the circle.

The Tree was always feminine and the branch was the child, the "Coming One." The Tree was made the symbol of the Mother as well as of Mother Earth, and all that gave nourishment in bringing forth the child or the fruit, symbol of renewal.

The mystical Tree belonging to the Fall was the Fig Tree, supposed to introduce purity among men. The doctrine of the fig tree belongs to the Hidden Wisdom. The human Fall was that of ignorance—ignorance that brought death into the world. Among the proverbs of Solomon we find, "Wisdom is a tree of life to them that lay hold upon her; and happy is every man that retaineth her;" and "To be allied to wisdom is immortality." The Tree of Knowledge of Good and Evil is the Tree of Divine Wisdom, the Tree of Life, not of death as our Bible would have us believe.

The Sycamore or Fig Tree figures very largely in many traditions. Its name is derived from Sycos, a Fig Tree, and Moros, a mulberry tree. It partakes of the nature of the mulberry in its leaves and of the fig in its fruit and became chief type of the Tree of Life. In Africa this tree is always green and is a prolific bearer of fruit, being apparently unsusceptible to change of climate, time or season. The fig is an emblem of the feminine reproductive organ, as it contains the seed within itself. As the Tree of Knowledge the fig is known as the "Tree that Told." In the New Testament it is the blasted withered Tree, the tree without fruit, typical of the degeneracy of the lunar darkness of the Piscene Era of the past two thousand years.

In an Arab tradition the divine Jesus is said to have been concealed in the trunk of a Gemaseh Tree by the web of a spider which had been spun over the entrance and which had hidden him from his pursuers. There is also a

Turkish tradition that Mary and her child when pursued by those whom Herod had sent to murder them, reached a Tree at Maturea which had the power to open and close, it opened to receive them both and they were saved, and to this day a Sycamore Fig Tree at Maturea is pointed out as the "Tree of Mary and her Child." This tree symbolizes the "Shrine, the Sekhem." The name Maturea comes from Mat, which is an ancient name for An, the birth-place. "The Shrine of the Child" imaged as the celestial Tree that offered food and drink to all, was called the Sekhem, birth-place sacred to their goddess mother Hathor. When the tree was portrayed with two extended branches it imaged the Mother of Life and the Cross in one, "The Bearer."

The Druids selected the most stately and beautiful tree as an emblem of their Deity. After trimming away all its branches, they chose two of the largest and fastened them like extended arms to the highest point of the tree, representing the Cross.

There is a tree in the Koran called Al-Zakum. Mohammed had this tree of Knowledge planted in a place called Hell, instead of in Heaven. The fruit of this tree, of which the damned were to eat, was represented by heads of devils and serpents. This interpretation was, in a sense, but a later revival of the tree and the serpent.

In Egypt the Ark, containing Osiris, floated on the water until it became entangled in the branches of a tamarisk which had grown to the height of a tree, and was enclosed with the child within its trunk, symbolizing the Tree of Life, the "Sekhem" or the "Shrine." Moreover the mother of Confucius was told in a dream she would bring forth her child in the hollow of a tree.

In India there is a legend that Buddha had been incarnated many times under the Asvattha, the sacred Fig Tree, their mythical Tree of Knowledge, Wisdom and Enlightenment.

Agni, the Hindu God of Fire, is said to have been born in wood, like the embryo in the plant. Curiously wood and fire have the same name in some languages, and Sun and Fire are the same in Hindu. In Hindu philosophy souls are supposed to issue from the soul of the world and return to it as a spark of fire.

The Palm Tree as an ideograph of time as well as of letters was a form of the Tree of Knowledge, and when Taht, the Egyptian scribe, carried a Palm cross in his hand it was a symbol of Time, representing the crossing (astronomical), not the crucifixion. It was the symbol of the equinoctial year. In Egypt the Buka is the Palm Tree, the branch carried in the hand of Taht, is the Book of Taht, and the bark of the tree was used for his writing. The Buka, or Palm-branch finally yields us the name of the Book. The Palm Tree was the Tree of Knowledge that first supplied the divine drink. The Toddy Palm of Central Africa yielded a liquid like milk, which was fermented and called Koumess. A fermented drink was used in the ancient mysteries to induce the gift of prophecy and divination, while the gods were said to become intoxicated in order to obtain immortality. In Deuteronomy xiv, 26, the Jew is told to save his money "for wine, or strong drink, or for whatsoever thy soul desireth; and thou shalt eat there before the Lord thy God," and this was to be his offering to the deity. The first wine, in a mystical sense, was the blood of the Tree of Life. The juice of the fruit of the tree was mingled with blood to prepare the Eucharist of the ancient mysteries.

Buka is the Palm Tree, the Palm Toddy. Buk is food-bread; and in a final phase it became the developed book, while retaining the ancient name. Book and food are both found in the Papyrus plant, the root of which is eaten as food, of which Hor Apollo aptly writes, "To denote ancient descent, the Egyptians depict a bundle of papyrus, and by this they initiate primordial food, for no one can find the beginning of food or generation." The eating of the book became synonymous with receiving knowledge, which assurance is given us in the Book of Revelation.

The Tree of Life and Knowledge derived from motherhood was wholly feminine. Duality came with the blending of the sexes. Then the Tree of Life became masculine and the Tree of Knowledge feminine, as the woman was the first to eat of its fruit. There is a curious engraving of a sacred Tree of seven branches on an early Babylonian Cylinder, in which there is a serpent, a man, and a woman. Of its branches three are given to the man and four to the woman. Back of her, elevated on its tail, is the serpent. It should be remembered that "Dwelling in the Microcosmic Tree are the manifested Serpents of Wisdom," and "in origin and in importance the Tree of the first day and the Fount of Immortality are indissolubly bound together." Our North American Indians have an instructive symbology originating in reverence for the starry heavens and their knowledge of the signs of Zodiac, and based upon the importance of the four cardinal points symbolized in the Tree.

The Lenni Lenape Indians of Delaware hold a festival, in their "House of Sacrifice," in honor of the God of Fire, recognized as the Sun. Twelve poles or trees are gathered, which they tie together at the top, and spread about below into a circle. This they enclose by folding rugs and blankets around it, so that it suggests a small furnace, into which they roll twelve stones, heated until almost red hot. These are sacred to their twelve spirits, four of which represent the genii of the four cardinal points of heaven. Twelve men enter this Temple of Sacrifice, and the duty of one of them, an old man, is to scatter twelve handfuls of tobacco on the stones, the fumes from which, being intensified in the enclosed circle, are inhaled by those inside. This is construed as an inhaling of the spirit, or the Great Breath, and produces a swooning, somnolent condition, which finally reaches a state of ecstasy, in which the supernatural is induced, creating or revealing to them the unseen world.

The fumes of tobacco suggest to the Indian a purifying process and an uplifting of thought, as incense does to other peoples. The smoke wreathing towards the Great Spirit expanded into the Great Breath and was their offering to the Most High. The puffing of the pipe, sending the fumes of tobacco to the four spirits of the four corners of the world, was an indispensable rite of the various Indian tribes and preliminary to any religious gathering. Brinton, writing on our North American Indians, calls the cult of the Red Indian "an adoration of the Four Cardinal Points, identified with the Four Winds or Spirits who were the Ancestors of the human race; and that the Indian speaks as if he carried the Cross inside of him and expresses himself according to the Cardinal points, even within his wigwam."

The Lenni Lenape Indians[1] when speaking of Manitou relate that he floated on the waters in the beginning, where he created and shaped the earth from a grain, and afterwards made man and woman from a Tree. The Sioux Indians thought, however, that for many years primal man stood with his feet held firmly in the earth, growing up like a tree, near which grew another tree. A snake appeared and gnawed them both off at the roots, and in their freedom they walked away as human beings. This was their primitive way of expressing ideas of the early garden of Eden, the serpent, the tree and the primal pair.

The Oak Tree, bearing the Mistletoe, source of many sacred legends, was said to have healing properties for both soul and body. The Oak was "The Tree of Knowledge" of the Druids.[2] They held nothing in greater reverence, using

---

[1] The Lenni Lenape Indians were those who made the famous treaty with Penn in the year 1682. Penn addressed them as friends and brothers, comparing the red and white men to the different members of the human body, making pledge to live in peace and friendship with them and their children of the forest, and they, being deeply touched by his truth and sincerity, announced through their Chief that they would "live in love with William Penn and his children as long as the Sun and the Moon gave light."

[2] Druids were Wise Men, Astrologers, who were ever watching the heavens. They had their sanctuaries in great Round Towers, which were observatories of the heavens.

its leaves in all their religious ceremonies, and they considered the growth of the mistletoe on it as a sign that the Deity had chosen this tree as His own, and that therefore its virtues were all-powerful, all-healing. In defining the word Mistletoe, "Mes is generation, birth, child. Ter is time, a shoot, a sign of time. Ta is to register, also a type. Thus Mis-tle-toe is a branch, typical of another birth of time personified as the child, the Prince or branch."[1] They called mistletoe their Branch of Pure Gold. The old gold of mythology was Fire. When gathered and kept for several months mistletoe becomes a bright golden color and was most sacred to them, as it revealed the treasures of both heaven and earth. On the sixth day of the Moon six Druidic Priests plucked the sacred branch of mistletoe. The Festival of the sixth day in olden times was called the Lunar Sabbath, and the sixth day of the Moon was anciently called Tabu time. The number six related to breath and was synonymous with conception. The gathering of this sprig also took place when the Sun was in the Zodiacal house Sagittarius, sign of the hunting season, and when the Moon was within a few days of its renewal the Mistletoe must be shot down with an arrow, and caught in the left hand without its touching the ground.

Similarly the God Shu was placed by the Egyptians in the sign Sagittarius, and represented great power. He was given the Bow and Arrow. Arrows symbolized the Sunbeams and the bringing down of the Light, and by the use of the arrow the divine properties and magical healing qualities of the mistletoe were thought to be retained if kept from contact with the earth.

There was a prevalent belief that Mistletoe contained the "Seed of Fire" and had remarkable properties for extinguishing fires, and it was therefore used as a preventive of fire as well as medicinally for burns by fire.

---

[1] Massey, Gerald.

At the time of the gathering of the Mistletoe the Druids prepared two white bulls with horns garlanded with flowers. The Priests, in pure white, cut the Mistletoe with a golden knife, or sickle, and as it fell it was caught in a cloak of pure white, after which came the sacrifice of the bulls with the prayer "That the deity may prosper his own gifts to them, to whom he has given it."[1] The death of a bull in the Druidic mysteries was a sacrifice to virility, which the bull in the different cults seemed to represent.

Again at the Summer Solstice, when the Sun was culminating in the longest day of the year, the mistletoe was gathered for both mystical and medicinal qualities. Because of its magical virtues, as it grew neither in heaven nor on the earth, and contained the purifying quality of the spark of fiery life from the Sun, it was not allowed to touch the earth, as this contact would destroy this spark of life. There was an "old superstition that the plant in which the life of the sacred tree was consecrated should not be exposed to the risk it incurred by contact with the earth."[2]

When certain tribes among the Indians of British Columbia are at war and desire to burn the homes of their enemies, they shoot at them with arrows made from Oak Trees that have been struck by lightning, or attach a part of this tree to the arrow, believing its fire to be contained in the wood.

The Oak Tree is more frequently struck by lightning than any other of the forest trees. Fire kindled by lightning was greatly reverenced by primitive peoples since they imaged their God coming down to earth as thunder and lightning. Great veneration was given the Oak and the Mistletoe growing upon it, for the life or spirit of the tree was supposed to be in the mistletoe, and therefore everliving.

The Yule Log was of Oak, which was the King of the Forest. Its wood was burned at the midsummer festivals

---

[1]Pliny.
[2]The Golden Bough, Vol. ii, p. 208.

as well as in winter, when the golden treasures of the Sun therein stored were released to find a home in the heart of the true believer.

The Apple Tree was also made sacred by the Mistletoe, and was called the Tree of Pure Gold. In ancient times covenants were made and troths plighted under this tree. With its berried sprigs of Mistletoe, so like the clustering stars, it was named the Tree of the "Lofty Summit," pointing the way above. Today we find the Mistletoe suspended overhead at Christmastime for the Christmas kiss. "The tree of the Summit" was a type of the Celestial Pole, Seat of Judgment, and was guarded by the celestial serpent, the Constellation Draco.

So extremely sacred was the Tree, that ancient Priests had the figure of a tree imprinted on their bodies, signifying that they had knowledge of the Secret Serpent Wisdom. The sign of the Tree was similar to the Swastika Cross cut into the flesh of the Initiates as a sign of loyalty toward this Wisdom. The Hindus called one of their trees "The Tree of Frankincense, whose fragrance was guarded by the Winged Serpents" (the Seraphim). A concealed symbolism is always found in these sacred mysteries.

The Divining Staff of the Rabbins was the Rod that budded, over which was cut the "Name" and "Sun and Lord." It was a branch of Fire that belonged to the mysteries. A legend of the first Staff, created in the evening of the Sabbath, has been written by the Rabbi Elizier, and is most enlightening.

The Chinese Tree of Knowledge was their Immortal Peach Tree, which bore fruit but once in every three thousand years, around which are woven tales and legends similar to those of the Tree of our Mother Eve of the Garden of Eden. The Chinese manifestation was a Justice one and stressed the three thousand year period, and their Peach Tree of Immortality produced only the one fruit in those years. It is said also of this Tree that three thousand years elapse before the Tree blossoms and another three thousand years before it sets fruit, all having mystical significance. The Great Mother in China was the Royal King-Mother who produced the Immortal Peach, or the forbidden fruit of knowledge but once in every three thousand years. It was the blossoming and the setting of the fruit at stated periods that made this Tree a cyclic symbol, for their Tree was an important type of Time.

In one of their legends Woo-te had eaten of this fruit, after which he built a terraced pyramid of mud, high enough to reach heaven and to the mother of this Immortal Peach. She descended to earth by means of this pyramid for seven days and seven nights, that she might discuss with Woo-te the "Principles of Reason" and the Hidden Knowledge. The primitive pyramid with its seven steps or stages is typical of the Great Mother or Goddess of the Seven Stars belonging to the Mount, who was the Royal Mother Si Wang Mu living high up in the mountain of Kwan Lun. Her Tree produced this Immortal Peach from which it was believed the Elixir of Life could be distilled, thus making the Peach a symbol of longevity or Immortality.

The word God in Chinese, as well as in Egyptian and in cuneiform writing, represents a Star. Under a horizontal line there are three perpendicular wavy lines, apparently bringing down "Light from the Sky," as the blue line above represents the firmament. This outpouring of Rays of Light from the celestial heaven or from the hidden Sun, their God, undoubtedly signified the pouring out of the Light over China every three thousand years.

The Shenu of the Hebrew is the Thorn Bush. In Egyptian the Shenu is the Thorny Acacia, a sacred Tree of Life from which the divine voice was supposed to issue.[1] In Deut. xxxiii, 16, the Hebrew divinity is spoken of as "him that dwelt in the bush." Diviners were placed in groves

---

[1] The Shenu also represents a point in the heavens or place of the Solstice recommencing in the sign of Leo, that of Fire.

of these bushes, from which the oracular voice was thought to issue. Sometimes they used pits for these ceremonies, surrounding them with thorn bushes, from which the divine voice was supposed to come.

The ancient peoples believed that the mounting of the Tree was a means of reaching Paradise, their place of Rest. It is difficult for us to understand this teaching today, or to comprehend that they found their divine rest and peace in loving adoration of the great Celestial Ocean of blossoming Stars and their contemplation of the Golden Gate, beyond which lay Infinity.

Tracing the Tree back to these early beginnings of knowledge, food and drink, we cannot wonder that the strangely reverent primitive peoples looked upon the Tree as the Mother of Life.

The May Pole was the Tree of the Sun or Fire. The above is an authentic May Pole with its symbolical additions. "In the Upper portion we have the Apex of the Phallus, the Quarter-feuilles and the Discus and Round. The lower portion is the Linga, Lingham, or Phallus wreathed; also the 'Pole' of the Ship 'Argo,' otherwise the 'Tree of Knowledge'." ("The Rosicrucians," etc., by Hargrave Jennings.)

CHAPTER VIII

FESTIVALS OF FIRE

The May Pole is a symbol of the Tree of Knowledge, emblematic of virile life, and garlanded with blossoming leaves, belongs to the Crossing of the Sun at the summer solstice. It has been called the Tree of the Sun or Fire. In one of its authentic representations the phallus encircled with leaves looms above, and just a little below is a circle forming the four-fold cross. The seven ribbons of the May Pole symbolized the seven rays of the Sun, the seven prismatic colors or the seven planets and belong to the Great Mother as do all Sevens.

Sirius, Sut, Seb and Baal as gods were connected with the Tree imaging the Mother, they all combined in Sut (Sirius) the first born son and typified the element of Fire, that great and glowing Sun of Fire we know as the Dog-Star. The name and the meaning of Baal also may be a Fire-Tree, a Fire-God, or a Fire-Star. Our Dog-Star is the Fire-Star which belongs to the midsummer because of its heliacal rising and is typical of a new year, a branching of the Eternal Tree, or a rekindling of the Fire of heaven.

Our Bible says that God showed Himself to His Prophets Isaiah, Ezekiel and St. John in the midst of Fire. The word of God is compared to Fire, "Is not my word like a Fire?" Jer. xxiii, 29, and Jesus is likened to fire. Jesus sent His Holy Ghost or Spirit upon his disciples in the form of tongues of flame, or like sparks of fire, Acts ii ,3.

The worship of the Sun in its ancient purity was a belief that the Divine Spark from the Great Spiritual Sun was a revealed manifestation of God. The ancient peoples strove to bring this Spark, which pertained to their God, the Absolute, close to their hearts. Today we have a materialized god, GOLD, the one thing in our present Era called Almighty. Two thousand years from now, when our history is reviewed, we too shall be called Worshippers—not of the Sun-god but of the Money-god, which is one of the great illusions of this cycle of the "Dark Star."

With the coming of Summer the burning of old brooms and the relighting of the sacred Fires took place. The "Need Fires," or the "Forced Fires," as they were sometimes called were kindled by the spark obtained by the rubbing together of two pieces of wood, usually of oak. To obtain this Spark, wooden axles belonging to wagon wheels were symbolically used, around which they wound two ropes, which were worked with the greatest speed by powerful men in opposite groups, thus releasing the Fire that had been imprisoned by the Sun. Reading back in the Egyptian Ritual, the stars and the planets are found to be hauling the Sun by ropes, the bringing of the Sun out of the night. The relighting of the Fire by the Spark thus obtained was similarly imaged in these Fire Festivals.

In the ancient Sabean cult, Kar-tek was one of the names given to the goddess of the Great Bear, whose son, Sut, became the Baal of the solar rendering. Kar-tek means a Spark Holder. The "Need Fires" or "Baal Fires" were always sacredly produced by a Spark at their annual ceremonies. This was the divine Spark of the Druids, found at the dawn, which gave them their inspiration through the Fire from Heaven.

The Tree was superseded by the pyramid, and small ornamental trees, pyramidal in shape, were carried about during the Christmas festivals. The Fir Tree is pyramidal. Fir and Fire are from the same root, from which we have the Fir-tree or the Fire-tree at our Christmas festivals. Ta is an ideograph of the pyramid, and has the meaning "to give." Through this we can trace back to its origin the giving of the gifts at Christmas, which were originally offered to the youthful Sun-God during his festival, which occurred at the time of his rebirth in December. We irreverently call this ancient festival Pagan Sun-worship, though it is continued today, when Christians throughout the world joyously gather about the gift-laden Christmas Tree.

The Mummers at Christmas time, who wandered from house to house, masked, had their origin in the old Sabean cult and symbolized the darkness from which the Sun would arise. Christmas Eve, December 24, was the darkest period of the year, when the lowest ebb of all life was reached at midnight. The Pantomime is also very ancient, having been born from the stars above, and given in many types, with representations according to times and customs.

The Pyramid and the obelisk are male symbols, but their bases are feminine and typical of the birthplace. The apex represents, Fire, Virility. The triangle is feminine at its base, but masculine at its apex. The nave of the church is feminine, its spire is masculine. The tomb in the earth is feminine, but the stone above is masculine. "In the First Epistle of Timothy, Paul likens the Church *to a house and a pillar*, . . . the pillar and House were both symbolically the same. Pillar, Seat, Mount, Tree, or Abode, was each representative of Motherhood, whose latest type was the Mother Church."[1] The myths and fables of the Tree first standing for the North Pole, the Tree that was likened to the Horn that produced the Golden Apples, that delicious fruit of the Garden of the Hesperides are today an integral part of our so-called Christian religion, which has seemingly failed to eat from the Tree of ancient Knowledge.

In Egypt the equator was known as the Horn Point of the world, called Apta. It was the beginning and the ending, and a point of endurance, or a foundation. The Ascendant of the horoscope, which shows the beginning as well as the ending of the great circle or wheel of life, was sometimes known as the Horn.

---

[1] Massey, Gerald—The Natural Genesis, Vol. i, p. 393.

The Circle Dance, solar in origin, danced by David uncovered before the Ark of the Covenant, was also a characteristically Sabean rite, denoting the motion of the planets around the Sun.

A religious dance is performed by the Kaffirs at the time a lad reaches the age of puberty. At this time the creative power, the reproducing spirit, the Ruach, as the descending dove, called the "Spirit of God," symbolical of rebirth and renewal falls upon him. It is a manner of celebrating the coming of the fatherhood upon earth. In the Hebrew tradition Ruach is said to enter the child at the age of thirteen, when he becomes possessed of Ruach, which is the "Breath of Life," or the coming to life of the spirit in embryo.

Another religious dance, Solar in origin, given at the turning point of the Summer Solstice, when the Sun entered the Zodiacal sign Leo, was called by the Greeks the "Pyrrhic Dance," from Pur, meaning Fire. The dancers imitated the coiling and gliding of the serpent, esetorically signifying the motion of the Serpent Fire. August, the month of the Lion, is a peculiarly Solar or Fire Month, and while named after the Emperor Augustus, was perhaps so designated to indicate its imperial authority in the Solar year. It was the month of the Dog-Star days, and was by the Western Indians consecrated to the Serpent Worship. The Serpents, by the way, are charmed and controlled by Feathers. Feathers symbolized Breath and were an early ideograph for Spirit. The well-known immunity of the Indian dancers to the serpent poison is easily explainable when the winged or feathered serpent art of Egypt is understood, and when we realize the power of the Serpent Fire, which is closely allied to the sign Leo, house of the Sun. This constellation with its subtle connection with the Serpent is probably one of the most famous of the twelve signs of the Zodiac.

Fire was the great secret of the Magi in the slaying of the lion and the control of the serpent. "The lion is the celestial Fire, while the serpents are the electric and magnetic currents of the earth;" and "That which is above is like that which is below and that which is below is like that which is above, for the fulfilment of all things."

In the first volume of the Secret Doctrine, on page 213, we read that "The highest group of hierarchies is composed of the divine Flames, so-called, also spoken of as the 'Fiery Lions' and the 'Lions of Life' whose esotercism is securely hidden in the Zodiacal sign of Leo. It is the *nucleole* of the superior divine World. They are the formless Fiery Breaths;" also, "the Hierarchy of Creative Powers is divided into seven (or 4 and 3) esoteric, within the twelve great Orders, recorded in the twelve signs of the Zodiac; the seven of the manifesting scale being connected, moreover, with the Seven Planets."

The death of the Scandinavian Sun-God Baldur, the Beautiful, the Good, at midsummer, and the Fires that were to light him through the underworld and greet him on his return to life, were the same as those used in the burning of the yule log and the hanging Lights on the Fire Tree. Baldur could be killed only by the Mistletoe. He was the personification of the Mistletoe on the Tree, which was thought to contain the life and spirit of the tree, yet it was the Mistletoe that caused his death.

The Divining Rod was gathered on the mystic midsummer eve. It was thought to be made of four kinds of wood, of which Mistletoe was one. In England a sprig of mistletoe was always carried by the Priests on Christmas Eve to the High Altar, at which time liberty and pardon were granted to the wayfarer and the wicked who came and stood at the Gates, which symbolized the four Quarters of Heaven and Earth. This branch has been poetically said to bring back to life those who wait at the Golden Gate, the Eighth, leading to infinity.

The Russians have a belief that if the golden bloom of the fern seed is caught at midnight on the mystical midsummer eve and scattered about in the shadowy darkness, it will fall to the ground like sparkling stars, directly on the spot where great treasures are hidden. This is a key to the hidden mystical treasures of divine knowledge.

Regarding the Eve of St. John fancies innumerable arose, beautifully interwoven with the gathering of the flowers and plants, golden and glowing from the entrapped rays of the summer Sun, guarding against sorceries and disease. It was thought that when the Sun had reached its greatest culminating point, its magic entered the flowers, which must be culled before the witching hour had passed, which brought together the youth and the maiden under the enchanted spell of midnight, when they plighted their troth with each other. Among those that were considered of the greatest importance to be gathered for magical healing and divination was St. John's wort, which some think should be gathered on the day immediately following St. John's Eve when the sun enters the sign of the Lion. Its bright yellow blossoms and golden stamens are tiny types of the great Sun above. The edges of the calyx and leaves are marked with dark purple spots, which yield a red oil, believed to be the blood of St. John, hence its great healing property, and value for endless other safety guarding purposes.

Magical flowers of the Solstices are chosen for their brightness, their golden colors shedding light, like lamps in the darkness, and should be gathered on the longest day of the year, when the radiant fire and heat of the Sun at the very moment of its greatest power carries its mystic message into the heart of the plant.

We lovingly tread on enchanted ground whence man looked toward heaven and the glowing Sun whose light and fire were stored in the leaf and blossom and had dreams of magic and healing, extracting the divine spark for wonder-working, as it were, from God Himself, who was thought to manifest at the time of the two solstices, celebrated by festivals of Sacred Fire.

The Summer Solstice was preeminently a feast of Fire or a

Fire Festival.   In many lands huge bonfires were built on the summits of high hills and wheels of Fire were sent blazing down the hillsides, typical of the descending Sun, the wheel with its spokes representing the sun and its rays.

At the Summer Solstice the lifting of children over the dying embers of the fires, the joyous leaping through the flames, the swinging and leaping around the blaze in their circular dance, the sacred lighting of the flame by releasing the embedded fire of the Sun, were all for purificatory purposes.   They reverently and joyously believed that the new born Sun would bring riches through the golden summer and a plentiful harvest, and would dispel the evil witchcraft of the sorcerer.

Midsummer fires are continued in our present era, but are regarded as superstitions, whereas in olden days they were reverenced as symbols of the Sun's crossing at the Summer Solstice.   At the Winter Solstice the Tree of Fire has become the Tree of Light on our Christmas Eve.   We have the burning of the Yule Log.   Yule means the Sun, whose Fire is transfigured in the green-leafed Christmas Tree of renewal and rebirth, the light of which symbolizes the return to life of the Sun-God.

December the twenty-fifth was originally devoted to the worship of the Sun-God Mithra, and was adopted and introduced into the Western Church in the Fourth Century, climaxing as the anniversary of the birth of Jesus in the later Christian religion.   The origin of both the Maypole and the Christmas Tree however are to be found in the crossing of the Sun in the two Solstices.

Mithra was the name of the Solar God of Light and Wisdom among the Persians.   His birthday was celebrated on the twenty-fifth of December, date of the rebirth of the Sun at the time of the Winter Solstice.   The Mithraic cult was introduced into Rome by the early Emperors, and the date of December twenty-fifth was adopted as a special festival by Aurelian A. D. 273.   The Solar character of this festival was well known by the Roman Emperors, and not until the Fourth Century was December twenty-fifth introduced and accepted as the birthday of their Christ. "Augustus and Gregory discoursed on 'the glowing light and diminishing darkness that follow a nativity'."[1] "Pope Leo the Great recognized the day as the birthday of the Sun, and denounced it as the birthday of Christ. He was Pope of Rome in the Fourth or Fifth century. Gregory the Great became Pope about the year 590."[2]

Mithra was said to have been born in a cave at the Winter Solstice, which occurs in the Zodiacal sign Capricorn.[3] Abba-Udda, the Akkadian name for the tenth month, which corresponds approximately to December, means "The Cave of Light," and indicates the birth of the Mithraic Messiah. This Mithraic cult with its aspirations towards moral purity and immortality, proved a formidable rival to Christianity. Our Christmas is borrowed directly from it, and close relation is found between the Sacred Books of Revelation of the two cults—the Persian Zend-Avesta (the Parsee Book of Zoroaster), written about 1000 B. C., and the Book of Revelation of John of Patmos. The foundations of both these books are astronomical and prophetic. All ancient prophets and priests were astrologers.

A comparison of the two books will reveal the Christian form of the Mithraic Revelation. To attain knowledge of God and see the future, Zoroaster drinks of a special magnetized water which produces a trance lasting seven days and nights. In Revelation we are told that John eats a little Book that he may prophesy. The Serpent, which was the constellation Draco, called the Serpent, or the Dragon,

---

[1] Olcott—Sun Lore of All Ages, p. 230.

[2] Special Reports, Leo the Great and Gregory the Great.

[3] On the twenty-fifth of December, the day of the Nativity of the Sun, the days begin to lengthen, and the Sun's power is on the increase. This was the time when in Egypt and Syria the celebrants entered the inner shrine, and issued at midnight crying, "The Virgin has brought forth"—"The Light is Waxing." The log burned on Christmas Eve was in celebration of the birth of the divine child as the Solar Sun-god.

figures largely in both visions. In one book the Dragon swallows one-third of mankind, cattle, sheep, and other creatures; in the other he draws the third part of the stars from heaven with his tail. When the ancient religion of the Mother and Son was changed into that of the Father and Son, the change was symbolized by the falling of a star from heaven. This is the demoralization or dethronement of that "Old Mother,'" who became the degraded Venus in one cult and the harlot in the other. "When the Star Jupiter comes to its culminating point and casts Venus down, the sovereignty comes to the Prince," and there is the "Woman clothed with the Sun whose Prince comes when the Star falls from the sky." Zoroaster describes the seven regions of the world founded on the seven heavens, or the Tree of seven branches with its divisions of time and space. John describes the seven Churches of Asia and the seven-branched Candlestick, or the Tree of seven branches. In the fulfilment of the prophecies, the heaven of seven, or the early seventy Princes or divisions, are replaced by the Zodiacal Tree with its twelve branches or signs, and its thirty-six decans or seventy-two duo-decans; from which Tree was derived the Cross, symbolized in the four corners, or the four cardinal points of the world. It was originally the Tree of Healing and of Light, which vanished with the lost Paradise. Both cults were Kronian and Solar and followed the cult of the Mother and Son, and were established when the Sun was proved to be the true time-keeper.

The priestly ceremonies of the Mithraic mysteries were in imitation of the motions of the heavenly bodies. The Initiates were given the names of the Constellations, and were dressed like the animals that were represented in the signs. Their purification was by water, and in honor of "She of the Celestial Waters." They had their Confessional, and also a kind of Eucharist, or offering of bread. The "bread" used in the Mithraic sacraments was a round cake, emblem of the Solar Disk, and the "Cup" is usually found on the altar or "table." All concerning the worship of Mithras and the caves used for initiations, were destroyed after A. D. 400. There is a tradition of the Rabbins, concerning the origin of the Wafer, given by Alfonso de Spira, in his Fortelicium Fidei, vol. ii, 2, which "says that its circular form is a symbol of the Sun, and that it is offered to the genius of that luminary as a victim. 'The Wafer has ever been styled the *Hostia,* the victim,' in Hebrew 'Messah'."

The worship of Mithra was introduced at Rome after the conquest of Pontus by Pompey, as a distinct creed, which became very popular during the second and third centuries of the Empire. The religions of Mithra and of Serapis were the sole forms of worship, penetrating far corners of the Empire, the Mithraic Festival was called the "Birthday of the Invincible One," and celebrated chariot races took place during this festival later dedicated to the memory of Christ. Its exact date is not known, but it is not surprising that "Leo the Great (Serm. II on the Birth of the Lord), blames those Christians who gave offense to the weaker souls through the shameful persuasion of some by whom this festival of ours is reverenced not so much on account of the Christ's Birth as on that of the 'Rising of the New Sun'."[1]

Mithra was undoubtedly admitted to be a type of Christ, and the Jews when they were living in Persia obtained a great portion of their spiritual wisdom from the Mithraic Creed. At that time they brought into their worship a belief in a future state of rewards and punishments, the latter carried on in a fiery lake. Both Jews and Christians by misinterpreting the mithraic ritual of the "sacred fire" founded a fiery region named Gehenna by the Jews, a name which in the New Testament is transferred by an easy metaphor into Hell which figures so largely in their beliefs. The Jews have also a Holy Order of the Angels, as well as Devils, a Last Judgment, and the Immortality of the Soul, all of which are borrowed from the religion of Zoroaster.

[1]King—The Gnostics, pp. 49, 50.

Justin Martyr declared that the Mithraic mysteries were so like those of the Christians that they had stolen them to deceive the people. A final severance of these two cults—biblical and non-biblical—can never take place, because both are purely astronomical, and upon them much later theological history has been founded. Our Era of Light, however, now superseding the Era of Darkness, will dissipate the fogs created by false interpretations of the myths. Truth will finally reveal itself in the Light.

Millenia belong to the end of cycles, and are the fulfilment of prophecies. In the new era, as in other precessional periods of the past, prophecies will be fulfilled. In the thirteenth chapter of St. Matthew, in speaking to the initiates Jesus says, "It is given unto you to know the mysteries of the kingdom of heaven." To the unbelievers, indeed, it has not been given!

Kircher tells us that all who entered the Temple of the Epicine divinity Serapis[1] bore on brow or breast the letters or sign of 10 (IU). IU was the Egyptian Messiah, their Coming One, their Prince of Peace. Serapis, like all other gods, was a double type of deity identified with Iu-Em-Hept, and was made a double type of the Solar God Apis, and Sirius, or the Sun and Sirius. Tracing the Egyptian myths to their source, we find basic truths underlying their mythological structure. Sut, son of the ancient Mother, was called the long-eared Ass, or IU, as the Hearer, who became a type of the Bull God AU. AU was the Lord of Victory, and resided in the house of Shu, the Egyptian Moses. This was the house of the Lion-Gods, who light Atum, or AU (in other words the Sun) in and out of the generative abyss of darkness. Hor Apollo says the ear is a symbol of a future act. AU means to be, and thus as Iu-Em-Hept he

---

[1] In all temples where Isis and Serapis were worshipped, images with the finger to the lips were seen, meaning that silence was to be maintained regarding all that concerned the great Mother Mystery, symbolized by the Shekinah of heaven, the Sacred Spirit as Mother of all.

is the future being, the Coming One. Cosmically and astronomically the Sun-Gods were always Sons of the Sun, but when they had ceased to be housed in their mythological and astronomical houses, they became through theology "Sons of Righteousness."

In the Second Century in the city of Alexandria which was a hot bed of Gnosticism, a sect sprang up which gave an almost fanatical worship to Isis and Serapis. They believed Serapis the prophetic type of Christ, Lord and Creator of all, judge of the living and dead. Portraits and statues of his head were undoubtedly the first conventional head of Christ. In Payne Knight's "Ancient Art and Mythology" Serapis is represented as wearing his hair long, "formerly turned back and disposed in ringlets falling down upon his breast, and shoulders like that of a woman. His whole person, too, is always enveloped in drapery reaching to his feet." Serapis and Sarpa mean Serpent, and both Serapis and Jesus are later found represented as a great Serpent, an indication of Divine Wisdom, and symbol of Spirit. "The Egyptian Priests chanted the *seven* vowels as a hymn addressed to Serapis, and at the sound of the *seventh vowel,* as at the '*seventh* ray' of the rising sun, the statute of Memnon responded."[1]

Throughout all the celestial myths of Egypt, Horus, the Egyptian Messiah, figures most prominently. Two Horuses were given and yet were as one, symbolizing both sexes, male-female. The child Horus, son of Isis, remained a child until twelve years of age. All the children of Egypt wore what was called the Horus Lock until they had reached the age of twelve. Full manhood was attained at the age of thirty, at which age Horus was anointed, as the son of Osiris.

Horus the adult was the revealer of the Father in heaven, when his worship superseded that of the Mother and Son. The child Horus was the shadow of the real, but when at the

---

[1] Blavatsky, H. P.—Isis Unveiled, Vol. i, p. 514. .

vernal equinox he became the Sun of the Resurrection, he was the potent, pubescent Son. The name Horus denotes one who ascends as a spirit. As the adult Horus, the revealer, his mythical character is given in all the histories or legends of the world, and is always identified with the ending of an Age or a Cycle.

In the Egyptian myth this youthful Messiah was manifestor of the Seven Powers. He was known under different names in other cults. In the Sut-Typhonian he was Har-Khuti, Lord of Light and of the glorified elect. Har, the younger type of Horus, was spiritual, had the power of becoming invisible, and typified the resurrection of the Osirian cult. He was the Horus. In that of Iu-em-Hept he was Atum, the Eternal Word. He was also Khunsu, the child in the cult of Amen-Ra, introducing the Solar cult, and we finally find him as the Good Shepherd, the Saint of God, the Bread of Life, as Truth and the Life, the Fan Bearer, and the Door of Life.

"Horus represented the Path over which the dead passed out of the sepulchre, the God whose name is written in the Road." As Khunsu in the Denderah planisphere he is seen in a disk of the Full Moon of Easter, offering a pig for sacrifice. In the judgment scenes, given in the "Book of the Dead," the return to primordial matter is pictured as entering the bodies of swine. As Ra, the Sun, he is sometimes called Remi, the Weeper. It was Horus who sent fire into the "Place of Destruction," and was "God of the Furnace" —that is, the Solar Fire, which the theologians have construed into "Hell Fire." Its origin lies in the scorching heat of the African summer sun.

There are at least thirty-six different languages in Africa, and in every one of them the word Fire is the same as Hell. In Africa the heavens were looked upon as a "Hell of Fire" and in one instance was called a "Heaven of Ashes" because of the intense heat of Africa. Even today the heavens are termed "Fiery Furnaces."

Six thousand years ago, when the Vernal Equinox was in the sign of Taurus, the Bull, the Constellation Orion arose as "The Star of the East," and the three large brilliant stars seen in the belt of the Constellation were mythically given the names of the "Three Wise Kings." According to the Precession of the Equinoxes, the next sign to arise was Aries. The constellation of the brilliant Triangle was the new star arising on the horizon in the East, and was said to beckon to the Wise Men, pointing to the coming of a new Sun-God or Messiah. This Triangle, the pyramid of Horus, belongs to the young Egyptian God Har-Khuti. Har, as the younger God was type of Horus of the Resurrection, and spiritual. He is pictured in one of their ancient Zodiacs holding a Triangle in one hand, the rule or flail in the other. Horus of Egypt was their Lord, their Alpha and Omega, the important events of whose mythical life are found in counterpart in our New Testament. All events given in his life were never human, but were of divine significance because they were born from above, created out of the configurations found in the heavens. Similarly the Fall in the Solar cult was an astronomical myth, which has been surrounded with that halo of glory which very frequently clothed their humanized heroes who were all so called "Heathen Gods?"

When the sun rises at the time of the Winter Solstice, and the Christmas celebration takes place, the Zodiacal sign Virgo appears on the horizon. The twenty-fifth of December is a date given not only for the birthday of the Sun, but also for the births of Jesus, Buddha, and Mithra. Virgo, the virgin sign of the Zodiac, is represented as a Mother, and looking at a very old planisphere of the heavens, we can see her there symbolized, holding a child in her arms, and apparently pursued by a serpent which is directly under her feet, and as if about to be trodden upon. This same symbolism obtains for Isis and Osiris of Egypt, Maya and Buddha of India, as well as in China, and in the Book of

Revelation. The Woman and the Child later found in Rome as Mary and Jesus are an example of it. The unity of the ancient myths found in various countries of the world, slightly changed in some renderings, due to elaborations, but identical in their roots, is unmistakable. The myths of the Serpent, emblem of Eternity and type of the night which encircles the world in an endless embrace are similarly identical. And what of astrology, "Astrology is a synthesis, because the Tree of Life is a single Tree and because its branches spread through heaven bearing flowers of Stars . . . are in correspondence with its roots, which are hidden in earth."[1] And these Stars are reflectors of great and mighty splendors, while our Sun, symbol of the Great Central Sun, which is the source of all Truth and Light, is but the phanton shadow of that great primal Source from which all glory emanates and which manifests in man as a spark of Divine Fire.

[1] Ballanche—Orphic Initiation.

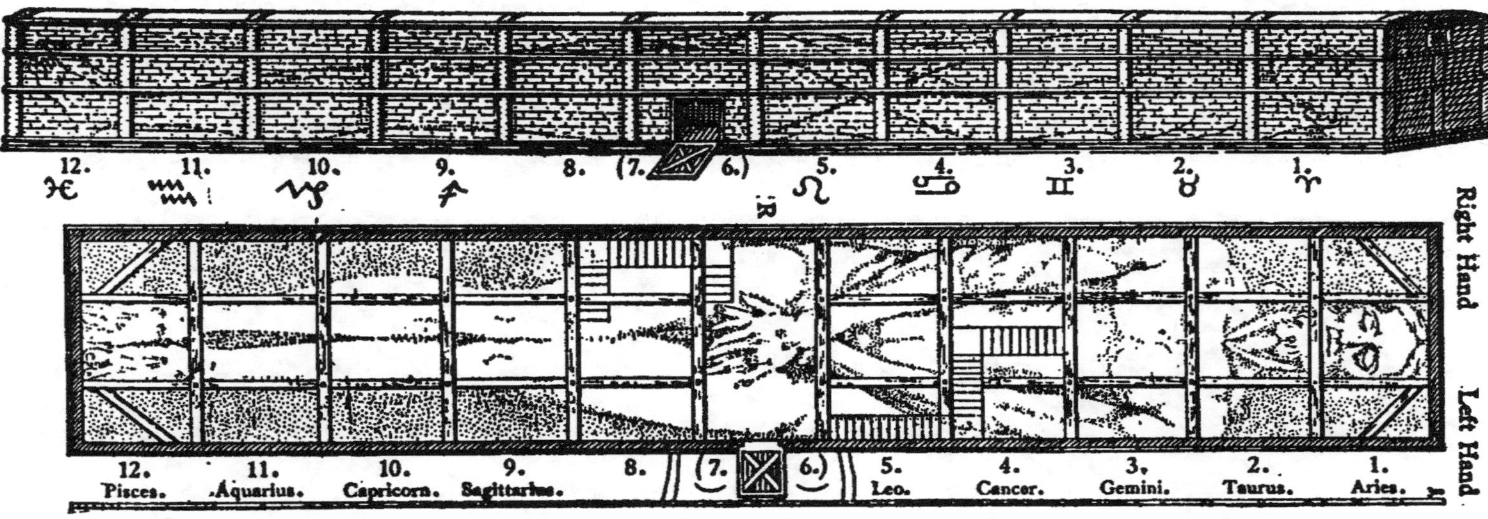

5 "SIGNS," or "Zodiacal Spaces"—"Preadamite." (5. ☽ 12 Signs— (5 "SIGNS," or "Zodiacal Spaces"—"Preadamite." (5. 1593 : ANNO.

ROSICRUCIAN SYSTEM.
Structure (Symbolic) of the "Argha," or "Arc." Also—
(Forms—exterior and interior—of the "Ark of Noah," from the description of Moses.)

Left—∗

∗ Place of the "Escaped" Signs.

147

CHAPTER IX

CELESTIAL WATERS

Every symbol in esoteric philosophy is said to have seven keys. The Dragon also had its septenary interpretation. Its symbol was the constellation of the Dragon, Draco, sometimes called "the Scaly One," giving significance to its Seven beautiful Stars, which in their highest symbolism became identical with the self-born, the Logos. The Dragon is one of the most ancient of all symbols. Terrestrially the name Dragon was given to the "Wise Men," who were astrologers. The mystics were also called Dragons of Wisdom or Serpents.

In China the Emperor's throne was known as the Dragon's Seat, inherited from the Initiates or Dragons of Wisdom. The Chinese profusely display emblems of the Dragon, of which the Twan-ying-t'u says, "His Wisdom and Virtue are unfathomable . . . he does not go in company, and does not live in herds, he wanders in the wilds beyond the heavens. He goes and comes, fulfilling the decree; at the proper season if there is perfection he comes forth, if not he remains (invisible). And Kong-fu-tyu says of the Dragon, "The Dragon feeds in pure water, and sports in the clear waters, i. e. Wisdom and Life."

As far back as the third "Deluge" of the third Lemurian race, that old Dragon "Whose tail sweeps whole nations out of existence in the twinkling of an eye," that ancient "Old Dragon" of the heavenly constellation was identical with the great Flood. "We know that in the past the constellation of the Dragon was at the pole, or boss, of the celestial sphere. In stellar temples . . . the Dragon would be the uppermost or ruling constellation . . . it is singular how closely the constellations . . . correspond in sequence and in range of right ascension with the events recorded respecting the (Biblical) flood."[1] The first great flood was heaven-born and cosmical. There have been numbers of terrestrial floods.

The pyramids are closely connected with the constellation Draco, and the deluges as are the Initiates, who were the Dragons of Wisdom. The "Secret Doctrine" tells us that "The Great Dragon (Deluge) had respect for the Serpents of Wisdom, whose holes are under the Triangular Stones," i. e. the Pyramids at the four corners of the world, records of which have been well preserved, together with the history of human evolution traceable in the heavens.

Anciently pyramids existed at the four corners of the earth, and belonged to no single nation. They have been found scattered over the two Americas, under and above ground in virgin forests, on plains and in valleys all over the world. They were built with geometrical precision corresponding to the heavens, showing that the ancient peoples realized that "God geometrises." Endeavor to reach their origins brings us to a time almost unimaginably far distant. Pyramid, Dragon and Deluge became associated with the Flood, and the floods of the Nile in Egypt were regarded as a divine reminder of the Great Atlantean Flood.

The story of the Deluge is undeniably a universal tradition. The Smithsonian confirms the existence of many deluges and glacial periods dating the earliest one 850,000 years ago, and the last one about 100,000 years ago. "But which was *our* Deluge? Assuredly the former, the one which to this date remains recorded in the traditions of all the peoples, from the remotest antiquity; the one that finally swept away the last peninsulas of Atlantis, beginning with Ruta and Daitya and ending with the (comparatively) small island mentioned by Plato. This is shown by the agreement of certain details in all the legends. It was the

---

[1]Proctor.

last of its gigantic character . . . Noah's flood . . . at least, only, a moral connection."[1]

Within the memory and possession of the Aryans observatories of the submerged Atlantis are recorded at a period 850,000 years ago. Floods preceding this date were traditional. We are told that astronomical records had their beginnings in the early Atlantean period. Age-old records can be found in the planisphere of the ceiling of the Denderah Temple, showing that the Poles have been inverted three different times. The ancient Planispheres and Zodiacs, and their bearing on humanity, should be studied with earnestness, and great reverence.

"Deluges" were caused by the reeling motion of the world, when making the movement of precession. A great Zodiacal allegory, far earlier than the Hebrew, and based on astrological fact, is the Nimrod Epic, in twelve Cantos or legends, paralelling the Sun's passage through the twelve signs of the Zodiac, and containing distinct reference to the animal forms of the Zodiac. The eleventh canto was given to the God of Rain and Storms, Rimmon, whose place was in the Zodiacal constellation Aquarius, sign of floods. The Akkadians called this sign the "Curse of Rain." In an early Zodiac the Egyptians, placed the goddess Menat, their wet-nurse, in this sign, portraying her as the Mother from whose many breasts flowed the "Water of Life."

Deluges signified the end of a cycle or period of time. A first deluge is found in the conflict between Timelessness and Time, or Chaos and Creation. Ancient legends teem with stories of the Deluge, but all having a fundamental unity with the original first telling of Time and Creation, when the heavens were the Celestial Waters. In the symbolism of every nation the Deluge stood for unsettled chaotic matter, Chaos itself, and for water, which was the feminine principle. Today we are entering the sign Aquarius, and we shall find changes, prophecies fulfilled, and a chaotic con-

---

[1]Blavatsky, H. P.—The Secret Doctrine, Vol. ii, p. 141.

dition which will spread over the entire world, carrying us back in thought to those old traditions.

The flood has dual meaning, spiritual and physical, cosmic and terrestrial. Chaos or the Great Deep stood for the Moon as the Mother, whence proceeded all the germs of life. She was called the Ark of the Celestial Waters, while the Sun was the principle giving life to all. Ark was the mystic name for the Holy Spirit or Mother, whom the Jews connected with Israel, Jehovah and his seed. Ur (Urt) was the chief seat of the worship of the Moon-god, being the place from which Abraham came. The Moon was originally feminine, but later for a time was made masculine. The Akkadian Urdhu and the Hebrew Ararat are the Egyptian form of Arurut. Urdhu is the district of the Northern Mountain, which mythologically is the North of the Great Bear, "The Thigh!" Ur meant First, Oldest, Great, and Urt was the Enceinte Mother whose image "typified the very primitive crib and cradle (Apt) of the human race, or the time-births which began in the mountains of the north, Urdhu, Ararat, or Urrtu, afterwards called the birthplace of man, in all the oldest mythologies; the full form of whose name (Urt) is Rerit (or Ururat), the Sow, the Hippopotamus, the Great Bear."[1]

In all traditions of the Deluge the Ark was made to contain the Seed of Life, which in various miraculous ways was always saved for future generations. This germ of all living things was necessary for the repeopling of the earth. It represented the "survival of life, and the supremacy of spirit over matter, through the conflict of the opposing powers of nature."[2] The ark, oblong in shape, was used as the "Sacrificial Chalice" by the priests in the worship of the goddesses who represented the generative powers of nature. Hence the Ark as a symbolical representation of the mother containing the seed of life was the Ship of the

---

[1]Massey, Gerald—A Book of the Beginnings, Vol. ii, p. 521.
[2]Blavatsky, H. P.—Isis Unveiled, Vol. ii, p. 444.

North. "The Talmud books say that Noah was himself the dove (spirit), thus identifying him still more with the Chaldean Nouah. Baal is represented with the wings of a dove, and the Samaritans worshipped on Mount Gerizim, the image of a dove."[1]

The story of Noah's deluge is astronomical and astrological, based on the same archaic traditions of persons who were saved from the deluges or cataclysms in boats, ships, arks and canoes. Noah clearly a mythical symbol, cannot be rightfully claimed by either Jew or Christian. Noah is but a Jewish representation of the Pagan Gods, who were never men but types of astronomical periods, or solar or lunar years. Noah mythically means "One who rests," sometimes called the "Sun Setting." Also the Hebrew Nuach or Noah is related to Breath, breathing. Nu means a flood; so did Time as Seb, one of whose names was Nu, and Nua was rest, repose. "Nothing is older than water as an element of life and there is nothing more initial than its influence on the mind of man as an agent of destruction, of death, of an ending, the water of death being the natural antithesis to the breath of life."[2]

Water and Breath, in which baptismal regeneration finds its origin, are a symbolical representation of "from out of the water into a new life," or rebirth. Among the many names derived from the word Noah, that of No means a boat, feminine symbol of repose, rest; while Ah is masculine. No is also synonymous with habitation. The Noahchidae, who were the Children of the Boat, have belonged to different nations. All proves that Noah was never a human being, but belonged to the mythological stories of the heavens.

Mystically Noah is interpreted as spirit falling into matter. When so imprisoned the pure spirit is said to become intoxicated, thus we find that Noah, as soon as he finds himself on dry land, plants a vineyard and gets drunk. A mystical

---

[1] Talmud, Tract—Chalin, Vol. vi, col. 1.
[2] Massey, Gerald—The Natural Genesis, Vol. ii, p. 190.

interpretation extends to the two Falls given in the Bible, which are closely related.   The Fall of Adam came about because he had tasted of the forbidden fruit, celestial knowledge.   Noah's Fall was caused by his drinking too freely of the terrestrial fruit of the grape.   Celestially the fruit of the grape was divine wisdom.   Drunkenness represented the abuse of this wisdom in an irresponsible way, so "Adam gets stripped of his spiritual envelope; Noah of his terrestrial clothing; and the nakedness of both makes them ashamed."[2]   Noah's ark signifies spiritual rebirth, the emergence into immortality.

There are many historical deluges as well as local ones traceable in the traditions of many countries, but they have nothing in common with the mystical Noah.   Deluges, cataclysms or cycles of time at the ending of different eras do not destroy the world, but the general appearance is changed and a new type of humanity, races, animals and flora evolve from the old.

Kaemfer in his "Japan" gives a tradition of the Chinese flood—"The Island owing to the iniquity of its Giants, sinks to the bottom of the ocean, and Peiru-un, the King, the Chinese Noah, escapes alone with his family owing to a warning of the gods through two idols.   It is that pious Prince and his descendants who have peopled China."   It seems evident that this flood also points to Atlantis, indicating a Chinese belief in the divine dynasties of kings.   One of the traditional deluges described in Hindu books bears an interesting resemblance to the same tradition.   Viavasvata saves a little fish which turns out to be the Avatar Vishnu, who warns him that the globe is about to be submerged, and that the inhabitants will perish.   He is told to construct a boat upon which to embark with his family, "And the seeds and plants and pairs of animals" are to go with him.   At the coming of the rain an enormous fish places itself at the bow. It has a large horn and to this Viavasvata fastens the cable

----

[2]Blavatsky, H. P.

of his boat, and so is piloted through the turbulent waters.
When the storm ceases the boat is landed on the summit of
the Himalayan Mountains. This traditional story was never
considered sacred, but in some books was told concerning
a descendant of Viavasvata. It was carried into all countries
belonging to India East and West.

The metaphysical meaning of Fish is divine, but the
theological was made phallic. Jesus, Vishnu, Bacchus and
other great Messengers were all called Fish. The Chinese
term every great period or cycle of time, Deluge. "Their
River Scheme" with its written program, is brought up from
the water. An altar marks the spot where the Fish or Fish-
man emerges, and the River Scheme is laid upon the altar.
The same story is related of Xisuthrus, hero of the Chaldean flood, while the Egyptians placed an empty boat in the
scales (Libra), which is their sign of the altar. Viavasvata,
Xisuthrus, Deukalion, and Noah were all heroes of world
deluges. Natural phenomena furnish names and records of
the causes leading to these events, whose mythical origins
are discoverable, as are all beginnings, in that wonderful
birthplace in the north of the heavens.

In the traditions of the terrestrial deluges reference is
made to the mystery of mankind's being saved from utter
destruction at the end of the third race by the woman, who
was mortal and was made the receptacle of the seed. There
were three Dynasties preceding human rulership, namely,
the DYNASTIES OF THE GODS, of the Demi-gods,
and of the Heroes, or Giants. In every tradition concerning
these ancient floods or deluges the Seed is always miraculously saved, sometimes spiritually and sometimes physically,
while Seven also figures very largely in all accounts.
The Incas, seven in number, repeopled the earth after
the deluge. Xisuthrus, or the Chaldean Noah, being saved
was translated to heaven alive with the Seven Kabirim
Gods. The Chinese Yao has seven figures sailing with him
to be animated as human seed on his landing. Osiris, when

he enters his Solar Boat, takes with him the seven Rays. The Titans who were especially associated with the flood, were seven. A meaning of Titan is derived from Tit-Ain— "The Fountains of the Chaotic Abyss," while Tit-theus, or Tityn, means "Divine Deluge." Through all these names if properly read, will be traced records and causes, originating in the constellation of the Dragon and its Seven Stars, and leading to the Deluges.

Babylon owed its foundation to those who were saved from the deluge. These were the Giants who built the Tower and were great Astrologers. They had received their instructions of secret wisdom concerning the heavens from their fathers, the "Mighty Ones," who had left records of the periodic catacyclisms which they themselves had witnessed. "This is in flat contradiction to the Bible narrative, which tells us that the deluge was sent for the special destruction of the Giants. The Babylon Priests had *no* reason for telling lies."[1] The Giants were the astrologers in whose temples were kept records of all great periodical upheavals, of which they were witnesses, and "As the star glimmering at an immeasurable distance above our heads, in the boundless immensity of the sky, reflects itself in the smooth waters of the lake, so does the imagery of men of those antediluvian ages, reflect itself in the periods we can embrace in an historical retrospect. As above, so it is below, that which has been, will return again. As it is in heaven, so on earth."[2]

The Tower of Babel, one of the most ancient astronomical temples, was called the Temple of "Seven Lights," or the "Celestial Earth." It was an edifice embodying the astronomical knowledge of antiquity. Herodotus tells us that there was a road on the outside of the Tower of Babel that went eight times round in its ascent, giving the appearance of eight towers, and filled in from top to bottom with many stars. It was built in the latitude of thirty-

---

[1] Blavatsky, H. P.—Isis Unveiled, Vol. i, p. 31.
[2] Blavatsky, H. P.

two degrees. This is a fact of very great importance, as it shows the "pericyclosical" motion of the poles around each other, commemorating eight revolutions of the poles, or "The Serpent coiling Eight times Around." The Babylonian astrologers made use of this tower as an observatory. The Jews have coupled with this wonderful monument, the history of one they called Nimrod, who was not a man, though they would convey the idea that he was. The meaning of the word "is compounded from Naim, beautiful; Ur, heaven; and Ad, father; Nim'r-ad then, means the Beautiful Father of Heaven." It is stated that the Giant Naboad (Nimrod) was a son of Kush, Ethiopia, and of the race of Ham (Kam), who built Babylon.[1] In Genesis x, 6-10, it says, "the sons of Ham, Cush, and Mizra-im . . . and Cush begat Nimrod; he began to be a mighty one in the earth. . . . And the beginning of his Kingdom was Babel and Erech, and Accad, and Calneh, in the land of Shinar." This history pertains to the birthplace of mythological astronomy in the North. Biblical allegory reveals that Nimrod became a Gibbor (Kibor) giant on earth, and was called the greatest of the Gibborim (Egyptian Kabiri) who were the Seven Great Stars "considered to be a brotherhood of sailors through the celestial waters." Kabiri or Kab-ari were the Seven companions or watchers, that made the circle and cycle of time. (Kab, Egyptian, means to turn around, ari, companions or watchers.) In the Ritual there are four Kabiri, lords of the four cardinal points, the four genii that guard the four corners of the sarcophagus. These four belong to the Seven Great Spirits of the Great Bear, identified in mythology as the seven Kabiri. The four earliest corners, called the four corners of the Great Bear, were typified by the Hippopotamus, the Lion, the Crocodile and the Monkey. The next following were called the four quarters of Nimrod. They were the four royal stars, the great and beautiful fires of heaven, Regulus, Antares. Alda-

____

[1]Bunson—Egypt, Vol. i, p. 229.

baran and Fomalhaut. Anhar-Nimrod, as the Great Gibor, was the elevator of the heavens, founded on the four corners, and became the Angel Gabriel. Shu-Anhar in planetary phase was Mars, a fact which is an aid in tracing the original Nimrod, chief of the four Kabiri, the four Royal Stars. Mars is god of generation and breath, as well as god of War, and is the ruler of the zodiacal sign Scorpio, representing the generative organs, and whose brilliant star is Antares, of the royal group of Four. Gabriel was the Announcer of the Coming Son, and Nimrod, "whose Tetrapolis above was the model of the Tetrapolis below in the plain of Shinar"[1] was chief of the Kabiri of the four corners.

Nimrod, Shu and Kepheus are the same. Shu is portrayed as the hunter with his dogs. He was the Lion of the Sun. On the Nineveh tablet it says: "If the star of the Great Lion is gloomy, the heart of the people will not rejoice." When transformed into the leopard, or cat, he becomes the Lion-leoparded of Heraldry. Nimrod (Kepheus or Shu) was the Hunter, Shepherd, Lawgiver and King of Kush. "Kush begat Nimrod." Kush (Kam) or Ethiopia was the primeval parentage of the black race, and Nimrod was son of Kush. Kush was a name of the birthplace of the North —"The Thigh" (the Great Bear).

The City of Nineveh, the latitude of which is four degrees nearer the Pole than that of Babylon, could have seen nine revolutions of the pole of the Ecliptic pass between the North Pole and its horizon, and from this circumstance "Nineveh received the name Nin'-ophi, i. e., "Nine Serpents."[2] There are other monuments of ancient origin erected to reveal and perpetuate knowledge of the pericyclosical motion of the Poles blended with the latitude of the different countries. Every four degrees of latitude represented a coil, or spiral, called a serpent, because of the two slow motions of the Poles.

"The Serpent round the Solar-fire-place—the Solstice, or

---

[1]Massey, Gerald—A Book of the Beginnings, Vol. ii, p. 516.
[2]Mackey, S. A.—Mythological Astronomy, p. 72.

the Pole, is the *pericyclosical* figure described by the pole of the ecliptic round the pole of the earth; which is known to form a *volute,* increasing in size every 25,000 (or more) years, 'till it reaches the Equator; when, by the present rate of the Pole's apparent motion, there must have been traced, an imaginary SPIRAL, having 22 or 23 rounds. The present rate and order of the polar motion, would in *forty-five* times 25,000 years *invert the order of the Poles!* describing among the stars, a *winding stair-case,* called the CLIMAX or *scale of heat,* from whence is derived the word climate, a measure of heat from *cali, heat,* and med or *metre,* a measure. Hence it is very probable that the ancients, in, or about the *Age of Horror,* divided the earth into forty-five climates, i. e., twenty-two and a half on each side of the equator, allowing four degrees to a climate. And as this number four is measured out to us by the ascent or descent of the pole at every round made by the recession of the equinoctial points, it became a number highly venerated by all the ancients. The Pythagoreans called it the mystical Tetrad; but this does not mean they worshipped the *number four as a God.*"[1]

This spiral motion has been the foundation of nearly all religious history. The mind of man needs only to rise above the prejudices of the past to realize a wealth of primitive knowledge concerning "the Solstice, i. e., the Sun-stand— the *boundary of the sun* which in the Eastern language, is Gibe-on." The North Pole was called the Mountain. The highest point in the ecliptic, called the Mount of the North Pole, was reached by the Sun at the summer solstice ere it began its descent.

The different nations agree so exactly in respect to this point that there can be neither doubt nor suspicion as to their knowledge of this pericyclosical (Precessional) motion. Towers and Temples modeled after the coils of the serpent, given as rings, and connecting their country with

---

[1] Mackey, S. A. Mythological Astronomy, pp. 63-64.

the heavens, were erected to register this fact, and show conclusively that peoples belonging to a remote antiquity understood the Precession of the Equinoxes. Babylon, with her thirty-two degrees of latitude, had her tower with its eight coils; Nineveh at thirty-six degrees, is named from the nine coils. Pluto (Egyptian) at twenty-four degrees, is portrayed with six coils of a serpent about him. Pekin at forty degrees of latitude has her Porcelain Tower ten stories high. Moreover there are many statues of human figures with serpent coils representing latitudes of two, four, six degrees, etc. About every twenty-five thousand years by precessional reckoning the ecliptic is removed four degrees from the Pole of the heaven, the angle of the pole varying four degrees with every round or revolution. Each of the motions ascending or descending every twenty-five thousand years with these four degrees of change, was symbolized by serpents, each according to the latitude of the country being represented by a volute, a coil of the serpent. When the ecliptic is within sixteen degrees of the Poles, it would be, every day, in the plane of the horizon in that latitude. "By placing the sign Cancer at the North, that of Capricorn at the South, Aries East and Libra West, the entire Zodiac would be seen in the heavens every morning at sunrise, for six months, and for the next six months would be seen at sunset." In the latitude of eight degrees it would take the ecliptic 100,000 years to go from horizon to pole and back again; at sixteen degrees the period would reach 200,000 years, and so on. (Deduced from Mackey's Mythological Astronomy.)

During six periods of time the earth was subjected to heavy ravages of the elements which caused floods and havoc of all kinds. Subsequently the earth would become a better place to live in. When the Great Star Aldabaran coincided with the Equator, astronomers of that time could forecast the exact number of years the havoc of waters would continue. About 31,000 years ago Aldabaran coincided with

the Equator at the Vernal Equinox. This star was a point
in the ecliptic used to measure the longitude of the Equator
and regulate time, from which new cycles could be deduced
after the Zodiac had gone through all parts of the Equator.
Aldabaran was called "The Leading Star of the Heaven,"
and also known as "The Guardian of the Sky." It is one
of the four Royal Stars of the Cardinal cross, the four great
Sacred signs, and is known as the Ruler or the Regulator.
Aldabaran is in the sign of Taurus, the Bull. Six or
seven thousand years ago, when this star again coincided
with the Equator, Babylon began her 1903 years of
astronomical calculations,[1] and festivals were held to commemorate their great period of devastation by flood, which
they called "God's Wrath." Some people have mistaken
these floods for the beginning of the world. Plato in his
Timaeus claims the Egyptians believed the world subject to
conflagrations and deluges, while the Stoics adopted a system of catastrophe destined at times to destroy the world,
and ever recurrent at the ending of the great sidereal cycle
of approximately twenty-five thousand years. The ancients
thought that when the gods could no longer bear the wickedness of man they sent deluge to overwhelm humanity.

The Jews were not astronomers, their knowledge of the
stars was gathered when they were held as slaves. The
Jews received much instruction when in Babylon, in which
city Ezekiel was thought to have taught them. It has proved
difficult, however, to make astronomers of the Jews. Ezekiel had his marvelous visions when in Babylon; Daniel
had his when in Persia; and John when on the Isle of Patmos. Both John and Ezekiel must have had knowledge of
the pericyclosical motion of the Poles. John's vision
belongs to a very remote antiquity. Jewish history covers
nothing that is new, but the early Jews had great ingenuity

---

[1]The beginning of astronomical observations at Babylon was 2234 B. C. In
the year 331 B. C. Alexander the Great found an unbroken series of observations running back 1900 years.

in "turning *singulars into plurals;* and plurals into singulars; and what was *feminine* with their masters, they made to be masculine; in working it into their histories; and in some places *things inanimate* have been turned into men by adding the sign of the masculine gender; this was frequently done by the Greeks."[1]

It is of interest to note that at the Feast of the Passover, when the ecliptic and the equator met or crossed in the sign Aries, the Ram or Lamb, all Egypt was gay, homes were decorated with branches of trees and door posts surrounded with wreaths of beautiful flowers. The Lamb was decorated with ribbons and flowers and led around the city in triumph, to show the gratitude of the people to the Giver of all good things for the favors that would evolve from the Sun when going through this sign. Nevertheless the Jews slew the Lamb, and smeared their doors with its blood, Exod. xii, 7, disregarding entirely the astronomical significance of the springtime and thus repudiating all astronomical reckonings. Although the Jews began their records at the Vernal Equinox when the Sun was in the constellation of the Bull, there is no relation whatever between them and the beginning of the knowledge of astronomy. The Hindus can trace their knowledge back to an astounding antiquity, yet they have been termed "Benighted Hindus." "These *poor benighted Hindus* have registered a knowledge of astronomy ten times 25,000 years, since the *Flood,* or *Age of Horror,'* in the latitude of Benares."[2] Benares was the chief seat of celestial science in India, and astronomical tables were constructed for the meridian of Benares, just as ours today are calculated from the meridian of Greenwich.

Going back in memory to those ancient peoples and realizing their reverence for the heavens and their Creator, one instinctively feels that their sublime devotion was trying to bridge the distance between then and now with an urge

---

[1]Mackey, S. A.—Mythological Astronomy, p. 149.
[2]Mackey, S. A.—Mythological Astronomy. Appendix p. 23.

or a prayer that a similar spiritual impulse might awaken the sleepers of today. It is incomprehensible how writers, men of learning, continually speak with contempt of the Hindus, whose "Mysteries" came direct from their study of the stars, that Great Book of God. Their imagery of the heavens was both symbolical and poetical, so why denounce them because scholars have misinterpreted both symbol and language? Their religion was infinitely superior to that of the masses today. They were called worshippers of idols, and what will be said of the Christians today? Perhaps they call us also worshippers of idols, because we have our symbols of the Lamb, and the Dove, and the Shepherd. Our miracles are nearly all borrowed from the ancients, although we sadly distort their meaning. Astrology is intimately connected with the piety of the ancients. Their spirit and mind were awakened to a knowledge of the Supreme and His Works. We are gradually approaching ancient scientific wisdom today for the moving finger seems to be pointing backward indicating that finally we shall ultimately identify in the dead past the everliving present Truth.

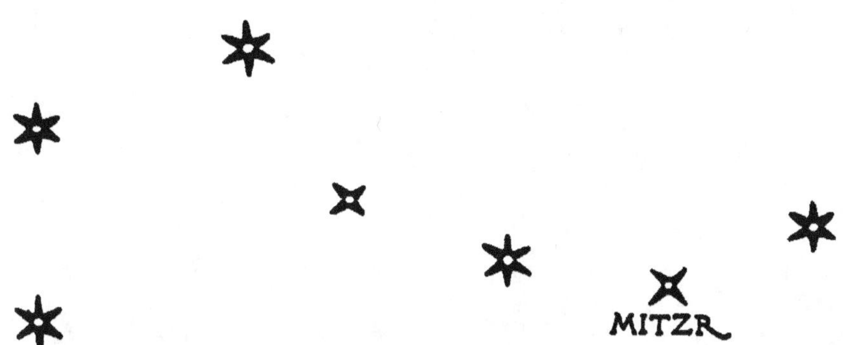

THE SEVEN GREAT STARS

The Seven Stars of the Great Bear, which in the course of evolution became spirits, genii, gods, planets, and endless other typical
Sevens belonging to all the countries of the world.

CHAPTER X

CELESTIAL ORIGIN OF JEWISH RACE AND HEBREW LANGUAGE

SEVEN, TEN AND TWELVE

Egyptian myths became miracles in the Hebrew writings, the name "miracle" having been substituted through ignorance. The Jews undoubtedly commingled with the Hekshus, the Shus-en-Har, and the Typhonians. They were known as the "Mixed Multitude." As the so-called Shepherd Kings, they were Typhonian and not of foreign birth. The earliest rendering of the name of the Hebrews is Gabari. These were the Kabiri, the children of the Goddess Mother of the Great Bear constellation, the Typhonians. The Hek-Shus (Hek-Sos) were called the ancestors of the Israelites. The Jew, the Hebrew, or the Israelite belonged to the pre-monumental cult of Sut-Typhon, the ancient Shus-en-Har. The Disk worshippers theologically have the same meaning as the Hek-Sos. The Hek-Shus and Jews were identical and with the Shus-en-Hars were worshippers of the God Har, or Sut, whether as the Sun or the Son. Manetho tells us that the Hek-Sos were the so-called Shepherd Kings, who were styled Captive and were known as the servants of the Egyptian God Horus. They were finally driven into a city called Avaris. Their efforts to hold this city being futile, they departed from Egypt through the desert toward Syria and there built a city in the country of Judea, and called it Jerusalem. Judea was named from the outcast Jews of Egypt, and the city, Avaris, was called Typhonian. Josephus claimed that his people were followers of the Hek-Shus religion, the Typhonian, which was the worship of the Mother and Son, the earliest ever known, belonging intact to the mythology of the heavens.

The rulers of the Shus were called Heks. The Hek was an Egyptian regent or governor. They were worshippers of Hek, who was the earlier Kak, god of darkness. The Shus-en-Har did not cease with the reign of Menes, whom tradition claims was King of Egypt about 4560 B. C. following the Divine Dynasties. Violent agitation ensued when the supremacy of the new cult of Sebek-Ra arrived and strove to replace the worship of the ancient Son, Sut, and Sebek, the crocodile.[1] This was the quarrel between Sut, the Sabean Son, and the Egyptian Amen-Ra, the Solar Son, resulting in alliance of the Ammonians with the Osirians against the Typhonian cult. Sebek personified the solar Ra (Sun). Sut and his Mother, belonging to the Sabean time, were compelled to make way for the truer time-keeping kept by the Sun. Sut and his Mother were, as the angel Uriel poetically tells Enoch, "the stars which transgressed the commandments of the Most High God." At this time vandalism ravaged the monuments from which whole records of dynasties that had maintained the cult of Sut-Typhon were erased.

The wars and struggles of the Hek-Shus began under the Pharaohs of the Egyptian Monarchy, commencing when Amen-Ra, the Solar God, became the generator. Contemporaneous elevation of the male above the female instituted the degradation of the Mother and Son, whose cult before the Fatherhood had been established, was a worship embraced by the entire world under different names. Theologians have been unable, even in the present day, to blot out this worship of the Starry Child and Mother, denounced as "Temple Closers" and "Enemies of God." It was a faith too strong to be shaken. For a time the Osirian cult devastated the worship of the Great Mother and her Son, yet it loomed up

---

[1] In the adoption of the crocodile type there was a custom in the town of Har for everyone to eat some part of a crocodile on a certain day set apart for this. —Manetho.

again in the year 2300 B. C. As captive kings and servant
rulers, the Hek-Shus find identification with the Hebrews in
Deut. v, 15, "Remember that thou wast a servant in the
land of Egypt."

The Government of the Shus-en-Har belongs to the most
ancient in the world. "The original service was that of the
Shus-en-Har. . . . The ancient theocracy represented a government assumed to be divine with no monarchy but that of
Divinity. It is the oldest form of government in the world,
earliest everywhere." Priests or Judges were the Law Givers and representatives of the people. The Hebrew "Mixed
Multitude" most certainly adhered to the Typhonian religion
until it was looked upon as odious and an abomination.
After the expulsion of their last king, who was called SUT-
Apehpeh, the Osirians and Ammonians again came into
power. Their city Avaris was depicted as the "Home of the
Leg." This was the constellation in the North and seen in
the planisphere as "The Hinder Thigh," symbol of the Mother
Typhon and the Matrix of the world. There surely can be
no denying that the origin of the Hebrew "Mixed Multitude"
is in the Egyptian Mythological Astrology of the Heavens.

The Jewish glyph and the Hebrew language are not original, but are borrowed from the Egyptian and are considered
sacred. Hebrew is composed of the hieroglyphs, symbols
and myths of the Egyptians and their gods. The imagery,
allegories and divinities found in old Hebrew writings are
Egyptian and appertain to the Typhonian cult. The Jewish
"New" departure and developments were made out of the
oldest of all materials, originally mythical in Egypt, but converted into the historical by the Jews. Celsus says, "The
Jews were a tribe of Egyptians who revolted from the established religion." Their Jehovah can be traced back to the
Great Mother.

The Eighteenth Dynasty overcame the Sut-Typhonians.
Ramese II was a follower of the Typhonian religion, and
must, therefore, have befriended the Jews. His wife also

adhered to this early religion of the Mother and Son. The persecution of the Jews was due to their religion and to the fact that they placed the male element in superiority—the Father and Son above the Mother and Son.

About 2466 B. C. Amenhept I, of the Twelfth Dynasty founded a special temple for the ram-headed god of Thebes. Osiris, the great celestial god of the orthodox Egyptian religion, was succeeded by the ram-headed god of one cult and by the Sebekhepts of another. Sut was god of the Nashi, the negroes, and when he became the Aten Sun of the horizon was especially worshipped by the Ethiopians and by Amenhept III, whose mother was an Ethiopian, and therefore a worshipper of the Aten Sun. Amenhept III reintroduced the Aten, or Sun-disk worship, and called the youthful solar god Aten-Nefer. The mother of Amenhept III had marked influence on both politics and religion during this period, foreshadowing the religious revolt that was impending at this time.

A hymn of the Fifteenth Century B. C. to Aten was used in the worship of the Sun-disk as a symbol of God:

> "Thy appearance is beautiful in the horizon of heaven,
>   O living Aten, the beginning of life!
>   Thou fillest every land with thy beauty.
>   Thy beams encompass all lands which thou hast made,
>   Thou bindest them with thy love . . .
>   The birds fly to their haunts—
>   Their wings adoring thee . . .
>   The small bird in the egg, sounding within the shell
>   Thou givest it breath within the egg . . .
>   How many are the things which thou hast made!
>   Thou createst the land by thy will, thou alone,
>   With peoples, herds, and flocks . . .
>   Thou givest to every man his place, thou framest his life."

Amenhept III built a large basin or lake on which he launched a boat of the solar disk, emblematic of his worship, and called it Aten-nefru. It was a symbol of the young sun-god, Aten. His mother represented the boat as the

"Bearer," or the genitrix, which carries us back to the Mother as the Ship of the North. This is the bark or boat representing the Mother who impersonates the Virgin Mother of the Only One. She is portrayed upon the walls of the temple of Ra at Luxor as the earthly image of the mother who gives birth to the child Christ or Messiah representative of the Aten-Sun. In mythology the Messiahs were always born from a virgin mother. This mother was known as the Maiden Virgin Queen, Mut-em-Ua; Em-Ua means "alone" and signifies the mother in the line of the Typhonian descent who gives birth to the Only One. The Aten-disk is the emblem of the divine and only Son of the Mother, or mythically the Sun on the horizon, of which this Virgin Queen Mother, Mut-em-Ua is the physical representation on earth. In "The Shrine" or "Holy of Holies" of the temple at Luxor, she is depicted as the Boat of the Sun. In this sacred room four marvellous scenes, which bear close resemblance to those of the birth of the Christian Messiah are engraved in hieroglyphics on the walls. In the first the God

Taht, the messenger of the angels, the "Annunciator of the Gods," appears to be telling the virgin queen that she is to give birth to the Coming Son, who is to be the symbol of the Aten Sun. In the following scene the god Kneph—Spirit, Divine Breath or Holy Ghost—who causes conception, and Hathor, Nature, are with the Queen Mother. Each takes her by the hand and holds the Ansated Cross, symbol of Eternal Life, to her mouth. This entire scene is typical of spiritual incarnation or conception. In the next scene the child is discovered surrounded by his nurses, one of whom holds him in her hands.   In the last scene the child is enthroned, receiving the adoration of gods and men, and behind the god Kneph three men are seen kneeling offering the Ansated Cross and three gifts to the child.

These four scenes of the Annunciation, the Immaculate Conception, Birth and Adoration, are quite familiar to Christians. The Immaculate Conception, by the Great Mother, Mut-em-Ua, of the child worshipped as the Aten-Sun, constituted the grandest and most sublime mystery of every ancient religion.[1]

Aiu, the husband of the nurse of Khu-en-Aten, was said to be a protegé of Amenhept III. He was priest or holy father and fan-bearer at the king's right hand. He was given the title of the Royal Scribe of Justice, and was considered a Judge, a Sep, and as Aiu-Sep he prefigures the Biblical Joseph. The Queen of Khu-en-Aten had a sister who was thought to have been the wife of Tut-Ankh-Amen, and afterwards of Har-em-Hebi.

Amenhept III was followed by Amenhept IV, and "he was supposed to have changed his name to Khu-en-Aten, the Adorer of Aten.[2] He changed the name of the city called after him into Pa-Aten-Haru, the city of delight for the solar disk, or rather the youthful Sun-god Adon, the Lord, and he would appear in public riding on the golden chariot like the disk of the Sun."—Inscription of Amenhept IV.

Amenhept IV was the last of the Twelfth dynasty, and the ram-headed god in all probability was adopted as Amen-Ra and as Sebek Ra about the time that the Sun of the vernal equinox entered the sign Aries the Ram in a date coinciding with the ending of the Twelfth dynasty, in 2410 B. C. Amen was a title of Sebek, the Typhonian

---

[1] "In the great Harris Papyrus Rameses III complains that the revolters and the insurrectionists have the gods in the human likeness, and Queen Mut-em-Ua and her son assumed the human likeness, as the Mary and child-Christ of the Aten cult."—Sharp, "Egyptian Mythology."

[2] The latest researches point to these two as being different personages.

Sun-god. Amen-Au was the hidden Au, a god of the Sebek family of gods, and Amen-Ra was the god of later Egyptian naming, who was called the DIVINE FATHER.

According to monumental history there were several Exoduses, under both religious and symbolical names. The Children of Israel were the sons of El, Al, Ar, or Har, the highest type of which was Sut,[1] the Dog-Star, Sirius. Later Saturn as Sabaoth, son of the mother Typhon in the North ruled over Israel. Sut-Typhon fleeing from Egypt, riding on an ass, mythically signifies the Great Exodus.[2] Ass in its symbolical rendering is Iu, Sut, or Ius—Jews—all one and the same, the son, and hence this very early Exodus symbolizes the exit of Sabean time at the advent of Solar reckoning. The first religion was Sabean, and pre-monumental, and originated with the Star of Joudi, that great mother in the North, and her son Sut, one of whose types was the Ass. To mythology can be traced the idea of a male Eternal Being. "First was the Iu, the one who for ever comes and becomes; the divine youth, the son of the mother, the eternal boy, the universal lad.[3] Next is the Being who is, and ever continues to be; and lastly, the Being who inferentially *was* and has been forever."[4]

The Ever Coming One, continuing to come can be identified as born and reborn in the cycles of the Sun. IO, the Lunar Goddess, the "White Wanderer of the Heavens," is an early feminine form traceable to the Great Mother of Iu, the Jew, whether Sabean or Solar. Iu-Sa, Iu-Su (Jesus) or Iu-Sif, was the coming son or the Messiah of mythology. In thought the doctrine of the Coming One

---

[1]Sut was the Sabean Son; Khunsu, the Lunar Son, and Adonai, the Solar Sun.

[2]The Ass was one of the types of Sut, the Dog-Star; similarly Iu (the Coming One) is a name for an Ass. These types belonged to the Cult of Sut-Typhon, during the Sabean period which preceded the introduction of Solar time-keeping by Moses. Sut-Typhon was called the ass and its foal.

[3]Records, iv, 102, Hymn to Osiris, 17.

[4]Massey, Gerald—A Book of the Beginnings, Vol. ii, p. 439.

goes far back to the beginning. IU as the son of the mother, the Coming One, was the double Horus of the Becoming, type of futurity, and not the earth born Messiah. This fact has given rise theologically to many false interpretations. The Egyptian A. U. was the coming being, the embryo, and was similar to Ptah, who personated the embryo, and also to Sut, the Ass-headed. IU is the ancient name for Ass, and this is expressed in the Book of Revelation by A, O, the Egyptian AU, signifying who was and is, and is to be. The letter U is the letter O, thus the IU has the varient AU, the A, O, the Alpha and Omega of the Greek alphabet. "The Jews," says Petronius, in characterizing their cult, "calls unto heaven's ears." The followers of Sut, whether as Egyptians in Egypt or Hebrews out of it, were the followers of Sut-Typhon, the long-eared Ass.

Iu-em-Hept (Hept means peace, plenty) was the peace-bringer, and Nefer-Hept (Nef-breath) was the breather of peace. A male-female dual nature runs through all ancient myths. Bacchus and Horus were bi-sexual, and there is even a Greek statue representing St. Sophia, the Christ, as a bearded female. Iu-em-Hept reappears in the Hebrew writings as Ecclesiasticus, the Preacher. The Apocryphal Book of Ecclesiasticus is called the "Wisdom of Jesus the son of Sirach, or Ecclesiasticus." The Prologue of the book admits it to be a work brought out of Egypt. In the Hebrew collection the Preacher is identified with Jesus. Iu-em-Hept wore the Long Garment, typical of a female gown, just as the Jewish High Priests and the Roman Popes do. In the "Book of the Dead" Iu-em-Hept wearing the long robe is addressed as follows, "Hail to thee coming, approaching in peace, whose garment was that in which was the 'Whole World'." Chapt. xviii, 24, of the Book of Solomon, says, "For in the long garment was the whole world, and in the four rows of stones was the glory of the fathers graven." The name of the mystical Solomon signifies "Peace." Sol-Om-On represents three names of the Sun in different languages. Iu-em-Hept was the Egyptian Jesus known as "The Eternal Word" in the "Book of the Dead." IU the root word means to come; the ever-coming one—he who comes with peace.

"The only satisfactory ethnological designation for a people like the Hebrews must be derived from a religion that had its rootage in mythology."[1] In a certain sense the Israelites never were in the Terrestrial Egypt. The Children of Israel were the sons of the early Astrological Mythology of the Mother and were the Seven Stars, whose leader was her son, Sut, who became Saturn, the tribal god of the Jews.

The Jews are said to be a racial remnant from the Golden Age. The Golden Age in Mythology was that of Sut-Nub, or the Typhonian period. The Jews came from the northern part of Ethiopia, crossing the deserts, and seem to have been builders of pyramids, which is perhaps an evidence of their Egyptian origin. On the plains of Africa there are remnants of pyramids undiscovered, save by the Wild Tribes who regarded them as holy, the foundations of which will one day be laid bare.

The Phoenicians, whose kings were the Hek-Shus, according to a tradition of Manetho, were identified with the Shus-en-Har, who had rootage in Egypt extending to pre-monumental times. They were called Israelites, and belonged to the Typhonian or celestial religion. They returned from their wanderings under the leadership of their priests and fell into captivity. When Moses led them forth they were briefly rewarded for earlier services, but their true destiny will be world leadership at the end of the reign of Justice, which will precede the Capricornian era, and Moses will be the Law Giver in this coming age, of which all learned Jews have foreknowledge.

The world Serpent is typified in the zodiacal sign Scorpio, and the heavenly Serpent is in that of Capricorn. The Jews

[1]Massey, Gerald.

are represented by the sign Capricorn. The Jewish Serpent worship was a priestly rite, performed in the service in the Synagogue, and the Jewish priests were supposed to heal the sick with the Serpent power. The Egyptians grew up in the essence of the Light, of which the Jewish people had knowledge. When the Jews returned from their wanderings their leader, Moses, who was an Egyptian, knew they were the people destined to rule the world in a later cycle. Moses was educated, as Manetho tells us, in the Temple of the Sun in the City of the Sun. He was a great Egyptian Priest and knew that the Israelites, or Jews, would rule at the culmination of the present age of Justice, and he knew he would return in that period, and as a world leader, give forth the real justice of the Mosaic power under the new polarity which will not manifest in its entirety before the new axial progress shall be established. At that period the planet Saturn, their ruling planet and ruler of the sign Capricorn, will come to the conjunction of the unseen planet. Capricorn is service justified in evolution.

Among the various names given in celestial allegory to the Sabean birthplace were the Egyptian Mitzraim and Mazaroth, names originating in the heavens above that were later applied to the Egypt below. The star Mitzr in the constellation The Great Bear gave its name to the Celestial Mitzraim, which with Mazaroth belonged to the primal Sabean birthplace. The first circle evolved by this constellation and its Seven Stars was divided into ten degrees or ten divisions of heaven, or ten tribes, and was again subdivided into seventy. From this we have the earliest knowledge of the Ten Tribes of Israel, which were purely Typhonian and were ruled over by the Seven Stars of this constellation. These Seven, Ten and Seventy were primarily celestial before they were associated with the Nomes of the Egypt below. The name Astronomy comes from Astro-nome, or the arrangement of the stars into nomes, constellations or divisions, from which originated the first

Celestial Chart, with its naming and noming afterwards adopted in many lands. Therefore, Mitzraim and Mazaroth are the truth-tellers forevermore of the early Egypt, and her astronomical measurements. Mazaroth means the Fires of Heaven or the "Lights," and the first Nome was given to the Dog-Star, Sirius. Paradise, the early Garden, was also one of the earliest nomes.

In the tenth chapter of Genesis the Seven Sons that came forth from Mitzraim are given. These Seven appear under various names in every ancient mythology and are always the Seven Stars of the constellation of the Great Bear. From this first Sabean circle of Seven, called the heaven of the Elohim, came the division into Ten, the subdivisions of which created the seventy degrees or Nations that were anterior to the Solar Circle of the twelve signs of the Zodiac.

In Rabbinical lore the earth was divided into seven climates, and every climate into ten parts. "These were the seventy nations divided among seventy princes the blessed God taking no part in them, because he is pure, wherefore they are not children of his image, nor bear any resemblance of him; but Jacob is the portion of his inheritance." In the Hebrew version there were ten generations or patriarchs who followed the Seven, who were again followed by the Seventy, between the Deluge and Abraham, and they certainly coincided with the celestial allegory.

Atlantis was an immense Island beyond the Pillars of Hercules. It was said to be governed by Neptune, who had ten sons, to each of whom he gave a portion, or one-tenth, of the Island. His eldest son was called Atlas, from whom the Island was named. It had been an island of peace, plenty and harmony, but the people degenerated and finally it disappeared because of earthquake and deluge.[1] The ten

---

[1] "Atlantis" is the Fourth Continent. . . . The famous island of Plato of that name was but a fragment of this great continent. Since the destruction of Atlantis the face of the earth has changed more than once. . . . The last serious

divisions, the ten sons, coincide with the Hebrew ten divisions, and they were the ten races of men mentioned in the Persian Bundahish, which preceded the Chaldean. But Egypt tells us of no similar legend. Their knowledge of a deluge belonged to the cycles of Time. There were two lists of patriarchs who preceded the flood called that of Noah. There were seven names in one list and ten in the other, wherefore the number of nations into which the new earth was arranged was seventy-two, representing the duodecans of the solar Zodiac which superseded the Seven, the Ten and the Seventy.

The covenant of Abraham follows the flood, ending the first period of the ten patriarchs. The bow or the circle in heaven was one witness of this covenant connected with the Zodiac, and circumcision was the other.

On the two lists of the names of the Patriarchs that preceded the flood of Noah, the first seven are Adam, Cain, Hanoch, Jerad, Methusael, Lamech and Noah. The second comprises Adam, Seth, Enos, Qunan, Mahalalal, Jared, Hanoch, Methuselah, Lamech and Noah. These are commonly called the Elohistic and Jehovistic records, and are two forms of the Hebrew Generations given in one of the creation legends.

The Patriarchs were sidereal, cosmic and numerical symbols and signs. Volney in his "Ruins" frankly says, "All pretended personages from Adam to Abraham and his father Terah were mythological beings, Stars, Constellations, and Countries." Patriarchs of Vedic origin were the earliest known and were accepted emblematically as representations of the different signs of the Zodiac, by Christians as well as by so-called heathens. Fundamentally the patriarchs were

change occurred some 12,000 years ago, and was followed by the submersion of Plato's little Atlantic island, which he calls Atlantis after the parent continent. Geography was part of the mysteries, in days of old. Says the Zohar, 'These secrets (of land and sea) were divulged *to the men of secret science*, but not to the geographers'."—Blavatsky, H. P.—Preliminary Notes, The Secret Doctrine, Vol. ii, pp. 8, 9.

spiritual as well as physical types of evolution belonging to all ages.

Deuteronomy xxxiii is an astronomical chapter of the Bible describing the twelve tribes of Israel to be the twelve signs of the Zodiac. Contemporaneously Jacob became the Father or the Sun-God of the twelve signs.

In Deuteronomy xxxii, 8, 9, it is written, "When the Most High divided to the nations their inheritance, when he separated the sons of Adam he set the bounds of the people according to the number of the children of Israel. For the Lord's portion *is* his people, Jacob *is* the lot of his inheritance." In the Septuagint the text reads, "According to the number of the Angels." These were the mythological Israelites, later brought down to earth as a race of human beings, and the God of the descendants of these children of Israel was Jehovah, deity of the Seven Stars, tribal God of the Jews, who were worshippers of the Lord God of Sabaoth. Sabaoth in planetary form was Saturn, the Individualizer, the Bridging Planet, connecting the material, mortal side of man with his higher spiritual immortal nature, Saturn regenerates through pain and suffering as he lifts the veil revealing the great Light beyond. Beyond his Bridge lies the great enfolding love enveloped in the wondrous Light of the world.

The seven sons of the Egyptian god, Ptah, and the seven sons of Sydik, as well as many, many others, can be traced to the Seven of the Great Bear. The seven spirits associated with this constellation are mentioned in the Egyptian ritual—"These same are behind the constellation of the Thigh, Ursa Major (The Great Bear) of the Northern heaven." They were appointed chiefs and given power over the seven constellations. The Persians later gave the constellations to the planets. The seventy Shepherds, Princes or Angels of the Kabala, who were said to appear on earth during the downfall of the Tower of Babel, were rulers of the seventy divisions. All Seventy can be found in Rabbinical writings under the names of Shepherds, Watchers, Elders, and so forth. They all had a common origin in celestial allegory or the phenomena of the heavens.

"After King Damascus, came Azelus, and then Adores, Abraham, and Israhel, who were the Kings. But a prosperous family of ten sons made Israhel more famous than any of his ancestors. Having divided his kingdom in consequence, into ten governments, he committed them to his sons, and called the whole people Jews."[1]

A rectification on astronomical grounds of the original Seventy resulted in a total of seventy-two, representing the duo-decans of the Solar Zodiac, and when the latest arrangement was based upon the twelve signs and the seventy-two duo-decans of the Solar Zodiac, the ten Tribes became twelve.

"The Afghans call themselves Ben-Issarael (children of Is(*sa*)rael from Issa 'woman and also earth,' Sons of Mother Earth." There remains no doubt concerning the Afghan tribes, "the names of the oldest Arabic tribes, re-transliterated, yield the names of the Zodiacal signs and of the mythical sons of Jacob likewise."[2]

When Jacob, of the ten, was changed to Israel, of the twelve, it was said that the seventy princes were not the children of the true, i. e. later, God. They were not born in his image, and bore no likeness to him. In the old allegory there were seventy souls of celestial bodies appointed Watchers and Timekeepers in the heaven of the seventy divisions, or degrees, that preceded the seventy-two divisions or degrees. The first mention of the name of Israel is found in the 33rd chapter of Genesis, where we find Jacob elevated to the position of "El," Lord. The name Israel is derived from Isaral, or Asar, the Sun-God, and Isra-el means "Striving with God."

Jacob wrestled all night with the Angel, or opposing

---

power, till break of day, but his thigh was put out of joint. This was in the place called Pen-i-el, and he had "seen God face to face" . . . "As he passed over Penuel the sun rose upon him and he halted upon his thigh," the hollow of which had been touched by the Angel. The place Peniel is found in the heavens at the beginning of the Zodiacal sign Sagittarius and in the constellation Scutum Sobieski. Astrologically this is a point which induces spiritual vision when favorably aspected. Always at the beginning of a new cycle or age spiritual Light spreads more profusely over the world, and to "see God face to face" becomes the privilege of the attaining Seer who has developed his higher consciousness. The constellation Scutum Sobieski is called the Coal Sack, as it is a dark place in the heavens, where shooting stars are seen in the month of November. From out the dark come these creative birth-giving elements, Light out of Darkness always.

No historical evidence of these tribes is given. Herodotus, who was born 483 B. C., and who was in Assyria when Ezra flourished, does not mention the Israelites, and Brugsch Bey gives it as a fact that "nowhere do the inscriptions contain one syllable about the Israelites." In the mythology of the heavens proof is found of the Children of Israel and of their belonging to the Sabean beginnings. Their birthplace was that great "Ship of the North," and their journeys were from out the land of Darkness into the Light, or mythologically out of Night into Day. The story of the Exodus was common property to all nations and can be found in the ancient Book of Enoch, which is called "The Book of the Revolutions of the Luminaries of Heaven," and is the history of the Sabean, Lunar and Solar cycles of Time, from the earliest known down to the Precessional Periods belonging to astronomical reckonings, or from the circle of the twenty-four hour period to the great cycle of 26,000 years. The Book of Enoch is filled with secrets concerning the heavens, and with allegories that have been turned into history. In the Egyptian "Book of the Dead" these tribes and children are introduced as a Solar Allegory. Their home of bondage was located in the nether Northern region. When Moses came from Egypt he was a full Initiate with knowledge and wisdom of the mysteries, which were of the heavens. The circle of the Exodus was both Solar and Zodiacal, and represented the wanderings of the Children of Israel. Gerald Massey states that it is apparent that had the journey of the Israelites been a real one the Israelites at Moseroth would have almost described a complete circle around to a point at Baalzephon, the place of their departure, this circular movement being Zodiacal.

It has been said that the Jews had but two tribes, those of Judah and Levi. The Levites, however, could not have been a tribe, as they were said to belong to a caste, a priestly Caste, and were represented by the Zodiacal sign Aquarius. Their knowledge of the Serpent went back for generations. Leo, the opposite sign of the Zodiac, is Judah's natal sign, through which the present Aquarian era will be ruled. Judah represented the God of the Twin Lions of the heavens, who was the Law Giver, the "Triumphant One." Judah also represented the Hebrew Kingdom of the Twelve Tribes, as distinguished from the earlier ten Tribes of Israel. These tribes, because of their relation to the Zodiac, are very easily identified in the 49th chapter of Genesis.

Jacob foretold to Judah that "The sceptre shall not depart from Judah, nor a lawgiver from between his feet, until Shiloh come; and unto him *shall* the gathering of the people *be.*" Genesis, xlix, 10. Shiloh or the Messiah was the Returning One, whether Stellar, Lunar or Solar, for the Shiloh was periodic in the celestial myth. The Solar Shiloh was the Sun of the Resurrection. The Hebrew Shiloh was called the *afterbirth,* typifying the adult youth. The root of the name denotes renewal, rebirth. He became the revealer of the father in heaven, when the masculine-minded cult arrived. The ever coming one also belongs to the father, "whose power came and forever came with the transformation at puberty," when the creative power descends.

Cruden says that the full meaning of this prophecy is in regard to the people of Israel in their relation to the Tribe of Judah; and "this tribe alone returned entire from captivity with some relics of the Tribe of Levi and Benjamin. From that time the nation was distinguished by the title of the Jews in relation to it, and the right to dispose of the sceptre was always in the tribe of Judah. The Levites received power from them." The sceptre means Power, Command.

The name Israel, derived from El[1], the Lord, belongs to the celestial Ten Tribes, in Je-shu-run. Jeshurun is identified with the first circle of four quarters, in which the reckoning by ten preceded the twelve signs of the Zodiac. The ten signs made way for the coming of the twelve Tribes or the twelve signs of the Zodiac having seventy-two duo-decans. The ten "lost tribes" were of heaven. They remain above, veritable storehouses of knowledge, revealing for all time in mythical language the great wisdom and heavenly mysteries of the ancients.

The Egyptian god Ptah[2] was called the founder of the Solar Circle. Atum, his son, was typical of the change from

---

[1] El was the supreme deity of the Hebrews and a male, son of the Great Mother, identified by the Greeks and Romans with Kronus, Saturn. El is the worn-down form of Hal or Har, equivalent to the Egyptian Makheru, or true voice. El or Al was the supreme god of the Babylonians. There is no other origin for the Hebrew El. El interchanges with the Sabean Baal, Baal-Zebul, Baal-Zebub, Bar-Sutekh, Bar-Typhon (Egyptian), Baal-Zephon and Baal-Kivan (Hebrew). In the Babylonian and Phoenician mythologies they all were the son (Al) of the Great Mother, goddess of Stars, Moon and Sun. In the mysteries of Baal-Poer, Baal-Poer and Bar-Typhon were the Openers. Baal-Poer was lord of the Openings, and is identical with Sut or Bar-Typhon the Opener. Kivan is identified with the Hebrew Jehovah. El-Shadai, Adonai, Baal were all personifications of the son of the cult of Sut-Typhon, the First Great Mother.

[2] The first form of Khepr-Ra is Ptah. Ptah was the image maker of the gods. He was the Potter who shaped the Vase that contained the Seeds of all living, the Vase being always a feminine symbol. Ptah formed the circle of the Sun or Solar Zodiac.

seventy to seventy-two divisions in the Solar Zodiac. The god Ptah was the Hebrew Terah. Ptah and Terah were divine artificers. Terah or "Old Time" was seventy years old before his three sons were born in Ur of Chaldee, clearly defined in the myth as "representing the time of the seventy Angels, Princes, Elders, or Shepherds, who presided over the divisions of the heavens, as the seventy years of Terah before the birth of Abraham."

In the 46th chapter of Genesis we are told that all the souls that came into Egypt were three score and ten, the traditional number of the house of Jacob. These were the seventy that preceded the Solar Zodiac and were synonymous with the seventy Elders who judged the people of Israel. "Terah was the Father of the Fathers of Israel, Abraham, Isaac and Jacob, whose children were to swarm in multitudes, numerous as the stars of heaven or the sands of the sea," and with his twelve sons went into Egypt and "grew into a multitude 2,000,000 strong." The Egyptian god Ptah was also called the Father of the Fathers of the Gods, and one of his symbols of Time was a frog or tadpole, a sign of swarming millions. Ptah is portrayed as beetle-headed and frog-headed, sometimes as a double type having a scarab placed over the frog-head. And when the bounds were set according to the number of the children of Israel, Deut. xxxii, 8, the division represented the time at which Moses instituted the Solar or final Zodiac. ·The twelve tribes received his blessing, its bestowal being the last act of life. Gen. xlix. Moses was king in Je-shu-run at the gathering of the Tribes. Je-shu-run was the celestial four quarters of the heavens, later called Solstices and Equinoxes, and representing the sacred animals of the Zodiac—The Bull (Taurus); the Lion (Leo); the Bird (Scorpio); and the Man (Aquarius). "There is none like unto the God of Je-shu-run, who rideth upon the heaven in thy help, and in his excellency on the sky." Deut. xxxiii, 26; also "Sing unto God, sing praises to his name; extol him that rideth upon the heavens by his name, JAH, and rejoice before him." Psalm lxviii, 4. The god of Je-shu-run is Jah-Adonai, introduced by Moses as the Solar God.

Terah, Father of Abraham, was a "Maker of Images,"[1] the Teraphim. Time in Egypt is Ter, a name given to Khepr, the Beetle. Ap is likewise a name of the Beetle and the Frog. Hence Terap. Its plural in Hebrew is Teraphim, Images of Time. The "Teraphim were consulted in Israel for oracular answers." The Teraphim were the Gods worshipped by Micah and others. See Judges xviii. The Teraphim were also called the Kabiri. The name Kabiri is derived from Abir, one interpretation of which is Great. Ebir was an astrologer. Abraham was an astrologer. The Kabiri were the sons of Eber of Sutekh or Kefa, who are readily traced back to the seven sons of the old Great Mother Typhon.

Teraphim and Seraphim became identical.[2] The latter were serpent images representing the fiery serpent of heaven, the one fabled to have guarded Mount Meru, which was the Garden of Eden, so that sinful man might not approach. They were sacred symbols of immortality, and were the images received as a dowry and carried by Dardanus to Samothrace and on to Troy. Teraphim and Seraphim were worshipped ages and ages before the Christian era. Seldenus in explaining the Teraphim says they were made and composed after the position of certain stars and planets, and according to figures that were located in the sky and called *tutelary* gods. Maimonides writes that the worshippers who carved images which were Jewish oracles "claimed that the light of the principal stars (planets) permeating these through and through, the angelic VIRTUES (regents of stars and planets) conversed with them, teaching them many most useful things and arts." The Teraphim, made by the astrologers, under certain constellations, were at times connected with sorcery, witchcraft and idolatry.

---

[1]"The temple images were human in shape and made of wood." (cf. I Sam. xix, 13, 16.)

[2]Sometimes they were winged wheels.

The Cherubim, or Cherubs, were esoterically identical with the Seraphim, being images or likenesses of the Celestial Constellations, "The Heavenly Hosts," or "Cosmic Angels," and having exquisite knowledge. It is said of the Seraphim that they know most, but that the Cherubim love most. Cruden in his Concordance interprets the word Cherub as meaning in Hebrew "The Fulness of Knowledge; and Angels are so called from their exquisite knowledge, and were therefore used for the punishment of men, who sinned by affecting divine knowledge." Cherub has the meaning of a serpent in a circle. Kr is circle, and Aub serpent.

Adonai, Jah, the Hebrew El, or Lord, has a Biblical connection with the Cherubim, as the Lord of Israel is spoken of as dwelling between the Cherubim and the Ark that was in the midst of them. This was the Ark, that point of covenant between heaven and earth, the constellation of "The Thigh," known as the Ship of the North, the Holy of Holies for all eternity.

Clement Alexander thought it likely that the two Cherubs were originally the constellations of the two Bears. They are found as Solar Cherubs and at a later period as the two Beetles or Scarabs which formerly symbolized the Zodiacal sign Cancer.[1] "These two Beetles were figured in an Ark, facing each other with wings outspread." Josephus declares that Moses had seen these Cherubs beneath the Throne of God, which astrologically represented the North Pole, under which are the two constellations of the Bears. The Beetles were the transformers. There was a "gate that opened one way for the descent of the Sun, and afterwards of the souls to the earth, the lower of the two regions; the other way being the outlet to the land of eternal birth, in the eschatological phase of the celestial imagery."[2]

By tracing history back to its starry Sabean origins one is sure to find a safe original anchorage. All astronomical myths

---

[1] So copied by Rosellini.

[2] Massey, Gerald—A Book of the Beginnings, Vol. ii, p. 310.

began with the dark or night, in the primal Typhonian cult, originating in that wonderful birthplace, the Celestial North, home of the ancient Mother Typhon. In Inner Africa the symbols and types of the primal Typhonian cult still remain extant in primitive form, as they obtained, previous to the immigration down the Valley of the Nile, which initiated the civilization of Egypt itself.

The mapping out of the heavens, the measuring of Time and the Revolution of the Stars, were conceived by the ancients for purposes of practical usage and human guidance. Their observations became facts and were recorded in their astronomical mythology. They observed and connoted with great accuracy the motions of the Sun, Moon, and Stars.

In the Biblical Genesis we are told of divine creations, and that when they were accomplished the Elohim saw that everything was created Good. Who were the Elohim? Mythological Astronomy will tell us. They were the Watchers in Heaven, the Seven Sons or Stars of the Great Mother. They were also the Seven Great Architects of the world, progenitors of man, and by their periodic revolutions Heaven and Earth, the Upper and Lower, Night and Day, Darkness and Light were created. "Wisdom hath builded her house, she hath hewn out her Seven Pillars," (Prov. ix, 1), and her foundations were laid by those Seven Great Stars that were first noticed encircling the Pole. The Egyptian word for Create is "Ker-at." Ker means a Curve and At a Circle, and "by the circle of Time was curved, carved and created the heaven of Symbolism." The earliest circle makers were the Seven Stars, the Elohim, who founded the first Celestial Chart of phenomenal or visible origin.

Legends of all countries instinct with great beauty and uplift of thought, tell of the Seven. The Rishis of India, the Hohgates of our California Indians, the Spirits of the Great Bear in Egypt, China and Japan, the Seven-branched

Candlestick, the Seven Spirits before the Throne, the Seven Pillars of Wisdom as well as the Seven Gifts of the Holy Ghost typifying the Seven Stars revolving about the ancient Mother, who in those faraway times was known as "The Living Word."

In the Egyptian "Book of the Dead" these Gods of the Circle and of the "Seven Aahlu" were termed the "Ancestors of Light." The Hebrew Elohim created Light. In Genesis we read "Let there be Light, and there was Light," which indicates that the Seven were the primal Light Bringers of the first creation, which was Sabean in origin. Indeed "These Generators and Ancestors of Light were so ancient they had been sublimated, divinized, and relegated to a kind of spiritual realm beyond the phenomenal creations described in the book of Genesis."[1] Generations were of heaven and astronomical. Esoterically the Seven Stars were the "Sons of God," Divinities of Power, who knew and could impart all the secrets of nature to man, and who could reveal the wonderful but now Lost Word. "The Word that is no Word," has to be sought in the seven names of the seven first emanations, or the "Sons of the Fire" in the secret scriptures of all the great nations."[2] The Seven were the all-embracing manifested deity only when considered as One. In later theology they were materialistically transformed into the One God, Jehovah, who was the Great Mother, one of whose names is the familiar Eve. When Adam and Eve had eaten of the fruit of the Tree of Knowledge the Elohim were made to exclaim, "Behold the man has become as one of us, to know good and evil; and now lest he put forth his hand and take also of the Tree of Life and eat and live for evermore."

In the first chapter of Genesis the first creators are called Elohim; in the second, the divinity is called Jehovah. Upon the authority of Biblical chronology, the Elohistic Texts were

[1]Massey, Gerald—A Book of the Beginnings, Vol. ii, p. 142.
[2]Blavatsky, H. P.—The Secret Doctrine, Vol. i, p. 438.

written 500 years after the date of Moses, while the Jehovistic were written 800 years after his day. Jehovah was first the Mother, and the Elohim her progeny. The Elohim were always Seven in number. There were Seven Powers of Eternal Nature, first born in space; then came the Seven Stars of the Goddess Mother, later represented as the auxiliaries of Kronus, when with Time and the measuring of Cycles, creation began. All are readily identified with the Sevens of many myths, and are the Egyptian, Akkadian, Babylonian, Persian, Hindu, Britanic, Kabalist and Gnostic prototypes of the Seven Powers, who were considered the creators as it were of human beings, before the Supreme Being had become anthromorphised.

Jehovah-Elohim was supreme as Jah. The Hebrew Lord as Iao, Jah or Jehovah, the Supreme was symbolized by the number 10. One Jewish sign of the Trinity is a circle of three yod letters. Their numerical value is 30. In the earlier lunar reckoning there were ten days to a week and three weeks to a month of thirty days, which makes Jehovah into a Lunar deity, and a trinity in unity. The Egyptian God Aten, the Coming One, or the newly arising sun, was given a title of "Highness," and was signified by the number 10.

The Most High God of the Jews, El, Eloi, Elohim, plural, and Shadai, co-existed with Jehovah. The Hebrew El was the male supreme deity. El is also the child. El-Shadai is Son of Shadai. He was also called the Lord of Hosts or Angels and was the greatest of all the gods, goddesses or divinities of the primal Seven in heaven, Jehovah, the Mother of the Seven Great Stars. The God of the Jews was frequently written of in the Pentateuch as She, but was changed to He after the divinity had changed sex. Because of its feminine origin it was thought blasphemy to speak the Ineffable Name J H V H, the male, and female symbol, which was primarily the feminine principle in all things spiritual and material and hence it became sacred. Elohim, Jehovah and Shadai meet in one divinity and starry constellation, the

Great Bear, the Mother who is sometimes called the Multa-mammae, the many-breasted. This makes apparent the feminine nature of Shadai, who, says the Book of Genesis, "shall bless thee with blessings of heaven above, blessings of the deep that lieth under, blessings of the breasts and the womb," and who was worshipped by the Hebrews under the name J H V H.

The tribal God of the descendants of Israel was Jehovah. The Jewish natives who were born under Saturn when he had become Jehovah were the worshippers of the Lord God of Sabaoth.

El in Egyptian is also the Child, who in the early Sabean days was Sut, in planetary type Saturn. Later El was transformed into Satan, whom Job introduces as one of the sons of God. Satan was accounted a son and an Angel of God by all Semitic nations. The learned Kabalist Eliphas Levy speaks of Satan thus: "It is the angel who is proud enough to believe himself God; proud enough to buy his independence at the price of eternal suffering and torture; beautiful enough to have adored himself in full divine light; strong enough to reign in darkness amidst agony, and to have built himself a throne on his inextinguishable pyre." He further says that the true name of Satan is that of Jehovah reversed, for Satan is not a black god but the negation of Deity. The devil of the early Christians, with horns, hoofs and tail was introduced from Babylon through the Jewish Talmud. The Christian religion, transposes Satan into an enemy of God, whereas in reality by Satan the highest divine spirit or Occult Wisdom on earth is meant.

The Roman Catholics speak of seventy planets that preside over the nations of the globe, meaning the Regents of the planets. "Each people or nation has a direct Watcher or Guardian and a Father in Heaven, which is a planetary spirit." This cannot be denied.

Philo, the most illustrious and devout Jew of his race, recognizing the true nature of all sacred writings, treats the

Pentateuch as allegorical and symbolical. It is known that the Pentateuch arose out of the older primitive documents by means of a supplementary one. The real Hebrew Bible was a secret volume, unknown to the masses, and is far more ancient than the Septuagint. The Pentateuch was written on papyrus by a scribe's pen from the ancient hieroglyphics, which were carved in stone. The Hebrews, retaining these hieroglyphics, turned them into the square letters. It is said the Pentateuch was given to Israel in the Holy Language, and in the Ibri writing. The hieroglyphs were secret signs and gave to the Egyptian writings their sacred character. Later the Pentateuch was translated into the Aramaic language and the Ashurith writing. The Hebrews retained the ancient language with the square letters. Ibri writing and Holy Language identify the oldest Hebrew as Egyptian. Ezra was a scribe of the Law of the God of heaven and was said to have worked with supernatural guidance and divinely strengthened memory when he retranslated the Law from the Ibri writing into the Chaldee of Ashureth, the square type. He was the author of the modernized version of the lost books of Moses, which the Israelites were the latest to adapt and make their own.

Talmudists insist that the five Books of Moses were engraven on stone, and written in seventy languages. The present Hebrew writing is no older than the fourth century of our era.

The names Jehovah-Elohim are derived from the two words each of which is male-female; Jehovah, a compound of Jah, male, and Hovah or Eve, female; and Elohim, a compound of El,[1] male and H. female. Numerically Jehovah is the diameter of the circle and Elohim the circumferance. Jehovah-Elohim was the Mother of the Seven ele-

---

[1] El was the highest god of the seven, the Dragon with Seven Heads, or the Constellation of Draco when combined with that of the Little Bear. He was the same son of the first Mother who was the Moon-god Jah of the lunar Trinity, which became duad as mother and child, and evolved her consort, forming the trinity that preceded the luni-solar Father, Mother, and Son.

mentary gods, combined in the one divinity, the one constellation. A seven-fold god is mythological, whether Jehovah or Iao-Sabaoth. Sevekh, the seven-fold, Ea with the seven fins, Ra with his seven souls, the Hindu Agni with his seven arms, the Gnostic Chnubis with his seven rays, the Dragon with his seven heads, and El of the seventh Planet, and many others, were the vehicles of many imaginings, and finally became converted into gods in relation to celestial phenomena,[1] when "the Gods were seen in their ideas as Stars, and all their signs, and the Stars were numbered with all the Gods in them."[2]

---

[1] The seven properties assigned to nature are, Matter, Cohesion, Fluxion, Coagulation, Accumulation, Station, Division.
[2] Hermes Trismegistus.

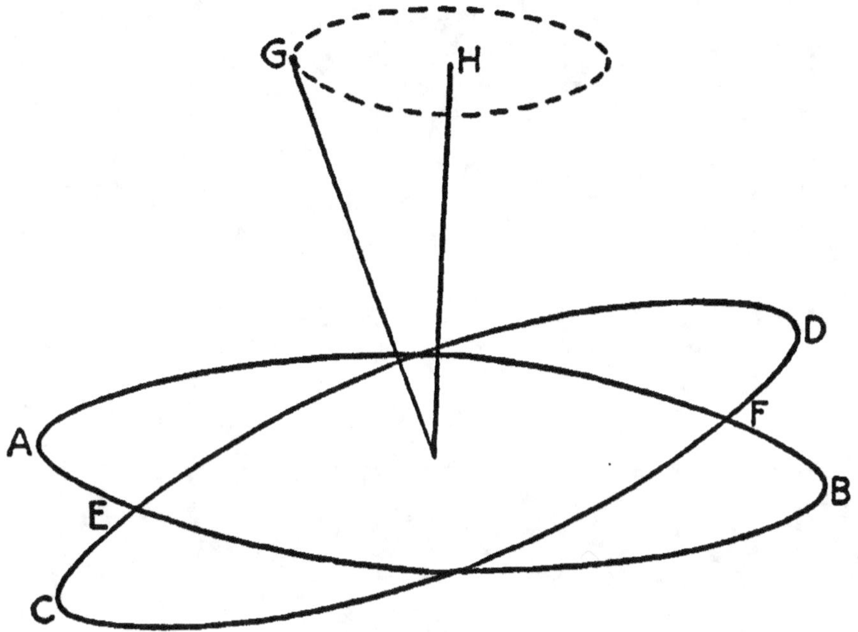

POLES OF THE ECLIPTIC AND THE EQUATOR

The circle A B is the Ecliptic or Zodiac, the apparent path of the Sun. The circle C D represents the plane of the earth's Equator. The line H shews the Pole of the Ecliptic and the line G that of the Equator. The two points of intersection E and F are the Equinoxes. The Precession of the Equinoxes is caused by the movement of the Pole of the Equator G around the Pole of the Ecliptic H, which takes 25,920 years to make the Great Cycle of Precession. From "The Faith of Ancient Egypt," by S. G. P. Coryn.

CHAPTER XI

HEAVENLY MEASURES

If theology is to be truly interpreted, astrological knowledge cannot be ignored. The false concepts concerning astrology, most ancient of sciences, will one day inevitably meet with annihilation. Astrology is the gospel of the stars giving man insight into the mystical and leading his thoughts into cognizance of divinity. Symbols conveyed abstract qualities of the Deity, ancient fables conveyed facts. When our theologians dip into the great and wonderful past and apply its eternal truths to the present, a glorious day will dawn for humanity. As Buchner says, "The whole past of the earth is nothing but an unfolded present." The Creator was the foremost thought in the minds of ancient peoples who worshipped Him with a reverence rarely manifested in our materialistic age. They believed that "They that be wise shall shine as the brightness of the firmament; and they that turn many to righteousness as the stars forever and ever," Daniel xii, 3, and that "He telleth the number of the stars; he calleth them all by their names." Psalm clxvii, 4.

Volney says, "If at some future period some one united Astronomical Science to the erudition of Antiquity, too much separated from it, that man will instruct his age in many things, which the vanity of ours has no notion of."

Tradition relating to the Poles is of inestimable astrological value. "Axieros" was the distinctive appellation given by the ancients to the two poles, which were called, conjointly, the "Kabirim." These were names suggesting the "principle of generation" and "most powerful Gods." "The pole of the heavens generates the season according to the

angle with which he penetrates the center of the earth—
when parallel, we have constant spring; but when he penetrates through the equator, the ravages of the elements must
be dreadful"![1]

Polar motion was known to the ancients from time imme-
morial. In certain temples of antiquity polar motion was
made a special study, the results of which are a priceless inheritance for us today. There is a city and river in
Africa called "Axim," where undoubtedly this motion was
known and recorded. The ancients had many fancies
regarding the angles formed in heaven and on earth by the
changing positions of the Poles. A story is frequently
quoted from Herodotus, that when Cambyses entered one of
the temples of the Kabirim in Egypt, he was convulsed with
laughter at seeing what he thought to be a man standing
erect, and a woman standing on her head in front of him.
The Egyptians had used this fanciful method to represent
the passing of the North Pole of the earth to the South
Pole of the heavens.[2]

In Perry's "View of the Levant" a figure of the South
Pole of the earth in the constellation of the Harp is given in
which the Poles appear as two straight rods, surmounted
with Hawk's wings, to distinguish the North from the
South. The Poles were often figured as serpents with heads
of hawks, one at each end. These symbols also represented
the Poles inverted "in consequence of the great inclination
of the axis, bringing each time as a result the displacement
of the Oceans, the submersion of the polar lands, and the

---

[1]Mackey, S. A.—Mythological Astronomy, p. 73.

[2]These Poles are represented in a great Kabalistic symbol in the Zohar.
A figure of them is given in the "History of Magic," by Eliphas Levi, p. 53,
where the man (white) is seen standing erect, and the woman (black) standing
on her head. They seem interlocked, with the arms meeting at an angle on
each side. These figures in stone are found in Egypt. Eliphas Levi interprets
them as being God and Nature; or God (Light) mirrored inversely in Nature
and Matter (Darkness). They are but figures of the Kabiri in existence in the
temples of Egypt over 2,500 years ago, and they personified the passing of the
North Pole of the earth to the South Pole of the heavens, also the inverted Poles.

consequent *upheaval* of new Continents in the Equatorial regions, and *vice versa*."[1] These marvellous types of the Kabirim, or so-called "Deluge" gods, have been distorted by modern interpretation, which supposes them to have been worshipped as gods.

Eusebius gives an account of one of these symbols, a serpent, representing either the pole of the earth or the pole of the heavens. It is taken from Epeis, an Egyptian, whose works were translated into Greek by Arius. "He is of every *serpent* the most divine, who opening his eyes fills all things with Light in his primogenial residence, and if he closes them total darkness ensues." Eusebius also quotes from two Persian writers, Zoroaster Magus and Astanes: "The God has the head of a hawk, he is the first of beings, immutable, eternal, unbegotten, indivisible, indefinable, the giver of every good, *immutable,* of the holy most holy, of the wise most wise, the source of equity and justice, self taught, natural, perfect, intelligent, and the sole inventor of the sacred powers of nature." Eusebius also speaks of the Egyptian representation of the Universe as a circle of fire, and a serpent[2] having the head of a hawk, or a circle dividing heaven and earth. S. A. Mackey in his "Mythological Astronomy" explains this as follows: "Here is the pole of the earth within the plane of the ecliptic, attended with all the fiery consequences that must arise from such a state in the heavens when the whole Zodiac in 25,000 years must have 'redden'd with the solar blaze,' and each sign must have been vertical to the polar region."

Astronomically the Poles are the heavenly measurers. Their name, Cabirim, means measure of the stars, the lights. In this word beginning with a C instead of K, Cab means a measure, and Irim or Urim means the heavens. They were

---

[1]Blavatsky, H. P.—The Secret Doctrine, Vol. ii, p. 360.

[2]The Astral Light, the Milky Way, the path of the Sun to the Tropics Cancer and Capricorn, and the circles which form the sidereal years, were always called Serpents. Hawk and Serpent conjoined was a well-known type of the primordial divinity of a dual nature.

always known as Great, Beneficent and Powerful Gods, and under so many different names that much confusion has arisen concerning them.[1] An esoteric understanding brings light and a perfect explanation which straightens out many of the riddles not easily divulged to those without intuitive or perceptive knowledge. Esoterically the Kabiri Dioscuri were the two poles, later called by the Greeks Castor and Pollux, the two brilliant stars which are given to represent the Zodiacal sign Gemini, which has been called the two Pillars of Heaven. The Kabiri Titans were the seven great gods cosmically and astronomically. As Titans they were called children of the Sun, because of their being connected with At-Al-As, "the Divine Sun," and with *tit*, the deluge. The Titans were called Atlantes.

Diodorus ascribes the invention of Fire and the art of manufacturing iron to the Kabiri Titans, and Pausanias proves that the original Kabiric deity was Prometheus. The Kabiri were not only cosmically generators of the Seasons, but also as presiding gods were great volcanic energies. They brought Light into the world, symbolized in Prometheus, who had also brought Light into the world and had endowed humanity with reason and intellect. The name Kabeiros means "The powerful through Fire," and wherever cult of the Kabiri was recognized, it was always connected with fire. They built their temples in the most volcanic regions. Possibly in this we find a key to the Christians having made of them "Infernal Gods." So sacred was their Temple at Memphis that only Priests were allowed to enter. For many long ages the Kabiri lived in the memory of the nations as the benefactors of man and whether called planetary spirits, angels or messengers, taught the mysteries of the art of Agriculture. Osiris-Isis, as the Great Kabir of Egypt, was. said to have revealed wheat, by producing it.

---

[1]Kabiri, or Cabiri, is a generic name. They were called Mighty Gods as well as Mortals of both sexes, and were Celestial, Terrestrial, and Cosmic. Cabiri is a first rendering of the name by the Hebrews.

The origin of the Semitic Kabirim, "The Powerful and the Mighty, the Great," has disappeared in the shadowy mists of time. "The word guebre[1] comes from Kabiri, or Cabiri, and means the ancient fire worshippers, or Parsis. As gabir it has remained as an appellation of the Zoroastrians in Persia."[2]

In the Samothracian mysteries, the generic name of the Kabiri was the "Holy Fires." They were the founders of the Seven Localities of the Island of Samothrace, sacred to Vulcan. The "Kabir born of the holy Lemnos" whom Pindar describes as the Adamas, was "a type of primitive man, born from the bosom of Earth" physically, and from the divine Fire of progenitors spiritually. Hence derives the Seven Adams who were preeminently the Seven Stars or Fires of the Constellation The Great Bear. According to Babylonian accounts the first race to fall into generation was Adami, the Dark Race, comprising those ancient primitive peoples whose records were ever written in the heavens. In Inner Africa the name of the most ancient Great Mother was "Khebma," whose children were the Kamara or Kabiri (Kam means Black), the black race.

The Kabiri of Samothrace were said to drink at two fountains, Lethe (oblivion), and Mnemosyne (memory). They like the most ancient deities of the Egyptian temples were the Great Cosmic Gods, the great Polar Gods who were the presiding powers of the Sidereal 26,000-year cycle and agents of the upward progress of the race. In Grecian temples their rites became phallic, and their worship indecent. In the Egyptian "Book of the Dead" they are called the Lords of the four cardinal points, the Genii that guard the four corners of the sarcophagus, belonging to the Seven Spirits, the Seven Stars of the constellation The Great Bear. In the Kabala they are the Watchers in Heaven, Councillors of the Most High. Noah was called a great Kabir. He is

---

[1]Gibbor, Hebrew, in the Septuagint is translated Giant.
[2]Hyde's De Religione Persaum.

either a myth, or a legendary hero evolved from the Kabiri of Samothrace of Titanic tradition. Cain, represented by the planet Mars, is god of generation, Tubal-Cain was a Kabir, an instructor. He was Vul-cain, greatest of all the gods of a later period, and in Egypt termed the greatest of the gods.

The Deity of Israel was called the Great Kabir. The Hebrew word Kab means "To roll around" and Khab in Egyptian is "to give birth to." Ari, or aru in Egyptian are the Watchers, the Companions, the Keepers. The Kabiri were the Seven that gave birth to and made the first circle of time. The Watchers, the grouping of the original Seven made by the clustering together of these stars was called Kabbing. The Kabala itself, means the doctrine of the stars, their revolutions, repetitions, hidden wisdom, and sacred powers relating to the cycles of time. The Jews claim that the Kabala was taught by God to a select company of angels in paradise, while an astronomical myth tells us that paradise, or the Garden of Eden, was formed by the Seven Great Stars that circled the pole, called the Kabiri or kab-ari.

Occult science proves that the founders of all root races have been connected with the North Pole. Gods, religions, beliefs, myths, have all come from there. No wonder we find it alluded to as the "Cradle of Man," for when the Pole star energises the earth's axis humanity receives an upward urge or spiritual rebirth.

The ancient topography of the nature of the Arctic and Antartic regions of which the ancients had clear understanding is unquestionably accurate. "If we hold at present only to the astronomical and geographical significance it may be found that the ancients knew the topography and nature of the Arctic and Antarctic regions better than any of our modern astronomers."[1]

. Early astronomers divided the heavens into three great divisions. The point called the Mountain, denominated the Highest, was the middle of the first division which always

---

[1]Blavatsky, H. P.—The Secret Doctrine.

seemed to remain above the horizon, and stationary. It was made the seat of the Empire, whose monarch, from his throne, could behold the whole world and every nation night or day. This was the Great Judgment Seat, from which even unto this day, at certain periods in world changes, proceeds the powerful Justice Ray of a Balancing Manifestation.

Henry Melville in "Veritas" very fittingly speaks of the "Pole Star" as the rock of ages. " 'Trust ye in the Lord forever; for the Lord Jehovah is the rock of ages.' Isaiah xxiv, 4. This Polar star is the rock, or Mount Olympus of the Latins, which was so high that no bird could fly to the top, nor were clouds ever seen on its summit. This Polar Star is the Mount Meru of the Buddists, and the Mount Zion of the Hebrews. 'They that trust in the Lord shall be as Mount Zion, which cannot be removed, but abideth forever.' Psalm cxxv, 1. David says, 'Lead me to the rock that is higher than I." Psalm lxi, 1. From our world nothing can appear higher than the Polar star which is the pivot or point of axis on which the earth performs its diurnal and annular motion. David exclaims, 'thus saith the Lord, the heaven is my throne, and the earth is my footstool; where is the house that ye build unto me? And where is the place of my rest!' Isaiah lxvi, 1. Cephas, or Cepheus, means rock. Cepheus is seated in the highest heaven, and he has Mount Olympus, or the Pole Star, for his footstool." Celestial Astrology and Astronomy are spoken of as lost sciences, and we are told that until the position of the dark planets is known, astrology can not become an exact science, yet it can and will again be raised to its former sublimity.

The North Pole of the heavens was represented as the Mountain, the South Pole as the Pit. The Mountain and the Pit explain the meaning of Helion and Acheron, which, according to S. A. Mackey, were made use of in astronomical calculations by the ancients. Helion or the Sun, was the Sun in his highest, Acheron was usually translated as Hell, or the last condition or state of the Sun in its disappearance among the Southern constellations. Could we look down from the North Pole to the South Pole into the great abyss, the point of our vision might lead us very quickly to the discerning of a Christian Heaven and Hell, for many an absurd misinterpretation has been generated concerning these primordial parents, the Poles.

"The North Pole of the Heavens has a circular path among the stars." The star Polaris in the tail of the Lesser Bear is the present Pole Star. It is about one and one-quarter degrees from the true Pole. It has been and will remain the Pole Star for centuries to come. "Yet owing to the precession of the Equinoxes, the real Pole is continually, though slowly, changing, following a circle around the Pole of the Ecliptic, which lies in the Constellation Draco. It takes the North Pole about 26,000 years to complete its great circle, which has a radius of $23\frac{1}{2}$ degrees. About the year 7500 A. D. the star Alpha in Cepheus will be the North Star; about 13,500 A. D. the brilliantly beautiful star Vega in Lyre will hold that position; and about the year 21,000 A. D. the star Alpha in Draco will again be the North Star."[1] The discovery of this motion of the Poles belongs to antiquity. And invariably the wisdom of antiquity found its written expression in the symbolism of the Heavens, through which came anciently our knowledge of The Supreme, The Absolute, God.

"The two slow motions of the Pole are so proportionate to each other, and produce such a complex figure in the heavens, differing everywhere in the exact proportion of the different latitudes, that the different nations never could have agreed in their descriptions, had not each nation observed and registered for itself."[2]

Mackey also explains that the periclyclosical motion calculated according to the rate mentioned by the ancients, keeps the angle decreasing, at a rate which will make the Pole of

---

[1]Barritt, Leon—The Evening Sky Map.
[2]Mackey, S. A.—Mythological Astronomy, p. 73.

the Earth unite with the Pole of the Ecliptic in something over 100,000 years, a period which would produce universal Spring.

Meru, the home of the gods, is the North Pole, the Garden of Eden, whither the gods were supposed to ascend and descend periodically. It was guarded by the great serpent, the constellation Draco. These were the Zodiacal signs or Gods, passing from the Pole of the earth up to the North Pole of the heavens, according to the Precession, and then gradual sinking, towards the Pit in the South. One ascends as another descends, which leads to the understanding of the spiral and its symbol, the Serpent, which is best explained by S. A. Mackey in "The Sphinxiad :" "At noon, the ecliptic would be parallel with the meridian, and part of the Zodiac would descend from the North Pole to the North horizon; crossing the *eight coils of the serpent,* which would seem like an imaginary ladder with eight staves reaching from the earth to the Pole, i. e., the throne of Jove, up this ladder, then the Gods, i. e., the signs of the Zodiac ascended and descended. It is more than 400,000 years since the Zodiac formed the sides of the ladder. Did the Jews receive some faint traces of antiquity from their masters?" To explain he says, "If we assume a time when the Poles were Parallel; the Pole of heaven, in eight times 25,000 years, would seem to have described a pericyclosical figure round the Pole of the earth like a serpent coiled eight times; and as each volve is *four* degrees asunder, the figure of the serpent described by the Pole of the heaven round the Pole of the earth, in 200,000 years would sweep a circle, the diameter of which would be 64 degrees, i. e. 32 degrees above the Pole, and 32 degrees below it. It would be the circle of perpetual apparition in the latitude of 32 degrees." People have certainly woven strange romances from the ascending and descending signs of the Zodiac, and how determined the Christians have been to find in this, the serpent of Genesis, instead of a Cosmic Metaphor. There was a time when

> "The Pole return'd not to *her* former place,
> But seem'd to seek the other pole's embrace;
> And by a *spiral road-way* round the skies,
> At *four* degrees each step, was seen to rise."

and at this meeting of the Poles there was everlasting spring and " 'Twas nature's honeymoon—a time divine." It was the Golden Age when Saturn created a reign of Justice. Our American Indians have preserved a knowledge of distant ages, when the Sun disappeared in winter, and must have known of the Polar Motion.

The Labyrinth in its spiral windings is a transcription of the path of the North and South Poles of the earth, passing from the ecliptic to join the North and South Poles of heaven, illustrating the Precession of the Equinoxes, or the lessening of the angles of the Pole. In the Labyrinth there were three Spiral staircases. Opening from these and facing inward, were from three to four thousand rooms. The labyrinthine windings began below, spiraling upward and then downward to earth. This arrangement, mysterious yet so simple, is wholly Egyptian in its suggestiveness. S. A. Mackey, in his "Mythological Astronomy," asserts that the three spiral staircases show that the Poles had repeated the ascent and descent three different times, giving an immense antiquity to the origination of the Labyrinth.

The Kabiri have been said to be one, two, three, four and seven in number. One Kabir represented a Great or Mighty Power in nature. Venus was called a Great Kabir when enceinte and typified the first Mother, whose seven children as Stars, were the Kabiri. The two Kabiri were typified as the two Poles of Heaven, the Kabiri Dioscuri. Terrestrially Jupiter, Father of the Gods, and Bacchus, God of Wine, personified the Poles. Three and four Kabiri are found in the Grecian phallic worship, these numbers representing the male and female principles. The four were also the Genii or Spirits of the four corners or Cardinal Points belonging to the Seven Stars of the constellation The Great Bear. There are four

Kabiri who were called by Sanchoniathan, the sons of Sydik. If we identify Sydik with Noah as "a just man" of the Scriptures and with Melchizedek priest of the most high god after "his own order" both must have been the children of Justice and identified, as was Sut, the Star-god, with Saturn, who became the planet of Justice.   The Kabiri were called Axieros, Axiokeros, Axiokersa and Kadmos or Kadmillos, the latter being Hermes the Great of the sacred writings. They represent modes of Force, and in their names should be noticed the introduction and transportation of letters. The letter A has been from most ancient times connected with the parent Sun, while the X seems to relate to the cardinal cross of the fixed stars, and S to the Serpent power. The Greek word for the ancient wisdom (Wisdom of the Serpent) is Sophia.   Note the presence of the o, i, a and s in Sophia and similarly in the names of the Kabiri.   Originally letters were symbols of heavenly powers or modes of force.

The Kabiri were said to have invented the letters of the alphabet and the language of the gods.   They taught mankind architecture, law, legislation and different kinds of magic, and the use of medical plants.   The names Kabiri, Kadmus, Noah, Hermes, Orpheus, Asklepios, etc., were all generic names.

The Kabiri Titans are identical "with all the rulers and instructors of the primeval races which are referred to as the Gods and Kings of the divine Dynasties."[1]   These were likened to the gruesome individual whom we call the devil, by godly or religious symbolists and by many theologians, who seem to rejoice in rejecting all proofs to the contrary.

"We modern Europeans feel surprised when hearing talk of the Spirits of the Sun, Moon, etc.   But we repeat again, the *natural good sense and the upright judgment* of the ancient peoples, quite foreign to our *entirely material* ideas upon celestial mechanics and physical sciences . . . could

---

[1]Blavatsky, H. P.—The Secret Doctrine, Vol. ii, p. 393.

not see in the stars and planets only that which we see, namely: simply masses of light, or opaque bodies moving in circuits in siderial space, merely according to the laws of attraction or repulsion; but they saw in them *living* bodies, *animated* by spirits as they saw the same in every kingdom of nature. . . . *This doctrine of spirits so consistent and comformable to nature*, from which it was derived, formed a grand and unique conception, wherein the physical, the moral, and the political aspects were all blended together . . . "[1] "The telluric, metalline, magnetic, electric and fiery elements are all so many allusions and references to the Cosmic and Astronomical character of the diluvian tragedy."[2]

Fortunately, from the myths of the past are emerging great truths of which science is becoming aware. Our blinded eyes may yet be opened to a truer revelation of the truths taught by Jesus, who derived them from that mighty past, of which so little now remains undistorted by modern lust for gold and the tottering power it brings.

---

[1]Creuzer—Egypte de Merville, pp. 450 to 455.
[2]Blavatsky, H. P.

Cyclic Tree

The above illustration is copied from an old Egyptian Zodiac, in which the Tree, Bird and Dog symbolize Cycles. The bird in the tree represents the Phoenix Cycle of 500 years, which multiplied by 52 gives the Great Cycle of 26,000 years. The dog, type of Sothis, which also represented the Phoenix Cycle of 400 years with 365 days to the year, which multiplied four times gives the 1,460 years Cycle. The Sothic year was called Four-fold because of the heliacal rising of the star Sothis, which was found to be one day late every four years. It completes its Cycle in 1,461 years, every year representing $365\frac{1}{4}$ days, and being called one-quarter of a Sothic year. The Tree as a Type of Time becomes the symbol of the Great Cycle of Eternity or the "Cyclic Renovation," the Precessional period of 26,000 years.

207

CHAPTER XII

MESSENGERS OF THE ETERNAL

The star Sirius is undoubtedly the most interesting, and in its surpassing brilliance the most glorious of all the "Fires" above. Its renown is as ancient as the human race, it having been known to all races and worshipped by all peoples without cessation. It was the star of Eternal Dawn, the "Herald Star which measured whole ages by the rising light as it dawned for a moment in the eastern horizon."

Over 500,000,000 stars are observable within range of the telescope, and these have untold distances between them. As to our earth, it is "but as a grain of sand on an infinite seashore"—a thought which all should make their own. Our Sun is 1,300,000 times larger than our earth, and yet is insignificant beside the great and glorious Sirius, which may possibly be outshone in light and size by many other suns that dwell in infinite space. We should accept with inward thankfulness the traditions and relics of the great past which seem so indestructible, and persist with such tenacity, and despite the destructive periods and peoples that would obliterate that which has outlived a seeming oblivion.

Sirius was watched with great solicitude by the ancient Egyptians, as it foretold the time of rising of the river Nile, upon which their prosperity depended. The river was their single source of life, and its rise depended on the rains which fell in remote places unknown to them. This southern star, "The Spy and Watch of the Gods," signalled the coming inundation, which began when the Sun was in the sign Leo, the Lion, morning risings of which preceded the inundation. The blending of these two fiery luminaries gave forth intense heat. In a later day, which was even then far remote from the twentieth century, the name Dog-Star was given to Sirius, which rose in the beginning of August and remained above the horizon for forty days. At the present time the rising of this star in July precludes its having any influence whatever over the dog-days, as its rising varies with the latitude of different countries and also with the Precession. The Egyptian sacred year began at the time of the rising of the river, coincident with the rising of Sirius, producing in the Egyptian an overwhelming desire to look above and note the movements of heavenly bodies, which registered times and seasons creating unchanging foundations.

The first registering of the cycles as measures of time, was based upon the annual heliacal[1] rising of Sirius and the revolution of the cluster of stars near the pole. Planetary time came much later. When these stars failed to keep true time, Sut-Anubis (Mercury) was given to Sirius as her messenger and was the lunar Taht which became her bright and better half in the period of time-keeping by the Moon, which followed that of the stars. The myth of the Deluge is attributed to Sirius, when found losing time, for Sirius unloosed the waters, called the Deluge, but these were finally checked in their course by the Moon, the male lunar Taht, when time became reckoned by each new Moon and by the month instead of the year. It was in his lunar character or type that Taht came to the assistance of the lagging star Sirius.

This was the origin of the myth of the dog that let in the deluge—or admitted the devil into Eden; the "Little Dog"[2] that can be seen in the branches of a tree in the old Egyptian Zodiac, keeping watch from a distance over the Garden of

---

[1]There is always one day in the year when a star will arise, just before the dawn, to vanish in the increasing splendor of the rising sun, called the "heliacal rising."

[2]The Egyptian phoenix is seen in the celestial tree as a little dog, and also as the bird in the same tree. The phoenix bird and a phoenix tree are found together under one name. The tree that began as one became two, then four, then seven and nine and twelve, and finally, as a Tree of Time became the symbol of the great cycle of 26,000 years, a type of immortality and the eternal.

Eden.   As Mercury he was known as the "Southern Sentinel."
Sirius as the Dog-Star can be seen in the branches of the
cyclic tree peering about and spying into the promised land
of—"Springtime, and the Golden Fields of the Setting Sun."
There is a Russian tradition that the dog was placed in
the Garden of Eden to watch over Adam and Eve and to
keep away the Evil One, but that the dog, being tempted by
a piece of bread, yielded to Satan's wiles and allowed him to
enter.   Another tradition ascribes to the guardianship of
the dog the fact that enough corn or seed was left to supply the
world.   One of the gods had become very angry, thinking
that this seed which was heaven-born had been abused, and
wished to destroy it entirely, but the dog pleaded that at
least a little of it be left, and his wish was granted.   This
is the same little dog watching over Eden in the tree belonging to the sign Virgo, the Virgin, which as the planet
Mercury is a watcher over the treasures of both heaven and
earth.   These legends as well as scores of others were
related of the Goddess Mother of the Great Bear and her
son Sut, when they were discovered to have been unfaithful
in their timekeeping, nevertheless the dog remained the
keeper of the Sothic year and of the Sothic or Phoenix cycle.
The Phoenix, bird of Fire and type of the resurrection is
identified with the Egyptian Bennu.   The Phoenix constellation contains one of the conspicuous stars of the heavens,
Acharnar, the symbol of the Phoenix[1] and said to denote
Victory after Death.   This constellation was said partly or
wholly to correspond with Aquila, the Egyptian Eagle, having as its beautiful star Altair, sometimes called the Bird of
Jove, and also with the constellation Cygnus, the Swan of the
Greeks.

---

[1]"The Phoenix was an image of the Sothic year. This constellation came to
the meridian at the time of the rising of Sothis. A star of the first magnitude, Acharnar, belongs to it. . . . Akar (Eg) is a name of the underworld; Nar
signifies victory; thus Akarnar in Egyptian denotes the victory over Hades,
symbolized by the Phoenix, the bird of resurrection."—Massey, Gerald—A Book
of the Beginnings, Vol. i, pp. 107, 108.

Hor Apollo states "when the Egyptians would symbolize an aged man they would portray a Swan, for when it is old it sings its sweetest melody." The Swan became a type of renewal, of immortality and with the approach of a new dawn it raised a song of great sweetness and joy, because of the coming of the Light, and youth, and a new beginning. It was a very beautiful and softened song of resurrection. Sirius was guide of the resurrection as she rose shining and majestic on the meridian bringing in the circling years.

Ancient Egyptian Calendars of which Sothis (Sirius) was the determiner were corrected by observing the heliacal rising of this star, for corrections had become necessary, before knowledge was obtained of the lunar periods leading to the determination of the true length of the solar year. Years were numbered by means of festivals.

Sut (Sirius) was the earliest form of the divinity of Fire and can be traced by means of the monuments down to Sebek-Ra, the Ram or Lamb of the Zodiacal Aries, considered the type of fulfilment. Sirius has been identified as a type of Fire and of Gold and was that "Fiery flaming sentinel of the fiery hosts of Space." Associated with Sirius was the Golden Dog, and also Sut-Nub, the black-and-golden Sun-and-Sirius god of the Golden Age.[1]

The great pyramid was considered by the Arabs to be the

---

[1]Sut-Nub or Sut-Nahsi was the black Christ of Egypt, and has been worshipped in Europe as the Black Bambino of the Italian Church, and in India as Krishna, the black Christ. The black Sut-Nahsi was a negro image of the earliest god. This black god was continued as Sebek, Solar God of Darkness or the crocodile of darkness. No matter under what line of descent, it was direct from the motherhood and this single god is such only as the child of the Virgin Mother. When the fatherhood had been established, the one born of the Virgin as the descending dying Sun was the god, Jah, of the Hebrew god of darkness, the black divinity.

"To this origin of the negro god and this line of descent through the black Star-god, the black-and-golden Sun-and-Sirius god, and the black god who was the sun of darkness, the Typhonians remained devoutly attached . . . the god of darkness, the black divinity, who becomes the black Iu . . . and finally the black Jesus of the Christian cult, the Son of the Virgin Mother in the Romanish Church, and the pre-monogamous worship of the Africans."
—Massey, Gerald—"A Book of the Beginnings," Vol. ii, p. 346.

treasury of knowledge of all hidden wisdom from the beginning, and was called "The Lights."   The pyramid is a figure of seven founded on the square and the triangle, and is identified with Sut (seven) or Sirius. It was oriented to Sirius.

Nine or ten thousand years ago the Sothic cycle, suggestive of the Typhonian worship, was still used by the Egyptians, who were most learned astrologers and builders of pyramids. They had profound knowledge of cycles, both great and small, and fully understood the difference between the Fixed Stars and our planets, for they looked upon the Fixed Stars as the "genii that never moved" and the planets as the "genii which never rested."

There are very powerful aspects between the earth and the satellite of Sirius, which do not seem to be mentioned either in astronomy or astrology. It is invisible to human vision, but is the refractor of Sirius' light to the earth, and is the so-called "Dark Planet," because the refraction of Sirius makes it invisible to human vision. It is not very far removed from our own Sun. It is obedient to Sirius and to the solar system of Sirius, and yet within equatable distance to our earth and is a great influence in reviving on earth the ancient souls who will minister to the Light. Should this fall in opposition to the Moon in the ninth house of the horoscope, the house of Light, from the third, it gives a very unusual perception of cosmic destiny.

The myth of the birth of Time, coming from above, was created by the motion of the Stars encircling the Pole, and establishing forever the Circle of Eternity. This is not an abstract conception, but a basic fact, from which arose the cycles that belong to the greatest antiquity. They were calculated by two very ancient astrologers—Narada and Asuraya, the Atlanteans—so very long ago that they seemed to and do belong to a mystic past, and are so ancient that sceptics as well as many theologians deny their existence, but the Secret Doctrine gives undeniable proofs, and Occultism has demonstrated the infallibility of these anciently computed cycles, which have reached us today intact. Narada and Asuraya were the great Giants of Archaic time. Narada in occultism is known as Pesh-Hun, "The mysterious guiding intelligence which gives impulse to and regulates the impetus of the cycles, 'whose symbol is in the serpent Sesha, that carries within itself 'Infinite Time.' He is reputed to have given dates for cycles in cyclic figures with records of all the astronomical and cosmic ones to come. He taught his science to those who were known as the first people who looked above for knowledge, the first observers of the Fixed Stars.

Asuraya-Maya founded his astronomy on those records, together with the length of the coming cycles, until the final great cycle was reached. It is said of him that he was "one to whom God imparted knowledge of the stars." He was known as a most powerful magician and a wonderful astronomer, as well as the Greatest Astrologer of Atlantis. The Egyptian Priests had these records and arrangements of the stars, as did the Hindus, who still have them today.

The Circle and the Cycle are synonymous. A circle is Sar-Saros, or cycle, and with every race was the symbol of the Unknown. It is "Boundless Space" and "Limitless Time in Eternity" born from above, based on the myth of the birth of Time and the Circle made by the stars that had neither beginning nor end. Thus the Eternal was founded on the cycle and the circle, and continual cyclic repetition, just as in the creation of the four cardinal points from the circle, the "Four Times" of Egypt represented "Forever," through the continuity of one circle mingling with another. The transformation of one cycle into another can be found in the Hebrew word "Everlasting," meaning ever-repeating. The Hierophants of Egypt created from their philosophy the "Circle of Necessity," the fate to which all are doomed as well as judged, the circle that is symbolized in the twelve signs of the Zodiac.

Time cycles in the Books of Genesis, Daniel and Esdras are all prophecies, and every prophecy is astrological, the prophets themselves being astrologers. Death, renewal, or destruction and reproduction of worlds in ancient times were thought to be by Fire and Water. The end of the world or the Great Cycle was believed to occur in either the sign Cancer (fire) or Capricorn (water), one being the antithesis of the other. Berosus taught that when all the planets should coincide in the constellation Cancer, the planets being so placed that a straight line could pass directly through their orbs, all earthly things would be consumed (pralaya) but that cataclysm by flood would occur when the same combination of planets took place in Capricorn. The devastation by fire belonged to Cancer, and cataclysm by water when the Moon was in Capricorn. The Beetle in ancient times was placed in the sign Cancer, as it was thought that the world was renewed in this sign, ushering in birth and rebirth, an early cycle being typified by the Beetle. The beetle was called the God of the resurrection of the Sun or its renewal and a redeemer of the dead by his begetting. When the beetle has his wings folded he represents his metamorphosis or transformation. The beetle rolling his own seed into a ball symbolizes both Sun and Soul, and is identified with the Phoenix, whose transformation is by fire.

When a repeating cycle of time culminated at midsummer, the beetle was interpreted to mean a Giant Cycle. The giant Repha of the Hebrew writings "Had on every hand six fingers, and on every foot six toes, four and twenty in number." II Samuel xxi, 20. Six fingers and toes are traceable to the beetle, who had six tarsi on its feet and had thirty joints, representing the six months of ascent and the six of descent, with the thirty days to the month. The Rephaims of Genesis, xiv, 5, who were in Ashtaroth, were the "giants of the old world who carried themselves insolently towards God and man and were drowned in the deluge," and were the Seven Stars of The Great Bear, "who came not in their proper season" and so deviated from the ways of wisdom. The deluge was the ending of a cycle.

A Giant personified a Goliath cycle of time. The cycle of Sut was a year, and that of Taht, the Moon-god, who superseded Sut, was a month. All cycles symbolized the ebb and flow of life. In their ascent they reached towards the highest, and by the immutable law of opposites, their descent was towards the lowest, but every returning cycle in its reemergence reached higher and higher. Our present cycle has touched the lowest point of transition, a dark period unproductive of understanding, and has seemingly failed to recognize the divine spirit within, materialism having superseded the Light.

Our great solar cycle or circling of the Zodiac brings periods of Light and Dark, life and death or resurrection. The Egyptian Great Years were the precessional periods called Cyclic Renovations, a return of time and seasons to their original place. An Egyptian year represented four of ours, and to "represent a current year," says Hor Apollo, "they depict the fourth part of an Arura, a measure of land of an hundred cubits; and when they would express a year, they say a quarter, . . . four of these quarters *Squared* the four-fold year." This failing of Sothis being one day late every four years in its heliacal rising was allowed for annually and rectified in its great cycle. This irregularity "was considered to be the work of opposing powers of disorder, falsehood and chaos."

Two periods of time in connection with the Egyptian Great Years were of extreme importance. One was known as the Sothic cycle, which covered a period of 1460 years, and the other as the Phoenix cycle, covering a period of 1500 years. Herodotus tells us the Phoenix appears every 500 years, the ancient Phoenix that went down into Egypt to die or be transformed into the young one, which took place in the city of the Sun, the city where Abraham taught Astrology, and where the transformation of the Star-god into the Sun-god took place, and where the god Atum transformed into the son as Iu-em-Hept the Jesus of the Apocrypha who is associated with the 400-year cycle.   The Secret Doctrine states that Phoenix came from Phenoch-Enoch, symbol of a secret cycle and initiation.   This bird was also thought to live a thousand years, when it kindled a flame in which it was self-consumed, becoming reborn from itself and living another thousand years.[1]   One form of the Phoenix of Egypt, called the Bennu, is the Nycticorax, a bird that appeared at the time of the inundation,[2] and which had the double plume on the back of its head.

In the Book of II Esdras, Chapter xii, 13-16, a parallel to the Phoenix occurs where it says, "And the whole body of the eagle was burnt, so that the earth was in great fear." Further it says, "there shall rise up a kingdom upon earth, and it shall be feared above all the kingdoms that were before it.   In the same shall twelve Kings reign one after another. *Whereof the second shall begin to reign, and shall have more time than any of the twelve.*   And this do the twelve wings signify which thou sawest."   If, as Gerald Massey understands, we take this vision to refer to the founding of the Zodiac of twelve signs, and the introduction of the year or cycle, to which the quarter of a day was added to be calculated as one day in every four years, and the one day taken into account in the *second month* of the year as in our February, then the second King may be said to have more time

---

[1] The bonfire, whose origin was Sabean, was a fire connected with and consecrated to the reappearance of Sothis, when it crowned the summit of the year, just as the Phoenix or Bennu coming to the meridian typified the fire in which the bird was fabled to have been transformed.

[2] The Nyticorax is an owl called the Night-crow, which announces the time of sunset almost as truly as an almanac. This peculiar bird, says Gilbert White, can only be watched and observed during two hours of the twenty-four, and then in the dubious twilight—an hour after sunset and an hour before sunrise.—Massey, Gerald—A Book of the Beginnings, Vol. i, p. 108.

The bird was a type and was continued as a figure of the Great Year coinciding with a Talmudic legend of the bird over which the angel of death had no power. This was the one who had not fallen, as it had refused to eat of the forbidden fruit when it was offered to Eve.

than any of the twelve, because the leap year of four fold length would be reckoned and dated by the month of his reign. The difference of a day corresponded exactly with the day intercalated in the sacred calendar of the Egyptians every fourth year, as in the case of our own Leap Year.

In the divine Dynasties the reign of Osiris is given as 400 years. The cycle of 400 years belongs to the Astronomical Allegories in the Books of Genesis and of Esdras. The prophecies of the Apocrypha belong to the period of 400 years called the Sun and Sirius period, to which the Jesus of the Apocrypha belonged. There is an Egyptian legend telling us that Osiris in the 365th year of his reign took Horus as companion and left Nubia, with the purpose of driving Sut-Typhon out of Egypt, so that the ushering in of the correct Solar time of 365¼ days might be accomplished.

The ancient Sut-Typhonians were very learned astronomers and had a thorough understanding of the cycles of Precession, and knew of the longer axis of the earth's orbit (the apsides) which reduced the actual period of precession in the 500-year cycle. "It carried the axis of the orbit completely around the whole circumference of the Ecliptic in 20,984 years."[1] The length of the year calculated by this second motion is about 21,000 years, or fifty-two times the Phoenix cycle of 400 years.

The ancients always regarded the Angels as the repeaters of the periods of time. We know them today as the heavenly or celestial hosts. The Talmud states that "one angel is taller than another by as many miles as a man could travel in 500 years." This 500 years determines the Phoenix period or cycle of time. In Rabbinical history the Angels are placed in the lower heaven, Seven of them being Archangels with as many as 360 under their charge. This lower heaven is the third created, and is the solar circle or ecliptic of 360 degrees. Job's joyous stars are the sons of Elohim, the circle makers, the Seven Stars or children of the

---

[1] Herschel.

Great Mother, the constellation of the Great Bear. We know that Sut, her first son, was called Satan and was the mightiest, the most beautiful, as well as the wisest of God's Archangels. He was Sabaoth, the Lord God of Israel, later theologized into Satan, the adversary, who is finally identifiable as the planet Saturn, symbol of Justice.

Knowledge of the Angels came directly from the Pharisees, who based their angelology on the Babylonian account of creation, which is found on the Assyrian tiles. Their Angels, of which there are Seven, are placed in the lower heaven. The second and third tiles read "The Angels who are in rebellion, who are in the lower part of heaven, had been created."

The Gnostics claimed that our earth had been created by the lower Angels, the inferior Elohim, and taught that the God of Israel was one of them. The Sadducees, who were guardians of the Laws of Moses, rejected the doctrine of the Angels. The Essenes had the knowledge of time-cycles and periodicity, which constituted the Jewish Kabala.

The "Sons of God" are the only angels mentioned in the Book of Genesis, but "The chariots of god *are* twenty thousand, *even* thousands of angels; the Lord *is* among them, *as in* Sinai, in the holy *place*." Psalm lxviii, 17. In the solar myth the Lord is the Sun in the midst of the stars in heaven. The Stars, the Angels, myriads and myriads of them, and the little ones, "sun themselves in one beam of all their glory and are gone."

Shennu, the Hebrew Sinai is the region of the time cycles. Shenah, Hebrew, and Shena, Egyptian, denote a place of repetition or transforming one into another at the end of a year. Shennu is a circle, orbit, and the Shennu of Egypt means millions, crowds, attendants, typifying time and periods which were personified as Angels just as today, they have been called "Saints of God."

Angels were the "Messengers of the Eternal," that is, they were the announcers of Time, and their doctrine was knowledge of the time cycles, which was a sacred and hidden wisdom in ancient times and originated with the great and first mother who created the first circle or cycle with her earliest known Angels, the Stars. In the "Book of the Dead" the messenger or Angel of divine vengeance was called Apt, the "Living Word," and was this same mother. Apt was a type word for Angel. Ap was to manifest, make known, announce, and Apt was the feminine manifestation.

In archaic teachings the Fall was the incarnation of the angels who had broken through and were in the chains of flesh and matter, in contradistinction to the Fall[1] of the Seven early Stars, which were said to be inert and lazy, as they had failed to keep time and the time cycles correctly. In the Zohar the Fall of the Angels refers to those who have broken through the seven circles. The "Seven Circles" are "the seven planets and planes, as are also the seven invisible spirits, in the angelic sphere whose visible symbols are the seven planets," the seven of the Great Bear and others.

After the Fall in Eden the Angels were said to have imparted their celestial knowledge to man that he might regain his lost Paradise. The doctrine of the Kabala was centered in the cluster of Seven Stars in the North. They were the Angels first noticed and construed as the periodic messengers of heaven, keepers of the cycles of time and makers of the circle of Eternity, of which they were messengers. They still keep watch at the gates of the Solar Zodiac, especially at the gates of the four corners in their last material manifestation, when, consciousness rising above the Cross of Matter, (formed by the four corners) is represented by a type, sign, or angel pointing the way to that path in which life can be most nobly expressed.

---

[1]The Scriptures speak of the Giants who lived before the flood. They were called Nephilim, the "mighty men of old." The word means to fall, fall from heaven. They were the celestial Giants of the primary world, the Seven great Stars belonging to the first great mother, who had "transgressed the commandments of God" or whose time-keeping had been found untrue.

Draco was called the "Counsellor of Treasures" and as the Dragon was part of all primeval revelation, "the fetishism of the dark because primeval." Draco surrendered its character of the Good Demon to undergo eschatological change. As the encircling Dragon or Serpent, it was the symbol of Eternal Going Round, or Eternity, and from its revolving around the pole originated the Serpent coiling around the Tree, thus Serpent and Tree become inseparable.

CHAPTER XIII

KEEPER OF SUPERNATURAL TREASURES OF KNOWLEDGE AND WISDOM

Hor Apollo tells us that "The earliest observers gave the first fact, revealed by the darkness as the whole starry Vast above slowly crawling round and round in one general movement like a serpent, whose variegated scales were the stars." From the rising and the setting of the stars, so like the motion of the serpent, many types were created. Among the elements above, the serpent was a symbol of Fire and Air, and below of Earth and Water, these being the four elements that were sacred over the entire world.

Serpent worship is as old as the heavens, and has been practiced since the beginning of time as we represent time on earth, and was symbolically interpreted by the primitive peoples. The earth was spoken of as the "Queen of the Serpents and the Mother of all that moves," which titles typified the time before the earth had become globe-shaped or round, and was "A long trail of cosmic dust or Fire-Mist moving and writhing like a serpent." The spirit of God was thought to breathe upon this Fire-Mist until it became cosmic matter, and finally circular, representing to the people of early days, the ring-shaped symbol of the serpent with its tail in its mouth, emblem of Eternity and Infinitude, whence came all the globular[1] bodies found within the universe.

---

[1]"The simile of an egg expresses the fact taught in Occultism that the primordial form of everything manifested, from atom to globe, from man to angel, is spheroidal, the sphere having been with all nations the emblem of eternity and infinity—a serpent swallowing its tail. To realize the meaning, however, the sphere must be thought of as seen from the center. . . . The 'Mundane Egg' . . . is found in every world-theogony, where it is largely

The primordial Serpent seen in the heavens, was composed of myriads and myriads of small stars forming a "luminous Zone," called the Astral Light. Moreover the path of the Sun through the Sidereal Year was always allegorically called a Serpent. The Serpent was a symbol of Divine Wisdom and was a synonym for initiation into the secret mysteries of the Magi, the Astrologers.

The Gnostics of the first three centuries were philosophers and formulators of the Wisdom or Gnosis which they taught.[1] The Gnosis was a spiritual and sacred knowledge obtained only through initiation into spiritual mysteries. The Gnostics of the Second Century found in their Serapis (Serpent) an accepted type of Christ to whom the latter day Christians gave the name of Messiah. Serapis was represented as a Serpent, just as Jesus was later. All ancient religions were symbolized by a Serpent. In Egypt the resurrection of Nature was represented by a Serpent having human legs. A Serpent on two legs, also meant a high Initiate. It is commanded in the "Book of the Dead" that Chap. clviii should be read in the presence of a Serpent on two legs. The Serpent was the emblem of Christ to the Ophites. Similarly the Brazen Serpent which healed those who looked upon it was an emblem of Christ, and as the good genius, the Agathodæmon, the Serpent is found engraved on many of the Gnostic gems.

"The *Way of a Serpent,*' and the workmanship, are among the most amazing in all nature. It has no hands, and yet can climb a tree to catch the agile monkey; it has no fins, but can outswim the fish; no legs, yet the human foot can-

---

associated with the serpent symbol; the latter being everywhere, in philosophy as in religious symbolism, an emblem of eternity, infinitude, regeneration, and rejuvenation, as well as of wisdom. . . . The 'Virgin Egg' is the microcosmic symbol of the macrocosmic prototype—the 'Virgin Mother'—Chaos or the Primeval Deep."—Blavatsky, H. P.—The Secret Doctrine, Vol. i, p. 65.

[1] The Gnostics taught that Light and Shadow, Good and Evil, were veritably one and have so existed through all eternity and will continue so to exist as long as there is a manifested world. "Shadow is not evil, it completes the Light, or Good. It is its creator on earth."

not match it in fleetness. Death is in its coil even for the bird on the wing, which the springing reptile snatches out of its own element. The Serpent slays with a dexterity that human destroyers might look upon as divine. One of the most arresting sights is to see this limbless creature turn its coils into a hand to grasp its prey, and lift it to the deadly mouth. The serpent in the pangs of sloughing is a phenomenon, once witnessed, never to be forgotten. There is a startling fascination in the sight of that image of self-emanation proceeding from itself, the young, repristinated, larger life issuing of itself from the mask of its old dead self like a spiritual body coming forth from the natural body, the unparalleled type of self-emanation, of transformation, of a resurrection to new life, of *'Time, or Renewal coming of Itself!'* "[1]

The early Christians were Serpent worshippers, and among those called the Naeserians the Serpent was known as the second person of the cosmical and astronomical Trinity, symbolized by the constellation of the Dragon, which celestially was said always to have within it that which was sacred and divine. The true objective of this worship was undoubtedly more obvious at the time when the constellation Draco and the other most northern constellations were more universally noticed and studied.

It can readily be seen why the Serpent, as the Constellation Draco, winding itself around, as if guarding the Pole of Heaven, or the Garden of Eden, was called the "keeper of supernatural treasures of knowledge and wisdom," and that he might be a truer transmitter of the Light than an anthropomorphic god. In some countries the people ate certain parts of the Serpent and drank its blood, in order to acquire knowledge, which would enable them to understand the language of animals and birds. It was the unexpected tasting of the Dragon's blood that opened the eyes and ears of Sigurd so that he heard what the birds had

---

[1]Massey, Gerald—The Natural Genesis, Vol. i, p. 293.

to say, immortalized in the exquisite music of Wagner. Eve in the Garden of Eden was faced with the serpent temptation. The original Kamite record of this is found in the Tale of Setnu from "Records of the Past" and of most precious wisdom. "Thou shalt know what relates to the birds of the sky and the reptiles, and all that is said by them. The divine power shall raise the fishes to the surface of the water. If thou readest the second page it will happen that if thou art in the Amenti thou wilt have power to resume the form which thou hadst on earth," and to quote from The Natural Genesis of Gerald Massey, "This marvellous book had been placed in a box of iron, inside a box of brass, inside a box of bronze, inside a box of ebony, inside a box of ivory, inside a box of silver, inside a box of gold, and concealed in the middle of the river Coptos. Iron, brass, bronze, ebony, ivory, silver and gold make up the symbolical number seven, equivalent to the Seven coils of Fafner the Dragon."

The star Alpha Draconis of the constellation Draco was the Pole Star about 2793 B. C., and was held in very great reverence by all the early nations, who called it by various names, such as "The Judge of Heaven," "The Proclaimer of the Light," "The High Horned One. It was an object of worship to the early Christians.

The central passages of the Temples of Hathor, Denderah and Thebes were oriented to Alpha Draconis, then the Pole Star, as were other temples and pyramids of later date. Our own astronomer, Serviss, speaks very beautifully of these orientations, "to square their work by the stars, and to construct long rows of sphinxes and majestic columns to conduct a ray from the sky to the eye of God in his dark and hidden chamber, where no impious foot dared follow."

The Hivites of the Old Testament were known as the Ophites, and were connected with the Sabeans, worshippers of the Stars and the celestial Serpent. No other people or nation gave to the serpent the significance the later Christians have given it, for to all the older nations it was the symbol of Wisdom, and of great Seers, and never the devil of evil that has been manufactured into a belief in the lives of the people of today.

The Brazen Serpent of Moses was the Divine Healer. Why has it been Christianized into the dreaded reptile? Originally by the ancients the Serpent was regarded as the " 'First Beam of Light' that radiated from the abyss of 'Divine Mysteries'." And the Serpent Mystery was given only to the "Little Ones"—God's Little Ones who were the perfect Initiates, as was Jesus who knew and taught this sacred divine mystery.

To the Ophites the Serpent of Genesis and the Saviour were one. They held the Serpent in unusual veneration. "Moses was a descendant of Levi, the Serpent tribe; Buddha was of Serpent lineage, through the Naga (serpent) race of Kings who reigned in Magadha. Hermes-Thoth in his snake symbol is Tet, and according to the Ophite legend, Jesus or Christos is born from a snake (Divine Wisdom or the Holy Ghost) i. e. he became a Son of God through his initiation into the serpent wisdom." The Ophites assumed a definite existence about the Second Century, although the source of their worship was ages older, and like other Gnostics, they did not accept the teachings of the Old Testament, because they considered them inferior in knowledge and not containing the true Divine Wisdom. They worshipped the Serpent as the author of supreme knowledge. A brief and most interesting summary of their views is given by Epiphanius. "The supreme Aeon, having produced other Aeons, one of them a female, *Prunnicos* descended into the waters; whence, not being able to escape, she remained suspended in mid-space, being too clogged up by matter to return above, and not falling lower where there was nothing of affinity to her nature. Here she produced her son Ildabaoth, the god of the Jews, who in his turn produced seven Aeons, or Angels, who created the seven heavens.

From these seven angels Ildabaoth shut up all that was above him, lest they should know of anything superior to himself. They then created man in the image of their father, but prone and crawling on the earth like a worm. But the heavenly mother, Prunnicos, wishing to deprive Ildabaoth of the powers she had involuntarily endowed him with, infused into man a celestial spark, the soul. Immediately man rose up upon his feet, soared in mind beyond the limits of the eight spheres and glorified the Supreme Father, him that is above Ildabaoth. Hence Ildabaoth, full of jealousy, cast down his eyes upon the lowest stratum of matter, and begot a virtue in the form of a serpent, whom they call his son. Eve obeying him as the son of God, was readily persuaded to eat of the tree of knowledge."

The angels recognized by the Roman Church were included in the Ophite planetary group. Michael is figured as the Lion; Suriel as the Bull; Raphael as the Serpent; and Gabriel as the Eagle.

There were renowned subterranean caves or crypts under the cities of Memphis and Thebes. Those of Thebes were on the western side of the River Nile, extending towards the Lybian desert. They were known as the "Serpent's Catacombs," or passages wherein were performed the sacred mysteries " 'of the Unavoidable Cycle' generally known as the 'Circle of Necessity', the inexorable doom imposed upon every soul after the bodily death, when it had been judged in the Amentian region."[1]

In Egypt the "Circle of Necessity" was called the "Inevitable Circle," that of gestation, and the serpent became a supreme emblem of this mystery of the mysteries.

All the legends of the Serpent, whether allegories in our Bible or myths of ancient times, can be very easily traced to Astrological Mythology. The Sun conqueror of the Dragon of Darkness, the Celestial Virgin, the Dragon of the Book of Revelation, and many others can be brought

---

[1] Blavatsky, H. P.—Isis Unveiled, Vol. i, p. 553.

from the far off past and traced to their primal origin in the Fixed Stars, the Zodiac and the Constellations.

"Fiery Serpents" was an epithet given the Levites of the priestly caste, after they had departed from the *good law*, the traditional teaching of Moses, and to all those who followed *Black Magic*. They were the "rebellious children" against whom the prophets thundered because of their sins and iniquities, and who were to carry their riches "into the land whence came the viper and fiery flying serpents" (Isaiah, xxx, 6) or Egypt and Chaldea whose Initiates at this time had degenerated (700 B. C.). "But these 'Fiery Serpents' must be carefully distinguished from the 'Fiery Dragons of Wisdom,' and the 'Sons of the Fire Mist'."[1]

There was an ancient teaching, which called the earth "The Great Sea" and the "Sea of Life," and told of primordial Chaos and the evolution of the Universe, comparing it to the uncoiling of a Serpent "Extending hither and thither with its tail in its mouth, which was a symbol of eternity and also of cylic periods, and every thousand days it manifested itself." These were the days of Brahma, representing a period so great as to be almost inexpressible.

Mythologically the Serpent encircles the world, clasping all in one embrace, and when travailing in the pangs of a new birth, during the painful process of its sloughing, it was made the symbol of transformation and resurrection. Hor Apollo says of this wonderful serpent, "moreover every year it puts off its old age with its skin,[2] as in the Universe the animal period effects a corresponding change and becomes renovated, and the making use of its own body for food implies that all things whatsoever that are generated by Divine Providence in the world, undergo a corruption into it again." The Serpent evolves into an image of Time, like

---

[1] Blavatsky, H. P.—The Secret Volume, Vol. ii, p. 212.

[2] One of the Rabbins relates that "when the old serpent shed its skin presently after the fall of man, the Creator made a garment of it to clothe Adam and Eve.

Kronus or Saturn, who devours his own children—that is, the days of the week, or hours of the day, or the years. The Serpent Draco was one of the early Time Symbols in the heavens. By the rising and the setting of the stars Time and Seasons were indicated, and later the Stars as divinities became the keepers of Time and the Seasons. Plutarch feared unfolding the secrets of certain constellations lest they declare war against the length of Time.[1] He also held the idea that all the elementaries or forces of nature got their souls from the stars. There is a myth that when the constellation Draco, the Serpent, went once around the Pole Star, it laid an Egg. This was the Egg of the primary year in heaven. That the Universe was shaped like an Egg, was in the beginning a universal belief. In Egyptian symbology and worship the Egg was always associated with the Serpent. They were really inseparable. The Serpent was a phallic symbol only when dissociated from the Egg. Since the Serpent was oviporous the symbol not only connoted Wisdom, but became an emblem of the Logoi or self-born. It was often depicted with an egg in its mouth which esoterically has reference to the World Serpent bearing the Cosmic Egg in its mouth. The Egg was the symbol of life in Immortality and Eternity. Chaos and Darkness, and the embrace of the primordial waters by the wind (breath and fire) are all connected with the Cosmic Egg, "with the thought that the soul would gestate in the Egg of Immortality, to be reborn into a new life on earth. It not only relates to the incarnation of man but to his spiritual rebirth, or regeneration."[2] In Egypt eggs became sacred to Isis and on this account were never eaten by the Priests. Diodorus states that Brahma and Osiris were born from the Egg. The Brahmans will not eat Eggs, fearing lest they destroy the latent life within and thus commit a sin.

There was a Chinese belief that the dropping of an egg

---

[1] Of Isis and Osiris.
[2] Blavatsky, H. P.

by the god Tien from heaven to earth and into the waters created the first man. "This symbol is still regarded by some as representing the idea of the origin of life, which is scientific truth, though the human *ovum* is invisible to the naked eye. Therefore we see respect shown to it from the remotest past, by the Greeks, Phoenicians, Romans, the Japanese, and the Siamese, the North and South American tribes, and even the savages of the remotest islands."[1]

In Adams County, Ohio, United States of America, on a great mound has been discovered the figure of a serpent emanating an egg from its mouth, showing knowledge of the serpent mystery. It measures one thousand feet in length. The Mound Builders of America outlined their enclosures in the forms of birds and serpents and their hieroglyphs were raised in enormous reliefs. Egg and Age have become synonymous as a cycle of time which is retained at the present time in our Easter Egg.

In the Books of Genesis and Hosea is given the story of Jacob and Esau. Jewish tradition tells us "that Esau when born, had the likeness of a serpent on his heel." Esau personified the "Light-god that bruised the serpent's head," and Jacob, who in Genesis laid hold of Esau's heel was a demon of darkness, the Egyptian Kak "the Elemental Darkness continued by name Kak or Ka, the Nocturnal Sun." Jacob appears in both phases in the Biblical story.[2] Twin brothers belong to a myth incalculably old primarily belonging to ancient Egypt and found in the folk-tales of many lands.

There are many allusions in the Bible to the serpent, as Fiery, Brazen, Flying, but unfortunately these are seldom understood. Moses and the Israelites in the wilderness were assailed by Flying Fiery Serpents. "The Lord sent fiery serpents among the people, and they bit the people, and much people of Israel died." Then Moses was

---

[1]Blavatsky, H. P.—The Secret Doctrine, Vol. i, p. 366.
[2]The name of Jacob is sometimes derived from a Hebrew word meaning the "heel."

told to make a serpent of brass and elevate it on a pole, and "it came to pass that if a serpent had bitten any man, when he beheld the serpent of brass, he lived." Num. xxi, 9.

There was the rod of Moses which turned into a serpent and the rod of the Egyptian Taht, the caduceus twined about with two serpents. The army of Moses was saved by his using the Ibises.[1] He is said to have invented baskets, made like Arks, of sedge, which he filled with Ibises (the Ibis is the Stork), which he let loose when he came to the land which bred the serpents which were destroyed. Taht wears the Ibis on his head.

Both the Brazen and Fiery Serpents were Saraphs, the "burning fiery" messengers, or the Serpent Gods, the Nagas of India. The Brazen Serpent was the divine healer. In the symbolical meaning of Brazen is found the feminine principle, and in that of Fiery the masculine. The "burning fiery" messenger and the brazen fiery serpent signified Cosmic Creation.[2] A word in Hebrew for Serpent is Nachash, which is a term for brass, and a title of the Serpent is "Brass of Earth," which tallies with the Hebrew Nachusta, Nachus meaning brass, and ta is in Egyptian a word for earth. Brass was a metal that symbolised the nether world, the mother earth, matrix of creation, where life was given. The Serpent guarding the sacred tree that held the treasures of knowledge was the Serpent of Wisdom offering the fruit for the enlightenment of mankind, wherefore the Gnostics were continually calling upon the Serpent for his services to mankind. The Gnostics had full knowledge of the Tree of Good and Evil, and to what heights of wisdom man could be lifted, and what knowledge he could

---

[1]Josephus.

[2]The *creative* God emerges from the egg that issues from the mouth of Kneph—as a winged serpent—because the Serpent is the symbol of the All-Wisdom. With the Hebrews he is glyphed by the 'flying or fiery serpents' of the Wilderness and Moses, and with the Alexandrian mystics he becomes the Ophio-Christos, the Logos of the Gnostics."—Blavatsky, H. P.—The Secret Doctrine, Vol. i, p. 364.

attain by the eating of its fruit. The Gnostics knew that the Tree and the Serpent were divine images.

By calling their Serpent the evil one, Hebrews and Persians in their later theology perverted and degraded the Starry Intelligences of heaven. "The Archaic Snake, as a malignant Deity, a fiend of Cosmic proportions, is but the creation of theological fancy."[1] Perhaps much of the demoralization of the present time may be due to listening to the doctrine of the theological Serpent, or Satan, created for the credulity of our present humanity. It seems incredible that this symbol has been so deeply misconstrued in Bible interpretation, when it meant to ancient peoples, from whom we derived our Bible, nothing less than a symbol of Eternity, Wisdom, God. Some one has said that perhaps, after all, Hezekiah was justified in ordering all the old symbols broken into pieces, when we consider the evil imaged concerning them. The symbols of Egg and Serpent have been handed down since the time of Moses, who was versed in the Serpent Wisdom, but latterly were purposely misrepresented.

It is unfortunate that so much of the beauty and reverence once a part of religion has been destroyed, by the intrusion of the vicarious atonement and the forgiveness of sins. Some one has said that we have become manufacturers of misery, and to this we can add the saying of Hermes that "The wickedness of the soul is in its ignorance." H. P. Blavatsky has most truly said of today, "All is doubt, negation, iconoclasm and brutal indifference in our age of 'isms' and no religion, every idol seems to be broken but that of the Golden Calf."

The mythical dragon or serpent has been interpreted variously. In the beginning there was the genitrix Typhon,[2]

---

[1] Blavatsky, H. P.

[2] The constellation Hydra was called the serpent of the south, and was followed by the serpent Hapu of the four corners or cardinal points of the world from which were developed the twenty-eight mansions of the lunar Zodiac, that existed prior to the solar Zodiac of twelve signs. From the one

whose son Sut or Sevekh was typified by the crocodile when he signified the number seven, because of his superior intelligence the crocodile became synonymous with the soul.   This Star-god crocodile was changed into the Sun-god Sebek-Ra and converted into the Lamb.   This is the same lamb that is found in the Book of Revelation, which "had two horns like a lamb, and . . . spake as a dragon."   Hor Apollo tells us that "the crocodile lays sixty eggs and is sixty days hatching them, and lives sixty years."   Sixty is the measure the Egyptian astronomers were supposed to have used in their first operations.   Sut, Sevekh or Sebek in planetary type is Saturn, and under this type Saturn in Chaldee is Satur, i. e., Stur.   Its numerical value is 666.   The Greek S, as well as the Coptic, has the same numerical value as the 6, while S is the symbol of the serpent.   Gerald Massey in his Natural Genesis gives very interesting information as to the value of the 666 and SSS and says that old Sut became identified with 666 number of the Beast.   Sut, Saturn or Satur end in another double Christian continuation, for he became canonized as the "Saint Satur," known as a martyr, in the Roman Calendar, whose festival occurs on the 29th of March.   Theological martyrdom of the heavenly constellations is unique.   If theology is the final phase of mythology, it has a strange way of interpreting ancient expression in modern thought.   In one of the Hibbard Lectures, Renouf, who was a Roman Catholic, exclaims, evidently with fervor, "Mythology is the disease which springs up at a peculiar stage of human development."   Possibly he may have meant its modern interpretation which has converted the Most High God into Satan, the Devil, and who in the end was reconverted into a Saint.

The Dragon of the Deep, as Darkness, was ever known as

------

came the many depicted in the planespheres, and when the first was referred to, whether as the serpent, or as the mother, or as Typhon of the abyss who emenated from chaos, she is finally identifiable as the Virgin of the Zodiacal sign Virgo who was the original of our Eve, the serpent woman of mystery and eternity.

"The Adversary of the Light." It is the same old Serpent of whom "Theology has made the primal shadow substantial and *permanent in the mental sphere; and from the darkness of the beginning it has abstracted the Devil in the end.*"

Mosseau says that "The Christians were the first to make the existence of Satan a dogma of the Church, arch enemy of God and Prince of Darkness, Spiritualism and Magic the twin brothers. Rome sends her preachers and advocates to rescue these from the 'Bottomless Pit'." And Father Ventura suggests that "To demonstrate the existence of Satan is to re-establish one of the fundamental dogmas of the Christian Church, which serves as a basis for Christianity, and without which, Satan would be but a name."

The Apophis or Akhekh Serpent of the Egyptians was a wicked monster of the deep, symbolized as the crooked serpent, with sword blades set all around it, typical of destruction, and also as a door-keeper to the gate of death. It is depicted on a sarcophagus of Meneptah in the valley of death. It suggests Job's crooked Serpent "Have the gates of death been opened unto thee? Or hast thou seen the doors of the shadow of death?" Job xxxviii, 17. In Isaiah 1, xxvii, both the crooked and the piercing serpent are mentioned, when "in that day the Lord with his sore and great and strong sword shall punish Leviathan, the piercing serpent, even Leviathan that crooked serpent; and he shall slay the dragon that *is* in the sea." The crooked and piercing serpent of Hebrew Mythology is the Egyptian Bariak. Pra, Egyptian, and Bra, Hebrew, mean to manifest, to eminate, Akh in Egyptian means Fire. Bariak signifies a "Fulminator of Fire."

In Egyptian Tan means division, cutting in two, to divide, to turn away, a separator, and the Serpent covered with sword blades was the piercing, severing Serpent. This was Job's monster of mythology, the Serpent of night, representing powers of darkness and death, which armed with piercing

---

[1]Massey, Gerald.

blades severs the light of life in the "bend of the great void" where it lurked. "The lunar eclipses are *Tennu*. They cut off the light and occur at the dividing place."

The Akhekh Gryphon is a Dragon with wings, wings and feathers were types of Fire. The winged dragon was pre-figured by Winged Lightning or the Bird of Thunder. One form of the Egyptian Akhekh is a Gryphon having the winged body of a beast, the tail of a serpent and head of a peacock. This is the Winged Dragon, which became the mythical Cockatrice, mentioned several times in the Old Testament. "A picture of the Temptation of Christ, from a French miniature of the twelfth century, shows Satan as a survival of the Akhekh Gryphon, with the head of a Cockatoo instead of the Peacock, and a serpent for his tail."[1] The Peacock and its feathers are thought to bring misfortune even in our day.

There were three types of Serpent. The dark Serpent was lightning, a physical evil in nature and the enemy of man. The Agathodaemon or good Serpent was a type of Time, renewal, eternal life, immortality. And the third Serpent has been called the Devil, or evil on the physical plane. This was Sut, the first son of heaven who once upon a time took care of all souls and their rebirth, but who later became the personal Satan of Theology, the Akhekh, or the Aphophis, monster of Darkness.

"Both two and four-winged snakes are depicted among Egyptian sculptures, and are considered by Mr. Cooper to be emblematic of deities, and to signify that the four corners of the earth are embraced and sheltered by the supreme Providence."[2] They gave the name Apta to a Serpent bearing four mystic signs which denoted the four corners or ends of the world. There was also a Serpent called Hapu which had four heads, symbolizing four secret places or corners. Coatepautli, the Snake-Circuit, was the name

---

[1]Didron, Fig. 70.
[2]Gould, G.—Mythical Monsters, p. 185.

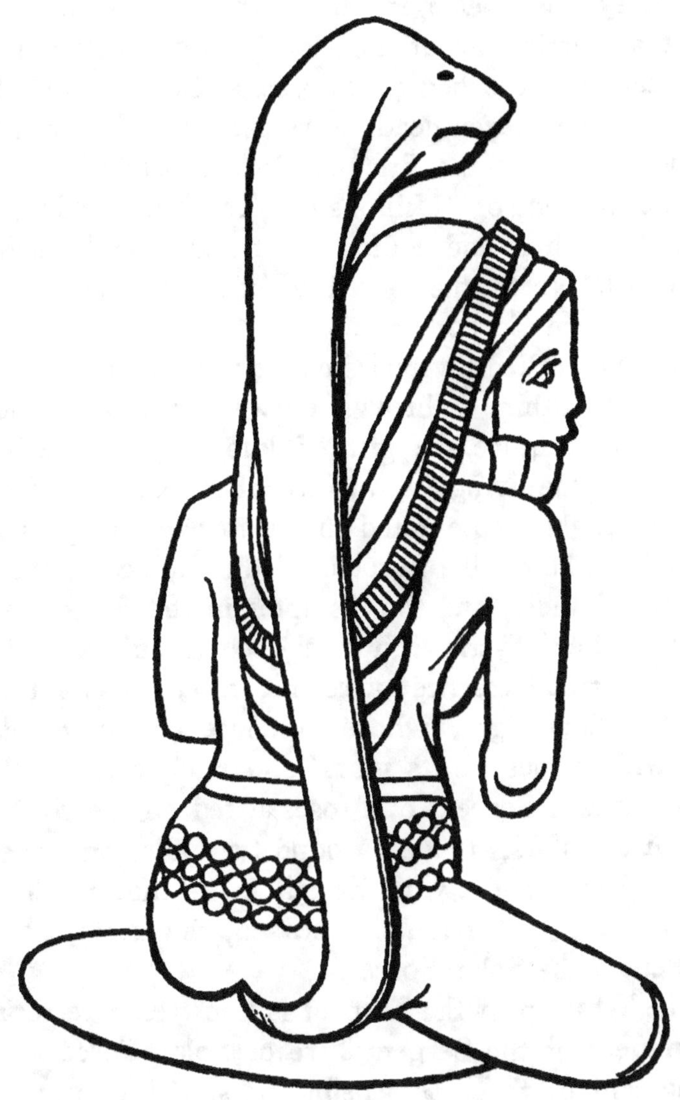

THE MYSTICAL SERPENT

The Naga (serpent) found in Hindu sculpture is here represented in its most hidden and mystical meaning as an emblem of the mystery of the mysteries. Its hooded crest towering above and overlooking the human body is visibly displayed as coming from the human body. Sometimes the serpent is portrayed with five, nine, and ten heads, all being typical of periodicity.

of the great Temple of Mexico, which was built of stone in the shape of Serpents tied together. The Mexicans represented the four cardinal points by putting four twisted knots in the serpent forming the circumference. Endless are the serpent symbols belonging to the mighty Serpent constellation that circled about the Pole. More than one arcane significance is attached to the primal Serpent and its Seven Heads. "The seven heads were the seven Logoi, reflections of the Logos, as the first manifested Light." For Draco was the Serpent of "Millions of Years" in the High Hill of Heaven, circling and coiling itself about, and enclosing the Hill of the North, the sacred Mount Meru, later discovered as the Biblical Garden of Eden.

All the so-called mysteries convey knowledge of the spirit, the Christ within. Through outward manifestation of the Christ, we acquire the gift of knowing and realizing the mystery of the living Astral Fire of the earth, and dual currents of Light, represented in all ancient theogonies by the Serpent. The double Serpent of the Caduceus, the Winged Dragon of India, and the Tempter in the Book of Genesis, in whom the "Mystics intuitively see an animal emblem and a high spiritual essence; a cosmic force super-intelligent, a 'Great Fallen Light,' whose influence circumambulates the globe with respect to its moral and intellectual COILS."[1]

The Brazen Serpent of Moses lifted on the rod, the Serpent Girdle of Isis twined around two poles on ancient monuments, the Serpent with its tail in its mouth, the Serpent as Lightning that fell from heaven, the Fiery Serpent, all represented the Solar Force.

"The Wisdom of the Serpent is knowledge resulting from government of the Serpent Fire or Solar Force. . . . The unfoldment of the supersensible or spiritual nature of man is but the progressive manifestation in him of the vital energy derived from the Sun, and its Divine Source, known throughout the ages as the Solar Force or Serpent, and

---

[1]Blavatsky, H. P.

proceeding from the Creator of the Sun and Worlds, the Great Architect of the Universe. 'By His spirit He hath garnished the heavens; His hand hath formed the crooked serpent. Lo, these are parts of His ways; but how little a portion is heard of Him? But the thunder of His Power who can understand"? Job xxvi, 13, 14. *The Solar Force is the Serpent in the ancient symbol of the egg and the serpent."*[1]

"I beheld Satan as Lightning fall from Heaven." Luke x, 18. This is the fiery Serpent or Solar Force which arouses man's brain centers.

Sun and Fire were synonymous. Anent the First Cause, the Word SUS, or Sun, the Sun behind the Sun, was once anciently written *SUƧ* . The likeness between this and the serpent Sun of the Egyptians can be seen. The U is feminine and the word represents the matrix of the Serpent Fire, macrocosmic and microcosmic, i. e., Super-solar and mundane. The letter reversed is a symbol of the Serpent Force or Super-solar manifestation. SUS denotes involution and evolution, the descent of the Serpent Force into matter and the return upward through evolution. The Serpent Solar Disk is often seen on Egyptian monuments *SOƧ* (the S reversed) the Sun, with the Serpent on either side. The word written *SUƧ* shows the Serpent evolving through the Great Mother into the counterpuntal apposition of the Super-solar system. Letters of the ancient alphabet were keys unlocking the originating causation in manifestation of all things.

The S.S. or Z.Z. symbolically used, are interchangeable. Often the "S.S. on sigils and talismans are suggestive of serpentine evil influence and denote a sign of *black* magic upon others, the double S.S. are found on the sacramental cups of the Church and mean the presence of the Holy Ghost, or pure wisdom."[2]

---

[1] Comte de Gabalis, Dudley Edition, p. 42.
[2] Blavatsky, H. P.—Isis Unveiled, Vol. ii, p. 449.

Knowledge of the manifestation of the Solar Force has been sacredly guarded in all ages. This force when conquered by man in his lower nature leads to the highest spiritual development. In the Caduceus of Hermes, as in the Rod in Revelation, the Serpents are entwined, representing the spirally moving creative energy in man as well as in the Universe. This energy is the positive and the negative polarization of all life, and was the true Tree of Life, whose trunk was the Rod. The Serpent or Rod was reverenced by all the peoples of antiquity; the Christians alone forgot even the applied wisdom and prudence of the serpent of which Jesus said, "Be ye wise as the serpent and harmless as the dove."

Through research one comes upon a revelation of the importance of this Force. In the ancient mysteries mastery of the Serpent Force was the means of unveiling the secrets of the unseen world. The Gnostics had two Serpents representing good and evil forces. One was known as the Serpent of the Dust; the other was the Serpent of Divine Wisdom, the Solar Ray. The Solar Ray was known in the Celestial Hierarchy as Serapis (Serpent), an angel of the highest order. Many strange and horrifying instances are given of the endeavors to create clairvoyant vision through the use of the Serpent of the Dust.

The Serpent Wisdom had its primordial home in Africa, where the Gnostic Christians paid it highest honors. The Creative Force of the Kabala makes "sketches and spiral lines in the shape of the Serpent," and the Uraeus worn on the forehead by the Egyptian Kings is the Serpent Emblem of this Cosmic Fire.

The beguiling in the Garden of Eden[1] is a profound allegory concerning the Serpent Force in its dual aspect. The

---

[1]The zoological serpent that crawled on the earth and bit the dust likewise was created long before Adam and Eve and before there was the so-called "original sin," but Eden finally evolved as a real garden of Paradise, and the serpent a real one, and because he was said to tempt Eve was made to crawl on its belly and bite the dust forevermore, or so it is related in a later period.

Tree of Life represented the everlasting wisdom of the Most High, wherein the Serpent is at home, while the apple represented the sex knowledge that tempted Eve, and shut her off from spiritual development, which is the Fruit of the Tree of Life. The Serpent Fire to the pure in heart brings wisdom, but to the sensualist a descent into the darkness of matter. Prophets, Seers, Wise Men all have mastered the Serpent Fire and eaten of the Fruit of the Tree of Life. The Garden, the Tree, the Serpent, the Great Mother—Eve as we call her, all belong to the mythology of the heavens, and are found without trace of evil in the monuments of Egypt. All the great religions of the world were under the influence of the heavens, and our own Christian belief and dogma are intimately related to them. The same significance can be found in all, the same meaning which is told over and over again in birth and rebirth, generation and regeneration, in both stars and man. We follow, we shall always follow the course of the Stars, for "as it is in the heaven so shall it be on earth." Irenaeus frankly admits the Gnostics have truly said that all the supernatural transactions given in the Gospels "were counterparts of what took place above."

It is well to keep in mind that a Serpent was an emblem of Christ, and also to reflect on the words of Pococke: "Myths are now proved to be fable, *just in proportion as we misunderstand them; truths, in proportion as they were once understood.*"—Italics mine.

"For the dragon (the Constellation Draco, or the Serpent) while sacred and to be worshipped, has within himself something still more of the divine nature of which it is better to remain in ignorance."[1]

-----

[1] Homer.

INDEX

VOLUME II

ASTROLOGY

The word Astrology is a compound of the Greek $\varLambda O \varUpsilon O \varSigma$ (Logos) i. e., the Light made manifest through the Sun and Earth into material inversion, and ascending through Earth and Sun to its Serpent Source. The "Astro" in Astrology stands for Star or Stars. Astrology may be said to be the science of the Word or Primal Cause in its manifestation to man through stellar influence, hence Astrology's sacred priority among the sciences of the ancient world. Astrology is the Mirific Word operative through stellar force.

CONTENTS

Book Two

"As it is in the Heavens so will it be on Earth"

ILLUSTRATIONS

Book Two

ZODIAC FROM THE CENTRE OF THE CEILING OF THE TEMPLE
OF DENDERAH

The temple was dedicated to Hathor the Virgin Mother. This
Zodiac, properly called a Planisphere manifests intimate connection
with the path (celestial) taken by the departed, "the holy dead in
their entrance into light. . . . The mystical symbols representing the
starry groups, image forth the supernal powers and spirits, which
the holy departed, according to the creed of the Egyptians, encountered
in his progress through the heights as he mounted from the plane of
earth to the burning throne of Ra . . . girt by the Zodiac like
an azure belt of gleaming gems." From "The Book of the Master,"
by Marsham Adams.

xi

CHAPTER I

TRANSCENDENT FORCES

In the traceries of tradition we find that man, when he emerged from his primitive state, was inspired by the awakening of his higher consciousness and by the call of the stars. He absorbed knowledge from their Book of Revelation and mystery, or the Book of God. He gradually came to realize how intimately he was related to the celestial sphere, as a living link between heaven and earth, and that the rising and setting of the stars not only affected him, but created the seasons of the year and many mysteries needing interpretation. As far back as we can trace the mind of man, his knowledge growing out of his meditation on the stars and the symbols and signs of the immutable laws of heaven, have remained fixed as they have reached us today. Upon them the science of Astrology was founded, and though so sadly misconstrued by the ignorant, it will be lifted from darkness and will again take its place in the Light of the incoming Era. The mathematical foundation of this science of the stars, is so solidly based on a general theory of Nature from which it is inseparable, that it will survive forever, for "It is in the imperishable rock of Numbers that the fadeless footprint of Astral science was first set, like the mighty seal of an eternal compact made between Urania and the Law."[1]

It is the wisdom of the Supreme that guides the stars. Sympathy and attraction between man and the stars operate through the astral. Astrology is not a combination of myth and symbol for the credulous to quibble over or the modern priesthood to deny. Every sign, every symbol, is a divine

---

[1] Sepharial.

bond or union with a Divine Truth.   There is no uncertainty in this; man's intellect and intuition pierce the past and prove the immortality of tradition and its symbols.

The earliest books of our Bible are astrological, and are filled with priceless ancient wisdom told in myth, fable, and allegory.   Events of every description and kind, whether historical or otherwise, were anciently recorded.   It was a method of learning and assimilating great truths, which were true prehistoric realities.   Through misinterpretation, however, the modern world has been denied many of these truths embodied in myths, but in the coming days of dissemination, these are to be freed from their numerous false renderings, many of which have been deliberately conceived during the past two thousand years.   Astrology has been handed down to us in its scientific aspect, unaltered, from a time so far in the past as to be almost beyond human reckoning.   It was the mother and precursor of Astronomy; it was once a power sublime, built on the mystic connection between the stars and mankind, including the great secret of initiation and the occult mysteries.   "Modern wisdom is satisfied with Astronomical computations and prophecies based on unerring mathematical laws.   Ancient Wisdom added to the cold shell of astronomy the vivifying elements of its Soul and Spirit, *Astrology*."[1]

When we penetrate the mists of the past, we find Astrology as a Wisdom Religion, the teachers of which were believed to have descended from the planet Venus, under the direction of those who were known in this ancient religion as "Lords of the Flame."   This seems somewhat misty or cloud-wrapped, but those who love the mythical or mystic and are willing to search and research, until the great wonders of heaven and earth unfold to them in marvelous and almost inconceivable splendor, will find many truths becoming manifest through the little rifts in the veil of materialism that let down the Light.   The planet Venus was

---

[1]Blavatsky, H. P.—The Secret Doctrine; Vol. i, p. 645.

named after the Great Mother Typhon, Mother-Goddess of the Great Bear, which mythically represented the one, original and initial birthplace in heaven of all motion, time and creation, with many copies to be found below on earth.

In the beginning of each new cycle of human evolution, according to the need of the age, a quickening or spiritual rebirth occurs, coincident with and acting through the prominence of the Zodiacal Cross which is evident at this time. This has been proven from the beginning, when humanity was in its childhood. Astrology is the basis of all things. Originally it was pure religion, the heart itself of religion. Subsequently a period was ushered in when it became a philosophy, and finally a science. The conflict between science and religion at that time undoubtedly had much to do with the lowering of its high standing. Through astronomy a materialistic form of astrology was evolved, yet as a science Astrology preceded and was known as the soul of Astronomy.

A modern theological idea was quite freely circulated in ages past that Satan, or the Devil (Saturn in planetary form) is responsible for the wickedness of the world, and that he has a host of evil spirits with him to do his bidding. From this materialistic view of the devil the idea is adduced that he is to be chained for a thousand years before being let loose again.[1] The man-made adversary is a remarkable creation of human thought, and one wonders what the ancient peoples would think of this degradation of one of their most spiritual and powerful symbols, not only of Wisdom but of Justice. Yet this idea has come in spite of the knowledge that God made all things good. It belongs to the age of illusion from which we shall be freed.

---

[1] In Egypt Satan is actually found chained to a cross. The cross was used by the Egyptians as a talisman for protection and as a symbol of saving power. As the Apophis, "Monster of Darkness," he is the enemy of Ra, the Sun. "The Apophis is overthrown, their cords bind the South, the North, the East and the West, their cords are on him." These are the four points of the cardinal cross, and symbolical of the above. represent the evil passions which the Sun destroys.

Ancient Astrology taught concerning ministering angels who would influence the world for what we have termed good and evil, in accordance with the duality of all created things. Satan (the planet Saturn) has been greatly misinterpreted and very much maligned. His influence as a planet is of great power when in aspect, being the planet of duty and pure justice, and though he may take us through paths of pain and suffering, it is the road which leads to regeneration and which frees from material bonds. Saturn, it should be remembered, was the Lord God of Sabaoth of the Jews, their tribal God. When Saturn is adversely aspected in the heavens it shows that some serious lesson must be learned on earth. This is the part he has played in "The martyrdom of Matter, implying that the general break-up of material conditions, as well as the sacrifice of life, was in reality liberating powerful spiritual forces hitherto pent up in matter."[1]

Every thousand years for a short period of time Saturn joins the planet Neptune in the Zodiacal sign of Leo. Leo represents the element of Fire. Saturn is known as the Purifier, and while in this fiery element is sure to regenerate all who come under his administration of Justice. On August 1, 1917, the Super-Lunar planet Neptune was conjoined with Saturn. Neptune gives the finest vibration of all our sacred planets, being farthest from the earth, and when posited in the sign Leo bestows the purest love the heart can give. These two powerful planets were polarized by the Super-Solar planet Uranus in the opposite sign Aquarius, the sign of our incoming Era, bringing about co-operation between them of tremendous force and importance. Uranus is the planet that destroys completely but never a building soul or condition, liberating from habits that have become crystallized and have ceased to serve. The aspect between Saturn and Uranus was completed in 1918. On August 1, 1917, when Saturn was conjoined with Neptune,

---

[1]Bond, Frederick Bligh—The Hill of Vision, p. 40.

Uranus was at 22 degrees in Aquarius, the opposite sign in the Zodiac. Saturn reached the exact opposition of Uranus in October, 1918. Another thousand years must pass before Saturn can again form these unusual connections with Neptune and Uranus, causing the "chaining of Satan for a thousand years."

The transit of Uranus through a sign covers a period of seven years. He entered the sign of Aquarius in 1914. In all Bible history seven years of famine, catastrophe, epidemics, wars, plagues, etc., preceded the coming of a new Era. Cyclic law is inevitable, it being the instrument, as it were, of spiritual activity impelling man onward and forward. "There will be signs in sun, moon and stars; and on earth anguish among the nations in their bewilderment at the roaring of the sea and its billows, while men's hearts are fainting for fear, and for anxious expectation of what is coming on the world. FOR THE FORCES WHICH CONTROL THE HEAVENS WILL BE DISORDERED AND DISTURBED. Isaiah xxxiv, 4. . . . But when all this is beginning to take place, grieve no longer. Lift up your heads, because your deliverance is drawing near."[1]

Astrology is as incapable of error as Astronomy. When failure through its interpretation comes, it is proof that the interpreter is not infallible, as he often fails to realize that he is dealing with a world of transcendent spirit beyond our visible world of matter.

Recently an astrologer stated that an opposition of the planets always means unmitigated evil. This is untrue. The stars impart to us no more than we are able to assimilate. Signs and planets in themselves are not evil, nor are their vibrations, therefore how can there be evil from them in the horoscopes? The opposition and squares formed by the planets are often mistakenly thought of as evil, and they are most forceful in their application. They give and

---

[1] Weymouth, R. F.—The New Testament in Modern Speech; Luke xxi, 25, 26, 28.

should give strength to overcome whatever experience they disclose, although weaker natures, or those lacking in character, which would be revealed in their horoscopes, would take the easy road downward instead of rising to the heights made possible.

It should never for a moment be forgotten that Astrology is and should be sublime in its character, and it is out of the strength indicated that the sweetness and beauty of life are given. It is in these so-called, and wrongly called, "evil" aspects that we find the stepping-stones leading us upward and onward, while those which are called benefic, though. they suggest an easier path into pleasures and in places where there are no hills to climb, do not give the glory that comes through victory in trial and combat; or the rugged beauty and joy of reaching the mountain top, where the influence of pure spirit can act, enveloping us in its harmony and clear vision—that harmony which is Love, God. Aspects, therefore, whether so-called evil or so-called benefic, mean always cooperation between·the forces.

In all manifestations of life there is always the interaction of the two opposite poles, the two unchanging governing forces, the negative and the positive, and whether of high spiritual vibration or of lower and more material voltage these forces control everything visible or invisible in the Universe. Each man must meet his crossroads and decide which way life will lead. Interest in one's personal life and in that of the world should be very great today, as we enter upon a new Highway, a new Cycle, one of the critical periods in the evolution of the world. This is a fact known to all astronomers, but they seemingly are not concerned with the manifestations that will take place upon the earth induced by the changing positions of the heavenly bodies.

Every individual is said to be born under the direct influence of one of the planets, and his chief characteristics are invariably under the guidance of the constellation or planet

under which he was born. One can never escape his ruling
destiny, but the two paths are always open according to
desire, one towards the higher spiritual development and into
a closer touch with the Infinite, the other leading to misery
and the downward path. These are the two conditions, spiritual and material, that should be given a balanced judgment
in the interpretation of the horoscope, and the astrologer
who gives judgment should be well on the upward path.[1]

The changing of the Poles is always of very great importance. The pole of a country is its latitude. "As we recede
from the equator to the poles, the Pole Star, which when at
the equator we observe on the horizon, gradually rises in
the heavens until at the pole it would be at the zenith—its
angular distance above the horizon being equal to the geographical latitude of the place from which it is viewed.
This is called the 'elevation of the pole,' or polar elevation,
or more briefly the 'pole of the ascendant'."[2]

At the present time the pole of the ecliptic is a little over
one degree from the pole. It will reach the exact degree of
the pole about the year 2000. Our earth has been passing
the celestial pole, which means a changing of polarity, as earth
now passes out of the sign Pisces that has represented the last
great cycle of two thousand one hundred and sixty years,
and makes its way into the sign of Aquarius, introducing our
new Era. It takes the pole of the equator 25,920 years to
travel around the pole of the ecliptic, and we know that this
circle of the ecliptic is divided into the twelve Zodiacal signs,
and that the equinoctial points will occupy each sign 2,160
years. Each of these signs measures thirty degrees, or one-
twelfth of the circle. The equinoctial points will remain in
each degree seventy-two years.

---

[1]The judicial or predictive side of Astrology should be excluded entirely if
one is to reach a purer, a more rarefied existence through its interpretation.
Today it seems to be chiefly judicial, and used as a means of getting money, and
so the sacred science of the past has been betrayed and bedraggled in its use
today, for few are given understanding of the higher law and its spiritual side.

[2]Leo, Alan—Astrology for All, Part ii.

Astrologers all know that when these cycles of 2,160 years are ushered in, a new manifestation of Light occurs. At such a time everything undergoes change. It brings about a new demonstration of spirit, a new moulding, as it were, of spiritual forces that flow through the ether of space, piercing the darkness and creating powerful struggles with the materialism of the times.

In our world history, which we can consider as a horoscope, three of these great periods, as well as many minor ones, due to the motion of the earth and its relation to the cross or angle of the earth with the heaven, have taken place. In horoscopical charts these crosses or angles are called Cardinal, Fixed and Common. They affect the individual as well as the world, for we are all of the same substance as the stars, all members of one family. It is the false idea of separateness held by the majority of the world today that has brought sorrow and agony great enough to make the angels weep.

The cardinal points are the north, east, south and west points of the circle of heaven, and these are similarly placed at the angles of the circle of the horoscope. The cardinal signs of the Zodiac are the constellations—Aries, Cancer, Libra, and Capricorn, and when these form a cross or are on the angles of the horoscope, they bring critical times affecting the whole world, varied experiences of all kinds, wars and rumors of war, and out-rushing energies hard to control. Self-expression comes to the fore, good and bad conditions become public, things are outward in expression, events are inevitable.

The fixed signs are Taurus, Leo, Scorpio and Aquarius, and when these are in evidence at the angles, long periods of peace are ushered in, there is a dislike for changes, more conservatism and stubbornness, monarchs arise, governments are newly formed, statesmen appear, organizers and merchants are more numerous.

With the Mutable or Common signs, which are Gemini,

Virgo, Sagittarius, and Pisces, on the angles, there is less action than with the cardinal signs, impulses are more religious, there is a greater intellectualism, with many teachers ready to help in a spiritual awakening that arises, and conditions are dualistic. There is always more thought and less action. A cardinal cross has been in evidence in our present period, when all the latent energies and emotions and pent-up feelings of the world are rioting, their bonds broken by the on-rushing forces of a new world crisis, bringing out the opposition and the squares that have been formed, sometimes as discords, from the cross from which we are emerging. Eventually this cross will fulfil its message of pronounced benefits, unless its influence is held too long in abeyance by the hate, jealousy and miserly greed which the rich and the masses allow to take possession of their hearts, instead of accepting the great love, so patiently awaited, which the spirit of our incoming brotherhood will make manifest. Old orders are slow in their passing, great periods converge slowly, but the age of reconstruction is due, and though it may be slow in coming, it cannot fail to arrive. Unselfishness and compassion cannot be entirely smothered by the forces of evil, for the Light in places has already penetrated the atmosphere of earth, and from out of chaos harmony will eventually come.

A magnetic influence is said to be conveyed by the stars, and the planets to every living creature, animal, plant, or mineral belonging to our world. Planets belonging to our solar system are regulated within the limit of their orbits by the sun, but the sun consists of a reflected magnetic influence from other solar systems. The ancients never looked upon the sun as the cause of light and heat, but considered it the vehicle for these, or that through which they passed on the way to earth. The Egyptians expressed their idea concerning this as "The eye of Osiris, which is the mind and divine intellect of the concealed." Light is the first demonstration of the Infinite, "The First Begotten" creator of our planets and of our worlds. It should be noted that the ancient astronomers were Adepts, who had studied and held sacred their knowledge of the stars. The Parent Sun of all humanity was the Central Spiritual Sun, the Sun behind the Sun.[1] The term, Sun's Sons referred not only to the planets but to all heavenly bodies generally. The obeisance given by the primitive people to their Gods was offered to some supreme condition, not to God Himself. The Sun was the reflector of the Spiritual Sun, which they called "The Eye of the World,' our planetary world. You will often see it depicted as drawn by seven horses, or by one horse with seven heads, the former referring to seven planets, and the latter to their common origin, Fire." It was the Gnostics who taught us the planetary origin of the soul and its powers, and that every soul as it journeyed toward earth had to pass through the regions of the planets, every one being of the substance of Divine Light, and that the spirit (angel) of the star guiding each new birth of the soul was of his own essence. Man is the vehicle of soul, but does not realize it, and unless he becomes receptive to higher spiritual vibrations, may always remain in ignorance of this fact.

From an occult standpoint every one has his individual star for all eternity, which is a spark from the Infinite, our Oneness with God. It is the Christ within, our birthright, and our star through all cycles of manifestations or incarnations representing our individuality. We are also under our Astrological star applying chiefly to our Personality, and to the guidance of a planetary angel[2] or spirit that works through the planet whose vibrations intimately belong to us, and operate through the environment in which we express

---

[1]Beside the Central Sun, there is the teaching concerning a Polar Sun, said to connect the Central Sun with the equatorial planes belonging to our visible Sun.

[2]"Planetary spirits are the informing spirits of the stars in general of the planets in particular." They are not spheres in heaven shining for no purpose, but convey powerful influences in their connection with human beings, ruling over his life and destiny.

ourselves during any given life. Our characters are bestowed by our planet, our spiritual powers by the angel of the planet.

Stars, humanity, and these spirits are indissolubly bound together. If it is true that, according to an old legend, a knowledge of astrology was given by a higher race of beings, the more we study, pause, and consider, the more we shall find it the profoundest science ever given to man, and a pure, simple, and divine law. "Every Star in the great Universe is a Temple of a god, and the gods themselves, the Temple of the Great Unknown God." The exoteric theologies are undergoing a new spiritual baptism, old creeds and dogmas which were instituted by priestcraft in the early centuries of more modern times will become extinct. Our rising generation is gradually harking back to the ancient undefiled teachings containing the messages of the stars, which are wonderful today, when denuded of the blind superstition and ignorance which have beclouded them. There is one great Universal Law, which is God's, and the Book of God is written in the Heavens. The old love of power and of gold taught a false theology, which has.produced patched-up creeds and dogmas from which in our ignorance we suffer. Today the worship of the Golden Calf by the rich and of the Idol with its feet of clay by the masses deflect us from the wealth of heaven.

The study of eclipses was most profound in olden times when sacred temples were erected for their observation. A solar eclipse of unusual and deep import took place on December 3, 1899, when a satellitium, that is, a group of planets, six in number, was stationed in the double Zodiacal sign Sagittarius, with another just entering its cusp and one leaving, while the super-luminary Neptune, the most spiritual and mystic of all the planets of our solar system, was directly overhead, posited in the opposite double sign Gemini, suggesting a radiant downpouring of Supernal Light into what might be termed a reflection of the double warp and woof of life, represented by the planets; predicting a critical period of change in human as well as cosmic conditions pertaining to spiritual and universal causes.   Neptune will be benefically aspected, by every planet and will aspect every remaining planet in turn, the last of these occurring during the latter part of 1928-9, when it will aspect the planet Venus.   Neptune symbolizes divine love; Venus *is* love, the creator of beauty and harmony, never the degraded Venus of sex, so irreverently misapplied today.   We are told that the humanity inhabiting Venus is of a far higher order than that to which we have evolved on our Earth today, so this connection with Neptune will bestow upon our Earth a super-fineness and a delicacy of expression.   This sign Sagittarius in its double aspect is both material and spiritual in its application to our humanity, indicating in this world chart that physical man will have the opportunity of yielding to his higher impulses, and of redeeming himself from the desires of his lower nature, through the crucifixion of the animal passions.   This subtle Neptunian force, in its cooperation with Venus, because of its very fineness, will penetrate and inter-penetrate until it creates a world of more enduring light and harmony.

Neptune is in the double, positive, common sign Gemini, whose ruling planet is Mercury, the Heavenly Messenger, who is also ruler of the negative, common sign Virgo, which is rising on the Ascendant, the sensitive Eastern point of the chart, at this time.   Virgo, the Virgin, is the cosmic mother of the Zodiac, and from most ancient days has been depicted holding a child in her arms, typical of the advent of a new Era, and from this has become the signature of the Immaculate Conception.   The Child is the symbol of the new humanity which the Mother lifts up to the Light.   In old mythical or astronomical charts of the heavens she is seen holding a sprig of wheat in her hand.   Wheat grows in every country in the world, and has never, like other fruits or cereals, been discovered in a wild state.   It has defied every effort of scientists or botanists to trace it to its origin, indicating that it was originally not a product of the earth. The Virgin Mother of the celestial heavens holds in her hand wheat, symbol of Divine Food which is within the reach of all. This solar eclipse fell very close to the degree where the earth's orbit, the ecliptic, crosses the Equator, creating two of the most sensitive points of the Zodiac.[1]

The prophecy of Jesus foretelling the end of an age by the darkening of the sun and the moon or the overshadowing of the sun, is manifest in the heavens. Neptune on the material side, brings about chaos, a breaking up of physical conditions, and by its opposition to all the planets of this chart of December 3, 1899, will finally force a change through the disintegration of opposing forces which must eventually bring about peace. And what was conceived in this configuration was brought to birth in the solar eclipse of 1910, which is closely allied to our incoming Era. The planets in this new chart form a Cardinal Cross, at the foot of which, and diametrically across from its position in the previous chart, is Neptune. The glyph of Neptune is a semicircle representing a cup, through which passes a vertical line symbolical of the spiritual life pouring through. It terminates in a cross, which symbolizes spiritualized matter. The sun, the moon, and the super-luminary Uranus are directly above, pouring down their combined spiritual forces into this cup, three lines of which point upward, tipped with arrow-like heads, symbols of Light ascending, and signifying a mingling of Divine Will and Divine Love.[2]

---

[1]"At the time of this conjunction of the luminaries, they were in conjunction with the fixed star Antares, which is diametrically opposite Aldabaran. These two stars mark the positions where the earth's orbit, the ecliptic, crosses the sun's equator. The orbits of most of the planets cross the sun's equator at or near these two points, probably sensitive points in the Zodiac. They are about 10 Gemini and 10 Sagittarius."—Leo, Alan.

[2]"Uranus is the higher octave of the Sun—True Individuality. Neptune is the higher octave of the Moon—True Personality. Love and Imagination—Passion and Purity Out of these the Child."—Leo, Alan.

At one end of the horizontal line of this cross Saturn is conjoined with Mars, and these two planets are polarized by Jupiter at the other end. These positions suggest a retarding of evolution from the materialistic side, for Mars and Saturn in conjunction create great cruelty, wars and tyrannies, preventing the help that should be given to humanity. The Jupiter influence that might have been merciful is perverted. On its adverse side, the negative, it holds on to old conventional forms, and also gives an element of hypocrisy. But above, in the sign Capricorn, a sign that can bring about an inspired heavenly service, are Uranus, the Sun and the Moon. They are freed from their material condition, which could disappoint, because they have risen above and cooperate with Neptune, bringing an assimilation of the super-lunar and super-solar forces by which humanity will surely be saved. Those who selfishly seek worldly ambitions or continue along old lines of thought, or in any way misuse power, will certainly feel the adverse influences portrayed upon this cross. The Uranian forces are always powerful, positive, fiery and inspirational, while those of Neptune are imaginative, very fine and very subtle, bringing into manifestation the intuitive faculty which has been submerged in the darkness of the past lunar manifestation.

Neptune is the planet of Socialism, that Socialism which was preached or taught by Jesus, which will come, bringing with it freedom and liberty for self-development. Much distress will precede this changing of a cycle, Neptune never drives, never forces, but is always gently persuasive, relying on the development of the higher self. In this chart Neptune is placed at the foot of the cross. The power of Uranus and the spirituality of Neptune must and will be manifested through the Socialism of brotherly love taught by Jesus.

Emanations of Light have appeared over various places in the world. They were seen by a few people in 1918. These emanations were from the undiscovered planet now deflecting the orbit of Neptune, which objectifies, as it were, the force which has been wrongly considered Neptunian, but which is in reality relegated Super-Solar Force.

Judging from the 1899 grouping of the planets, Neptune when in powerful aspect to a planet associated with it, will play an important part in the new age. In September, 1919, Jupiter had come to the conjunction of Neptune, inaugurating a far more harmonious condition, with purer spiritual ideals, creating the inception of a new theology, on a truer foundation, whose priests will better understand the inner laws, those Eternal Truths which are the same today as in the beginning of the world. There is need of the priest as a mediator between the material and the spiritual worlds, for the propagation of a new purified religion, a truer conception of the inner life, an inflowing of astral consciousness. The commingling of the heavenly forces of Neptune and Jupiter will bring Peace, for it is written "as in the heavens so will it be on earth."

A new astrology and a new adjustment of life impulse will proceed from the Moon and the unknown planet, and be energised by the Sun and Venus, and balanced by Jupiter and Saturn, and will be recognized on the physical plane through Mars and Uranus, while Neptune will bring to birth Super-solar operation and reaction, and restrain the major planets from malefic action. Neptune will also be protective to the native who has progressed beyond temptation and has evolved a higher consciousness which is able to guide him, and protect him from personal adverse influences.

Jesus was betrayed to His Glory, the trial of the Master is glory to the Master and is retributive swiftly to the age. A Master is able to deflect planetary Karma by means of his Super-solar realization. There is a variation of voltage which can be employed to make a disciple receptive to a higher vibration than that of planetary Karma. This may be a new idea, the polarization of a disciple by a Master's vibration. You will note in the horoscope of a Master and his disciple a decided polarity in the Ascendant and in the synthetic vibration of the map.   The usual Zodiacal oppositions are not to be regarded, because they are contradicted through the harmony of the synthesis and the Ascendant, and there is a synthetic polarity and a radio-activity in the Super-solar aspects.

Attention should always be called to the importance of harmonizing the charts of Teacher and disciple by the application of the data which a careful inspection of the charts will reveal, so as to be able to determine whether the postulant should be given entrance to the inner refuge.   Also as a further outlook, consider the number of the degree on the horizon at the time of birth, and remark the inner meaning of the degree, and then it will be found that the meaning is in harmony with the synthesis and radio-activity of the charts.

There are three causations in the map—the degree on the horizon, the synthetic balance and the radio-centric energy. The Heliocentric method is very valuable in determining the radio-activity in forming the triangle of causation.

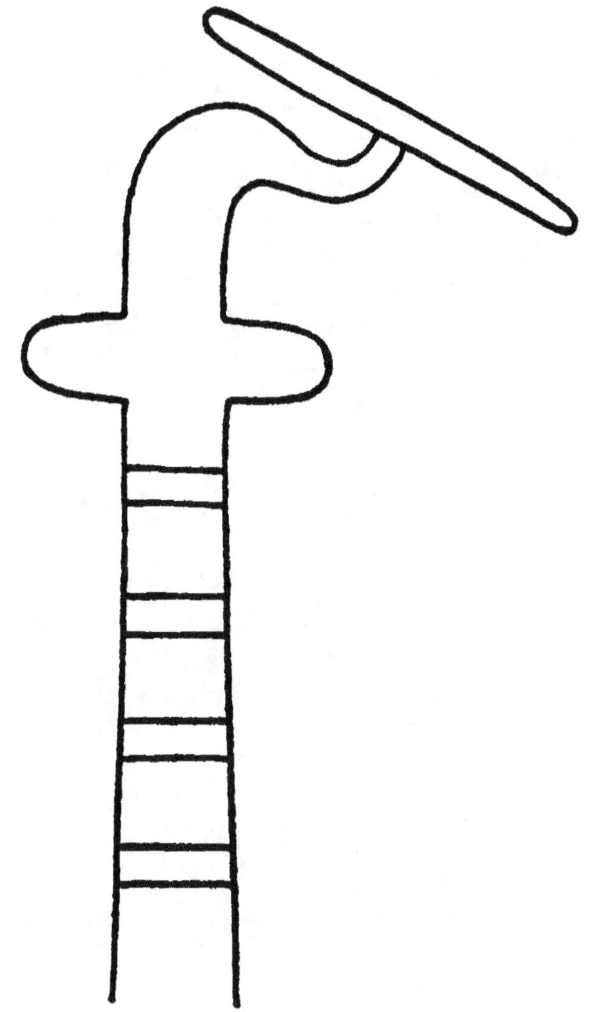

The Great Pyramid was called "The Light." It was mystically a tomb, tomb of a god, a risen god. In the masonry of the structure many mystic symbols are disclosed whereby "the priests so expressed the divine conceptions as to be intelligible to those alone who had been initiated in the Secret House . . . and if we represent the descent traversed by the Initiate from what was called the Head of the Well to the opening into the Chamber of the Fiery Ordeal, we have the form of the 'Sceptre of Ptah,' the Spirit of Divine Fire," Marsham Adams' "The Book of the Master," which is illustrated above, symbolized in the luminary, the Sun.

CHAPTER II

THE "EYE" OF THE GODS

We owe more today than is realized to the mythology of
the past, with its symbolic teachings and traditions of the sun
and the moon and the stars. Because of the distortion of
these teachings and traditions, and because of the lack of
interest and desire to penetrate the past through them, we
have failed to understand the reverent attitude of the early
races towards the heavens. They had evinced marvellous joy
in the unfoldment and understanding that came to them as
they watched and recorded the path of the sun across the
heavens, the approach of night with its darkness made luminous by the moon and the stars.

The ancient peoples learned to know and to love the
stars, and this aroused in them an inner sense, an awakening
within that gave them a key to some of the mysteries above.
From this they created their myths and golden legends that
have come down to us today, but we, being less imaginative
and having instilled within us a false understanding, have
been too easily led into believing that they contained the history of pagan idolatry, despite the fact that we have accepted
their mythical solar heroes born ages and ages ago as men
of historical renown, most of whom are referred to in our
Bible as living characters.

The Sun was always the great and mighty hero overcoming his enemy, darkness, personified in an endless procession
of myths and fables of heroes, many of whom were ridicu-
lously turned into human beings.

Allegories, or myths, of the ancients, especially those of
the luminaries, are filled with dramatic and even human

meaning. Mythical figures as heroes, kings, etc., were elevated to the heavens and given homes among the stars after their mythical demise. The fixed stars of heaven were said to be God's redeemed children, or were those who were under the jurisdiction of a higher state of consciousness. Mythical gods were all of a bi-une nature, and a double primitive essence. The one God finally became, as it were, a survival of the fittest.

It is only by separating the wheat from the chaff, and by directing our minds backward into that far away past, dreamland of mythical fancy, that we understand that facts were woven into nature studies as fascinating myth and allegory, in the midst of which was placed the Spirit, which was worshipped, and not the outer sign.

In the course of evolution, when the lowest level of the spiral had been reached, darkened days arrived, bearing close resemblance to those of our present dark Lunar period. We need to rejoice over this entrance of the new Era, the Aquarian, which is symbolically represented as the man with the Urn, from which rivers of Light are forcing their way through the night creating what those older peoples called the "Twilight of the Dawn," not that of the evening.

Worship of the Sun is as much a part of our lives today as it was in ages gone by, but this in our blindness we fail to see, have no desire to see. The very roots of our religion are found in the Luminaries and in the Stars. In the most ancient myths the Mother was deity, residing in "the endless expanse beyond the Earth, beyond the clouds, beyond the sky," in the Mother Space, coeval with Darkness as the Great Mother of all the fires, elements, gods and powers, from which the Sun, Moon, and Planets were born. As the Lunar Divinity she was the Mother with her Child, who, according to mythology, became the consort of the Mother, long preceding any idea of a fatherhood, or the Father-Mother-Son trinity. Time was once reckoned by the Mother Moon, the Child Moon, and the virile New Moon. When knowledge came that the Lunar Light was derived from the Sun, then and not before were the divine Father, Mother, Son accorded recognition. Profound significance was given to the event when fatherhood on earth was reflected in the new fatherhood in heaven, which brought in the Solar Regime. It was then that this early child became the son of the father, instead of the son of the mother. We read of the "Day-Star from on high," which refers to the Super-Sun, and fountains of the waters which are above the heavens. The word is, "The Sun—rising from on High; i. e., the dawn of the Sun behind the Sun, the Super-Solar Force. It is said that if we were to take the apparent Sun as a hole in space, this Sun behind the Sun would be seen.

The Sun was looked upon as a symbol of divinity. It was the life giver to the physical world. Early peoples knew of the Central Spiritual Sun that emits creative Light. Causality is latent. It was the Light as well as the Light giver of all spiritual realms, the Spiritual Sun that would send great teachers of Light into the world. This Sun that emitted creative light was called "The Center of Rest."

The Sun-Worshippers always looked upon our Sun as an emblem of the Spiritual Sun, the Super-Solar Force. They knew that when the Sun behind the Sun was in direct line with the star Sirius, the light from Sirius fell upon the square stone which the Egyptians in their "Book of the Dead" called the "Stone of God," in their Hall of Truth where Osiris sat to bestow upon the Illuminati the "Aft Crown of Celestial Light." This Aft Crown was imaged in the Zodiacal Light, that "Glory of the Supreme Heaven."

"Throughout the teaching of Egypt the visible light was but the shadow of the invisible Light, and in the wisdom of that ancient country the measures of the Truth were the years of the Most High."[1] In an ancient papyrus it is said "The God of the Universe is in the light above the firmament, and his symbols are upon the earth," and "This is the divine

---

[1] Adams, M.—The Book of the Master, pp. 141-2.

light that none may look upon in the flesh and live, Immortal, Invisible, Intolerable to mental eye."

"The Spirit beyond manifested Nature is the fiery *breath* in its absolute Unity. In the manifested Universe, it is the Central Spiritual Sun, the electric Fire of all Life. In our System it is the visible Sun, the Spirit of nature, the terrestrial god. And in, on, and around the Earth, the fiery Spirit thereof—air, fluidic fire; water, liquid fire; Earth, solid fire. All is Fire."[1] Fire is the fundamental source of all religions.

The subject of Light should be approached with the greatest reverence, as well as with humility. "The Supreme Being of the Sun is Light, for it is by the disk of the Sun that we receive the benefit of Light." Spirit is etherealized matter. Realizing this the Inca priests faced East, greeted the rising sun, "Extended their hands towards it" and threw kisses to it. A ceremony of most profound resignation and reverence, their prayer at Sunrise, "O Sun! Thou who art in peace and safety, shine upon us, keep us from sickness, keep us in health and safety. O Sun! Thou who hast said let there be Cuzec and Tampu, grant that these children may conquer all other people. We beseech thee that thy children the Incas may always be conquerers since it is for this thou hast created them."

Our North American Indians have most uplifting and beautiful myths of the Sun, which to them was the wigwam of the Great Spirit. A solar personification of the North American Indians was a great White Hare. In their legend of the catching of the sun, a fierce battle takes place when Ta-Wats pursues the Hare-god as he takes his appointed course across the heavens. In Ta-Wats' desire to subdue and hold the erratic solar god he shot arrow after arrow into his flaming face as he arose, each one in turn being consumed in his fiery breath.

The last remaining arrow, the "Magical Arrow," he bap-

---

[1]Blavatsky, H. P.—The Secret Doctrine, Vol. ii, p. 114.

tized in a "Divine Tear," and with this he conquered, but the gods condemned him for his act, and sentenced him to travel across the heavens until the end of time. By this decision days, weeks, nights, seasons and years were determined with recurring periods and were established forever in the Solar chart of the Zodiac.

The Divine Tear was symbolized as the weeping or shedding Sun, and was figuratively said to "Let water fall from its eye; it was changed into working bees; they work in the flowers of each kind, and honey and wax are produced instead of water."[1] The Sun as a deity in a later myth is said to shed one water that turns to blood, and also a liquid source of life, which was typified as wax or sperm. The long sperm candle is still held to be a sign of the "Light of the World," symbol of the Messiah, as is the tallest candle of the Roman church, while the red source is preserved or symbolized in the red wafer used by the Papists. The Divine Tear was a type of creative power in Egypt, and the Tears of the Gods were said to be the supernal waters.

Star currents tug and pull at our lives, and only high polarity can steer an unswerved course. There is deep meaning in the shortest verse in the Bible, "Jesus Wept." He was probably rising through tears into His Neptunian or Super-Solar polarity.

The mirific eye suspends a generative tear. The Indian intoning to the Great Spirit wept, and held up tear-wet palms to attract the influence of Wakonda, note the "Kon which is Mongolian, the Great Medicine" of the North American Indians derived from Asiatic source.

We are told in the "Book of the Dead," when Taht the Moon-god speaks, "I am the great Workman who made the Ark of Set-ar (Ptah) on the Stock." This was the origin of the ark, or circle of the sun, which finally created the Solar Zodiac, replacing the Lunar one. This circle was called the "Holy Nine dwelling in the water," and has been represented

---

[1]Records, Vol. vi, pp. 115, 116.

as the nine divisions over-arching the Abyss hollowed out by Ptah. His circle was called Put. Put means to open and divide, and is symbolized by a circle with three-fourths filled in. The hollow or celestial part was left open for the Sun as he voyaged over the earth.

Ptah or Put signified the number 9. From the Zodiacal sign of Aries to that of Sagittarius there are nine signs, and the "Holy Nine" were established with the last three signs of the Zodiac, which were called the Abyss, over which the Sun-god sailed or walked. The Sun-god was represented in various ways by symbols relating to the crossing of the waters. This was the quarter out of which the Ark was said to come forth, when created by Ptah and Ma (male-female), the potter and potteress of Egypt. Nine vases, nine divisions, nine signs are identical with the circle of Ptah. This three-quarter symbol connected with the number nine is a type of the Egyptian "Headless Cross" having three-quarters instead of four, and a figure of the nine divisions of the twelve-sign Zodiac, which was completed by the three watery signs. It was a symbol of the sacred nine months of gestation, and with the Abyss, represented the circle of the completed, or Ankh, cross. The Tau cross is the Alpha and Omega of secret and divine wisdom, and is formed like the letter **T**. The perpendicular ascending line in esoteric reading represents the male ray, and the horizontal one the female, and when constructed with the circle above, as the Ankh cross, it was made the attribute of the Mother. This cross was laid upon the breast of the mummy in preparation for rebirth, and was also placed on the coffins of women, to represent the feminine type. In the Ankh cross the symbols of both Venus and Mars are found. Venus has the circle above the cross. Reverse the circle by placing it below and it is Mars, and then we have the masculine-feminine sign.

The number nine frequently appears in myths in connection with brass as a feminine type. The Hebrews call the

brass vessels used in their ceremonies the "Nurses of God."[1]
Brass images the life-giving source or the breasts of the nurse
Menka, who was prototype of the goddess Ma, the "Measurer" of the moon and co-creator with Ptah as potteress of
the vases.   The vases are emblematic of matter, and represent the Seed of Life and the nine months of gestation.
Scores of myths arise from the number nine, which contain
facts relating to the prehistoric past and to its perpetuation
in the twelve signs of the Zodiac.

The history of Ptah takes us back to the mythical creations, and to the Sixth, when through him the solar period
was established.   In brief, the First heaven was Darkness
and Light, of which the Seven Stars of the Great Bear were
the Light Bringers.   The Second was the Celestial Water;
breath and water, male-female.   The Third is the sevenfold division; the seven elementaries, represented as Zootypes, that were later the Kronotypes of the stellar third
heaven.   The Fourth was given to Taht, as the manifestor
of the Moon, builder of the ark of lunar time, and founder
of the lunar four corners.   Taht was god of the Tat cross,
which he gives to Ptah as the emblem of the four cardinal
points, representing the four divine forces—fire, earth, air
and water—this cross was given to the Sun-god when he
made his circle of the solar Zodiac.   The Fifth was that
of Seb, Star-god and later god of earth and time.   The
Sixth was that of Ptah, when a Luni-Solar time was founded
with the four quarters and the Zenith and Nadir, as a sixfold heaven.   Ptah was a god who preceded the first sovereignty of Atum-Ra.   He was a first generator of light.
In the Harris papyrus it is written, "He moulded the gods,
made the sky, and formed the earth revolving in Space."
The Persians, in creating their heaven, Mount Alborz, say
that "it grew for two hundred years up to the Star station,
for two hundred more up to the Moon station, for two hundred more up to Sun station, and for two hundred more up to

____

[1] Plutarch.

the endless light." This is time as told by the Stars, Moon, and Sun.

Ptah was placed at the head of all the gods and was called the Father of the Fathers, like Terah, Father of Abraham. In his first form he was the Har, or Ptah, who preceded Ra, the Sun, and became the Sun-god Horus, the Egyptian Messiah, who has been made the greatest hero that ever lived in the memory or mind of man, because he was not made a hero of the flesh, but one to whom miracles were natural because mythical and therefore divine.

Ptah was later imaged as the creator spirit of Divine Force, and all previous gods were evolved into his attributes, when the solar Son or Sun-god was created. He was then the solar opener of earth, the Shaper, the Moulder by means of Fire, the Potter who sits at his wheel, forming the egg of the Sun and the Moon, i. e., the cycles and the vase. He was the measurer of space, and mapped out the New Heaven with the assistance of Ma, (Menke), "The True," as he builds the Ark of solar time (the solar Zodiac). One name of Ptah's son was Amen-Ra, the hidden Sun, of red or celestial making. When rising on the horizon he was personified as "The Judge of the Dead," and was called Iu-em-Hept, the Bringer of Peace, and the Prince of Peace. Amen-Ra's creation was comparatively late. He was evolved as time-keeper from the cycles. He was said to have had all the attributes of the one God. Amen-Ra, as the Father of Souls, is Atum-Ra in one cult, Osiris in another, Abraham of Israel in another, Surya in India, and Hu in Britain. Among the designs copied by Champollion is one taken from a mummy-lid, showing Atum as a green god, and the flesh of Ptah of the same hue. "Green was emblematic of the invisible world out of which life sprang in the green leaf."

Ra (Sun) was the first ancestor worshipped because he was typical of fatherhood, when representing the completion of the Sabean, Lunar and Solar time. He was enthroned by his worshippers, who also called him the "Eye of the Gods," as a symbol of the Sun.

When Ptah had finished his journeys below, Ra appears in a solar bark, with a serpent coiled around it in twelve coils, as a final symbol of the twelve-signed Zodiac.

In the Persian sacred book a completed year of 365 days is given, this being the Sixth Creation, meaning that the year was completed in 365 days. In the Targum of Palestine it says: "The Adamic man was created in the image of the Lord with 365 nerves," signifying a completed solar or sun year.

When solar time was established, cycles of the planets were introduced, and planetary time was calculated or worked out. A planet was assigned to each of the older gods or constellations. Time reckoning culminated with the 26,000-year period, its basis being in the Egyptian year of 360 days, a luni-solar year, having the moon or month reckoned by three weeks, of ten days each. The time of the ten divisions was succeeded by that of the seven. It is said that when the priests conducted Pharaoh into the Holy of Holies in the Temple of Isis, she bade him swear that he would not change this year of 360 days and the five Epagomenae,[1] and so it is to remain as the sacred year for all time. The great 26,000-year period, measured by the 360 degrees of the ecliptic of the heavens, dominated the 360 days and was retained after the true solar year was known. It was the prime factor in counting of the 26,000-year cycle of precession, marking the fulfilment of time, and with it ended this age of mythology, which was brought about by the Hebrew Ram or Lamb of Fulfilment. Even here there is a continuance of the Sabean cult, as Sevekh, son of the ancient mother, a type of Sebek-Ra, god of the Seventh Creation as the sun and Saturn combined, was transformed into the Ram or Lamb of the sacrificial Zodiacal sign Aries,

---

[1]Epagomenae—observed as birthdays of the gods.

preceding the Piscene manifestation, herald of the age of Christianity.

"In Egypt the Sun was assigned to Horus, the Moon to Sut-Typhon; Mars to Shu, Mercury to Anup, Jupiter to Seb, Venus to the genitrix, and Saturn to Sevekh-Kronus. The seven were continued by conversion in several forms of ruling powers, . . . recognized in the seven souls of Ra, the seven horses of Sûrya, the seven arms of Agni, the seven rays of Iao-heptaktis, the seven tongues of fire and forms of the Word, the seven Taas (Eg) or sages of Egypt, India and China.   These are the seven Rishis who lived on as the seven rulers in the circle of the great year, and made the cycle of the precession.   The seven time-keepers of the seven constellations that performed their first revolutions in the ark of the sphere became seven celestial personages in *an* ark that voyaged round the cycle of precession once in 25,868 years, which period they were fabled to fulfil by being continually reborn as men whose lifetime was reckoned at seventy-one or seventy-two years each."[1]

Gerald Massey, in his Book of the Beginnings, writes most interestingly of that which he calls a precious allegory of a primitive creation, which was found on an inscription in a tomb of Seti the First in the so-called "Chamber of the Cow," and which is a portion of the Books of the Prophets, or Horoscopus.   It is an allegory concerning Ra the Sun and the destruction of those beings, born of him, whom he thought had uttered words against him, and, because their hearts had become afraid, were fleeing from him.   The significance of the allegory is that when the true solar time had been acknowledged, those beings or stars of his early creation, thought to be false and rebellious against him, deserved to be destroyed and set aside because of their failure to keep true time.   So he creates or maps out the Fields of Aah-en-Ru, with the house of thirty-six gates (the divisions of the twelve signs into the thirty-six decans of the Zodiac),

---

[1]Massey, Gerald—The Natural Genesis, Vol. ii, pp. 322, 323.

and says, "I establish as inhabitants all the beings which are suspended in the sky, the stars."

A sort of prologue is seen. Ra is in his old age, with "limbs of silver, flesh of gold, and his articulations are of genuine Lapus Lazuli." Lapus Lazuli with the Egyptians was considered as a divine image, the True. He calls "before his face" Shu, Tefnut, Seb, Nut, fathers and mothers, and a few of the elders that had been with him before when in Nun. These were taken into the sanctuary, where he speaks "in the presence of the elders and fathers of the older gods, creators of men, and of wise beings." The Destruction, it says, takes place through Hathor, with the gilded horns, who is to destroy, and does destroy, men during three days of sailing. "She smote men over the whole land," and completed their destruction, with the help of Ra, who then feels that proper protection will be given to mankind.

During the destruction blood was shed freely over the land. This blood was mixed with the juices of fruit as a further protection of mankind, and from it a divine drink was distilled for the gods. This was called the Water of Life; sometimes the Drink of Immortality. This blood shed by Ra and Hathor and poured over the land is the covenant in making which Ra swears, "I now raise my hand that I shall not destroy men."[1]

These libations were made at the Festivals of Hathor (the Golden Heifer) in very ancient times, and they were kept in Israel as well as in Egypt. The shedding and pouring of blood for three days is mystically connected with the Red Sea, typical of the River Nile, when it turned red and imaged the mother source. Also at the time of the overflow of the river, festivals of a New Year were held, which were all symbolical of a new birth.

---

[1]"When the spirit was offered up to heaven, the blood was poured out in libations to the mother-earth, the Egyptian Neith, goddess of the lower heaven, that is earth."—Massey, Gerald.—"A Book of the Beginnings," Vol. i, p. 348.

After the destruction Ra feels weary and in need of support. As he cannot walk, he calls for Nut (night) who carries him on her back. Night is represented by the cow (Hathor). Ra (the Sun) then descends to earth, where all is darkness, to which he gives light and calls upon those who will support him. Shu is made the guardian of those who live in the nocturnal sky. Then Seb is called forth, with his serpents representing cycles and periods of time, and is made Father over this new land; then Taht is called with his luminary the moon, in which Ra.the Sun can make his nocturnal home, that he may shed his light in the night. After this he is lifted up into the sanctuary within the limits of the thirty-six decans, where he assembles and gives homes to the multitude, for he says, "Let a field of rest extend itself; and there arose a field of Rest. Let the plants grow there; and there arose the field Aaru." Then he finally proclaims, "Their sins were behind them, the destruction of enemies removes destruction."

The Aaru was the house of Osiris, founded on the thirty-six decans of the Zodiac, and the fields are the Zodiacal circle, where he establishes the multitude of stars. Aah-en-Ru was called "The land of the silver sky" and the "Place of Illumination and Union found with the Unseen Father."

When this extract, which is taken from the sacred books of Taht, was read to Ra by Taht, he (Taht) had first to purify himself for nine days, as all must do who would read from the sacred books. By such methods the thoughts of the ancient peoples rose to sublime heights. These are the people, who, by some ignorant writers, are called pagans, and derelicts. Those who lovingly delve into that great past know that their myths have been stolen and reproduced in our own Bible, which is considered unapproachable in its sublimity.

Astrology

If horoscopically the Sun and Moon are seemingly opposed, they are in reality counter-posed. It is an aspect giving a peculiar and essentially manly intellectual grasp, and an extremely feminine hesitation. It is a very acute counter position and is a lever on the Knower Consciousness. It may unfold amid a great deal of inward distress, and a great deal of outward discomfort, conditions necessary in all travail. At birth there is always the inner pain, with its outward painful disturbance. Birth is a generation of life, and the rebirth of the Knower Consciousness is a generation of infinite love and everlasting life. It is only possible through superhuman suffering borne without complaint. The fulcrum is in the super-solar world.

The great mystery about the lunar force is not recognized today as it should be. The Moon was the cosmic mother of the antique world. It was not only revered as a goddess, but as the Fountain of Generation. There is no need to make a separate lunar cycle in ordinary calculations, but to calculate the Sun in reference to the Moon; that is, make the Sun and the Moon correlative forces in judging a nativity. The Moon should be considered the background of life and the Sun the germinating factor. This will give a concept of the old method of evaluating the relative influence of the Sun and the Moon. A new method of astrology is sure to come, which will remove much of the uncertainty which has often been caused by the undervaluing of the lunar and the over-valuing of the solar forces. The solar god as a source of life was reborn in the Moon.

The Sun in the mid-heaven is a powerful generator of unseen force, bringing to the native worldly benefits which would otherwise be withheld through karmic insufficiency. The Sun in the mid-heaven does not involve any unheard-of wonders, but a practical solution of impending fortune or misfortune. It is supposed to denote the influence of the male, but it has been found to denote the generative force of spiritual benefit, which often operates contrary to the natal map. Under the Sun in its physical manifestation are included the vanities of the world, but great power and majesty are its birthright. The wisdom which rules over all comes from the Hidden Sun, as a Super-Solar Force. The symbol of the Sun is a circle within which is placed a black spot. In the Mysteries it was always taught that black was but the superabundance of light, hence the dot in the center. The very shadow of death is cast by the interception of the Light of Life everlasting.

Light illuminates the darkness just as it brings light and glory to the Moon, and even so can it reach the heart of man and permeate with light the innermost recesses of his being. All good and opposing influences come from the Sun, the Moon, and the Stars, duality is everywhere. In the Pymander of Hermes we are told that if we would see God we must consider and understand the Sun, consider the course of the Moon, and consider the order of the Stars, and "The Sun is the greatest of all the gods in heaven, to whom the heavenly gods give place . . . greater than the Earth and the Sea, and is content to suffer infinitely lesser stars to walk and move above himself."

Hermes also considers God as a circle, the center of which is everywhere and the circumference nowhere.

THE CELESTIAL SHIP OF THE NORTH

The symbolical navi-formed Argha is found in all sacred mysteries as an expressive type of the Holy Spirit who was The Ship of Life, the Celestial Ship of the North; and the Moon, symbolized by the crescent-shaped boat, became one of her emblems.

CHAPTER III

LIGHT THAT SHINETH IN THE DARKNESS

If sublimity of thought can be attained through the contemplation of the heavens, then one or more of the keys to the mystic Moon may be divulged, for the Moon is an occult mystery of the mysteries. She is the throbbing Virgin of Nature, Nature that conceives immaculately, whose magnetism not only generates life but can destroy it both physically and psychically. She is the giver of Life and Death on our globe. The Moon and Sun conjoined become the fructifiers, the Bringers Forth.

With the consummation and adjustment of planetary time the planets were assigned to the deities of Egypt. The Moon was given in the dual form as Sut-Typhon, the earliest Mother and Son, and as Venus represented the Great Mother (Typhon) alone. The relationship between the Moon and Venus is very close. They both symbolized the Argha, the Ship that contained the seed of all life, the Great Ship of the North.

The Moon was called masculine up to the fifteenth day as the Light period. The last fifteen days, as the Dark period, was feminine. With the Semitic races the Sun was female and the Moon male. This was a remnant of an Atlantean tradition, when the Moon was called the Lord of the Sun.

The Moon in Egypt or to the Egyptians was mystically known as male-female, and it was also called the Mother of the World. The Horned Moon introduced the male character of the Moon as a type of renewal. "The Mother was the Moon at full; the waning Moon was her dark child; the waxing Moon, the Child of Light, her horned and rebegetting bull." The renewed light in the new Moon gave promise of eternal youth.

Primitive man designated sexes, as well as all other human conditions, by means of phenomena. To him the full Moon appeared to be refilled with life, and from this he deduced the feminine characteristics which are found in all their symbols and ideographs of the feminine in relation to the Moon. When waning it was the impubescent child. The full Moon signified emanation, outgrowth; and the waxing Moon "became horned as the Procreative Power, the three were as one, the trinity in unity." Speaking of her power, the Moon called herself repeatedly, "The Light which Shineth in the Darkness," the "Woman Light." Hence it became the accepted symbol of all the Virgin-Mother goddesses. In all pagan theogonies the Moon was always intimately connected with the dragon, her eternal enemy.

There was nothing bewildering to the ancients in their early symbols. They represented one thing or condition by another, and the invisible by a corresponding type of power. Elementary types were of no sex. This was thoroughly understood by the ancients, consequently in some languages the Sun was made feminine and the Moon masculine. In the beginning they were neuter, later becoming male and female. To the primitive peoples Darkness and Light constituted the greatest dramas the world has ever known.

Long before it was ascertained that the Moon received her light from the Sun, many myths were extant which were especially connected with the waning of the Moon, the fourteen days from the full to the new, when the time of the Dragon of Darkness was supposed to reign. In some myths the woman is the slayer of the dragon or serpent (darkness), but it was the young son, the bringer of the Light, who crushed its head. To all primitive peoples she was the virgin Mother-goddess, and the dragon was her enemy, hence many portrayals of her crushing the head of the dragon, making him powerless. Sometimes she is seen

standing on the mythical serpent, which later became symbolized in astrology by the head and the tail of the dragon, the
head pointing to the north and the tail to the south.   They
remain today as the ascending and descending nodes or points
of the lunar orbits, where planets come from north to south
latitude, and their motion is retrograde about three seconds
a day.

The lunar myths and worship were based on knowledge of
psychology and physiology, with correct appreciation of
symbology and a profound understanding of nature.   Their
origin is untraceable unless we retain tradition.   Lunar and
Solar worships, which are included in the Roman Catholic
and Protestant religions and wherever Jehovah is deified,
show the most ancient of all religious manifestations surviving throughout the entire world today.   The churches worship
"Jehovah, pre-eminently a *lunar* god, and when both
Churches have accepted in their theologies the '*Sun*' Christ
and the lunar trinity" or 'Mariolatry' based on the ancient
cult.[1]

Jehovah was a lunar symbol of the reproductive and generative faculty of nature, and the Immaculate Conception
was a noble spiritual ideal of the Virgin Mother, spiritual,
not of "earth earthy."   Religious history of every nation
was expressed exoterically in symbology and never in words.
Pictorial expression was given to their allegories and fables,
which were deeply impressed upon their thoughts and
emotions.

The origin of the Trinity is lunar, the three-in-one in
nature.   "The moon was one as *the* Moon, which was two-
fold as sex, and three-fold in character as mother, child, and
adult male.   This child of the moon became consort of his
own mother!   It could not be *helped* if there was to be any
reproduction. . . . Through ignorance of the symbolism, the
simple representation of early time has become the most

---

[1] Blavatsky, H. P.—The Secret Doctrine, Vol. i, p. 388.

profound religious mystery in modern Luniolatry. . . . The Roman Church portrays the Virgin Mary arrayed with the sun and the horned moon at her feet, holding the lunar infant in her arms, as child and consort of the mother moon! The mother, child, and adult male are fundamental."[1] Remember the subjects of dispute at the Council of Ephesus in 431, when Mary was declared Mother of God; and her Immaculate Conception forced on the world as by command of God, by Pope and Council in 1858.

The Sun and Moon are most complex in their manifold meanings. The Moon, because of her waning, dying and reappearing every month, was always a symbol of Life, Renewal, and Reincarnation. The full Moon imaged the producer, whose child born on the wane, was the powerless one of the three, but the virile one was the refiller of the Moon. The waning Moon produced the dark child, and the waxing Moon the child of light,[2] who becomes transformed at puberty into what mythology has named "her horned or rebegetting bull," (the bull was always a type of virility). It was the crescent Moon, with upright horns, rising and setting that originated the horned phase as a masculine manifestation. The Sun between the horns on the head of the cow, or the Moon, in her feminine phase, were the bearers of the light, and represented a sustaining power. Horns were a type of male potency, and yet not solely male, as they are on the head of the cow, and belong to the Moon, both being typical horn-bearers. The female is the burden-bearer, carrying the Sun type of the masculine source on her head.

It is a matter of worldwide knowledge that the most ancient measurement of time was by the year of the thirteen periods of twenty-eight days each,[3] the lunar year of twenty-

---

[1]Massey, Gerald—Lecture on Luniolatry.

[2]In many lands the waxing and waning Moon were regarded as significant in that boys should be weaned whilst the Moon was waxing, and girls during its wane; and some preferred marriage at the waxing of the Moon.

[3]Both Persians and Chinese originally had twenty-eight mansions in the Zodiac, but afterwards reduced them to twelve.

eight mansions or Asterisms, and the thirteenth year became a year of great festival, feast and sacrifice.

Twenty-eight days is not a true lunar period but belonged to feminine physiological phenomena, the phenomena called by occultists "The Mythical Moon" of nature. It was also personified in Menka the wet nurse, who helped make the vase containing the seed of life.[1] All Orientals know the occult property of the Moon and its hidden influence for good or evil on generative power. If this influence on the human body were broadly known today in connection with the mysteries of conception, crime with its attendant immoralities would be less rampant. This world-old mystery seems beyond the ken of even the modern astronomer. The Moon was personified as Maia, Mother, Mary, even the month of May being made sacred to Mary. In its earliest rendering it meant "Inaccessible," and it is esoterically known as "Illusion." The Moon on the material plane is illusion; it is the Sun which radiates life. The importance of the Moon in illusion, meaning life on this plane, should never be lost sight of. The universal illusion is that of separateness from God —"He was in the world, and the world came to existence through Him, and the world did not recognize Him."[2]

The lunar month of twenty-eight days, or four weeks of seven days each, gives thirteen periods, or months, in the solar year of 364 days, or 52 weeks of seven days each, and this number seven becomes most prominent in exoteric religion.[3]

In Jewish literature the Moon was always found connected

---

[1] The month of Menat, the Potteress, creator of the Vase and the "measurer of the period of gestation, as ten moons in the year of thirteen moons of twenty-eight days, and afterwards the measurer of the month in three periods of ten days each, thus Menat was both the measurer of days and months, by the number 10, which is her name, and that name is the earlier form of Menoth or month."—Massey, Gerald—"The Natural Genesis," Vol. ii, p. 350.

[2] Weymouth, R. F.—The New Testament in Modern Speech, John i, 10.

[3] Whenever the number 7 is prominently given in Hebrew Scriptures, it is sure to be connected with the Moon. Their astronomy and observations of time were represented by the Moon.

with reproduction.   In the Jewish Tabernacle there were ten curtains, typical of the number of months of the lunar generative period that veiled the nine months of the solar.   In other countries the number seven symbolized cycles, forces, occult powers in the cosmos and its septenary plane, but the thirteen months belong to the Mother Mystery.   In the Talmud it is observed that there is one day of the year in which Satan is powerless.   This is the day of Yom Kipour.   In the other three hundred and sixty-four days he is all potent.   "Rami the son of Hami has said the numerical letters of Satan make three hundred and sixty-four days; during these Satan has power to do evil, but on the day of Kipour he is impotent."[1] The solar twelve months superseding the lunar thirteen was the origin of the superstition making the number 13 an unlucky number.   This was the placing of the masculine above the feminine, which, though it brought much rejoicing, also brought about much difficulty in its acceptance and understanding.   The number 13 is also related to Friday, a day very sacred to the Great Mother, and in the olden days was considered the luckiest of numbers.

The Russian serpent had 28 heads.   It was a form of the Apophis portrayed in celestial waters, and it had 28 double coils arranged in four sevens.   It is depicted on a sarcophagus of Seti.   The Chinese and the Akkadian division of the moon was three-fold, into the latitude, the longitude, and the orbit.   The Akkadian months were named after the signs of the Zodiac, and antedate the Chaldean.   The nature of the signs belonged to the ancient Kamitic astrology.

The Moon's synodical period is extended to twenty-nine days, twelve hours and forty-four minutes.   The solar reckoning was the termination of the mystery moon of twenty-eight days.

The year of 360 days was reckoned by the thirty-six decans of crossing stars that preceded the decans of the Zodiac which made their transits every ten days or three to the

---

[1] Treatise Youma.

month. The division of Egypt into the thirty-six nomes rests on the connection of the terrestrial division with the celestial, and the placing of the thirty-six decans belonging to the celestial houses of astrology in the Zodiac. The perfect year of 365¼ days was made to supersede the Sun-and-Sirius year of 365 days.

The Akkadians divided the monthly journey of the Moon into three parts of ten days each, and each of these ten-day parts they divided into two parts of five days each, assigned to the feminine and masculine alternately. This was according to the six-fold heaven, dividing the universe into six equal parts. "The distribution of all time, of all things above the earth and under the earth is done by the hexad of the Zodiac."[1]

The Festival of the Sixth day was called the lunar Sabbath. It is said of Osiris, "Thy beauties are in the midst of the Sacred Eye, Lord of the 6th day Festival." The Sacred Eye was lunar, type of reproduction, mirror of the sun, and opened on the sixth day after being closed or eclipsed during five days. The new moon, being the celestial image of renewal, or rebirth, came to represent Tabu time.

The number 6 related to breath, and breath was synonymous with conception. Pythagoras held this as a perfect sacred number and called it Venus, the Mother. The Chinese 6 breaths produced all things in silence. Maya was the queen of the number six, and as Proclus says "6 was allied to the soul."

Number 5 related to water, and was synonymous with the inundation (mystical) and identified with the cessation of activity in nature. It was always in all countries a symbol of the female generative principle.

It was after the fifth day of negation that the festival of the 6th was held. It was celebrated every new Moon, and was ever sacred to the period, held in purity as marking the

____

[1] Stanley.

coming of age of the female. It was observed with great reverence by all ancient races, and was called the period of Tabu, "The Ever-Sacred." It was on the sixth day that the Druids gathered the mistletoe, symbol of renewal, that was typified in the shoot. The "Annunciation" was on the sixth day. Manna was gathered on the six days, on the seventh there was none. On the Jewish Sabbath, the evening of the sixth day, the fruit of the Tree of Life and Knowledge might be plucked and eaten. The feminine manna was the Angels' Food. According to the primitive idea, sin or crime was an offense against the new moon. And in the legends of various lands the Moon was looked upon as an avenger of crimes, to whom the guilty must go for punishment. With some peoples this period was held so sacred that to make a noise on that day was punishable with death.

Puberty or the Coming of Age was a season kept sacred by most ancient races. It was called "The Ever Sacred," and was held sacred to the gods. Primeval revelation in its mystic aspect belonged to woman, incorporated in the five-day week period and amongst those old races the fifth day was followed by the festival of the sixth. The night of the fifth day was called the "laugh of dawn," typifying the joyousness which comes with the anticipation of motherhood. In Egypt, when this was attained the woman wore the double Crown of Maternity, represented by two serpents, one of which had five heads, and the other ten, representing the ten Moons or the period of gestation.

According to Philo, "the number 10 is the perfect number by which Noah the Just existed." Time reckoned by the number 10 is described as in the Ark, during the deluge of nine months or the ten lunar ones. The Ark was the receptacle of the seed of all life, and Noah as the Just man really signified the truer Time-keeper. Ten is the type of the lunar phase, just as 9 is the solar, and is mystically "the Begetter of souls."

The Holy of Holies and the sacred number 10 as a productive element are connected with the Garden of Eden. "The 10 is the mother of the Soul, and the light and the life are there united, since the number 1 is born from the Spirit, thus the unity has made the 10 and the 10 the unity."[1]

In the Apocalypse reference is made to God and the Holy Spirit, as A. O., which has mysterious allusion to the number 10 as the pillar and the circle, the most perfect of all numbers.

In "The Source of Measures," by J. R. Skinner, there is very interesting matter concerning the moon and the Garden of Eden, knowledge of which is of importance. The seventh day is a correlated part of the Garden of Eden, in the form of a circular day, allied in Holiness to the Holy of Holies, and to the perfect value of ten. Seven is nature herself, the master of the Moon. This seventh or circular day was set apart as the Woman's Day.

"The word 'sanctified' is Kodesh. Kodesh is to be fresh, new, pure, shining, young; which last word, as a substantive, has the meaning of *the time* of the new moon," marking its period by $7 \times 4 = 28$ days, $28 \times 10 = 280$ days as the period of gestation applying to human birth, and $28 \times 13 = 364$ days, a luni-solar, or week year as $52 \times 7 = 364$ days, "The idea of the Garden was to be a *source of the birth of time*, and of *distant measure* under feminine use."

In the Eleusinian mysteries "the priestesses had, for four centuries, walked in procession through the streets, carrying a *sacred basket; and* latterly it had become known that this *basket held a live serpent, supposed to be the author of sin and death.*"[2]

The mystic basket usually contained the figure of a serpent, and was surrounded by flowers and fruit. The flowers were of a kind that bloom but once a month, and the fruit is the basket or scrotum representation. "In the most ancient mysteries of the Greeks, they shouted *Eva!* and at the same time a *serpent* was shown." "The same Hebrew letter is the

---

[1] Hermes—The Divine Pymander.
[2] Sharp—History of Europe.

symbol of a basket and a serpent, numerically it is $3\times3\times9$, and is at the center of the Garden," and 13 was the number of the Garden of Eden, belonging to the Mother Mystery.

The light of night was known as the Eye of the Moon. The eye was a reflector, a place of reproduction. The filling of the eye with oil was typical of reproduction, like filling the lamp for light.

As a type of a reproducing circle, the eye reflected all images within itself, and as symbol of a cycle it was applied to Horus, to Taht of Egypt, and to Hu, who was the solar Overseer of the Druids, while in Mithraic sculpture it is seen as a disk on wings afloat overhead, with serpents attached.

When Draconis, the star in the Eye of the Constellation Draco, was at the center of the heaven, it portended great occult significance, and was known as "The Star of the Final Judgment," or the "Star of Judgment," because the rays of the Central Sun descended upon it. In the far distant future a period will arrive when this same star, as the Pole Star, will again become the center of heaven, the Eye of heaven which sees in all directions. Great prominence is given to the Eye in the well-known representation of the serpent with its tail in its mouth, as a symbol of the inner eye. The coiled serpent suggests a pyramidal form, with the head raised in the center of the resulting circle, in which the eye becomes the principal point, symbol of the creative point within the circle.

"It was essential to the symbol of the coiled serpent that the eye should be visible inside the circle."[1]   "It is a habit of the serpent to roll itself round and form a spiral heap with its head atop. The serpent built the primal pyramid with its eggs, and then coiled round the conical pile to hatch them. . . . Hence the serpent, with the head raised in the circle, thus made the eye a most essential point within the circle."[2]

---

[1] Pluto.

[2] Massey, Gerald—The Natural Genesis, Vol. i, p. 336.

The lunar eclipse, from which innumerable myths arose, was considered a forerunner of calamity in the struggles between the solar light and the dragon of darkness.   It mattered not to the ancients what symbol was used to depict the opponent of the light, whether bird, animal, or human being, but it had to represent some power in nature; such as Apophis, the serpent of evil, symbol of human passions, and the enemy of the Sun.   It was in the interpretation of just such symbols that the danger lay in converting the myths, especially of the Egyptians, into the Hebrew miracles.

When the Egyptians personified beneficent powers of nature they conceived them in their own images.   The destroying or opposing power they made into shapes of vicious or noxious animals.   The struggle between Horus —Light— and Set or Sut—Darkness—has been productive of many legends.   Light was always made the conqueror.

We are all familiar with the woman clothed with the Sun, with the Moon under her feet, about to bring forth the man-child, Lord of Light, which the crocodile or dragon of eclipse, darkness, is ready to devour.

In Egypt, China and India the earliest years of astronomical reckoning were calculated by the eclipses.   In Egypt the crocodile-headed dragon was called the Dragon of the Eclipse, and he was said annually to swallow the moon that contained the Lord of Light, the reflected light of the sun by night, imaged as the young child, a symbolical way of conveying a natural truth.   Three days whilst the Moon was concealed were allowed for the transformation of the new Moon from the old.   And so the Lord of Light was said to be swallowed by the crocodile.   The crocodile was also called the Water-Dragon, and was portrayed as the Great Fish, when the light was said to remain three days and three nights in the belly of the fish.   The crocodile represents both earth and water, and the legend gives three days in the heart of the earth as well as in the belly of the fish, for the concealing of the light.   This is the same crocodile that was said to swallow the lights, the stars, as they sank in the west below the horizon.

We called the myths and symbolisms of Egypt their mysteries. They have supplied the mysteries of the world, and are abundantly found in the miracles of the Hebrew writings. Even the headings of chapters of the Egyptian "Book of the Dead" are suggested by the arrangement of those of the Hebrew writings.

ASTROLOGY

Reincarnation and Karma, in its mortal out-working, are calculated by what, for want of a better name, we will call a luni-centric method. When you consider the relation of the Moon to female generation, you will at once see the relation between the Moon and Isis, the Great Mother. It is said in the Secret Doctrine, "Wisdom lies concealed under the couch of him who rests on the Golden Lotus, floating on the water." This is an allusion to the lunar wisdom. The Golden Lotus is the couch, the Wisdom is in the water which is underneath, and which is ruled by the Moon.

The number thirteen belongs to the Mother Mystery, thirteen being the overlapping or transmitting of the Zodiac, the cyclic ending or beginning. The Moon is the overlapping of another planetary chain. We are entering the Aquarian Manifestation in the forthcoming new era, and in Aquarius the Moon is in super-lunar exaltation. The number of the stars in the Water Urn of Aquarius is thirteen, which is the number of the incoming age.

It is through the illumination of the mind that service comes, through subjection and subordination of the lunar mind to the solar light, that such service is instituted. The lunar mind is the upper mind body which is above the astral consciousness, and it may be called the Neptunian mind, since it is through this stratum of consciousness that the higher evolvement of the new age becomes manifest. This is in no sense a psychic development, for it is beyond the phase of psychic functioning. There is a great interchange of forces taking place, to be developed and completed in the approaching period, for the Moon is undergoing a change in its earthly polarity, and will be receiving a new impulse from its parent Moon, or the Sun behind the Sun.

The super-solar systems are polarized alternately, the Moon being the outworn relegation of another and remote super-solar manifestation. The earth itself is travailing in the womb of the mother. The serpent power is opening the womb of nature, the Great Mother, and a new spiritual consciousness in its infancy is emerging, triumphing in the material pregnancy of ages. The heart of the child beats. The Light is the umbilical cord to the Cosmic Mother, not to the Earth Mother, the earth which brings forth ultimately, but to the womb of all nature, which is expressed life. The earth is not the planetary spirit which emerges in a new consciousness, but will be one with the spiritual influx of the higher solar systems. The earth is like the man who feels the divine light guidance, as a spirit within, and as a spirit without, remotely guiding and evolving him. The planet earth is in a state of spiritual rebirth, and the earth's spirit returns into incarnation and is the first fruit of a new reality. The earth is the great man or the grand man of alchemy. The Heavenly Man is the holy archetypal being.

The Moon in the ninth house of the horoscope is very potent, but the Sun is adverse in the map of a man who has been unequal to the bearing of civic responsibility. The Sun in the ninth indicates a conflict between the light and the more material solar impulses. The Sun has always been considered as a life-giving force; it is a generative agent when placed in the house of the Moon in a man's horoscope.

The Moon is the light in the ninth house, and the Sun is the extinguisher of the light, and makes conflict in a man's horoscope, but not in a woman's. In a woman's it usually means an early marriage and a fortunate one. In a man's horoscope it operates in later life and produces its effect upon the astral and mental rather than on the physical.   This is a peculiar and little understood position, and must be investigated to be appreciated.   In a man's chart the conditions, generally speaking, are operative later in life; when they act in a woman's chart the Moon's condition in the natal chart is precipitated into manifestation.   In most men's charts the Sun conditions are primary leaders, but with a woman they are apt to be external or secondary, except in material matters, when they usually act as a powerful force in changing the entire life.

The Moon in the Fifth House is apt to indicate a very unfortunate youth, which is due to great illusion in the sex relation, and to a very great illusion in the home and in worldly relations.   It shows that the Justice polarity is insecure, and that the native is destined to become a scapegoat, or considered as such.   Many insane people have this position of the Moon, and are very often driven to insane asylums unjustly by those who desire their worldly goods.

The Moon in the fifth house frequently gives sex perverts. A sex pervert is one in whom the lunar force is unbalanced in youth.   When the Sun is placed in beneficent aspect to the Moon in the fifth house, by trine, sextile or extreme opposition, the Moon is held in abeyance and the native is able to restrain his lunar, illusory impulses.   The native throughout his life is subject to the adverse influence of relatives, to his financial detriment, but he must never lose his faith in humanity, as he must become universal if he ever hopes to escape from his emotional Karma.   The Moon in this fifth house is the indicator of the reincarnated prostitute or pervert, and should be regarded as one of the serious indications of adverse conditions in any map, except in that of a person of noble Jupiterian or Saturnian aspects.   These two planets are intimately related to the Moon on the higher planes, and can bring the native relief and advancement if the fourth house indicates a pleasant ending to the life.

The Moon in the fifth house can be a most malefic condition, and very great thought must be given to substantiating this point. The aspect should be explained to parents, as a native with an aspect of this kind is peculiarly subject to cancer in later life. If Saturn is malefic to the Moon, Saturn can be very productive of cancer in a bad lunar chart. Saturn is constrictive and the Moon congestive, and both acting contrarily give a growth of tumor, cancer or goitre. It is very prolific of syphilitic conditions if Saturn is retrograde or malefic to the Moon in the fifth house in the progressed horoscope. The natal chart is not of so much importance in determining these conditions, but the progressed malefic aspect to the natal Moon brings about suddenly quite extraordinary results. This is but little known and will not be believed in to any great extent without much research in many maps. This can be done through an alienist who is in touch with astrology.

The Moon is very advantageous when placed in the tenth house, because it exalts the good influence of women in a man's chart, and in a woman's chart predisposes the native to inspirational guidance at critical points in the career. The Moon in the tenth house of a person who is undeveloped is the sign of a native whose highest consciousness is astral and who is intuitive and psychic, but never truly spiritual, unless the Moon and Mars are in benefic aspect, or the Moon and Saturn conjoined at birth. Then the native, whether man or woman, may be a great force, and the woman may be a ruler in her own sphere. The expert interpreter or astrologer has never dreamed that the Moon was the key to the worldly judgment of a woman's horoscope, or in a man's horoscope when placed in the tenth house, or when in the third, or twelfth houses, where it is a dreaded malefic, bringing over reincarnationally resentment and personal spite in the third, and a tendency to illusion in the twelfth.

A new Moon at birth is a benefic wherever placed in a horoscope, because it indicates a waxing fortune and a tendency to be little receptive to malefic aspects and to overrule them in the progressed horoscope. It can be worked out mathematically and is not usually taken into account in present judgment. The quarters of the Moon should be indicated in every chart, and the new Moon should be absolutely benefically judged. The waning Moon indicates a tendency to an early death. When adversely placed it will give added power to any malign influence which strikes its own house as well as its position.

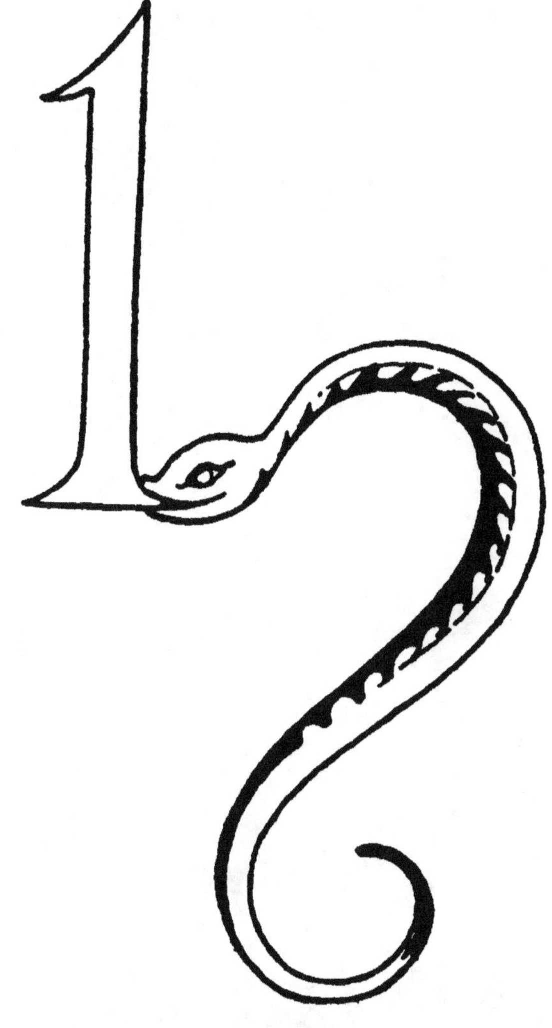

SATURN

The symbol of Saturn has the Hook also called the Crook of
Bishops from which originated the saying "By hook or crook." In
the symbol above, Saturn is depicted as the "Reconciler of the worlds
visible and invisible." The undulating curve of the hook, like the letter S is a symbol of the serpent. This is also called the "Shepherd's
Crook of the Second Person," and the "Crooked Sword of Paradise."

CHAPTER IV

THE BRIDGE

The earliest manifestation of Time was in the circling of the constellation, the Great Bear, around the pole in the North, combined with Sut, or Sirius, the Dog-Star in the south. In the primitive myth Sut was Sirius in one phase and Sevekh, manifestor of the Seven Stars of the Lesser Bear, in another. Sut was also superseded by Taht, who was known as "The Revealer" and "The Messenger." In a later phase he became the planet Mercury and Sut became the planet Saturn. In the Divine Pymander Taht is called the son of Saturn. He was an early form of Hermes, and always the swift-flying messenger. Both Sut and Sevekh signify the number seven, the number of Saturn in planetary form.

Sut was the first celestial hero. He was given the name of Fire-God, or God of Fire, the Fire of Sabean origin, but as time elapsed he became the Solar Son, traced to Sabaoth, God of Israel. In his early naming he was called the Prince of Peace, but in a later mythology he is discovered as Satan. When both Sut and his Mother became degraded by the Egyptian and the Jew, then Sut, Satan or Saturn was called the Adversary of Souls. "Sut is called a Semitic divinity and he comes back as such with his Ass. But he returns as an Exile to the old country, not as a new creation."[1] Nothing is older than the Great Mother Typhon and her child Sut.

The Golden Age of mythology and the worldwide traditions of the Age of Gold belong to the Sabean Cult of Sut

---

[1]Massey, Gerald—A Book of the Beginnings, Vol. i, p. 13.

(Saturn). He was called Sut-Nub. Nub means Gold, and the double Sut-Nub was typified as white and black. The white light god was golden, and the golden star was Sirius. The Egyptians represented a period of time by a star, and in feminine form Isis-Sothis (Sirius) was the original type of periodicity. The ancient mysteries taught that black was but a superabundance of light.

The symbolism of the exotericists carries us back to primal truths that originated in the starry happy fields of the ancients. Many of these belonged to the Golden Age of Saturn's manifold aspects. Saturn appears with the scythe as a symbol of the Golden Harvest. When he is Saturn-Kronus, Time, endless are the cycles that yield to his scythe, and no one escapes his Scythe of Time, for "it will not be made to tremble one millionth of a second in its ascending or descending course."

With the coming of the Osirian religion, when the Solar God superseded the Star God, gold became accursed because of its Sabean and Typhonian origin, since the time-keeping of the early stars was imperfect compared to the perfect time kept by the Sun. So it pleased the Solarites to condemn them in a thousand different ways. It is at this point, as time goes on, that mythology and history become strangely mixed, an understanding of the language of the ancients seeming to be wholly lacking. Even on monuments of great antiquity gold appears already tarnished and considered as the root of all evil, which is misuse or misunderstanding of its early symbology. Fire, the earthly form of heavenly light, was a symbol of gold, which was likened unto fire, and its corruption meant death in its symbolic significance. Symbols and ideas of the ancients did not lead to the worshipping of the symbol itself, but stood for information conveyed.

Plutarch tells us that at the festival of the Sun those who wore gold were forbidden to worship at the shrine. In the Talmud there is a story of the "Flute of Gold" that had been sacredly cared for since the time of Moses. "It was smooth and thin and formed of a reed, and at the command of the king it was overlaid with gold, which ruined the sweetness of its tones, but with the removal of the gold, it gave out its original purity and sweetness of tone."

In the Egyptian "Book of the Dead," Sut in his Dog-Star capacity alternates with Horus as the purifier of souls. Bennu was a God of Resurrection, and Sut "is the god of his house, belonging to the houses of the things of the gates." He is here pictured as the Great One, a God with the shining body. As Saturn he is always found as the keeper of the bridge which leads to Infinity. In the "Secrets of Satan," given by Dr. Kingsford in her book, "The Perfect Way," it is written, "Satan (Saturn) is the door keeper of the Temple of the King: He standeth in Solomon's porch; he holdeth the key to the sanctuary, that no man may enter therein save the anointed having the arcanum of Hermes" . . . and " 'The glory of Satan is the shadow of the Lord; The throne of Satan is the footstool of Adonai' " or the Universe.

In the "Book of the Dead" the Field of Aah-en-Ru is the "heaven of the gates," twelve in number (the signs of the Zodiac) and these were the gates of regeneration that lead to the Secrets of God. In the Sabean period there were seven gates that led to Infinity (the Seven Great Stars). In the following lunar period there were twenty-eight gates, called the mansions of the Moon.

Sometimes a dog was placed at the Angle of Fire, "eating of millions in his name." He was the gate-keeper of the "Fallen Ones," who were the souls or the stars which were sinking in the west. In the British myth this dog is named Dor-Marth, the gate of sorrow. It is the gate of the underworld or death, the night that leads to the path of resurrection.

The ear was one of the types of Sut (Saturn), who was the god of hearing, the "Listener in the dark" before the coming of the Seer, Light.   It became a token of a covenant[1] with divinity, and this primordial god Sut, Saturn in his planetary form is the Ear by which we can listen and take heed, for Saturn is the heavenly mediator.   He brings in the new, and fulfils to the last jot and tittle the old.   At the present time, when the conditions of the world are changing, he is a generative force in world affairs, and the forerunning influence of the Justice Star, and will not fail to bring the unregenerate to justice, but will bring new life to those who have seen regeneration.   Saturn at the zenith, if well conditioned, is very important in the horoscope of an advanced soul.

Anubis was also a type of Sut as the Dog-Star.   He was the opener of a new cycle or a new life.   As the announcer he was the primordial prophet.   As Anubis he prophesied the rise of the River Nile by his heliacal rising, and as the dog his bark became an early type of prophesy.   He was and ever will be the Voice of the Gods.   When the Sabean days gave way to lunar time Taht superseded Sut and became recognized as the divinity of writing, the Scribe, who later became the planet Mercury.   Still later Sut, the Sabean son, became Atum, the Egyptian Son in the Solar Cult.   A peculiarity of this cult is that it continues its Sabean phase in the tenets of the ancient Typhonian.

There is a Jewish saying that the Sun always shines on Saturday.   Saturday is the day of Sut, who signified a Sunbeam.   Saturn represents the number seven, and the Sabbath is commemorated as the seventh day of the week.   In early times the Jews had no names for the days of the week, but reckoned time as seven years or as seven periods of time, always making the seven prominent.   Saturn was most important to them, as he was their Tribal God, Sabaoth, and they made his day sacred.   Sunday was the day of the Sun

---

[1]The piercing of the ear became a religious rite, as a primitive mode of appealing to the Deity, who was the Hearer or the Judge.   The primitive races of the world even today continue this ancient custom, and a very beautiful one it was and is, even though we today regard it as belonging to the savage.   Yet it is adopted by us.

and belonged to the cult of Mithra, from which we have taken it as the sacred day of the seven, but the first Sabbath was Sabean, the day of Sut, long before the solar Sunday had been introduced.   Sut's day was a day of repetition or resurrection, Saturday; and that of Horus, or the Christ, was Sunday, day of the Sun.

Arabs of the Mohammedan religion considered Abraham as identical with Saturn, and in the Kaaba "he is represented as an old man with seven arrows, or 'lots of destiny' in his hand."   They recognized Saturn in his early form of Sut, who became the Hebrew solar God as the Father, Jehovah, and in his feminine phase was one of the types of the ancient mother.

There is a pronounced relationship between Abraham and Saturn-Kronus.   Saturn or Kronus offers up in sacrifice his only son, whom he had by a nymph, and who was called Ieoud, only-begotten.   It was undoubtedly his most beloved that he offered in sacrifice to his father, Ouranus.   After the sacrifice Kronus becomes circumcised, and demands the rite of his followers.   "And Abraham received circumcision as a sign . . . that he might be the forefather of all those who believe . . . and the promise that he should inherit the world was not to Abraham nor to his seed through the law, but through the righteousness of faith."—Romans iv.

A mystical sacrifice took place among the Phoenicians during a time of calamity, which was thought to propitiate an avenging deity, thereby turning his wrath aside, even though his vengeance was thought to be a just one.   The sacrificed son was to be the most beloved, was to be offered by a prince, and was also to be immaculately conceived.   Those who were devoted to this sacrificial purpose interpreted this rite mystically.

The rite of circumcision was founded as a covenant instituted as a rite of reproduction in the Sabean worship of the ancient mother, when manhood offered itself to the motherhood, and the bow, the circle in heaven, was a witness to this new covenant. The use of the circled wedding ring is a peculiar rite, with which the covenant of the bridegroom is contracted and the sacred bond sealed. This covenant became a guide and help in establishing the twelve signs of the Zodiac, through conquering which perfection could be attained. This was the earliest covenant in heaven, and in the stars are found the seven steps or degrees that reach to the summit of attainment. The Sanctus Sanctorum was the Ark of the Seven, the Ship of the North, "The Ark to build, the Covenant to keep."

The Seven Stars of the Great Bear are duplicated in the Seven of the Lesser Bear, and identified with Sevekh, as the Crocodile-headed god.[1]

Sevekh was also type of the Crocodile-Dragon, with his Seven Stars as the seven heads of the Polar Dragon, at the time Draco was a part of the constellation of the Lesser Bear. The mythological Dragon was this Crocodile-Dragon of Egypt. Sevekh was a type of intelligence, the supreme one of the seven, and as the Crocodile was the Seer Unseen, because of its seeing when in the water with its eyelids closed, while remaining invisible to others.

Sevekh as the sevenfold, when summed up in the One, became the supreme type of One God, the seven in one. The religion of Egypt from first to last was consistent, conveying various aspects of this simple truth. They had their one Supreme God symbolized under many different names. Whether their seven were gods, souls, elementals or stars, their seven-fold was summed up in the One, or the eighth as the Manifestor of the seven. When the fatherhood had been established which superseded the motherhood, the supreme one was called in Egypt Atum-Ra, found under different names in different cults as Osiris, Vishnu, Jehovah, etc., all typical of the seven in one.

---

[1] The crocodile as Typhon was the earliest form of the "Fish-Mother," Atergates, Hathor, Venus, and other fish-goddesses who brought forth the child from the water.

SEVEKH, THE CROCODILE-HEADED GOD

Sevekh identified with Sut was called the "Crocodile-headed God." He was the manifestor of the Seven Stars of the Lesser Bear. A star-god of darkness who was resurrected as the Sun-god, Sebek-Ra, in his type of sacrifice. Sevekh became the supreme type of the One God, the Seven in One.

The older races always considered they had what they termed seven souls unified in a permanent one. These were the Powers, Principles, Elements in the composition of man. They were the mystic seven of the primal seven-fold heaven, the seven-fold forces of nature. "Hermes describes the one soul of the universe as entering into the creeping things, and transforming into the soul of watery things, and this into the soul of things that live on the land; and airy ones are changed into men; and human souls that lay hold of immortality are changed into spirits, and so they ascend up to the region of the fixed stars (or gods), which is the eighth sphere, and this is the most perfect glory of the soul. . . . The eighth was the immortal blossom on the human branch."[1]

Sevekh superseded by Sebek through his resurrection from darkness, became Ra the Sun-god, called the Lamb, and continued as the Lamb with the Seven Stars in the Book of Revelation. This same symbolism was found in the catacombs of Rome.

At the end of the twelfth dynasty Sebek, Sevekh, and Osiris were frequently interchanged, which brought about a religious revolution, but the original Sut and Typhon were worshipped at the Shrine of Ombos, that of Sebek-Ra, shewing the continuance of the Typhonian cult, whose worshippers kept the Sabbath as the day of Sut, that of Saturday.

It was under the Osirian cult that the crocodile was made to occupy the three decans of the entire Zodiacal sign of Scorpio, which as the house of Death represented darkness. This was significant of the trampling under foot of the ancient Typhonian religion, now called evil and unfit. But darkness and death typified by Scorpio really led to resurrection and a new life. Even, today in the diversity or aftermath of the dark lunar period, the world in its agony is striving to reach up toward the incoming Light, in which Sut (Saturn) plays his great part as the Justice Bringer.

Among the Sevens that originated in the Mother as the

---

[1] Massey, Gerald—Lecture.

Great Bear, she can claim "the Seven Elohim; the Seven Rishis of India; the Seven Hohgates of the Californian Indians; the Seven Spirits of the Great Bear found in Egypt, China, and Japan; the Seven Khnemu or Pygmy sons of Ptah; the Seven Kabiri; the Seven Sons of Sydik, the Seven Dwarf Sons of Pinga, in the Mangaian mythology; the Seven Dancing Indians of the North American tribes; the Seven SINTOS of the Japanese, the Seven Amshaspands of the Persians, the Seven Sons of Aish, the Seven Sons of Jesse, the Seven Princes of the Chariot, the Seven Titans with Kronus, the Seven Heliadae of the Greeks, the Seven Companions in the Ark with the British Arthur, the Seven Associates with St. George, the Seven Spirits before the Throne, the Seven Eyes in the Stone, the Seven Bears, the Seven-headed Dragon, the Seven Hathors, Seven Persian Wise Women, the Seven Sisters, the Seven Korubantes of Korubas, the Seven Whistlers, the Seven Pillars of Wisdom, the Seven Great Gates of Thebes, the Well of Seven Springs, the Tower of Seven Stories, the Seven Doors in the Cave of Mithras, Seven Steps of the Masonic Ladder, the Seven Inclosures of the Jewish Temple, the Candlestick with Seven Branches, the Seven Tablets and the Seven Seals."[1]

All the Star-gods appear under various names or combinations of names, to represent the different attributes that applied to them, and because of this complexity are often difficult to untangle or understand. Fundamentally their symbolical rendering remains unchanged. They are like the roots of a tree bringing forth many branches. It is said, especially of the Egyptian Priests, that though they may have forgotten much, they altered nothing. Attributes of the original Star-gods were given to the planets that resembled them. At the present time many of these have either been forgotten or their symbolical meaning altered, through misinterpretation, has become unreliable in its application to the horoscope.

---

[1]Massey, Gerald—A Book of the Beginnings, Vol. ii, pp. 137, 138.

ASTROLOGY

In modern astrology we use the terms benefic and malefic according to the aspected number of degrees between the planets. The so-called "malefic" aspects are of great force and of the greatest importance in character building and inner meaning, depending upon our own weakness or strength as to how their vibrations will be met, they affect each one individually and are of greater moment than the "benefic."

Considering Saturn as the planet, and his influence in the horoscope, we find that there was a great energizing of this planet in the years 1923-4. Saturn is a planet of authority and potentiality in revolution. It is not alone Mars and Uranus which energize and bring justice out of revolution, but Saturn as well. Saturn is the bringer of newer and more just conditions, and when placed in the Nadir of the horoscope, is a great lever in any aftermath condition of life, karma, or world transmigration. When Saturn is polarized by Jupiter it gives static or statutory justice. Saturn is a reintegrating force which seems to crush, but it synthesizes and impels.

Saturn is a kingly ruler when found in the eleventh house of the horoscopic chart, for when placed there it gives a spiritual insight which overrides any adverse aspect indicated at this point of the horoscope. Saturn will not be in the eleventh house unless the native has some spiritual development, and unless well placed in the Ascendant, is better placed there than in any other house, in the horoscope capable of spiritual evolution. A person who has Saturn as a ruler is one not to be trusted always in money matters, especially in this age of tarnished gold, for the influence of Saturn is not always honest in money matters, and when placed in this position it is a very dangerous influence, for a woman who is in the least sensual. It is the ruling planet of many prostitutes. The reason for this is that Saturn contracts and the prostitute reacts to expansive astral influence.

Look into the horoscope of any great person, and Saturn will be found in a prominent position, and always aspected to the Super-Solar polarities.   Saturn is indeed a bringer of justice to the unjust and a bringer of mercy to the just. Saturn is not a so-called malefic planet.   It is only called malefic when aspected to another planet of similar tendency, as Mars.   When well aspected to Neptune it is highly benefic, and in the later life is an indication that the native is becoming an Adept, and that the Neptunian mid-wife is bringing into manifestation or birth the power of rulership, which was and will again become the native's birthright and privilege.

Saturn is a mighty refractor of lunar aspects.   It enhances their beneficence and increases their malevolence.   It is a great planet in every Initiate's chart, and is invariably placed in a position of angular importance in the chart of a struggling Adept, who has taken a heavy burden and must renounce his life in order to win immortality on earth.   That is the meaning of "He who loveth his life shall lose it, and he that loseth his life having loved it greatly, shall find it enhanced with immortal glory."   These are ancient mystery sayings which Jesus knew and often repeated to those who were being uplifted by his renunciation of life, his life which was superhuman, in order that He might be released from all human obligation in the coming round of evolution.

Neptune is the greatest planet in manifestation at the present time and will be for years to come.   It is the birth bringer of the Aquarian Age.   It is energizing Saturn with his Satellites, symbol of his eight powers or manifested Logos rays.   Saturn is the Neb-Kronus and Jupiter the Seb-Kronus.   Saturn is Neb-Kronus because it is the heart of evolutionary progress.   Every kind of Jupiterian influence is subsequent to the adjusting and balancing of the native through the eight powers of Saturn, which are infinite in their extent, but finite in their extirpation of all obstacles to the spiritual energizing of the native and his immortal solar body, which is again infinite or cosmic in its possible eventuality. The Cardinal Cross is to the Cosmos what Saturn is to the planets.

The Moon in trine to Saturn is a condition which produces reconstruction in the emotional nature. It is a condition which brings a man into the higher consciousness, and will not fail to make a woman psychic. It is a condition which brings a new intuition and which causes an emotional shrinking from former conditions and unwise affections. It is the condition which purifies the emotional nature.

Saturn is the death planet, because it is both infinite and finite in its manifested powers. Saturn could be called the planet of life and death. It is life to the living, and death to those who sleep in matter and know no resurrection of the identity, perfected in Light. Saturn is the ruler of the Jews and is ruler of the Zodiacal sign Capricorn. It is a symbol of the generating life in our solar system, and the unknown planet is the generation of the Light of the Cosmos.

Saturn square Mercury strongly contributes to inspirational work, unless the mind is governed by the illusion of illness.

When the Sun is found opposite Saturn it is energy in opposition, mal-adjusted energy, or vital energy in opposition.

Mercury quintile Jupiter is a Saturnian synthesis. The number of Jupiter is 5.

The number five is almost a Saturn symbol, and also a bridging symbol. Reverse the symbol of Jupiter and we have Saturn.

Saturn opposite its own position gives a strong Saturnian polarity, and a precipitation or balancing of judgment between the incarnational purpose and its fulfilment modified by the life karma incurred.

A triangulation of Saturn would mean that Saturn would be energized by itself and could hardly be more active, and that one result would be a pure strain of magnetic polarity to all Saturn types.

The tenth house is the key to the native's worldly history. It indicates the promise of the earthly incarnation, as it will construct or destroy its efforts.   Saturn in the tenth house is judgment to the native, and will bring him to earthly disaster without any doubt.   When it is under the benign influence of the Moon he may escape without any great loss of worldly goods, but if the Moon is opposite Saturn he is doomed to self-destruction, or to fatality through scandal, and he will never be able to avoid a loss of worldly influence.

A conflict between Saturn and the benefics means the transmutation of the personal life of this incarnation through the restoration of Karma. The opposition of Saturn to Neptune means the appulse and precipitation of spiritual justice.

The God Seb

The Egyptian Star-god Seb, copied from an ancient Zodiac. This god as a type of Time was connected with the goose or swan, the bird placed upon his head representing this symbol. The bird was the producer of the egg and the circle was a symbol of the egg as well as of the first cycle of Time. Seb was god or father of both heaven and earth and in his planetary phase is Jupiter.

"Jupiter assumes the form of a Swan, and Brahmá also, because the root of all this is that Mystery of Mysteries—the MUNDANE EGG." Blavatsky, H. P.—The Secret Doctrine, Vol. i, 358.

67

CHAPTER V

THE COUNSELLOR

Sut was primarily the son of the Great Mother Typhon and her messenger. Sut, Sothis and Seb belong to and are inter-related in the ancient myths; they cannot be divorced. Seb as Seb-ti is Sut in a dual representation of Seb, as Time. Sothis (Sut) was the primordial Star of Time, belonging to the phenomenal origin of time. Seb was more abstract as a presentation of time in general. Star-gods were all deities. In the cult of Seb he was the stellar Father-God; the first Father in heaven, but as a Sun-god he was Father on earth.

Seb was also the son of Sevekh, when Sevekh was represented in female form, but at Ombos, Sevekh was worshipped as the son of Typhon (permutation of the ancient bi-une relationship.)

The divine fatherhood was first represented in Seb as God the Father of Heaven. Later he became God of earth, and then was called the "Masculine Tree of Life." He was father of five Gods, his number was five and he was Lord of the fifth creation.

The myth tells us that the embrace of Chaos and the wind was the producer of the Egg. This Egg was revered as a symbol because of its form as well as for its inner mystery, and as a type of beginning. The Egg of the cosmos belongs to the most widely scattered beliefs, extending over the entire world. In the "Book of the Dead," Seb as Lord of the gods and god of both heaven and earth is mentioned as having laid an Egg, or the Universe, "An Egg conceived at the hour of the Dual Force" or form. But as Ra he exclaims, "I am the creative Soul of the celestial Abyss. None sees my heart, none can break my Egg."[1]

The Egg was originally ascribed to the Mother and was said to be prepared for the earth by Seb. The earth was called the prison house of fallen spirits, and when souls entered the Egg of Seb to be imprisoned in the human world, they were born into a world of time.

Seb as Time is connected with the Goose or Swan and the egg. He is seen depicted with this bird on his head from which endless fables have arisen and many fairy tales. The Goose of Seb was a representation of Apt, and Apt was another name for the Great Mother as the first producer of the circle in heaven. The circle was also a symbol of the Egg from which Time was conceived.

Seb, Jupiter, in his planetary form, was called the Wise One, the Counsellor, and, in connection with all early gods, represented a dual force and was therefore known as mother as well as father of the gods. It was said of Jupiter that he was a man and yet an immortal maid. Seb as father-god on earth was called especially father of the Sun-god, and the earth was called the "Back of Seb," the Bringer Forth, or the mother producing for the benefit of all.

Again, when Seb was made the consort of his mother in heaven, the Sun-god on earth became their child. He is also portrayed as an old man holding the young Sun-god in his lap, representing the Sun of the lower world.

Seb was a later form of Sevekh, Saturn, the Jehovah of the Jews, who follows out his dual form as Jehovah, which is a compound word meaning male-female. Hovah was Eve, mother of all living, as the procreative Earth or Nature. As Seb-Kronus he became a god of Time, a first time in heaven, and when mentioned as Seb-ti he represented the dual form of Seb, as a duplicator of Time. Seb-Kronus was god of

---

[1]Oviperous, or Egg-Bearing, appears to refer to the world serpent bearing the cosmic egg in its mouth, archetypal vision, also development of the auric body, which is oval.

Time, but not of Space. He was the divinity with authority over that part of heaven that was nearest to earth. "Lo, Seb (Jupiter) is god of earth and the heaven by day, who declines when Shu (Mars) uplifts the heaven of night."

In the origin of creations, evening and morning marked the first day, and the gateway of Light was opened by the Star of Dawn, and this star was assigned to Seb, who thus becomes the opener of Light and Star of the twilight with the dark of the night on either side. Herodotus calls Jupiter (Seb), the whole celestial circle and places him in both upper and lower heavens as star of the double horizon. No fatherhood had been established in the Egyptian myth until Jupiter had been crowned with the title of "Tef," meaning the "Divine Father."

The Akkadian cuneiform ideographic sign, used to represent a God in heaven, was a star. The Egyptian hieroglyph of heaven is also a star, and the star bearing the name of Seb (Jupiter) as the father-mother god was a type of soul and spirit, called "The Soul of the World," and the soul of a virile adult male. Seb (Jupiter), as the Soul of the World, by the Orphic sect, was called the beginning, and middle of all things—heaven, earth, fire, water, space and eternity. His eyes were the Sun and the Moon, and he was the essence of all life and beings. He was depicted as a man with the upper part of his body uncovered, for that represented the stars, but he was covered from the waist down, which was assigned to the terrestrial world and therefore more secret. His scepter was held in the left hand, being nearest the heart, the regulator of all actions.

In the "Book of the Dead," speaking of the soul, the people are besought to, "Keep it pure and bright and shining, starlike," knowing that sin against the Sun or Moon brought about leprosy and syphilis, which they called the "Divine Diseases," due to the non-observance of periodicity. It seems to be conclusively proven that syphilis originated in this non-observance of periodicity. Syphilis was one form of this divine disease, and leprosy another. The Persians called it a sin committed against the Sun, the Sun that was the judge of men at night, as the Seer unseen. On the tomb of the Egyptian Seti I, in the Hall of Ra, the Sun, a group of criminals is to be seen who are described as "Those who have insulted Ra on earth, those who have cursed that which is in the egg; . . . 'those who have uttered blasphemies against Khut;' who was the Sun of the Resurrection, and the future life."[1]

According to instructions found on a MSS of the time of Rameses II, leprosy was looked upon with profound disquiet some six thousand years ago. There is a collection of directions for curing this disease in a papyrus of the time of the Fifth Pharaoh of the First Dynasty. These were found in an ancient writing case under the feet of a statue of Sut-Anubis, a first Hermes, the Divine Scribe of Divine Words, who was said to be the scribe of the antediluvian Stelae of the Karuadic land, which existed before the so-called flood of Noah.

Leprosy was indigenous to Egypt and Africa. It was thought that the white negroes, the Albinos of the black race, were produced by it. Five materially was said to be an evil number with the Egyptians. The five intercalary days that were placed at the end of the Egyptian year of three hundred and sixty days were called the five days of negation, the Nahsi or black days (Sut-Nahsi was the early negro child). Seb as Time and the number five were synonymous and were correlated with this time of negation, the five days that were followed by the festival on the sixth in commemoration of the feminine periodicity, called Tabu.

Jupiter as the number five was the fifth planet, god of the middle earth or the fifth creation. The "Book of the Dead" says of him: "Five is the number of Seb, is bread of the earth, and seven was that of heaven, the bread of Ra" (the Sun).

---

[1]Records—Vol. x, p. 92. Authority, Massey, Gerald.

Jupiter as Kronus was thought by a very ancient writer (Pherecydes, B. C. 544) to be the "fundamental cause in all creation." All the oldest stars that were time-keepers were called Kronian. Jupiter marks a twelve-year course of time, and as a planet takes the year of twelve months to make his celestial revolution of the Zodiac.

In Sancrit, Jupiter is called the Lord of Expansion, for he brings about perfection. The ancients considered the world as unlimited in space and duration, the moving principle in all things being God, symbolized by Jupiter. His forehead they made of stars, his body of planets, and his feet of animals. Sometimes his symbol was the great serpent, studded with golden spots (stars). Jupiter typified 'the essence of motion, existence itself.

Diodorus calls spirit and ether You-peter (Jupiter) on account of the true meaning of the word, spirit, which is Source of Life. He was called Father, the generator of beings, Father and King of gods and men. He was god of earth and all that suggested early life, a vivifying soul of earth that produced fruits and vegetables. He was Lord of nutriment, of the fecundity of the soil, and in all ways he proved to be not only a star-god but was god of the earth as well.

Identified with Jupiter is the god Siva of India, who is depicted with serpents around his neck and others twining about him, as a measure of time or type of the cycles of time, and these time cycles are called the "Serpents of Seb." Ra says to Seb, "Be thou the guardian of my serpents within thee."

Seb-Kronus, Time, is a destroyer as well as a renewer, as was Siva, who is seen with a necklace of skulls around his neck, symbol of the dead past devoured or destroyed by him. Similarly Saturn-Kronus or Seb-Kronus is fabled to have swallowed his children, the past cycles. In one of the older Zodiacs Seb is made to occupy the decans of Scorpio. He is Lord of the Ark, the Holy of Holies;

Scorpio is just below the sign Libra (the balance between heaven and earth) and represents the world serpent, the great tempter, to be conquered and replaced by the heavenly one.

The Equinox was also a point assigned to Seb, and when the Hill or Mount was placed at the zenith, in the midst of it was a temple assigned to Jupiter, where he can for all time be found at his Judgment Seat.

The first circle made by the stars in heaven was called "The Bow of Seb," and the first drawer of this Bow was the Great Mother. It was the primordial Bow of Time, by which the ancients calculated the revolutions of the planets, and whereby they were enabled to register planetary time. The returning stars or circle makers were known as the benders of the Bow. Drawing the bow was a figurative way of making a cycle or circle of time. The bending of the bow was a symbol of the closing cycle or circle. As the Bow of Neith it meant a cycle of gestation. At the winter solstice it represented the ebbing and relaxing life of the old Sun, but the fulfilment of its mission, proving its divine descent, was in its resurrection.

Anup became associated with the lessening of the light in the shortest day, typifying the smallest bow of time. The bow drawn at the summer solstice being the largest and greatest of the bows, was given to Shu, the Lion-god.

There is the other great bow, or circle, the Rainbow, which in the mythical deluge became symbol of the "Dawn of Serenity," at the vanishing of all harmful forces of the earth. It was closely related to the goddess Isis, Nature. The endings of periods or cycles in ancient times were always called Deluges, heralding a new promise for man and this world, a rebeginning, the promise of fulfilment. This promise of fulfilment can be found in the well-known Cupid and his Bow. Cupid is always the child. On a rock sculpture (Persian), this child is seated on a rainbow, as the image of fulfilment, or of perfected time. This is the covenant completed in the child. Beneath him are nine men, typical of the time of completion for this new birth.   Both the bow and the number nine are synonymous, and are symbols of the nine months of gestation.[1]

A woman when known to have reached the age of pubescence was thought to be invested with her Iris, termed her "Messenger," which was mystically related to the rainbow of the heavens.   Ir is fire, and Is is water.   These are "contrasted powers," symbols of male and female.

But a greater and far more spiritual interpretation of the Iris is given.   "This Iris, the circle around the eye and the light of the eyeball with its crystalline humor, suggests the ineffable union of Fire, Water and Light."   "The formation," says Hyde Clarke, "of the human crystalline eyeball with the Iris gleaming within its surroundings is in itself a source of infinitely suggestive and esoteric study and as the seat of conceptive vision, has been accepted as such by illuminated minds and deep thinkers."   "He who would attain to the highest and most perfect state, and rise to the sphere of absolute bliss, must be purified by Fire, Air and Water."[2]   The blending of the water and the word, of the dew and the fire, as the covenant, is but the exemplar in nature of that dynamic union which transmutes in the human nature of the God-enlightened man.   In China and other countries the rainbow has been given adverse names, because of the mixture of the light and the dark, or fire and water, due to the Sun shining during a shower, and so became an emblem of sin, thus making the rainbow a token of failure to keep the covenant, and it became typical of the improper or the impure.   Many myths arose from what was termed the descent of the rainbow, or being led into the rainbow, which was anciently called the "Sin of Tapu."   In some myths the rainbow was identified with the serpent, the serpent that gnawed at the roots of the Tree of Life.   There were

---

[1]Cupid is found in the rainbow, riding on the back of a fish, sailing over the waters in a cup (the Argha), and also in a shell, all symbolical.

[2]Arnold, A. C.—History of Secret Society.

three dragons whose colors were given as those of the rainbow, which Saturn-Kronus (time) placed in the heavens as a token for short-sighted man.

If the rainbow sometimes meant the breaking of a covenant, it may have had reference to the transmission of a force beyond the Light and Fire to which both, as well as matter, are subservient.

The rainbow has been called the heavenly snake, maker of the Bobo beads. The beads worn by Neith as the gestator were called Bubu in Egyptian. She was represented as the rainbow and also as the Goddess of the Bow and Arrow. Through the rainbow she is identified with the Great Mother who *was* the Rainbow, whose Seven Stars represented the seven colors, and Rainbow, type of the Holy Spirit.

"Didron in his Christian Archæology represents the Messiah supported in a rainbow-like veil of a beautiful woman, and this is said to be taken from one of the sarcophagi in the Vatican, belonging to the first ages of Christianity."[1] In these first ages of Christianity the nimbus was made use of as a covering over the heads of those who were the Blessed. It changes in form, for it is seen as an oval, as a circle, and as a triangle, all sacred symbols and typifying the Holy Spirit. The nimbus belongs to very ancient times and was evolved from the Great Mother, as the Holy Spirit, the Shekinah; harmonizing with the sanctuary or tabernacle mentioned in the Apocalypse, and the rainbow around the throne, which is reminiscent of the Peacock Throne of the Orient and the Bird of Jove, as well as the Bird of Solomon, the Sun-Bird symbol of spirit, lustre and light. This puzzling symbol originated in the ancient recognition of God and the Word of God, the Holy Spirit. The beautiful rose windows of our churches, found in every corner of the world, are images of Light and type of the sacred spirit, said to be "like a caress from heaven." Treasuries of knowledge and understanding are found in all symbols and

---

[1] Kenealy—The Book of God.

are within the reach of all, unless one prefers darkness to light.

Three, 4 and 7 were the sacred numbers of Light, Life and Union, and the number 7 was particularly the number of a life cycle. The T or the Tau cross of Egypt is formed of this number and was the symbol of "Life Eternal." The Greek letter Z is a double seven found in the beginning of the word Zao, "I live," and in the initial of Zeus (Jupiter), the father of all living.

ASTROLOGY

The symbol of Jupiter represents the soul expanding beyond matter. As Father of earth he retains his material form, necessarily helping struggling souls towards the Light. Although Jupiter is a maker of form, he is the symbol of internal power and a strengthener of the spirit. Jupiter is expansion and fully develops the moral sense, and in his constructiveness enlarges and expands the consciousness. Moral construction is always fully developed in the genuine Jupiter person, and is the governor of all the cells and atoms of the body of the man. When found in the twelfth house of the horoscope, the house of darkness, Jupiter symbolizes the threshold, waiting there to guide his children into the Light.

Jupiter was known as King of the Gods, because he dispensed both benefits and judgments, and as the planet, is a benefic materially and to the undeveloped soul; but he is a judge to the Initiate and a kingly ruler to those who are on the Path. He does not advance the Initiate, he benefits him spiritually and holds him materially receptive to benefits which come through souls indebted to him. Jupiter is a great force in horoscopes of money men, and is a silent protector of the poor.

Jupiter will be of marked benefit in the next few years to those who have received the expansion of karmic reward and will be held receptive by Jupiter to the benefits of those never before met in life. This can be ascertained through the aspects of Jupiter and Saturn, which are not usually taken into consideration, but which are positively operative to a native of this character. A great application of Jupiter to the mid-heaven will be found during an intervening time before the retroactive karma becomes operative.

Jupiter when conjoined with the Sun in a spiritual chart denotes expansion of the regenerated spiritual life. This has never been interpreted in this way, but is infallible in its exhibition of result, in forecasting spiritual unfoldment. Jupiter conjunction Neptune suggests the so-called illegitimate children, who more often seem heaven-born, and are said to be more perfect in body and more inspired in mind, and history teems with records of their leadership. The Neptunian higher love brings universality of genius.

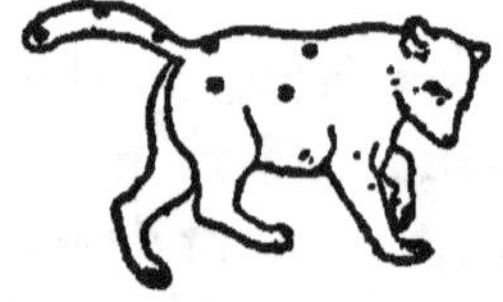

One of the Twin Lion Gods

The above illustrates the god Shu in one of his types, that of the Twin Lions, who were Lions of the north and the south or upper and lower heaven. He is here seen supporting the horizon in the east where the Sun ascends from the mountains of the plains to the high heavens. Above him is an ideograph of the sky. It is over this that Ra the Sun-god sails in his golden bark which at night is studded with stars. A star is the determinative hieroglyph of night, darkness. The horns are a type of courage, strength. In planetary phase Shu is Mars, ruler of the Zodiacal sign Aries, the Ram.

CHAPTER VI

THE "BOWMAN" OF THE GODS

The powerful, forceful and conceptive Star-god Shu was one of the most ancient deities. His origin and typology are somewhat obscure because of this, but he is readily traced back to the Mother who preceded all the gods, as one of her sacred Seven, being both guide and counsellor. In planetary phase he is Mars, whose life history and hereditary descent have fulfilled the promise of his mythical beginning, for he has been the warrior lord in the history of the present era, and the dual force given all gods or planets has been amply exemplified. In the readjustment of the myth concerning him he was made the adopted son of Ra the Sun and was called the "Heaven Bringer." "Thou leadest the upper heaven with thy rod, in that name which is that of An-Har."

Both Moses and Bacchus have a magic rod with which they perform their miracles, and both were saved in an ark, or ship or boat, typical of an ark. Shu was the god dwelling in the divine "Sekt," which was a very ancient name for the Ark (Argha), and as Shu-Anhar he was the lord of the tabernacle of the gods, which was the sanctuary of the stars in the sky, or the Ship of the North. In his dual capacity he was both Raiser and Separator of the heaven from the earth. As Anhar he was the god forcing the Sun along with his ropes, the celestial conductor, the Heaven-Bringer, not only the bringer to heaven. Raising the heaven is synonymous with beginning the circle; and bringing the heaven with fulfilling the circle. A day was a circle. Shu was the Bearer of the Sun, the Light of the Sun, the Bringer Forth. He supports the Solar Disk and as Anhar, the nocturnal heaven, and both represented the equinoxes when they supported the Sun on their backs.

Day was light and masculine, night, or the dark, was feminine. When Shu was given the color red, he was a symbol of the setting Sun, and his name was found written in the type of the Feather, while Anhar's was written in the symbol of the Vase, a sign of the Bringer, the Bringer Forth. When Shu wears two feathers they are the symbols of Light and Shade, representing the element of Breath and Air, or Spirit. He was the Child of the Sky. "I am Shu of divine company, my soul is God, my soul is Eternity. Shu, God of the atmosphere and the sky of light and air."

In another of his dual types he is given a sister called Tefnut, thus creating the male and the female, and symbolizing Breath and Moisture; the Breath of Heaven and Moisture its Dew. (Breath and the blood source were the mystical Waters of Life.) He was God of the Wind, which was said to be produced from the foam of the water. He was the Genii of the winds of the four quarters. His Pillars were the four cardinal points.

When he became Kafi-Shu as a divine type of Power, he wore upon his head the hind quarters of a lioness. The Kaf or Ape was a type of the star-god Shu, when he became the determiner of the Siderial Time, which was before the introduction of the lunar or solar time. The Kaf-Ape and the lioness were types of Shu and his sister Tefnut, who were placed in the sign Gemini, the Twins.

When Shu wears the two feathers he is the Light-God, God of Light in the Shade. He was also the light of the Sun, which was called the Lamp of Ra, as it shewed the position of the invisible Sun. He was the supporter of the Sun by night. In the earliest halving of the circle, when Shu upholds the heaven with his two arms making the north and the south, two lion-gods were placed at these gates representing the two solsticial stars as the two earliest law givers. They were called Kepheus in the north and Regulus in the south, Kepheus as the law giver of Aquarius the Waterman and Regulus the law giver of Leo, the Lion.   Kepheus as the ancient star-god, was represented in a dual character by the constellation of that name and by the star, Cor Leonis., in the constellation of the Lion.   The constellation Kepheus was called the Shepherd and his Sheep and was the Shepherd King of the heavenly flock.   This constellation rose when the Sun passed through the sign Cancer when he became the Shepherd of this domain.   Cancer was an early symbol of fire, and capricorn its opposite sign in the Zodiac was a symbol of water.

The Babylonians had "Shepherding Stars" for their celestial flock.   Anu, who was their god, selected certain stars as "Measuring Stars, Regulators, or Period Stars." They were Seven, the crossing stars of the mid-heaven.   In a very ancient royal tomb of the Twentieth Dynasty a calendar of astronomical observations was found, and these crossing stars were given as: 1, to the left shoulder; 2, the left ear; 3, the left eye; 4 was given to the middle; 5 was given to the right eye; 6, to the right ear; and 7 was given to the right shoulder.

Regulus and Kepheus marked the solstices in the signs Leo and Aquarius, and when the Sun passed through Aquarius, Leo or Regulus arose.   The Egyptians had two fixed points of commencement.   Kepheus was later symbolized by the planet Jupiter, and Regulus by the planet Mars, one of whose titles was "Lord of the fiery furnace."   Mars was also one of the Kabiri, the Fire Gods.

Sut, Shu and Taht the lunar God were the recorders of myths and the Hermetic writings of Egypt upon which the religious history of today is founded.   These sacred scriptures of Egypt are preserved in the great Temple of On, to be handed down from generation to generation.

Sut was called the first Hermes, Shu was the second, and Taht, superseding the first two, was the third and was known by the Egyptian Gnostics as Trismegistus.   These were the star and lunar gods before solar or Sun time had commenced. The Agathodaemon was added as the fourth of the divine scribes. Their writings were known as the *Hermean Books,* of which 1,100 were ascribed to Taht by Iamblicus, 20,000 by Salencus, and 36,000 by Manetho.

Shu as Shu-Anhar in one of his dual characters was known as the Twin Lions of Egypt, and called the Young Elder. The dual character of these Lion Gods is still found in the Judean imagery; "Judah is the lion's whelp. He stooped down, he couched as a lion, and as an old lion."

The lions were primarily given to the Solstices which marked the Egyptian sacred years. In their first representation they were lionesses, that they might signify a double force, strength and vigilance. Afterward they were given as Shu and Tefnut, or male-female, and later were made into the dual male type Shu-Anhar, and later still were symbolized by the planet Mars. As the lion goddess they represented the two eyes of the Sun, the left eye lighting the south, and the right eye the north. They blend into one as male-female, light and shade. Their most ancient form was that of the lionesses which in the "Book of the Dead" represent the endings of the journeys of the Sun. They were the conductors of the Sun on his way, and the makers of his festivals.

Shu was also the Bowman of the Gods, the Lion-god of the great bow, in which abode strength. He was a shield and buckler, a warrior, a supporter of the Sun, and the arrow was made his symbol.

As the hunter with his dogs, he is portrayed seated with the whip of rule in his hand, identifying him with Kepheus. The dogs of Shu were the punishers and devourers of the damned, the hounds of hades, our hell.

The Israelites, who became the Solarites, were the chosen of Ra, the Sun. They were the children of the wilderness of the Egyptian celestial myth, and their leaders were Iu, Au, and Shu the older star-god. The birth of Moses in the

Hebrew tradition is connected with the lion.   Ma-Shu seems to have been the Egyptian name of Moses, who was taken from the water and bred in the magical land that teemed not only with mythical but with mystical memories.   The head-attire of the two feathers of Shu was given to the Osirians as "The image of the Great Water."   Ma is a symbol of Truth as well as of Water.   A story is told by the Rabbins, whose traditions seem to be priceless, that Moses, when digging the foundations of the earth, came across a stone bearing the Great Name, upon which seven eyes were engraved and the seven stars that belonged to the northern heaven.

Shu as the great warrior was given two horns, typical of courage and strength, as were Moses, Nimrod, Bacchus and Dionysius.   In Shu's dual type Moses and Joshua of the Hebrew writings are identified with him.   Shu and Sut were both portrayed as an ass.   An ass was also a type of the Typhonian mother, and her sun-god was born as the ass. The ass and foal denoted the beginning and ending of cycles.

"There is a very rare representation of the Sun-god borne upon the ass.   The ass is portrayed as a person stretched upon the ground, hauling at the ropes of the Sun, as he draws himself up by means of it.   On his head he has the solar disk, by the sides of which are the two ears of an ass.   This is Shu pulling away at the ropes of the Sun.   Shu and ass are interchangeable."[1]

When solar time was ushered in, it was said that Typhon fled from Egypt on the back of an ass.   This was the period of the elevation of the male over the female, which caused the ancient mother to be cast out.   She was thought to have been disposed of forever, but lives today clothed in all her ancient symbolic purity, hidden only temporarily by the veil of present ignorance, for Zodiacal imagery is for all time. In celestial lore the stars and their leaders go out from the heavenly Egypt, under the guidance of the god Shu in his

---

[1]Book of Hades—Records of the Past.

type of ass.   The ass, tradition says, found water in the celestial wilderness above, as well as in the terrestrial wilderness below.   Tacitus says that the ass was placed in the temple and consecrated.   And Plutarch can be given as authority for the statement that the ass was worshipped by the Jews as the first discoverer of the fountains.   Ass and water are found in many fables of mythical origin which have evolved into a combination of religion and history.

Shu was made a lamp or a light for the young solar God. He was the marcher, forcing and hauling the Sun.   "Pull him along you glorious goers through the dark, you swift winged Mercury and blood red Mars, haul away at the ropes of the Sun."   This is applicable today as the light manifests through the sign Leo, the home of the Sun.

The supporters of the night, with all its hidden mysteries and powers, were the Star-god Shu and the Moon-god Taht, who became the faithful witnesses of Ra, the Sun-God. They were his two anointed ones of the night.   When planetary circles were revised, Shu was given to Mars as the young warrior, the Light God, and Taht the Moon-god was created that he, Ra, the Sun-god, might make his home in the luminary of the night.   These two anointed ones of Ra were the golden pipes that fed the seven-fold lamp of Light, which belonged to the old Mother and her Son, of the Seven Stars. Types of these, the Star-god and the Moon-god, witnesses for the Sun, can be found in the Book of Revelation as the two candlesticks and the olive trees.

In a mystical way the Pleiades were said to be the wives of the seven Rishis, the Seven Stars of the Great Bear, and were supposed to be the nurses of Mars, the God of War. Mars was "called the Commander of the celestial armies—or rather the Siddhas (translated Yogis in heaven, and Holy Sages on the earth)—'Siddha-sena,' which would make Kârttikeya (Mars) identical with Michael, the 'leader of the celestial hosts,' and, like himself, a virgin *Kumara*.   Verily he is the 'Guha,' the *mysterious one*, as much so as are the Saptarshis and the Krittikâs (seven Rishis and the Pleiades) for the interpretation of all these combined, reveal to the adept the greatest mystery of occult nature."[1]

Mars is said to be born of Fire and Water, "out of a Seed of Rudra-Siva (water), via Agni (fire), who dropped it into the Ganges" (the sacred river of India), a "boy bright as the Sun and beautiful as the Moon." He is called Agni's son, a fire-son, or star.

Rudra-Siva has the same meaning as the ansated cross of Egypt in its mystic and cosmic rendering. In the Rig-Veda Siva is called Rudra, the "howler," a deity both beneficent and maleficent, the Healer or Destroyer. Siva is the divine Ego aspiring to return to its pure deific state, and in its imprisonment in earthly form, on the personal side Siva is called the "roarer," the "terrible," and represents the powers of nature, which destroy that they may regenerate. And also as we liken Siva to the planet Mars, the passing of the *inner* man over the threshold from the narrow circle that will then divide or widen into the infinite one, as represented.

There is a very great mystic connection between the names Kumâra and Makara (Capricorn of the Zodiac). It is through their connection with Man that the Kumâra are connected with the Zodiac. As the five Kumâras they were Yogins[2] "who acquired entire exemption from passion." The Kumâras were the Virgin youths, "Eternal Celibates." The Kumâra as Yogins are five in esotericism, and their symbols were both *Aquatic and Fiery*. In their names we find their relation to the Zodiac, as Makara, "Ma," is five, Kara, a hand with five fingers, and five is the five-sided symbol of the Pentagon." Ma is also Water, and the mother, and Kumâra is the symbol of fire (spirit) and water (soul), the creator and the created.

Makara taken "in conjunction with the term 'Kumâra'—the numerical value of its first syllable and its esoteric resolution

---

[1]Blavatsky, H. P.—The Secret Doctrine, Vol. ii, pp. 549, 550.
[2]Blavatsky, H. P.—The Secret Doctrine, Vol. ii, p. 579.

into *five*, has a very great occult meaning in the mysteries of nature. . . . Makara is connected with the birth of the spiritual 'microcosm,' and the death or dissolution of the physical Universe (its passage into the realm of the spiritual"[1]) which is the beginning of the Night of Brahma.

In color Mars is red, both god and planet representing water and earth.   Water is the mystical blood of earth, and from Moses we have the saying that it "Takes earth and water to create a human soul."   In Mars is found the primeval generative principle within itself.   Mars, though the God of War, is also called "The Wrath of God" manifest in the desires of the flesh.   He is god of Life and Death, of Production and Destruction.   Mars, god of War, means bloodshed and "Blood was life and the shedding of blood was as much a type of conception as of death, in slaughter."[2]

No truer or greater conception of Mars can be given than that by J. R. Skinner in his "Source of Measure," p. 186: "Now Mars was the Lord of *birth*, and of *death*, of *generation* and of *destruction*, of *ploughing*, of *building*, of *sculpture* or stone cutting, of *Architecture*, or the *origin* of *measures*, and of *their uses;* in fine, of all comprised under our English word ARTS.   He was the *primal principle, disintegrating* into the modification of *two opposites for production*.   Astronomically, too, he held the birthplace of the day and year, the *place of its increase of strength*, Aries, and likewise the place of its death, Scorpio.   He held the house of *Venus*, and that of the *scorpion*.   He, as *birth*, was *Good;* as *death*, was *Evil*.   As *good*, he was *light;* as *bad*, he was *night*.   As *good*, he was *man;* as *bad*, he was *woman*.   He held the cardinal points (the pillars of Shu) and as *Cain* or *Vulcan*, or *Pater Sadic*, or *Melchizadek*, he was Lord of the

---

[1]Hindu exotericism represents them all as *Yogins*, whose piety inspired them to refuse *creating*, as they desired to remain eternally *Kumaras*, " Virgin Youths,' in order to, if possible, anticipate their fellows in progress towards Nirvana—the final liberation."   It was a self-sacrifice for the benefit of mankind.—Blavatsky, H. P.—The Secret Doctrine, Vol. ii, p. 243.

[2]Blavatsky, H. P.—The Secret Doctrine.

ecliptic, or *balance,* or *line of adjustment,* and therefore was
The Just One."

Going back to the ancient beginnings becomes very fascinating. Roots of words, symbols and myths, found in that
remote past, undergo strange graftings in the cycles that follow. All the planets originally represented as gods gra-
ciously look down upon humanity, ready to uplift those who
seek earnestly.

ASTROLOGY

Mars is strength and has a natural tendency due to his
double type as the Lion, to oppose forces as a means of
increasing his strength. Mars in his material robes represents
the grosser or lower forces of nature. When needing a balance of adjustment, the finer or more subtle forces of Uranus
should be called upon, which would give a super-solar vibration for the readjustment. This leads to a finely aspected
condition that would be powerful in raising one to the heights
of attainment, which can be found if Uranus is placed in the
sign Leo, home of the Sun, and a very friendly house for
Uranus. Adverse aspects between Mars and Uranus create
fatal inimical influences upon earth. Mars has the courage
of the martyr and energizes every symbolical sign of
the Zodiac. Mars is distinctiveness, and when he is in the
last, the twelfth sign of the Zodiac, all things reach their
fruition, and if an attitude of non-resistance can be acquired,
victory is given in the end, for then constructiveness affords
hope of spiritual attainment.

In planetary type Mars is made the symbol of matter, prevailing as it were, over the circle, symbol of spirit, to shew
that a struggle onward through the material activities of the
earth must occur in order to attain.

As the beginner of these struggles he was made the ruler
of the sign Aries, the so-called first sign of our Zodiac, where
he is enthroned in all his youthful splendor, and at the point
of increase of Light. He was also made ruler of the sign

Scorpio, a sign of Darkness, or procreation, which has been called the place of a "Chrestos in humiliation;"—but when Mars is found in the sign Leo, the Lion, heights of attainment are possible, for then he is "Christos triumphant."

Mars has been the energizer of this period of unrest, but in the coming cycle is to be the polarizer of spiritual generation. Thus sex will become an integral part of a new evolution instead of an excrescent growth requiring operation.

Mars is not likely to stir up unrest after the year 2000 for the Ram's (Aries) horns are heliacal spirals and indicate the double polarity of Mars and the subjection of the martial forces of Mars to the pole star or the Justice Ray, which was indicated in the old stories of Mars and his obedience to the Olympian fiat of the ruler of the gods.

THE HINDU GODDESS MAYA

The ancient Mother in human type as the Great Mother. From her breasts flows nourishment for all living creatures. Prototypes of creation surround her richly attired figure, as well as the many mystic and sacred symbols that belong to this Great Mother. In planetary phase she is symbolized as Venus.

CHAPTER VII

THE SHIP OF LIFE

The Great Mother, the Virgin Mother of mythology, was a representation of the human mother and in her matchless glory was the most worshipped goddess throughout the world. She was worshipped as the Virgin Spirit of ineffable loveliness beaming with splendor because transcendental and brightened with immaculate purity. She was the Virgin of God, the Word of God, the Mother.

The earth is now known to have existed even millions of years ago, and when we consider its incalculable antiquity, and that the Mother was placed at the beginning, we can scarcely realize her incredible antiquity and that through all the ages she has been an object of worship. It seems a peculiar desire of theologians to keep the masses in ignorance, not only of pre-monumental days but of monumental times, possibly through lack of knowledge or, with deliberate purpose, by preventing cleverly hidden primitive truths, from coming to light. It will be impossible to keep them much longer from the people, for out of the abyss of a dark material era we are entering into the light and the revelation foretold for the Aquarian Age.

The sublime truths of Astrology are, however, again becoming manifest and will cause man to lift his eyes towards the heavens where primitive man found his early religion which was beautiful in the extreme, today awaiting only our upward or inward sight to reveal to us the Great Truths. Their mystically conceived celestial symbolism, concealed in mysticism because so sacred, was a revelation coming direct from God the Eternal, and the personification of truths that have been and will be forevermore. The world is now in the agonies of a new birth, the pain must linger on until the divine perception of the reawakened soul comes into a realization of its birthright.

In mythical astrology the birthplace was always water, water being feminine. The primordial birthplace or Abyss, was the place of emergence and reemergence, or birth and rebirth. It was the "Piscina of Creation," and the Mother of the Abyss was this greatest of all Mothers. They called her Typhon and symbolized her in the constellation at the North Pole, the center of heaven. One of its names was "The Thigh" or "Matrix of the World," representing the covenant between heaven and earth.

The Thigh is portrayed in the Denderah planisphere as the leg of the Hippopotamus. The Hippopotamus was a primordial type of the Mother as the Great Fish, its large mouth being a type of the Ru, which means mouth, opening, gate, a place of emergence. Water with fish combined became the solar birthplace, found in the zodiacal sign Pisces, the Fishes. Hathor, Semiramis, Atergatis and other known Fish-goddesses were identified with the original waters of the birthplace, from which they brought forth the divine Fish Child. Two fishes represented Mother and Child, hence the two fishes of this sign. This is the child that was anciently portrayed as holding a rod of iron in his hand.

When the planetary cycles were calculated, ushering in new names and new phenomena, the ancient divinities were kept sacred, and Venus was dedicated to the Great Mother. The ancient Mexicans looked upon Venus as earlier than the Moon, and as the first light appearing in the world. In pre-solar times this Mother was accepted also as a Lunar Goddess, and once a year when the Moon came to the conjunction of the Sun in its place of manifestation, it was said, "The child of another year is born." The generations of the Sun, Moon and Stars were perfected in heaven, and were the peculiar attributes of the Mother, the "Begetter," the Bringer-forth, the Feminine.

In Babylon the Moon was held in greater esteem than the Sun, because Darkness came before Light. The Crescent, symbol of the Moon, was sacred among all nations. The Phoenician Astarte, the Babylonian Ishtar, the Egyptian Isis and Hathor, the Greek Diana, and other Lunar goddesses had the Crescent as their emblem, and it finally became the emblem of the Christian's Mary. There were three starry types of the Mother—the Constellation of the Great Bear, the Moon, and Venus, imaged in the trinities as the Two Marys and Jesus, similar to Isis, Nephthys and Horus, whom Champollion places at the head of his "Pantheon." The two women found in the Zodiac are the pubescent Virgin of the sign Virgo and the gestator in the sign Pisces, breath and the water source, in a double role of Light and Darkness, or one above and the other below the horizon. As the divine sisters they follow in line from Neith, (who wears a red crown, and Seti, who wears a white one "whose name is written with the arrow of Light the Sunbeam,") down to the two Marys of the Christian Era.

There were also the two divine brothers, Sut and Horus, and coming into our Biblical times, we have Cain and Abel, Jacob and Esau, and others, all symbolizing Light and Darkness, or the Celestial and the Terrestrial. There were also beings of a bi-une nature, male-female. Zeus was the immortal maid; Amen was the goddess Neith with four breasts; Merodach is made female in Jeremiah i, 2. "Her idols are confounded, her images are broken in pieces." In a Phoenician inscription Astarte is called King; Baal has been called a goddess, and the Chinese Venus of the Immortal Peach Tree was called the Western King. Venus was male at sunrise and female at sunset; she was called Har, the Lord, when above the horizon. The Peruvians called Venus, when a morning star, Chasca, the youth with the curling locks (Prescott). Astarte the Supreme placed horns on her head as a symbol of her lordship, says Philo; and Servius in a note says, "There is in Cyprus an image of a bearded Venus with body and dress of a woman, to which men sacrifice in female dress and women in a masculine one."

Jove, it must be remembered, was the Mother of the Gods and Eve was sometimes called the Ovarian Man. Belonging to lunar phenomena and as lunar goddesses they had a dual aspect, divine and infernal. Mythically they were all Virgin Mothers of an Immaculately born son. Exoterically the Moon was both female and male in allegory and symbol. What might be called the riddle of the worship of the Sun and the Moon, traceable in the churches derives from this world-wide mystery of lunar phenomena, "the correlative forces of the Queen of Night."

"In every religious system the gods were made to merge their functions as Father, Son and Husband, into one, and the goddesses were identified as 'Wife, Mother and Sister' of the male God, the former synthesizing the human attributes as the 'Sun, the giver of Life,' the latter merging all other titles in the grand synthesis known as Maia, Mâyâ, Maria, etc., a generic name. Maia, in its forced derivation, has come to mean with the Greeks 'Mother,' from the root *ma* (nurse) and even gave its name to the month of May, which was sacred to all those goddesses before it became consecrated to Mary."[1]

Astrologically the Zodiacal sign Taurus belongs to the month of May, and the planet Venus is the ruler of this sign and the Moon therein is said to be in exaltation.

The Goddess Mâyâ in a later human type is thus described: "She hovers over the waters of Source and presses her two breasts with both hands; the feminine fount, that stream of liquid life. The face and upper part of her body lighten with the radiance of the fire that vivifies, the spirit of life. . . . Within the cincture of her scarf she is seen as the bearing Mother. It is also observable that her figure and aureole of glory form the Cross symbol corresponding to the Ru,

---

[1]Blavatsky, H. P.—The Secret Doctrine, Vol. i, p. 396.

the three-quarter Cross of the Ankh sign. Her scarf also represented the Tie."[1]   In her relation to water and breath, representing the numbers 5 and 6, she wears the flower of five petals in each ear and a six-fold phallic symbol around her face. Six was the number made sacred to Venus, and Mâyâ is the Hindu Venus. Letters and numbers were mystically associated, and the letter M was the most sacred of all, whether feminine or masculine. It symbolized Water, The Great Deep, and in its origin was a portrayal of the Wave. Those born from this Great Deep were Mâyâ's sons. Indeed the most sacred names began with the letter M. Messiah was connected with Mar, the Sea, and with the sign Pisces water, and the Fish of the Zodiac, whose Sanscrit name is Minan.

The Lotus, which bears the seed within itself, was adopted as the emblem of the Virgin Mother of mythology. The Archangel holds in his hand the Lotus and presents it to Mary. Lotus and Water are among the most ancient symbols. The Lotus was called the Bark of the Gods, or the Sanctum Sanctorum, "The Temple of the Living God." Though this belief may seem pantheistic in conception, it was held with the greatest reverence. In the celestial world all was purity. The Lotus to the Hindu was the most exquisite of all flowers, and typified the mother. As Dr. Kenealy so truly expresses it, the lotus was as "some Transcendent Presence with the fragrance and beauty of a thousand heavens mingled into one." Similarly the Bark of the Gods, the Argha, the vessel of God that bears one safely over the waters, the Shekinah was symbolized as a *"blaze of glory"* surrounding God when he created. God was not looked upon as a man, but as a mystery not to be profaned, and it is well to keep in mind that "no impure thought was ever mixed with the symbology of the early archaic ages." The earliest idea of His spiritual life was filled with a light, almost indescribable and incommunicable. We fervently hope that the Initiates of the present time will redeem and reclaim

---

[1]Massey, Gerald—The Natural Genesis, Vol. i, pp. 465, 466.

pure primitive conceptions, coarsened and made gross by the materialism of our present day.

To quote Josephus, "The secret clue to mythology is physiological, the outer ring is Astronomical, because the imagery in which the primitive ideas, as well as others, were expressed, was figured first in the heavens," and its foundation is Water or blood as the flesh-making source. It was Mena, Menka, Menat, Ma, who was the wet-nurse in Egypt as well as in many other countries, and who in a mystical sense supplied this flesh-making fluid. Her name also means Dove, the bird of breath or soul, the Holy Spirit, whom we call the Holy Ghost. She is also well-known as the Black Diana of Ephesus. Menka was a title of Artemis, as the many-breasted wet-nurse, to whom the month of May was made sacred. In an ancient Hermean Zodiac she is depicted as a female Wateress, placed in the sign Aquarius, sign and symbol of our own new Era, and from her breasts flow streams of nourishment, which mystically is that liquid fire which imparts life to the spirit, and is the Light pouring over our world today. The brass vessels in Hebrew ceremonies were called the "Nurses of God," when they were formed like breasts typical of Menka, the wet-nurse.

The goddess Ishtar, the Babylonian Venus, whose emblem was the eight-rayed star, was goddess of the Seven Stars, and the eighth was the promised seed, the child, type of Christ. An Assyrian tile deciphered by the late George Smith tells of the descent of Ishtar into Hades, forming a very beautiful allegory of the soul in search of the spirit. She was worshipped in the temples of Syria and Hierapolis, and on the head of her statue sits a golden Dove. She was one of the Fish-tailed goddesses, like Semiramis, daughter of Atergatis, the mermaid of the Hermean Zodiac. She was "Queen of Heaven," like other goddesses, "Lady of the Dawn," goddess of love and beauty, but later became degraded into the darkest feature of the Babylonian myth. As "Lady of the Mountain," she reveals her identity with the ancient mother. Atergatis, like the Egyptian Venus in her fish-type, rose from the foam, and the Greeks turned her into a woman of great tenderness, or "tender fleshiness." Ishtar and Atergatis were called the "Begetters of the Universe," showing their oneness with the ancient mother.

Ashtaroth like Ishtar has been represented as the Moon accompanied by the Seven Stars. These Seven were known as the first "Flock," a form of the Host. The name Ashtaroth means, creating the "Hosts of Heaven." A name of the Great Mother in Hebrew is Herds or Flocks, and the stars were her children. Festivals were given for Ashtaroth and the New Moon, whom the Jews worshipped both before and after Jehovah was accepted as a male divinity. The hidden mystery of the Moon, in its dual nature was connected with Jehovah. "For the 'Fathers'—such as Origen or Clemens Alexandrinus—the Moon was Jehovah's living symbol: the giver of Life and the giver of Death, the disposer of being—in *our* world."[1]

Jehovah was a lunar symbol of the reproductive and generative faculty of nature, and was preeminently a lunar god, yet as male-female he was the Great Sea, the Holy Mother.

Ashtaroth like the Moon and Venus was the Great Mother, a symbol of Nature, called "The Ship of Life" (The Ship of the North), "carrying throughout the boundless Sidereal Ocean the germs of all being. And when she was not identified with Venus, like every other 'Queen of Heaven' . . . became the reflection of the Chaldean Nuah, the 'Universal Mother' (female Noah considered as one with the ark.) . . . The *Navi,* or ship-like form of the crescent which blends in itself all those common symbols of the Ship of Life, such as Noah's ark . . . and the ark of the Covenant is the female symbol of the Universal 'Mothers of the Gods' and is now found under its Christian *symbol* in every Church as the *Nave* (from *Navis,* the ship)."[2]

---

[1] Blavatsky, H. P.—The Secret Doctrine, Vol. i, p. 387.
[2] Blavatsky, H. P.—The Secret Doctrine, Vol. ii, pp. 462–463.

Ashtaroth and all other Virgin Queens evolved into Eve, the latest evolution being the Virgin Mary, who stands on the crescent Moon. The goddess Neith was also a Virgin Mother, knowledge of whom can be traced back 7,000 years. Her festival is still in existence on Candlemas Day, as a purification of the Virgin Mary, whose Immaculate Conception was demanded for over 1,800 years. Some of the doctrines of the mysteries, or of the Sacred Schools, are known to have been preserved in the Vatican, but their disclosures have been so distorted and disfigured as to be hardly recognizable. From them has been derived the doctrine of the Immaculate Conception, which "was publicly reaffirmed in the year 1855. This proclaimed the non-human nature of Mary." We have been told that our world is 6,000 years old and with the Bible as authority, people en masse believe this to be true, but it is a false belief and should not be allowed to continue unchecked. The Great Mother, the prototype of all Immaculate Conception, is so ancient that one needs almost to speak her age in whispers. The goddess Neith, or Female God, was thought to be "The only god without form or sex, who gave birth to itself, and without fecundation is adored under the form of the Virgin Mother, having given birth to God." (Deveria.) As type of the Great Mother she is most mysterious, as mystically she had come from herself, and had given birth to God. She was the Aditi of the Hindus, their Mother of God, the Hindus and the Aryanists began with little less than infinity. She was the boundless Heaven as opposed to the limitation of Earth. "She is not only the celestial vault or ether but is made to appear as a Tree, from which she gives the fruit of the Tree of Life" or pours upon her worshippers some of the divine waters of Life, and she is Time without limit. Astrologically she bears relation to the fish-goddesses, as the virgin of Virgo and the gestator of Pisces, and is the "Celestial Ship of the North," the Ship of Life. There are pictures of her with a Lamb, also with a shuttle, for she was the knitter of net work, as was Athena.

This net of Neith with which she fished her child from the water was the prototype of the caul in which some children are enveloped at birth.

Neith wears the head of the Vulture, another symbol of the Great Mother, and according to Hor Apollo, there was no male of this kind of creature. The female was impregnated by the wind, signifying Mother Nature and the Wind that became the Holy Ghost (the Holy Spirit). It is no wonder that in the "Book of the Dead" she is called "The Only One," and "Mightier than God." A sentence of the Commander Cambyses when he was introducing the King at the temple at Sais, is quoted by de Rouge: "I made known to his Majesty the dignity of Sais, which is the abode of Neith (Isis), the great producer, the *Genitrix* of the *Son, who is the first born, and who is not begotten, but only brought forth.*"

Isis[1], Issa, is the Virgin Mother as nature personified, was Mother of the Gods. Neith, Isis, Hathor, Venus, and others, are all one and the same. Isis was symbolized as the Lotus and as Mary of the Lily. She always wears her veil of divinity that no mortal hath lifted and the fruit she bore was Helios, the Sun. Helios, the Sun-god, called "The Light of the World," was the Light-Born, i. e., born in the cycles of time. Isis was called the sacred heart of Ra, the Sun. A description of Isis engraved on a sard is given in King's Gnostics, "She holds a sistrum in one hand, and in the other a sheaf of wheat, with the words, 'Immaculate is our Lady Isis'."

Notre Dame of Paris was formerly a temple of Isis, portrayed as the Virgin, carved as a Siren, with the body of a woman and the tail of a fish. The signs of the Zodiac were sculptured upon it, minus that of Virgo, symbol of Isis, showing that the church when a temple was dedicated to her, who

---

"[1]Issa, or *woman*, or Egyptian Isi-s, Isis. . . . But Isi was Jesse, the father of David, who was the father of Jesus, as Isi. So, indeed Isis, Egyptian, was the feminine form of Isi, or *Jes-*, Hebrew, as a form of *aish, man*, was *Jes-us*." Skinner, J. R.—The Source of Measures, p. 224.

in her origin was the Great Mother, the Holy Spirit. Isis is always represented with a veil, and the planet Neptune represents the intuitional force which pierces the veil of nature, and no man may lift that veil but the man who has become a god and sees through it. In the dissolving of the Veil there will be found a strong indication of lunar disillusion applying to the synthetic aspect of the mental condition by progression.

Isis as a Lunar Goddess wears the cow's horns, which identify her with "Vach." Vach was "The Melodious Cow," from which mystically mankind was produced. The Cow in every country was a symbol of the unresisting generative powers of nature, mystic and physical, with all "her magic ways and properties."

Isis standing on the crescent moon, with her infant son Horus in her arms, has been duplicated in the many beautiful Madonnas of the Christian Era, but as the Holy Spirit she was above and beyond any later identification given to her. It was said that she was worshipped on earth after the Sacred Books had been assigned to Taht, the Books that were written by the command of God, or by "Divine Revelation." Taht as the instructor of Isis and Osiris was the celestial incarnation of the earliest Hermes.

An inscription on a coffin says of Isis that it is she "Who opens for thee the secret places of those mighty names of thine. Thy name is Infant, Old Man, Germ, and Growth, Son of heaven, who makes the road for thee according to his Word. Thy name is Everlasting, Self-Begotten, the Dawn, the Darkness. Thy name is the Moon, the Heart of Silence, the Lord of the Unseen World." It is not out of place here to add a few closely allied words of Osiris: "I am yesterday, I am He who was before time began, I am the Dawn, the Light of the Second Birth, the mystery of the Soul, Maker of the Gods, by whom are fed the hidden ones of Heaven," and Isis was his sacred heart.

Osiris was represented as the Sun, god of life and reincarnation, and he was therefore made Lord of the Celestial Ship which carried the souls of the dead to their final judgment in that eternal progress of the Soul. Isis was represented by the Moon. She is nearly always depicted with the symbol of Venus, the Crux Ansata, in her hand, symbolizing the Eternity of Divine Love. Metaphysically Osiris is fire, the Sun, and Isis is water, the Moon, to signify which the ancients used the Bull and the Lamb, "To go forth is Osiris, to rest in meekness is Isis." The beads worn by Isis were nine in number, representing the period of gestation.

The Temple at Denderah was dedicated to Hathor, Mother of God, herself the "Habitation" of the Holy Light, the Sacred Mother whose child was the second person of the Egyptian trinity. She was the Virgin Hathor, of ineffable beauty, "the living tabernacle of the Sacred Light." She was designated "Daughter of the Water." Her lute was strung with sunbeams, her cows were seven in number, and her statutes were often gilded.

Eve, Mother Eve, also harks back to early times. J. M. Arnold in his "Genesis and Science" makes mention of a negro Eve. Eve was the first woman whose name signified Life and was called IYE (Eve). The Y represented an earlier F, IFE, which was a place of beginning, the abode of the gods. She is type of the ancient Mother, the original of all the Eves. In the Soudan the natives have a legend of Eve who had so many babies that the Father-God demanded that she have no more, so she hid them all in an oven, from which they issued forth as darkies, black with soot. In other words, they were negroes, this being explained in Eve, Cabin, Oven. All myths meet in types of the ancient Mother. The Cabin, as Eve's Oven, is the cabin of the primordial Ark. The soul on its passage towards rebirth was said to be "going in the cabin." "The 'Black Virgin,' so highly reverenced in certain French Cathedrals during the long night of the Middle Ages, proved, when last examined critically, to be a basalt figure of Isis."[1]

---

[1]King—The Gnostics, p. 71.

There is a mystery concerning the planet Venus. The conjunction of Neptune through Venus with the Moon was symbolized in the *black* goddess Diana of the Ephesians, the many-breasted, all-conceptive. The super-solar was manifested by black, a superabundance of light blending into blackness to mortal vision. The leopard skin of the mysteries showed the super-solar black upon the yellow solar ground and the astral moon light ever shimmered above it, visible to the clairvoyant.

When the super-solar manifests, the polarity changes and in woman becomes positive. Hence the divine woman is Father-Mother, the Jehovah Mother-Father. The symbol of the planet Venus is a circle or globe above a cross, representing Spirit above Matter, Spirit dominating, which was operative some two thousand years ago, when a message of Love and Truth was given to the world, but this past age has seen an inversion of the symbol, and matter and materialism have risen above the Spirit and the Truth. Thus the world has been brought to its chaotic upheaval of today, but all the pent-up love will release itself with the breaking through of the Light in the dawn of our Aquarian period, when the planet Venus will herald the Woman's Era. Venus is very occult and mysterious, and presides over all creative conditions. Her symbol is the ancient Ankh, the sacred symbol of Life, a covenant, a pair, negative and positive, or Female-Male. Since the Roman period Venus has been identified with Lucifer and Satan, or the Dragon degraded. This was the Dragon with the seven heads (Stars) that was said to draw the third part of the Stars from Heaven. Lucifer as the Devil of theology, identifies himself with Sut or Satan of mythology. Venus as Lucifer was the bright morning star, the Light-bearer over the earth in both its physical and mystical meaning. Small wonder that an Asiatic proverb says, "The Gods of old are the devils" of today. Lucifer was the genius of the morning star. "How art thou fallen from heaven, O Lucifer, son of the morning." Isaiah xiv, 12.

Venus was the star of the morning, and the star of the evening which made the first day, and so was thought to be older than the Moon. She was dedicated to the Heifer, the Pure and Sacred, or the Golden Calf, which was considered as of either sex.

The great Arabic Venus was called The Kabir the Great, when bearing her child, and greatness has ever been the name of the Mother. The Kabiri were the Seven Stars of the Constellation of the Great Bear, the great Goddess-Mother. The primitive girdle of Venus was made of wampum hair, fur and other sacred coverings, and was the loin cloth, symbol of pubescence, the early form of which was made with leaves and has remained sacred.

Venus as the Great Mother always rose from the water, the Universal Matrix, the Great Deep, the Abyss, and later they pictured her rising from the foam. Both Syrians and Phoenicians claim that a dove sat for several days in the Euphrates, the River of the Garden of Eden, on the egg of a fish, whence Venus was born. All fable and legend prove the origin of this Mother to be found at the Pole of Heaven, which point was the primordial Pillar of Heaven, the foundation and support of all, and was her Home. This Mother has been worshipped throughout all the world under different names, each adding its immortal tribute.

ASTROLOGY

Horoscopically the North Pole is to the heaven what the Zenith is to the horoscope. The Mid-heaven is to the progressed horoscope what the Pole Star is to the Mid-heaven. This axiom involves a new judgment of the progressed chart. It is a polarizing force which counterpoises the aspects operative at birth and brings forth into operative manifestation the opportunity for advancement.

When Venus is in the map of an Initiate who has been a great soul, but who has been suppressed in affection by the Yogi or preceding hermit, or had disappointment in genuine love, there will always be found an affliction of Venus, which is the polarity necessary for the higher expression of universal love and wisdom. Venus is invariably of extreme importance in such a map, and if well aspected to Uranus gives a leverage in the unseen world which no other planet can approximate. Venus in a watery sign indicates a strong relation to the Light, and awakens the astral in the human. When the progressed chart is pivoting on the natal, Venus is, if spiritual force predominates, imperatively Justice-bringing, being the turning of the tide energised by the tides of the super-ruler Neptune. Venus is Love. Uranus is higher Love, and Neptune is higher still, and after that comes the Unknown. The mission of Venus is Love in its purity. Venus is also a symbol of the "Creative Word," and is metaphorically spoken of as the instructor of the Giants, energising the creative work of the geniuses when placed in her own powerful and virile sign of Taurus the Bull.

If in the horoscope we calculate the difference by degrees between the natal and progressed lunar cycles, the number will be an index of the new conditions that will begin to manifest.

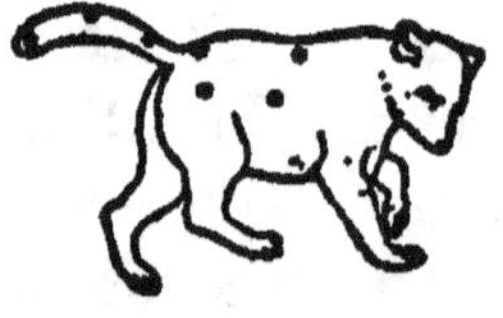

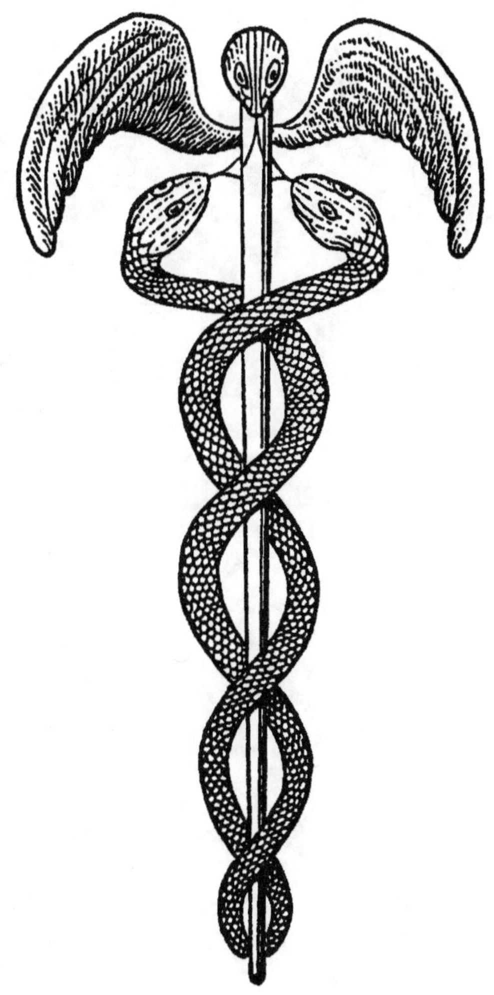

The Caduceus

The Caduceus was changed, modified by the Greeks. "The original symbol—with the triple head of the serpent—became altered into a rod with a knob, and the two lower heads were separated, thus disfiguring somewhat the original meaning." The rod was a symbol of the Tree of Life, and the outstretched wings were those of the Sacred Swan of Life. "Says a commentary in the esoteric doctrine: . . . *'The two serpents, the everliving and its illusion (Spirit and matter) whose two heads grow from the one head between the wings, descend along the trunk, interlaced in close embrace. The two tails join on earth* (the manifested Universe) *into one, and that is the great illusion,"* O Lanoo!—Blavatsky, H. P.—The Secret Doctrine, Vol. i, pp. 549-550.

CHAPTER VIII

HERALD OF LIGHT

First knowledge of the god Taht harks back to his identity with Sut, the Dog-Star. Like other fatherless gods, he was pre-monumental, and therefore very ancient. According to mythology at this early time he was both child and consort of Sevekh, who was symbolized in a feminine form as the Great Mother, "Mistress of the Writings" and register of the records made by Taht.

Taht in his lunar phase was called the bright side of the Moon, the side which contained the essence of creative wisdom of which he was the "Revealer." He was the "Divine Scribe," "Lord of the Divine Word," the "Divine Healer" and "God of Medicine," whose medicine was "Magic." As a God he was most mysterious, and as the Word or Logos existed far earlier than the monuments. He was known as the "Divinity of Writings" at and after the time of Menes, which was about 4000 B. C., when a period of great civilization obtained in Egypt.

Originally a Star-god he became a Moon-god, and when perfected time arrived or had been discovered, he was turned into a Sun-god (Ra), became a reckoner of solar time and then was named the Savior of Souls (stars), as they emerge from the dark or night. This placed Taht under Ra's supremacy, but Taht ever remained the "Revealer of Secret Wisdom giving Truth its Splendor," the Scribe and the Messenger of the Gods. He was also the Messenger of the Sun, making his revolutions in the shortest space of planetary reckoning.

As Moon-god he built the temple of the lunar zodiac,

establishing the twenty-eight mansions of the Moon and the four corners or quarters symbolized in the Tat Pillar Cross, and made sacred to the planet Mercury as was the number four. He was Lord of the fourth creation and was said to be born on the fourth day of the month. The Tat Cross was the emblem of the four cardinal points of the world designed by Taht and given to Ptah. This is the cross that led to the Hermetic path of the cardinal cross, the ends of which were lost in infinity. By the bending of the corners of this cross, the Swastica, the Fire-cross of India, is obtained. It was the symbol of Life representing the vivifying fire.

When Sirius, Sothis, or the Dog-Star (the same star under different names) was found to be losing time in its heliacal rising, losing four minutes each day, creating an extra day every fourth year, Taht in his lunar form as Hermes Anubis, the Golden Dog, symbolizing the Light or better half of the Moon in its reckoning, came to the assistance of this lagging star. At a later period Taht is seen traveling in a solar boat, crowned with a seven rayed disk, typifying the 365 days of the Solar reckoning, and the seven rays represent him in his lunar phase as god of the seven days of the week, Moon time. He jumps out of the boat every fourth year (leap year).

Taht as Moon-god[1] kept the horizon of the resurrection showing the way up from the underworld or night, and like Nebo, was keeper of the morning and evening "Gate of Souls." Taht was the double-headed watchdog of the Twilight, guide of souls (souls of the gods were the bright and beautiful stars) that were going into the dark or the underworld. On their rearising, he became the Golden Guide, the Herald of Light, for their resurrection. While on this journey he assumed the title of the Embalmer and Keeper of the Gates. As Mercury he was called the child of the sky

---

[1] Taht as the male lunar deity was impersonated by the half moon, and this horned moon was a symbol of the drinking horn. Drink and drinking were sacred customs long before they became profaned.

and the light of the sun, because of his youth and golden color.

Statues of Mercury (the Messiah of the Egyptians) as a young god were erected and placed at turning points in highways, and on doors and gates as a protection from harm. These statues were cruciform in shape, and represented Mercury as the interpreter of the gods by word of mouth.   There is an unexpected and incredible potency and strength belonging to the spoken word, which in modern times is rarely believed in.   When Mercury spoke through the oracles, his message was, "I am he whom you call son of the Father (Jupiter), having the key of the heaven (the Sun).   I come to young mortals."   Once a year these statues were garlanded with fresh flowers by the Priests, and every seventh day they were anointed with oil.

In the Denderah planisphere within an emblem of the full moon, eight gods are seen.   This is called the place of Smen, or the Full Moon of Easter, and was and is still given as the place of the resurrection of the child Christ, the Egyptian Messiah.

The eight primary gods of Egypt were the rulers in chaos, before a cycle of time had commenced.   They did not belong to Egypt alone.   Smen existed before the "firmament was lifted by Ra" in the Sabean time.   When lunar time was established Taht became Lord of Smen, but when solar time was introduced, the son as Horus was annually established in this place, symbolizing the changing of the feminine Moon-god, into the masculine Sun-god Ra.   It was the change from darkness to light.

Egypt considered the octave divine.   It was the numerical sign of the primary eight gods.   The eight-rayed star was their ideograph of divinity.   It became a symbol of Horus-Osiris when manifestor of the eight, and also of the constellation of Orion, the mummy constellation called the "Only One" who rose again.   It was an emblem of the child, also of the mother.   An eight-rayed star was found in the Catacombs of Rome as a symbol of Christ. It was also a symbol of Buddha. It was continued as an abstract of divinity. The number eight has the numerical value of the place of the beginning, out of which all comes, and was a type of Infinity. "The *Ogdoad* or 8 symbolizes the eternal and spiral motion of cycles, the 8, ∞, and is symbolized in its turn by the Caduceus. It shows the regular breathing of the Kosmos presided over by the eight great Gods—the seven from the primeval Mother, the One and the Triad."[1]

Smen was the place of the first Seven Elementaries, Powers and of the Great Mother, existing before the division of heaven into upper and lower realms. It was the place where souls were purified and prepared, where darkness was transformed into light, renewal and resurrection.

The lunar Zodiac which had been established by Taht, was superseded by the solar one which introduces the young god Khunsu, the young "Prince of Peace," called the child of the Sun and the Moon. The blending of the Sun and the Moon produced a perfect fulfilment in the solar son, herald of the solar timekeeping. The lunar son completed the circle of the Moon, the solar son then completed the circle of the Sun, and became one with the Sun-god, Ra, maker of the solar temple or Zodiac. The Moon-god Taht wears the half Moon on his head; Khunsu the child wears the full Moon, as the "Fulfiller." This full Moon still determines the time of Easter, which marks a Sabean, Lunar and Solar year of the Metonic cycle, a cycle of nineteen years, a period of eclipses and the number of the Egyptian "Book of the Dead." By dipping into the far past one finds that the Talmudic traditions go back to the very beginning of time when the first temple or circle was built by the very ancient Mother and son. This same son built each temple in turn, Stellar, Lunar and Solar, and though his name was changed at the entrance of the different cults, he was always the new-born Prince of Light, a Messenger, and a Messiah,

---

[1] Blavatsky, H. P.—The Secret Doctrine, Vol. ii, p. 580.

because he was heaven-born.   He comes down to us with all his golden glory of the past, as the planet Mercury, who was the inheritor of the Word from his ancient mother who was called "The Living Word."

The Books of Taht were preserved in the temple at On, and were filled with the original myths of Hebrew mythology, and their fragments persist in the Hebrew writings and scriptures. Taht is similar to the Hebrew Thuah—meaning to speak—and is a Hebrew symbol of Tongue, Speech, Mouth, etc. Hebrew language cannot be understood without knowledge of symbolic interpretation.   Tradition claims that these books of Taht contain the records of 36,500 years.   Taht persists throughout three periods of early reckoning. We have known him as the god, Sut, when he was the "Voice of the Gods;" as Shu when he was the "Keeper of Records of the Law;" and as Taht when he was the "Transformer," all being represented by the planet Mercury.   In the Divine Pymander of Hermes Trismegistus, fragments of these ancient books are found in which Taht is called the son of Sut (Saturn), and in the "Book of the Dead," Taht is Sut, the first form of Hermes (Mercury).   Hermes Trismegistus was the Greek name given him.

Taht was the Psalmist of the "Book of the Dead," which describes the descent of the soul and in its wanderings through the darkness of the underworld, thence passing onward and upward into the presence of the Sun.   The One Hundredth Psalm is assigned to Taht.

Taht, Hermes, Sut, Satan, Typhon and Seth were all generic names of the first Initiates, who were the founders of the Mysteries and who wrote the Books of Taht, in hieroglyphics and numbers, conveying the secret wisdom.   They gave enlightenment concerning the solar and planetary gods, during a very early period of time, as well as allegories concerning initiations into adeptship that were connected with the eclipses, which mythology fully explains.   They also gave the key to oracles and elementary works on science.   They were in existence long before the Books of Moses were known. Josephus writes of these as containing a strange wisdom concerning stars, and a message to the effect that the world was to be destroyed by fire and flood.[1]

The earliest of the books of Taht were undoubtedly antediluvian. Their hieroglyphics were found on columns or pillars, called Stelae, and were said to have been written by the "Sons of the Dragon," the Hierophants of Egypt and Babylonia. The title, "Sons of the Dragon," was known before the Great Deluge and was applied to the Atlantean Initiates. The Egyptians have been called the descendants of the Atlanteans, and the East Indians the descendants of the Lemurians.

Lemuria seems to have been closely connected with Australia. There should be great interest in Australia, the eastern starry land. The numerical value of its name is said to be superior to that of any other country save that of America. Australia will become a great center of esoteric research, but will not be known as such for some years yet to come. Australia is said to be a fragment of ancient Lemuria, which joined Lemuria to a great inland continent, about which nothing has ever been found out, and which will only be revealed through astrological and psychic research. Australia was not a civilized part of Lemuria. It had a very ancient civilization of its own, and was not an integral part of the Lemurian civilization. Australia will not come into its own until America has redeemed the world. Then, and not till then, will Australia become a great Republic, internationally famous as the home of the greatest culture and the birthplace of the most extremely developed sensitives.

---

[1]"The Prisse Papyrus has been called the most ancient book in the world (this does not refer to the Books of Taht). It was discovered in the Eleventh Dynasty, and contained copies of far more ancient documents, dating from the Third and Sixth Dynasties five or six thousand years old. This contained the literature of Egypt, whose people were great lovers of books. In this are found the precepts and maxims of Ptah-hept, and among them the fifth commandment of the Mosaic Law—'Honor thy Father and thy Mother, that thy days may be long in the land'."

By finding the date and casting a map of the time of the first English settlement in Australia, a prophetic aspect may be found between the Moon and Uranus, which could foretell the later destiny of this Australian treasury of antediluvian progress and aspiration. Australia, peopled with the dregs of Europe, will become the flower of our later development. A land which could redeem the criminal from his crime can reclaim an Empire and can make a world aware of its upward trend.

The stone or pillar, called the pillar of Hermes, was known as "The Emerald Tablet," a legend about which says that it was found by Alexander the Great in the tomb of Hermes, which had been hidden by the Priests in the very depths of the Great Pyramid; and the writing was thought to have been done by Hermes himself on a large plate of emerald, by means of a pointed diamond. The emerald was dedicated to Mercury by ancient astronomers.

In Egypt magic attained to a state of completion, and was a perfect science or doctrine, and nothing has surpassed the wisdom engraved upon this Stone of Hermes, called "The Emerald Tablet." It contains the doctrine of the unity of all things, the immutable law of equilibrium, ideas and expressions relative to the Creator and the Created, and an illuminating treatise on the Astral Light; in fact, the Emerald Tablet contains all magic and the key which unlocks the mysteries of Egypt or the wisdom of untold ages. It was said that in concealing his books under a pillar, Hermes found there the two pillars of stone upon which the great wisdom was written, showing that they had belonged to those ancient forefathers, the Atlanteans, the "Sons of the Dragon." Undoubtedly symbolical copies of these primitive records, which were covered with hieroglyphs, were reproduced and placed in the most sacred corners of Egyptian Temples, from which, it was said the Egyptians had gotten their great wisdom.

In the sacred writings of Hermes Trismegistus containing

an account of the old Mitzraimic philosophy, we find that *"nothing in the world perishes, and that death is not the destruction, but only the change and translation of things, . . . that when the world becomes degenerate, then that Lord and Father, the Supreme God, and the only governor beholding the manners and deeds of men, by his will, which is his benignity, always resisting vice and restoring things from their degeneracy, will either wash away the malignity of the world by water, or else consume it by fire, and then restore it to its ancient form again."*[1]

Destruction by fire and flood is described in the legends of many countries.

There is an Hermetic axiom that "the cause and the splendor and variety of colors lie deep in the affinities of nature, and that there is a singular and mysterious alliance between color and sound." Silver and green were associated together in the days of Hermes. White and black equated with the blue and red of the solar colors, blue was of heaven as the spirit, and red of the sun, as the flesh. The Hebrew heaven is paved with sapphire stones under the feet of the Eternal. "And *there was* under his feet as it were a paved work of sapphire stone, and as it were the body of heaven in *his clearness.*"—Exodus, xxvii, 10. There were two pillars in an ancient temple at Tyre said to be dedicated to Hercules, belonging to a period between five and six thousand years ago. They were of gold and emerald stone, symbols of and representing God and the Holy Spirit, God as the Golden Pillar, and the Holy Spirit as the Pillar of Emerald. The Apocalypse was sometimes called the "Pillar of Hercules," the "Pillars of Heaven," and the "Table of Emerald." "Pillars of Hercules" was a name given to a Rock, a word, so often used in the Bible as a religious symbol.

The Agathodaemon, or Good Serpent, that was endowed with the knowledge of good and evil, or divine wisdom, is shown by Champollion to be a deity called the Great Toth-

[1]Kenealy—The Book of God, pp. 145, 146.

Hermes. Hermes or Taht in human form was Hermes-Trismegistus, the "Thrice Great Hermes," founder of the Hermetic philosophy, on whose tablets were found the mysteries of the ages.

In the terrestrial incarnation of Taht he was called Trismegistus of the Rosetta Stone. The Rosetta Stone with its trilingual inscription was found in 1799 near the town of Rosetta, and supplied a point of commencement for the deciphering of Egyptian hieroglyphs. It was in 1822 that Champollion first interpreted these, and to him we owe the translation of that weird picture writing through which "Egypt, though dead, yet speaketh."

Taht, as the Light side of the Moon, was supposed to contain the essence of divine creative wisdom, represented as the serpent. The winged disk is a luni-solar symbol, showing the two halves of the lunation or the conjunction of the Sun and the Moon. The combining of the two in one, represented by the winged disk, was the emblem of the Lord in heaven the giver of light.

Both Sut and Taht hieroglyphs are Tet, an earlier sign of Tset, a two in one origin. Great interest attaches to this, as the Tet or Tset was a serpent. Eliphas Levi states that "Hermes duplicated the Serpent, setting it against itself, and in an eternal equilibrium, he converted it into a talisman of his Power, into the glory of his Caduceus."[1] The Caduceus is derived from the Egyptians. It consists of two serpents entwined about a rod, and as a symbol is both cosmic and astronomical, for the head and tail represent the points of the ecliptic, where the planets and the Sun and Moon meet together. The rod probably meant the cerebro-spinal system and the central cross; in the earth sign, may in one of its aspects have indicated the crossing of the super-solar force from the sympathetic to the cerebro-spinal system. The rod is that of Mercury, and sometimes is turned into the head of a serpent. The Uraeus worn on the heads of the

---

[1] The History of Magic, p. 134.

Egyptian gods was their rod and staff of power. Taht, when keeping record of good and evil, as the recorder and reckoner of the earth, uses a sort of tally-stick, or staff. "Thy rod and thy staff they comfort me," is written in the Shepherd Psalm, and Mercury was a shepherd of the Stars. The rod of Hermes (Mercury) is a serpent symbol. The rod of Moses turned into a serpent. Taht (Mercury) wore upon his head the Ibis, and by means of the Ibis Moses saved his army from the serpents.[1] The typical Word, Logos, or messenger, is a universal symbol, and Taht, as the lunar word, in various languages has the Egyptian name of the Voice, or the Word.

In a fresco of the Second or Third Century there is a picture of Elijah ascending in his fiery chariot and the figure of Mercury (Taht) appears in the picture, "He that cometh" was a name of the Ibis of Taht (Ibis is the stork). He was the messenger, the returning one, as was Elijah. Taht was the recorder of occult wisdom, the maker, the fecundator of Truth. He was the Word, not the Flesh, made True.

In the new solar creation he became the home of the Sun. "Behold thou shalt be called Taht, the abode of Ra . . . and he was given the north and the south of the sky, and there arose the Moon crescent of Taht," a type of the Returner. The Cynocephalis, or Aan, called "Luna's sacred beast," was the sacred animal of Hermes or Taht. This animal performed its devotions in front of a column crowned with a triangle and covered with hieroglyphics, evidently intended for one of the Pillars of Taht conveying the great wisdom. This lunar deity was also the oracle of the gods of periodic time, and to quote Hor Apollo, was the only animal that at the equinox utters its cry twelve times a day.

---

[1]Taht also wears the Atef-crown and the lunar disk, the Atef-crown denoting the solar god as the Father of Souls in the lower world, night.

ASTROLOGY

Going back into the early Sabean childhood of Mercury, and following him down through the ages to the present time we find his messages and his mysteries connected with all the planets, as he seems to enfold each in turn, for anciently he bore relationship to all other gods. He was their scribe, their messenger, and especially the bringer of the Light, for he was the "Herald of the Light" in his golden days. The symbol of the planet Mercury is the crescent Moon above the full Moon, and is a Christ symbol, representing a manifestation of the child Christ, the child of the Sun and the Moon, who rises above the Cross that belongs to earth, while the creative Word or Voice pierces the universe. It is a symbol of the Caduceus referring to that mysterious fiery power, the Serpent Force, which needs to be fully controlled before it reveals knowledge of spiritual things. It is the spiral creative energy in dual form, the positive and negative of all life power, and brings Cosmic consciousness.

When Mercury is posited in the ninth house of the horoscope, the house of Light, and is aspected to Venus in the third, it is a reciprocal relation of great power in the chart of an Initiate. The third decan of the sign belonging to this house has the sub-influence of the Sun, and Mercury in his lunar phase is made the home of the Sun that he may shine through the darkness, whether this darkness be mental or physical. For Mercury is one who heals the blind in their night wanderings and restores sight, as he emerges with the Sun into the light. Astrologically he is said to be more occult than Venus. He is the Shepherd who watches over his golden flock in heaven, and the true seekers of his occult wisdom on earth, for the divine wisdom he received he has imparted in books, and in him is the latent memory which he is ever ready to restore to the earnest seeker. His creative wisdom is found in his Caduceus. The Moon and Mercury have always been closely related, and aspects between them are most enlightening, especially when Mercury is in his own house. The Moon is always represented as being under the feet of the Virgin or on her brow. In all ancient religions the Moon was placed upon the brow nearest to the brain. Mercury governs the brain and the symbol of Mercury is intimately connected with the Moon. The Moon and Mercury are interchangeable in their wisdom. The Moon represents the higher wisdom in an Initiate's chart and Mercury the lower mind body, which is under the Moon or lunar wisdom instruction. Mercury is not a lunar planet nor a solar one, it is liaison officer between the solar and lunar forces. He was the messenger keeping time daily during solar and lunar phenomena and was connected with the god and goddess of Light and together with them gave inherent intellect and a ready exchange of ideas.

If the Sun is badly aspected in a chart to the Moon and the Moon is benefically aspected to Mercury and the Sun benefic to Mercury, the evil of the bad solar aspect will be counteracted in a very great degree. This is one of the judgments which will give results, for Mercury is the planet governing the intellectualists, and many people are finding and having a conflict between the Solar and Mercurial aspects which are neutralized by the Moon placed as described. Such a position indicates the progressing soul who is susceptible to an advancing realization, and who changes his creed, as it were, with his breakfast food, for the intellectualist is made changeable by a lunar aspect benefic to Mercury. The Moon is a powerful deflector of the mind, and can be a great hindrance to any mental achievement unless the native is ruled by Mercury or Mercury is in the house of the Sun, in which case Mercury is in super-solar exaltation and should produce the inspired mystic or leader. It is written of the men of Mercury that they are metaphorically immortal, through their wisdom.

Mercury's connection with the cross is of deep importance. "Eusebius says 'Hermes is the Emblem of the word which creates and interprets all' the creative Word that reaches through all the universe."[1] Mercury is also a god of cunning, both in his words and in his actions. Being quite capable of both fraud and theft, he has been called a thief (i. e. of the dark), a god of thieving, and it is not always well to find an afflicted Mercury in the horoscope.

But he was the Messenger flying everywhere conducting souls to the other world. He was the Sweet Singer of Heaven.

---

[1]Skinner, J. R.—Source of Measures.

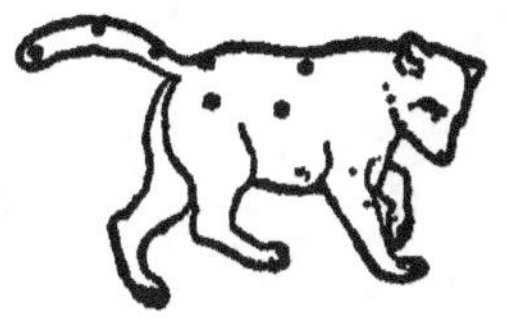

The Winged Disk is an emblem of new birth and resurrection and explains the verse the "Son (Sun) of Righteousness shall arise (in all his glory) with healing in his wings."

CHAPTER IX

GUARDIANS OF THE SUPER-REALMS

Both Uranus and Neptune were anciently held in great veneration.   They are truly occult and mystic, but very little has been revealed of their occult or mystic nature.   Investigation proves that they were known in very ancient times, and were given the deepest reverence, showing their Super-Heavenly origin.   Uranus was called "God of the Highest Heavens," "God of all Space," and may be said to typify the Saviour, because it is the operative reflector of that super-solar light through which alone this world can be lifted in vibration to that luminous heaven—world consciousness, which is the heritage of its cyclic progress.   Neptune was called "God of the Sea, midway between Earth and Sky." Uranus, unlike the other deities, who in some shape or form have been given to the world, has never been represented in ancient art.   His place in the celestial heavens seems to have been too remote.   Neptune is said to be the planet of Chaos. "Behind Uranus was Chaos, and beyond that the First Cause."

Undoubtedly Uranus symbolized that which had been too profound for the majority to understand, and he was too great in his conceptive function for the ordinary soul to grasp. It is said mythically that when Uranus was deprived of his power of generation, he fell into the vast ocean of Neptune, realm of the Astral, and that when the celestial waters had divided into heaven and earth, Neptune was given supreme authority over the finite seas.   Both these planets were known to the ancients, possibly under different names.

The Chaldeans had ephemerides of both, and of still another planet, evidently unknown to us.

There is a planet that is unknown to us, but known to the ancient Initiates of the Indian Temple, which is the greatest of the planets. It was called "The Revealer of the hidden and unmanifested Cause." It is unmanifested in the present cycle of evolution. It holds in eternal subjection and at inalienable distance the light solar system of the Cosmos. It is a planet of awe and incomparable majesty. It is unknown in the modern world but has been recorded in the ancient Indian Tables.

Neptune and Uranus do not depend entirely upon the Sun, like our other planets. Neptune receives nine hundred times less light than the earth, and Uranus three hundred and ninety times less, and their satellites show a peculiarity of inverse rotation as no other planets of our Solar system, being in closer relation to, and affected by the Sun behind the Sun. The Sun stands in greater occult and more mysterious relation with its seven planets than is generally known. The Sun was used as a substitute for Uranus when Uranus was seemingly unknown. There is an occult maxim which reads, "The real Sun and the real Moon are as invisible as the real Man." Uranus belongs to the Super-Solar region, and Neptune to the Super-Lunar. The Super-Solar is to the Solar as two to ten, or one to five, as the Quintile, which is of the greatest importance in connection with Neptune and Uranus. Both are guardians of other systems and planets besides our own. Neptune is the remotest planet in our solar system known to physical science.

The "Secret Doctrine" teaches that "the Sun is a central star, not a planet, yet the ancients knew and worshipped seven great gods, excluding the Sun and Earth. Which was the 'Mystery God' they set apart? . . . The ancients were led to introduce the Sun into the Scale of the Celestial Harmonies. Thus every time they perceived an influence that pertained to none of the six planets known, they attributed it to the Sun."[1]   Can this be an explanation of Uranus being Super-Solar?

In the ancient Kamitic, i. e., Inner African, myth, Urnas (Uranus) is a river running through the Fields of Aah-en-Ru (Paradise.)   This was the field with the twelve gates, which later became the twelve signs of the Solar Zodiac. Urnas, was bi-une in nature, but primarily feminine, as were all other ancient deities.   In a later period the Assyrians had their goddess Uuranie, the original feminine name of Urnas, continuing as the Assyrian as well as the Kyprian goddess Ouranie.   At Athens there was the shrine of Aphrodite Ouranie, the Great Mother.

"Urnas as the Water of Heaven preceded all other personifications."   Uranus with the Egyptians represented the Celestial Waters, or heaven above as the waters of the firmament, and the cutting of Uranus by his son Kronus (Saturn) Time, denoted the dividing or separating of heaven from earth, or light from darkness.   In all mythical creations creation began by the one becoming two, typified by cutting in two.   "The division by the Negro Eve was by the cutting out of the kneecaps, to form the first pair of beings."

Sevekh-Kronus, child of the early Mother of Time, was the true cutter of Uranus.   In the Greek myth Uranus is made to be the cutter of Kronus by his mother Gaea (earth), who formed the scythe or sickle used by Kronus, called Khepsh, who is both the Constellation of the Great Bear and the sickle of Egypt.   The sickle was made for the struggle between heaven and earth.   Uranus destroys his children from Gaea, in the struggle for supremacy, and confines them in the bosom of the earth.   Saturn destroys his children from Rhea by devouring them.   "An allusion to the fruitless efforts

---

[1]"Sir William Herschel, that eminent astronomer, gauging merely that portion of the heavens in the Equatorial plane, the approximate center of which is occupied by our earth, saw pass in one-quarter of an hour 16,000 stars, and applying this calculation to the totality of the 'Milky Way,' he found in it no less than 18 millions of SUNS."—Blavatsky, H. P.—Secret Doctrine, Vol. i, p. 576.

of Earth or Nature alone to create real *human* men." Astarte was the daughter of Uranus and had seven daughters. Rhea was the daughter of Uranus and Gaea, wife of Saturn, and had seven sons.

Uranus was said to be the first teacher of astrology to the Atlanteans, who claimed him as their King. The "Secret Doctrine" states that the Atlanteans were really the first purely human and terrestrial race, those that preceded them being more divine and ethereal than human and solid. The Giant Atlanteans perished some 850,000 years ago. They were the Gibborim of the Bible. The Aryo-Atlanteans perished on the last island of Atlantis, called Plato's Atlantis, which was submerged about eleven or twelve thousand years ago. By tracing the origin of the Nephilim (Genesis vi, 4), the Giants, we could come to an understanding of the hairy men and the satyrs. "Poseidon (identified with Neptune) is not only the personification of the Spirit and Race of Atlantis, but also of the vices of these giants."[1] His amours have been sung by poets and given in allegory in his personifications as the Dolphin, the Horse, and other animals. Neptune was called the grandson of Uranus and became a symbol of Atlantean magic. He is connected with the floods of Atlantis, being affiliated with watery signs, the feminine side of nature, and the Moon. He represents the Moon nature as opposed to the Sun nature. Neptune is always associated with the emotions and love.

Triton, the son of Poseidon, is represented as a man above the waist, but below, had the body of a dolphin. The dolphin was placed by Poseidon among the constellations, and became the Greek sign of Capricorn, the Sea Goat. This will account for the relation between Neptune and the Horns of the Capricornian sign.

Plutarch calls the first cube, Neptune, which is a figure six, chief of the six-fold heaven. When the upper and lower heavens were added to the cardinal points north, east, south

---

[1]Blavatsky, H. P.—The Secret Doctrine, Vol. ii, p. 775.

and west the cube was accepted as the six-fold type of support, the cube of heaven. Neptune as a cube is a fourth dimensional evolution. The symbol of Neptune was above the water, not under, and represented the super-lunar, and the super-luminary bridge.

To the ancients Science and Religion were one, as God and His Works were one. "Isis Unveiled," Vol. i, p. 267, truly says, "In the present century there is not one person out of ten thousand who knows, if he ever knew the fact at all, that the planet Uranus is *next* to Saturn, and revolves about the Sun in eighty-four years, and that Saturn is *next* to Jupiter, and takes twenty-nine and a half years to make one complete revolution in its orbit; while Jupiter performs his revolution in twelve years. The uneducated masses of Babylon and Greece had impressed on their minds that Uranus was the father of Saturn, and Saturn of Jupiter, and furthermore considered them deities as well as their satellites and attendants. We may perhaps infer from it that since Europeans only discovered Uranus in 1781, a curious coincidence is to be noticed in the Myths." Uranus was rediscovered March 13th, 1781, in the 25th degree of Gemini, and Neptune was rediscovered September 23rd, 1846, in the 26th degree of Aquarius.

ASTROLOGY

A great deal is heard about the influence of Uranus and Neptune in world affairs, but what the polarity of Uranus in human affairs is and what the pull of Neptune on the masses contains has not yet been found out. This Neptunian pull on conditions is not even delineated by common Astrology, but a new Astrology, or method of delineation, will be proclaimed and will be of extreme interest, which will be called forth in many unsuspected places on earth. There is a peculiar appulse of Uranus and Neptune during this present period, not so apparent in world affairs as in world aspirations. There is, as it were, a foreshadowing or forerunning in progress on the higher planes, which can only manifest on earth when the material world has assumed a more static and less volcanic vibration. There is nothing in the heavenly world causing the conditions operating in the world today. They are the retroactive impulses of the cycle that is passing. Even as the tide rises and falls, so a cycle drawn by planetary force to the flood-tide ebbs with resurgent impulse. There is no hope of an immediate betterment, but a clearer concept of direction will soon emerge. A new influence, that has not yet been clearly identified, will become operative in the old world; and the reality will be ascertained and will meet the mirage of a checkered camouflage when the awakening comes.

The world is in a cosmic vortex at the present time, because the Super-Solar influences are rushing into a vacuum in our Solar system. The advent of Uranus and Neptune and the unseen planet is very recent. The vibration of earth is void of any Super-Solar magnetically attractive polarity. On the higher planes many ancient souls or higher entities are laboring to reflect to earth in manifestation of matter, a reflex of the Serpent Power, but few can exhale the exhumation of this force on earth, the physical plane. It is disintegrating in its expression. Neptune is the mid-wife of the ancient Serpent Fire, and will not be operative in group activity on earth for some years to come. Then there will be a new inner teaching which will bear fruit exoterically in the succeeding years, making a cycle of extreme occult significance. Neptune is the Super-Moon ruler of the spiritual world. Our Solar system is in obedience to the upper Solar or Super-Solar system beyond the Neptunian integrity of revolution and obedience. Uranus is not so powerful in the coming era as Neptune, and the unseen planet is even more potent than Neptune. It is unseen because it refracts the light of the Dog-Star, which is inseparably connected with the Tree of Light and Life, that comes from the Pole, and has roots which are under the earth and in the tropical heaven, and are as intimate friends.

The unseen planet is of near cyclic importance, and initiates a new Astronomy, for there will be discovered certain magnetic deflections which are inexplicable on any other basis of calculation.

Uranus is the outrushing emanation of Light, and Neptune is the Super-Luminary Bridge. Uranus is the certitude of change, and is today evolving a changed order of the new Era, and is shaking the planetary spirit of earth into incarnation. There is a new expression to the Uranian force and a new earthly condition of change giving way to counter change. This is the sign of the incoming Justice Balance.

There is a definite mathematical ratio with Uranus and Saturn. The forty-two years of Uranus are related to the sevening cycle. Saturn is the modifier; Uranus the Agitator. Uranus is the Bolshevist of the planets. It is not true that he breaks down to build up. It is only when a building condition is indicated in the horoscope that Uranian changes are the radical realizers in progress. Uranus destroys completely, but never a building soul or condition.

By investigating counter aspects you can ascertain that a constructive power has been attributed to Uranus which properly belongs to Neptune and to a release of Saturn from affliction, but must take into account that the Moon or Sun in benefic aspect to Uranus are in themselves building forces. Jupiter has a great deal to do with luni-solar changes and benefits. It does not react very powerfully on conditions, unless there is a Moon in sextile to Jupiter. One must remember that the Moon is the handmaiden of the Uranian-Neptunian system, and will be magnetically enhanced as the Aquarian Era progresses in its relation to physical and astral life, while Neptune will replace or rule the Moon in the horoscope of the mentally or spiritually evolved.

Uranus in the twelfth house of the horoscope and opposite Venus indicates the conclusion of a love experience which has been preceding the entrance into incarnation of a remarkable spiritual Ego. The twelfth house is never Uranian with regard to the past or the future. It indicates the conclusion of causation and the causation of ending. It is a very benefic impulse in the chart of a spiritually evolved Ego, that has become superior to sex attraction. The opposition from other houses of Uranus to Venus is apt to bring a shaking up of the love life with a view to universalizing the love principle.

In regard to the influence of the Uranian cycle on the Moon or Cancer native, the Cancer nature is sensitive to the Uranian influence and is only protected from sudden death under strong Uranian aspects by the counter-poise of Neptune. Neptune is the neutralizer of Uranus to the Cancer native and is a powerful protector when placed in the fourth house, indicating a protection surviving to the end of life. This can be verified repeatedly.

Uranus, Sun and Jupiter are the great earthquake bringers in human lives. Their aspects change the course of events in accordance with Karmic adequacy, and their tri-une aspects in a natal chart will make a life of great exaltation and unheard-of suffering, and the first realization of their true influence will correspond with misunderstanding and reproach. Suffering is predestined to the evolving soul as the only means of spiritual exercise and perfection.

When Uranus passes through the sign Pisces, a dark watery sign, he represents both material and spiritual reforms. He entered this sign in 1919 for a few months and again in 1920 and will remain in it for seven years. He is performing his mission quite well, and has created a cauldron of unrest, with deeds carried on in darkness, the undercurrent that opposes the light, but a greater spiritual awakening will evolve, whose undercurrent will oppose the dark.

Neptune is the planetary manifestation of the incoming Era, the Super-lunar influence in the incoming cycle, intimately related to the Super-Solar force in nature, and to the human assimilation of higher forces, to sensitiveness if not sensed.

Neptune does not represent the churches. The Churches are represented by the signs of the Zodiac corresponding to their predominant symbol—as Pisces, sign of the Christian church. There is no planet identified with creedal religion, but there is a different planet for every religion according to the sign of the Zodiac rising at its birth. Cosmic symbolism can be said with truth to pertain only to the religion of the Light which is the religion of the Initiates.

Neptune plus Uranus in the M. C. and plus the Sun conjunction Jupiter in the M. C. of a progressed chart, which in the natal chart has been heavily afflicted in the world from birth, gives the yogi or master adept of the pre-Aquarian Era, because, when the Aquarian Era is really under way, the adept is a person that has been Uranized. The adept of the post-Aquarian or mid-Aquarian Era will be a person who has Neptune in the M. C. energized by Saturn and the Moon in conjunction and having the Sun in opposition under the earth, and the earth life benefically aspected, for the coming Era will recognize and adduce its spiritual guardians, and will relieve them of all unnecessary physical and mental strain; their emotional fabric will be tempered by great tenderness, and all adverse influences will be withheld by a very grave protection which will penalize any person attacking them, or injuring their lives or reputations. It is well to look up the Neptune native and cherish him or her with divine assiduity and reverent devotion.

Neptune in the twelfth house of the horoscope is invariably a spy, but in the chart of a soul of the greatest of the new order it may indicate the Forerunner sent into or out in the world to prepare the path of the Master, who desires information concerning national and international organization.

Neptune is the death-bringer to the spy or traitor. It is infallible in its disastrous consequences to the immediate family and to the immediate prospects and desires. Neptune in the twelfth house brings Nemesis in the immediate future of the spy or traitor when the aspects in the progressed chart energize a malefic opposition of the natal chart, it will be infallible. It may be unknown but is absolutely fatal to the native's hopes and unfulfilled desires.

Neptune in the Sign of Leo is the higher love of the heart, a central light as the reflector of the divine light. Neptune in Leo gives harmony of the heart. It is the exaltation of the Lunar above the Solar, or the Sun above the earth, and the "Moon above the Sun" on the generative or regenerative side. It is the heart center, the spiritual exponent of human evolution. Neptune is the great degenerator of Lunar force in the undeveloped. It is regenerator to the developed. Neptune will replace or rule the Moon in the horoscope of the mentally or spiritually evolved—Neptune is the Super-Moon ruler of the spiritual.

There is a mighty pull drawing Neptune into manifestation at the present time. Neptune is a planetary reflex of the Cosmic Heart's influence, as it were, a correlative door to the heavenly Cosmic Heart force now streaming to this planet. Neptune is, as it were, a planetary mid-wife, and is assisting in the birth of the new cycle by urging on the throes of the old. There is a correspondence between Neptune and the Fixed Star Aldebaran, one of the first "Crossing Stars," and a direct and corresponding polarity between them. There is much, according to myth, about Aldebaran as a guardian of the gate between heaven and earth, and of his having in his keeping the lives of the Immortal Fathers of the race who prayed to Aldebaran to keep the earth in its orbit and the heaven in its place. They believed that Aldebaran protected the Sages and gave them the key to the gate which led to the higher heaven. They looked to and called to Aldebaran and also to Sut-Anubis, the Dog-Star, watched over by Aldebaran. There is also another beautiful legend of the ancient world representing Aldebaran as the lover who watched for the immortal resurrection of his ravished bride. No trace of this legend can be found in any book, but there is a tablet in the British Museum which will some day be translated, which is said to have baffled Babylonian scholars for years. It was found in the archives of a Babylonian Temple to Ishtar.

"Abir signifies the BULL; which the Greeks corrupted into *Apis;* both names, however, are compounds, and are applicable to the Bull, in consequence of his being the most distinguished constellation in the zodiac, . . . In the circular and oblong zodiacs from *Tentyra* the *bull* is the *most distinguished* of all the animals, in the solar round, he was, therefore, the FATHER of the FIRES, i. e. he was *Ab-irim.* The bright star in that constellation, is the most brilliant of all the stars or *fires* in the zodiac, it was the FATHER FIRE, i. e., it was AB-IR, and this etymology is confirmed by the Arabic name of that bright star which is Al-de-'bir-AN, i. e., the-great-father of fires."[1]

---

[1]Mackey, S. A.—Mythological Astrology, pp. 168, 169.

EGYPTIAN PLANISPHERE OF ZODIACAL AND NORTHERN SIGNS
(According to Kircher.)

CHAPTER X

THE CIRCLE OF NECESSITY

"Let there be lights in the firmament of the heavens to divide the day from the night, and let them be for signs and seasons, and for days and years."—Genesis I, 14.

We are products of our solar system, and the motions of the Earth, Sun, Moon and Planets are performed with a precision that nothing in the mind of man has ever been able to imitate. Among the stars there is no inharmony, but a deep melody of silence that no music on earth can reach. There is no lagging above. It is the same today and forever, and by those who would delve and learn, mysteries will be unveiled and the key found that unlocks the past involved in the present. The unveiling comes only with long searching, and perhaps with many hours of failure, but if we would rise, though steep the ascent and straight, it leads towards the final gate, beyond which lies infinity.

Each and every one is surrounded by an aura, invisible to many but always visible to the clairvoyant. A magnetic aura surrounds the earth, and the signs of the Zodiac are in some way subdivisions of this, emitting an effect upon earth. They are at an angular distance between the earth and the sun, and are, as it were, within the sphere of the earth's aura.[1] This relative position between the earth and the sun, *is* due to currents of energy coming from the sun which interplay within the aura of the earth, producing an influence. Ancient astrologers considered the sun's path as the Zodiac of the earth. There is an occult spiritual side to the Zodiac,

---

[1]This vital magnetic aura and its forces, in their sub-divisions, radiate outward in every direction from our globe.

to which twelve spiritual Beings or twelve creative orders, which send forth manifestations of power belong, All life is under sway of spiritual beings, and the planets passing through the different signs of the Zodiac become natural centers of activity for them. The Zodiac is the matrix of theoretical astronomy and the Great Wheel of Necessity.

The groups of Fixed Stars from which our Zodiac is named lie at some distance beyond our solar system, but are in that same path through which the planets revolve around the sun. From an occult standpoint the planets have affinity with all planes. It is through the planets that the forces and energies of the higher planes are brought through to the earth as physical forces. The Fixed Stars are indices of the Super-solar force. The sun is but a means of this relegated fire. If we are to understand truly what the solar force means on earth, we should at all times regard the indices of the super-solar force which the Sun conveys to us. The Fixed Stars are reflectors of the Supernal rather than the solar. The rays which the Fixed Stars emit are darkness. Knowledge of this subject removes the static for Astrologers. The rays of the Sun do not produce the light we are aware of on our earth today; it is the reflected influence of other Suns that comes direct from the Central Sun, and striking our earth at various angles produces the energy of light. Due to the Precession of the Equinoxes, Constellations that occupied the signs of the Zodiac that bear their names have moved away some thirty degrees. The Constellations or groups of Fixed Stars begin with the first degrees of Pisces and the Zodiac at the first degree of Aries when measured where the ecliptic and equatorial circles meet. The same influences assigned to the Constellations, used in our Zodiac of today, are due to the occult property given to each of the signs, a property inherent and unchangeable, and in no wise dependent on the Constellations or groups of Fixed Stars, from which they received their names. Our Zodiac is a mystery language, and shows the relationship between God and Man.

Very great reverence was given in prehistoric times to this section of the heavens, and although there are many other constellations north and south, occult significance has not attached to them, or else the key that would have unraveled their mysteries has been lost.

"The zodiac is the *apparent* course of the sun and the *actual* course of the planets around the sun. The earth, on her yearly journey, passes along the belt of the ecliptic or the zodiac, and the sun is the center of the circle that she describes. Now it is evident that if the earth maintained an upright position as she traveled around the circle of the ecliptic, the terrestrial poles would correspond with the poles of the ecliptic. But they do not correspond because the earth, instead of maintaining an upright position, has her poles tilted away from the poles of the ecliptic."[1] The points where the plane of the equator, and the plane of the ecliptic cross, are called the equinoxes. The Precession of the Equinoxes is caused by the movement of the pole of the equator around the poles of the ecliptic.

Each time the Sun completes its circle of the Zodiac it crosses the equator a short distance back of the place it had crossed the previous year, consequently the equinoctial point is annually falling back at a uniform rate. It takes this point 2,160 years to fall back an entire sign of thirty degrees, remaining 72 years in each degree, and 25,920 years to complete the entire Zodiacal circle, and this is called "The Great Year."

The precession of the equinoxes is the key to all great cosmic cycles, causing manifestations in different ages. Despite disagreements regarding the exact time it takes for these cycles to arrive, the Egyptians were too exact in their calculations to make mistakes, and the proofs are too sound to question. There is no number in all occult science of such importance as 25,920. The Zodiac as we know, is divided

---

[1]Coryn, Sidney G. P.—The Faith of Ancient Egypt.

into the twelve houses, each containing thirty degrees of the three hundred and sixty degrees that comprise the whole. It is due to these that events of ancient times can be so clearly identified. History gives us these periods in the symbol worship of the different eras. About six thousand years ago, when the Sun entered the sign Taurus the Bull, there were the Bull-headed Gods; about two thousand years later there were the Ram-headed Gods, represented by the sign Aries, the Ram. The past two thousand years were represented by the sign Pisces, the Fishes. The changing of the cycles or the changing of the gods meant that a new spiritual impulse had entered the world, a new manifestation of The Light heralded by wars, cataclysms, etc., great and small. We are entering upon such a period today, as the Piscene Manifestation recedes to make way for the advance of the Aquarian Era ushering in a great extension of spiritual recognition.

An Age or Era takes its inception or impulse from the sign of the Zodiac which ushers out the vanishing past, for the evolving future. Man's spirit is of the same substance as the stars, and it is by placing one's self in harmony with God's laws that all things become possible. All teaching shows that the Zodiac was a foundation for the study of the laws of God, and that to understand these laws we must love nature. Our Bible proves to be a study of our solar system and gives knowledge of revolutions around other Suns of other solar systems, also showing the struggles between darkness and light, or black and white—magic. The first Bible ever written in the religious history of man was found in the heavens.

To read the Bible with a knowledge of the Zodiac and the heavens increases the interest and pleasure a thousand fold. Astrology is so little understood simply because it seems to deal with the supernatural, therefore remaining a blank to those lacking in perception. Two of the greatest needs of the world today are Intuition and Imagination, which would lift mankind from the spiritual blindness under which he has long labored.   These gifts are made manifest through meditation which reveals a power in silence.   Intellect does not always develop divinely given powers, but they can be born from the heart.   Interest in astrological lore would soon lead one into paths of great enlightenment not otherwise conceived of, for therein are found the laws of the Universe, which are the Word of God.

The Precession of the Equinoxes, which has helped to place the age of the Zodiac, is caused by the apparent motion through space of the Sun, which makes the Constellations appear to move forward against the order of the signs at the rate of about fifty and one-third seconds a year.   Therefore, at the beginning of all ages we find certain constellations in the first sign of the Zodiac, and from this fact is found the astronomical key to nearly all the religions of the world, our own Christianity included.   A world conception of religion is found in the interpretation of the Zodiac, the origin of which goes back to the very beginnings, when the primitive peoples became watchers of the sky.   Its antiquity shows that it contains both Divine Law and Power, and in this great circle of symbolism can be found the key to the history of the world, as well as to all the mysteries, which in character were astronomical.   In different periods of time different yet definite influences presided, but there was always a conception of One who was the Mother Supreme, and who in the solar reckoning of time was accepted as the Great Father, the Yah-vah or Jehovah of the Jews, who in a feminine phase was the Great Mother.

Heaven was the Bringer Forth, and the Egyptians represented this heaven as a woman arching over the earth.   This representation has lingered on in the use of the astrological Zodiac of today.   To them the Zodiac was a vast ethereal sea, and was often symbolized by a ship passing over the bent figure of a woman studded with Stars, to represent the sun's passage through the Zodiac.   The woman above, as heaven, and the woman below, as earth, were the first forms upon which physical geography was founded.[1]

Bailly found the earliest founders of the Zodiac to be antediluvians, with names of the Zodiac and planets applying in the same order and meaning everywhere. This could not have been by chance. The Egyptians have undeniable proofs and records of countless ages of the past, which have been found in their wonderfully preserved Planisphere of Denderah, filled with signs and symbols of their Zodiac. These records go back 87,000 years. The Hindus' calculations cover 33 such periods.[2] This planisphere proves what the Egyptian Priests told Herodotus, which was confirmed by S. A. Mackey, "that the poles of the earth and the Ecliptic had formerly coincided, and ever since the first Zodiacal records had commenced, the pole had been three times within the plane of the Ecliptic." This knowledge has been taught by the Initiates. The three Virgins given in this planisphere represent Divine Astronomical Dynasties.

A most interesting circumstance is told by Mr. Mackey in his "Mythological Astronomy," to prove how misled we of the Western Word have been regarding the famous and sacred city of Benares of Hindoostan, which was known as the seat of all celestial science of India "and the astronomical tables made use of in various parts of the empire are constructed for the meridian of Benares; as those in England are for the meridian of Greenwich, and yet the charitable mission-

---

[1] "In one of the tombs of the Pharoahs—Rameses, in the Valley of Biban-el-Molouk, in Thebes—Champollion Junior discovered a picture which according to his opinion was the most ancient ever found. It represents the heavens symbolized by the figure of a woman bedecked with stars. The birth of the Sun is figured by the form of a little child, issuing from the bosom of its 'Divine Mother'."—Blavatsky, H. P.—"Isis Unveiled," Vol. ii, p. 50.

[2] H. P. Blavatsy claims that the forefathers of the Aryan Brahmans had zodiacal calculations and a Zodiac from those born of Kriyasakti power, and "The Hindu nation has a registered knowledge seven or eight millions of years which is on a talisman of porcelain and which I have seen," says Mr. Mackey in his Sphinxiad. There cannot be the slightest doubt that in India and Egypt the Zodiac has been known for ages and ages, and the knowledge in those countries with regard to the influences of the stars and planets on our earth is far greater than our astronomers admit today.

aries do not call Greenwich the chief seat of *English Idolatry:* why, then, do they use such invective epithets about Benares?"

Art, Science, Astronomy, Symbolism including knowledge of the Zodiac, came originally from the Atlanteans. "That the septennial cycle or the week, the days of which were dedicated to the planets by the Chinese, the Indians, the Ethiopians, the ancient and modern Europeans, *not in any order regulated by the distance, or the size, or the brilliancy of them, but arbitrarily,* are a further proof of a uniform system of religious Astronomy, prevailing at one time among a most powerful people."[1]

All seems to be a part of one great system belonging to a common ancestor, and from Atlantis, as further explained in Mallet's Northern Antiquities. "All the Oriental nations except the Chaldeans agree to the division of the Zodiac into twelve signs, with similar emblems and symbols, further proving the common ancestor upon which the primal astronomical forms of religion were modeled, seed of which has spread down to the present day." A question is often raised in regard to this twelve-sign Zodiac, as at one time it was said to have had only ten signs, according to the Hebrew Kabala. This is known to be a blind, revealing truth in such a way that it will need explanation to the uninitiated. This could be read in the duodecimal notation, for in that scale ten can be read to correspond with twelve. An unraveling of the Ten-sign Zodiac is given in the "Secret Doctrine," Vol. ii, pp. 502-503. "In the same manner and on the plan of the Zodiac in the *upper* Ocean or the heavens, a certain realm on Earth, an inland sea, was consecrated and called 'the Abyss of Learning;' twelve centers on it in the shape of twelve small islands, representing the Zodiacal signs—two of which remained for ages the 'mystery signs,' and were the abodes of twelve Hierophants and masters of wisdom. This 'sea of knowledge' or learning

---

[1] Kenealy—The Book of God, p. 121.

remained for ages there, where now stretches the Shamo or Gobi desert. It existed until the last great glacial period, when a local cataclysm, which swept the waters south and west and so formed the present great desolate desert, left only a certain oasis, with a lake and one island in the midst of it, as a relic of the *Zodiacal Ring* on Earth. . . . Ten (signs) only were known to the profane; the initiates, however, knew them all, *from the time of the separation of mankind into sexes,* whence arose the separation of Virgo-Scorpio into two; (the two separate made manifest), which owing to a secret sign added and the *Libra* invented by the Greeks, instead of the secret name which was not given, made 12."

The Zodiac is properly divided into three groups of four signs each, as we use the twelve signs. If we use the ten-sign Zodiac it is properly divided into three and one-third groups. Every decan of Scorpio is related through its rulers to the other three groups. Water, Breath, Fire is a triangulation of the Zodiac. It is approximately indicated in the ancient myth of the Creation, in which the Universe came forth from the Water and the Breath and Elemental Substance. Primordial matter forms the basis and constitution of man in nature, because the term earth, in Genesis 1, 2, should properly be translated Elemental Substance. We are told that in the beginning was the Word, the articulated or differentiated Breath. The three signs and their intermediators are:

Taurus, Virgo, Capricorn, translator to higher expression
    —Gemini, Breath, Heaven and Earth;
Aries, Leo, Sagittarius, translator to higher expression
    —Libra, Justice Ray, Flame or Fire;
Cancer, Scorpio, Pisces, translator to higher expression
    —Aquarius, Light, Water.

The ancient Zodiac was divided or subdivided into sections of ten degrees each, called Decans. Three of these were given to each of the twelve signs, and to each of these thirty-six divisions was given an extra Zodiacal Constellation called a Paranatellon, which rises and sets at the same time with it.[1]

Hiparcus and Ptolemy pronounce the Zodiac in its present form to be of unquestionable authority, of unknown origin, and of unsearchable antiquity, as well as the base of all theogonies.

Connected with the Zodiac is the Zodiacal Light, a luminous light seen near the ecliptic and horizon, during morning and evening twilight. The hierophants know well its origin and occult significance. The Egyptian "Aft Crown" or Crown of Illumination symbolized this light, when placed on the head of the Illuminati who had made the "Passage of the Sun," North and South of which was love.

The Old Testament is filled with allusions to the Zodiac, especially the Solar one, its later form. Prophecy originated in the Zodiac, where the oldest theogonies can be traced, and the Prophets were Astrologers. These prophecies can be found at the roots of ancient Mythology, a method of giving profound facts.

The dying Jacob blesses his twelve sons, each one of whom represented a sign of the Zodiac. They *were* the twelve signs that *came out of Egypt* and camped according to the elements of Fire, Earth, Air, and Water, representing the four points of the compass, or four cardinal points of the Zodiac.

The Jews have a legend which relates that when Joseph told his dream of the Sun, Moon and Stars bowing in salutation to him, the father said to himself, "How did my child

---

[1]The first stars or crossers of the horizon were observed at regular periods of ten days and became the Decani; in Egypt the Tehani in the heavens were the conductors in the reckoning of the nights by tens. "The Egyptian Ephah measure is the hept, and hept is the number Seven. In Hebrew measures there are seventy-two zests to one Ephah. In this combination the seven (the revolving stars) of the beginning are related by measure to the 72 of space—the seventy-two duo-decans, into which the Ecliptic was at length divided."—Massey, Gerald—The Book of Beginnings, Vol. ii, p. 158-9.

The thirty-six decans of the Egyptian gates of Aah-en-Ru preceded the naming of the two Egypts, Celestial and Terrestrial, and their nomes, which were afterward adopted geographically by the Egyptians.

come to know that my name was, is, Sun!"[1] The twelve sons or signs also identify Jacob as the Sun in the twelve signs of the Zodiac.

In the building of the Zodiac, first was the Abyss, or the Mother. Division came as water and air, and these were subdivided into water, air, earth, fire, which symbolized the four quarters that were later assigned to the four Royal Stars, called the Four Quarter Stars. From these the constellations completing the Zodiac were formed by elements representing the seasons. The Zodiac was divided into twelve parts and then the thirty-six decans were evolved which as the duo-decans formed the Kabalistic tree of seventy-two branches.

The creation of the heavens and the cycles of Time is found in the building of the Zodiac. Mythology states that the Gods were created as the builders of the heavens, which were measured according to the cycles of Time and that they belonged to the religions of the Past, when the One God was the Mother.

The constellation of the Great Bear, with the Seven Stars or the seven constellations around the Pole, led the way to the Lunar and Solar Zodiacs. The seven multiplied by the four cardinal points would yield the twenty-eight lunar mansions,[2] which were followed by the twelve signs of the last and solar Zodiac.

The Gnostics, in Christian traditions used Ichthus, the Fish as symbol. In some astronomical charts the symbol of the month of twenty-eight days, the lunar month, is the Fish. The Hebrew name for Jonah is the Dove. Jonah goes into the Fish, but the Dove goes into the Ark.

---

[1] Bereshith rabbah, sect. 68.

[2] The Lunar Zodiac of 28 mansions was used by the Copts, Egyptians, Arabs, Persians, and Hindus many centuries ago, and is still used by the Hindus. "The year composed of thirteen periods of twenty-eight days was a world-wide institution, called a lunar year, and the number twenty-eight is registered in the twenty-eight lunar mansions, sieus, manzils, or asterisms, of the Egyptians, Chinese and Arabs."

The first circle and square were formed by the stars circling around the pole. The square is formed at an angle of 90 degrees, these four angles making the 360 degree circle of the Zodiac. The four quarters were first typified as animals, and symbolized the elements. The Hippopotamus, or great Fish, symbolized the water and was therefore the first to be humanized. It represented the Great Mother. The Lion (originally a bird, the Phoenix) represented Fire. The Crocodile represented the Earth, and the Ape Air. Two of these are still found in the Zodiac, as Leo and Aquarius. The latter was given as the Multamammae, the female Light-Bringer of the Hermean Zodiac. These are the same four found in the vision of Ezekiel and in the Book of Revelation. They have many variants, and as the elements, were held sacred in all ancient religions.

In the primary circle of time before the four quarters were established, there had been neither solstice nor equinox. The Egyptians marked their solstices as being on the horizon. Lepsius does the same, and places the vernal equinox up in the sky. Hebrews regulated their astronomy and observations by the Moon.

The Moses calendar was solsticial. The beginning of the year was with the month A-bib. "This day came ye out of the month of A-bib" (Ex. xiii, 4), and in "This month (A-bib) shall be the beginning of the months; it shall be the first month of the year to you." Several old calendars— Aramaic, Assyrian and Jewish—show that the year had at one time begun with Ab in July, when that month entered the Zodiacal sign Leo. This reverts to the oldest commencement of the luni-solar, or Cancer-Leo, year, and represents the Exodus from the mystical or celestial Egypt, under Moses.

The candlestick, the Tree, and the Zodiac all combine. The seven-branched candlestick was type of the seven-branched Tree. It was the master key to the flood gates of the waters above and to the Seven Great Stars, which made the first covenant in heaven. The Tree of Life and Knowledge imaged the Mother, who as two-fold was of earth and heaven with her heart at the center. This Tree had its roots on earth and its branches in heaven, and when it became four-fold was the Tat Tree or Pillar Cross of the god Ptah, parent of the Tau and the Ansated Cross.

The mother of the Book of Revelation sits on seven hills. Similar hills are mentioned, as existent in Inner Africa as well as in other localities. They are the Seven Stars of the celestial mount. Later came the planets. "And the heaven was visible in seven circles, and the planets appeared with all their signs, in star form, and the stars were divided and numbered with the rulers that were in them, and their revolving course was bounded with *the air*, and borne with a circular course through the agency of the Divine SPIRIT." (Hermes.)

The planets in ancient times were given two houses of the Zodiac, over which they presided, alternating as male-female, day-night, or luni-solar, an arrangement different to that in use today. The sun was given to Virgo and the Moon to Leo. During the reign of Antoninus Pius, A. D. 146, a series of coins was discovered on which the Sun was given to Leo and the Moon to Cancer, showing that the sign of the Solstice had been changed from the year of uncertain lunar reckoning, to the fixed year of solar reckoning.[1] The six double houses show the luni-solar month of thirty days, with divisions of five days each, in the year of 360 days, was in existence long before the solar time of three hundred and sixty-five and one-quarter days to the year had been established.

There had been two fixed points of commencement, and the Egyptians made use of both, one with the sun in Leo, of the first Zodiac of the four great stars, and the one in Cancer when the Zodiac of twelve had been instituted.

All chief characters in the ancient Kamite, or Inner African mythology were in the course of time placed in the

---

[1] Sharpe—Egypt Under the Romans.

Zodiac, filling in between the four cardinal points.   The signs and the decans can be identified with the Kamite Pantheon of Divinities.   Egypt has been called the mouthpiece of Inner Africa, and in going beyond Egypt for originals we get back to the Kamite.

Origination of the signs set in heaven having prototypes on earth belongs to the Egyptians.   All celestial types are reflections of nature, and those used in Egypt cannot be found elsewhere, their imagery was in Zodiacal phase and according to the Precession of the Equinoxes.   Their sacred year began at the summer solstice, when the Sun was in the sign Leo, at the commencement of the rising of the waters of the River Nile.[1]   This was figured in the Kamite Planisphere as the Constellation Hydra in the South, which rose heliacally at this time, becoming the sign of the Inundation, and making the serpent a symbol of the flood, which is also symbolized as Fire, the alternative type of an ending.   Their inundation ended with the sign Scorpio.   According to a papyrus, which is translated into Arabic, the deluge was supposed to take place when the heart of the Lion (Leo) entered into the first minute of the Crab's (Cancer) head, at the declining of the stars, rendered backwards, as the ending of a cycle of Precession.

CANCER

The Crab—The Egyptian year, had three months deluge and nine months dry, the deluge beginning at the summer solstice, the fourth sign of our Zodiac, Cancer.   Cancer is ruled over by the Moon.   In the oldest of the Egyptian Zodiacs two Beetles were placed in this sign, which later was represented by the Crab as we know it today. The Beetle became a symbol of great importance.   At the time of the summer solstice Beetles swarmed, preparing their eggs for the approaching rains.   When they were hatched

---

[1]The River Nile was the original of the Eridanus of heaven, and was called the "Mother Mystery."   This Mother is represented in the Herman Zodiac as Menat, the Wet Nurse.

EGYPTIAN ZODIAC ASSIGNED TO THE SECOND HERMES,
ACCORDING TO KIRCHER.

they were made symbols of an ark, a boat of the Sun, as the solar herald of the Sun's entrance into the following sign Leo, the home of the Sun.   Thus the Beetle was a luni-solar symbol of generation, creation and renewal.   "Ancient astrologers affirmed that Cancer was the horoscope of the world; it was, according to their tenets, the sign of commencement, of rotation, and growth.   They say further that by its creation the creation of the four elements became complete, and by their becoming complete all growth was completed."[1] The Egyptian god Ptah, creator of the solar circle, is closely related to Jupiter, who was said to prefer the sign Cancer, and who has been placed in the ascendant in a horoscope of the world.   Time cycles were symbolized by the Khepr (Beetle) which was made an image of Time.   The circle of Khepr-Ra, the Sun-god, was the Zodiac and he represented the point in the Zodiac where the year was renewed, hence typical of Becoming, Creating, Transforming, as the beginning of a new year.   This circle represented a renewed cycle of the soul, or re-birth.   The Spirit of Life and Immortality was everywhere symbolized by a circle.   Eden was a circle, where the "Goings forth were forevermore," as there was neither beginning nor ending.   Sometimes the beetle was called the Redeemer, the Eternal and Infinity.   Khepr was the Egyptian name for the Scarab.   Of Khepr-Ptah it was said, "Thou art fatherless; begotten by thine own becoming, thou art without mother; thou are born by the repetition of self."   Thus through transformation it became the creator, type of the only-begotten.   When the scarab is portrayed as a globe with two wings added, it becomes a most revered and sacred symbol of human and universal life, and of the resurrection and transformation of a liberated soul, showing a belief in reincarnation.   Portrayed with the wings folded it represented Metempsychosis.   It was also the transformer of the time-cycles, symbols of immortality.

The Egyptians consecrated a "Two-horned, bull formed"

---

[1]Massey, Gerald—A Book of the Beginnings, Vol. ii, p. 314.

Beetle to the Moon, and Hor Apollo tells us that the children would say, "The Bull in heaven is the exaltation of the goddess." It was written, "I am the Bull sharpening the horns of the Great Illuminator." This represents the position of the Moon placed in the sign Taurus, the Bull, which is the sign of the exaltation of the Moon. Scorpio appeared just after the inundation, and Cancer and Scorpio were made reciprocal. Scorpio became Cancer in the light of the lunar manifestation. "Manilius had learned that the Scorpion was a sign of increase; this was so on account of the inundation in Egypt. Serk (Scorpio) means to supply, is equivalent to increase. Water was a sign of increase. The vanished Scorpio appeared after just as the Scarabaeus appeared before the deluge."[1]

ASTROLOGY

Horoscopically the conflict of the Sun and the Moon in the sign Cancer gives malefic instrumentality, and operation unfavorable in most favorable circumstances, and a great change of polarity, and to an unsuspecting patient menaces almost certain death; also an operation indicated by the Moon opposed to Jupiter and conjoined with Saturn and Mars is fatal. The Moon is the Tide of Life, and a death planet particularly, and the Moon is the governor of the sign Cancer, which is a most unfortunate sign to anyone in trouble of any kind. It increases their receptivity to misfortune and makes them unable to gather their resistance to overcome their evil aspects. Cancer is the lunar sign and the Moon on earth is the merger of illusion with matter, and makes anyone inclined to overestimate the value of illusion and the valuelessness of common sense.

LEO

The Lion—The fifth sign of the Zodiac, follows that of Cancer. Half of the waters of the inundation had been

---

[1]Massey, Gerald.

poured out ere the Sun had left this sign, and from this originated the lions as water spouts and fountains that were used in the temples of Egypt and are still used for fountains over the greater part of the world. The Lion was a symbol of terror and of fire, and as a symbol of the elementary Fire was of great esoteric importance. The highest group of hierarchies were called, or named, the "Lions of Life," whose symbolism is hidden securely in the Zodiac. The Lion signified Strength, and its Tail, Power. The great brilliant star Regulus of this sign, one of the first "Crossing" stars, is exactly on the ecliptic, and was thought to be a radical point for the meteoric showers belonging to the month of August, that of Leo. The Messengers or Messiahs were called the Lions of the Holy Ghost (the Holy Spirit), the Great Mother. The Christian Messiah, Jesus, was called a Lion of the Tribe of Judah. His incarnation was prophetically symbolized as a "Winged Lion," and as "A golden serpent coming out of the Ark."

Sut, the earliest son known, was the builder of the First Temple, which was Sabean, with its Seven Stars or Pillars of Wisdom. This was followed by the lunar temple, built by Taht, with its twenty-eight mansions of the Moon. The final celestial temple was built when the Zodiacal circle of the Sun was completed. When Cancer, the sign of the Moon, emerged into Leo, the sign of the Sun, the young god Khunsu as a child of the Sun and the Moon was born. He was the mythological Sol-Om-On[1] (name of the sun in three languages), who as the son of this combination united the lunar and solar cults in one. The gold of Solomon was said to be "Moonshine and Solar Gold," the golden light of the Sun brought in by the vanishing darkness of the Moon. It

---

[1] The Precepts of Ptah-hotep, given about 4000 B. C., are twice as old as Solomon's Proverbs. A Papyrus in Berlin contains one of the oldest, if not the oldest book in the world (a complete translation is given in "Records of the Past," III). One extract reads, "If thou hast become great after being little . . . harden not thy heart. . . . Thou art only become the Steward of the good things of God." Another is, "Obedience is of God."

was at this period that the building of Solomon's Temple commenced. The mythical temple was not at Jerusalem.

Khunsu of one cult, Iu-em-Hept, prince of Peace of another, and Solomon of the celestial Israel (all generic names) rebuilded the sabean and lunar temples of heaven, perfecting the work their predecessors had begun.

The first twelve tribes that Solomon ruled over were the twelve signs of the Zodiac. There are many riddles of astronomical allegory extant, suggested in Psalm lxxviii, 2, 3, "I will open my mouth in a parable; I will utter dark sayings of old; Which we have heard and known, and our fathers have told us." Talmudic traditions go back to the origin of the circle, made by the constellation of the Great Bear as it circled round the Pole.

The temple of twelve signs was the arc "by which the twelve torments of darkness may be dispelled."[1] The Great Pyramid and the system of architectural measurements used in the temple of Solomon and Noah's Ark of the Covenant are the same, and they were built on the same foundations as their ancient pagan religions, which J. R. Skinner, in his "Source of Measures," so clearly identifies.

ASTROLOGY

The Sun, Moon and Saturn combined in Leo is an ancient sign and symbol of the Initiate who is to pay a heavy karmic debt. These are triplicate in expression, and in the house of the Lion are symbolic of the higher and lower nature as well as of the human heart, and if they are in conjunction, that is to say, if they are joined together in the lower nature, and if the solar and the lunar forces are bridging in the lower nature, this is a great danger to any man who holds an exalted position. That man will certainly be under great illusion at the bridging time and he will never be free from a condition of in-sol-ence,[2] a word meaning "Not sun, in sole,"

---

[1] Hermes.

[2] The Latin Word Solus is in relation to the one and only God. Solus very soon became Sol the Sun.

or "not a son of the sun," and would never be able to make an honorable demise because Saturn, ruler of the house of death, is in Leo, its opposite sign, the house of the Sun or life. The ancients regarded Leo as the house of the earth life of the Initiates entering upon their adeptship for which an earlier life had been a preparation. And it requires certain initiatory processes which are necessary just as the Greeks going into Egypt had to pass through certain experiences to fit them for the reception of the Solar Light operating at that period in Egypt.

VIRGO

The Virgin—The sixth sign of the Zodiac follows that of Leo. The constellation of the Virgin as the great cosmic mother is the symbol of pure undefiled substance and matter, the immaculate.

In ancient Zodiacs both the Vine and the Tree were placed in this sign. An old fable tells us that this was the Tree of Celestial Waters from which the Rivers of Light came forth. It is in this Tree that the Little Dog is to be seen watching over Paradise. The Vine was the symbol of vintage, and in this constellation there is a star called Vindemiatrix, the "Female Grape Gatherer." In the adjustment of the Zodiac, Virgo was given as the Virgin Mother, and the gestator was placed in the opposite sign, showing a correspondence between heaven above and earth below. Virgo was the symbol of seed, corn, the seed of life in the corn; also the symbol of wheat, and the Virgin Mother is depicted holding a sheaf of wheat in her hand, represented by the brilliant star Spica of this sign. The three stars—Spica, Denobola in Leo, and Arcturus in Bootes, form a spiritual triangle of great splendor in the heavens. Arcturus rising was looked upon as a foreteller of tempests. Another very beautiful celestial triangle is formed by the glorious Sirius in Canis Major, Procyon in Canis Minor, and Betelgeuse in Orion. Virgo with its sheaf of wheat, is, like the vine, a symbol of the harvest. The goddess of the harvest was called the Lady Repa. Repa, whose fruit preconceived by the flower appearing first, outcome of the harvest, is a name for Virgo. From this originated the names of many flowers prefixed by "Lady."

The Egyptians called the period following the passing of the Sun through Cancer, Leo, and Virgo, a time of rest and repose, and when the Moon was at full in the opposite signs they were called the "Lunar Water" signs. Originally the signs were alternated in a luni-solar combination. The sign Virgo was the Virgin of the Zodiac, mother of the coming son, and was so described in all ancient languages and so depicted in all pictures of the heavens. The Arabians make their Messiah the protector and genius of this celestial sign. This Virgin mother has been made to appear in the Book of Revelation as the Scarlet Woman sitting on the Dragon clothed with the Sun and the Moon under her feet. She is the Virgin of regeneration holding the child in her arms, as if she had risen above the illusion of life and was creating a new humanity, symbolized by the child.

Christmas Day was the birthday of the Sun at the winter solstice. At this time the constellation of the Virgin (Virgo) arises on the horizon, and this sign symbolized a Virgin with the child in her arms, and the serpent constellation beneath her. Isis and Horus of Egypt, Maya and Buddha of India, the woman and child in the Book of Revelation are all similarly portrayed and are witnesses of the many myths that have evolved from this imagery in the heavens.

The Twins in their early phase represented the two creative elements, Water and Fire. One was represented as Sut, the negro child of the dark (water), the Kamite Christ, whose shrine was the constellation of the Great Bear; the other as Horus, the child of the Light (Fire) who in the solar cult was the begotten of the Father, the Redeemer, and his sanctuary was in Rome. Two women became prominent in the early mythology. They are still with us. One belonged to the Zodiacal sign Virgo, the Virgin, who holds a child in her arms, the other as the gestator to the opposite sign Pisces, the Fishes, who holds the fish-child in her arms. Both Virgins were placed in the Hermean Zodiac. These signs are just six signs apart and have been made to typify sons of Elizabeth and Mary, John the Baptist, who baptized with water, and Jesus, who baptized with Fire.

Woman bears relation to the Great Deep, and this Immaculate Mother, who later was made to crush the serpent or dragon under her feet, was the "Virgin of the Sea." She *was* the Great Deep, the "Dragon of the Sea," even as she was the stately Ship of the North crossing the celestial waters, and finally bearing her children to the great Mount of Salvation whence they pass onward and upward into Infinity, presence of God.

VIRGO, LIBRA, SCORPIO

and their relation to the ten-sign Zodiac. Before the Fall, to earth, the old dragon or serpent represented divine wisdom; first as pure spirit, that was passive. It became active when enmity was placed between the woman and the serpent, representing physical existence, i. e., man born of woman only. During the Middle Ages the Zodiac was divided into ten signs, and in the old Syrio-Chaldean magic we find this change made in the center of the Zodiacal circle, by the combination of the signs Virgo-Scorpio. The Greeks placed the sign Libra between as a balance. Scorpio represents the organs of reproduction and was made an emblem of sin and matter, but Scorpio ascending was purely spiritual. Virgo represented purity, and the Immaculate Virgin. This arrangement resulted from unclean thought attributable to the delusion of an evolving world. The physical man superseded the spiritual, and the sign Libra was symbolically placed between these two signs of generation and regeneration.

The creation of the ten-sign Zodiac was given to the public as a blind to prevent the masses from knowing and understanding the secret of creation, that it might be kept pure, and the good separated from the evil. Libra, the Balance, symbolizing the turning point, was to be the mediator between God and man. When a low level had been reached on the downward course, this sensitive point or balance was to be the equilibrium needed to bring about spiritual harmony and justice. Enoch was said to represent Libra, and was called half divine and half terrestrial. It was also said that he went to God alive, which is here symbolically represented.

ASTROLOGY

The planet Venus is ruler of the sign Libra, and when it is placed in the sign Virgo and evilly aspected, it creates a great coldness, and in its sin is deceitful. When adversely placed in Libra its sin is more open, outrushing and brazen, but when occurring in Scorpio it can give great discipline, and through great suffering lead the sinner towards the upper spiritual side of this sign.

LIBRA

The Scales—The seventh sign follows that of Virgo. It was the equatorial sign symbolized by the Scales or Balance. The Sun's passage through the six upper signs represented the descent of the Divine Principle into matter and balance of the divine and material nature in man. The Egyptian Har-Makhu was made lord of the horizon. Makhu means balance or horizon. In a very old Zodiac Libra is pictured as a man with the scales in one hand, the rod of power in the other and a corn measure upon his head, but in the most ancient Zodiac Libra is represented by two Tortoises.

Cancer marked the summer solstice as the first quarter of the Zodiac, with Libra as the equatorial point or the second quarter, and these points were repeated in the following signs of Capricorn at the winter solstice and in Aries at the spring equinox. Each of the series or quarters ended with a double and common sign, Gemini, Virgo, Sagittarius, and Pisces.

Libra as the Tortoise became a symbol of the earth beneath the water, since this creature buries itself to arise again when the time comes. In many myths the tortoise became an arc of safety amidst the waters, and has been depicted bearing the world upon its back. And when the world thus built on its back sank beneath the waters the deluge was precipitated. This is highly symbolical. The Tortoise was held in great respect by our Indians, and was addressed as Mother Earth in its relation to water, flood and earth. "The great Circle of Time, on the face of which, fancy in India has represented the Tortoise, has the Cross placed on it by nature in its division and localization of stars, planets, and constellations."[1]

The mystic tablet of the Chinese, the KWA tablet, lies on the back of the tortoise, that appeared in the River Loh, and revealed the KWA secret to Fuh-Hi. The magic square is in the center of the back of a smaller tortoise surrounded by the twelve Zodiacal animals, the twelve double hours of the day and the twelve months of the year, and various other symbols representing lucky and unlucky days and the seasons of the year. It was their ancient custom to mention the hours of the day as "the rat hour," or "the tiger hour," etc., just as we speak of one o'clock, two o'clock, and so on. In the Mandan legends and ceremonies tortoise-shaped sacks, said to contain the water of the deluge, are used.

The Egyptians symbolized Cosmos by a large fiery circle, representing a serpent with a hawk's head lying across its diameter. This diameter as the Balance would be significant of the perfect service rendered by the Justice Ray coming through this point in the changing of the cycles. In an Akkadian calendar Libra is called "The Altar of Fire." Zoroaster like Noah built an altar for sacrifice after the flood. Various peoples have regarded this sign, Libra, as the Altar. In one planisphere another Altar full of burning incense is seen at the North Pole, a Holy Place.

Libra has also been called "The Claws of the Scorpion."

---

[1] Blavatsky, H. P.—The Secret Doctrine, Vol. ii, p. 549.

In an old Zodiac Sagittarius the Centaur, the ninth sign, is represented with a Scorpion's tail, and so we find the Scorpion with its claws in Libra and its tail in Sagittarius, showing there was once a Scorpion of the Western Quarter extending through three of the present signs and indicating that the Zodiac was founded in the beginning on the four quarters.

In a very ancient Zodiac Libra is represented by the claws of the Scorpion grasping an altar. The Babylonians discarded the altar but retained the claws, which the Greeks replaced by the sign of the Balance which had belonged previously to an Egyptian Zodiac.

SCORPIO

The Scorpion—The eighth sign, follows Libra. In a very ancient and primitive calendar Scorpio is given as the starting point of the year. One of the earliest reckonings, points to the commencement of the year at the autumn equinox, which is still observed by the Jews. The most ancient year of the Hindus also began at the autumn equinox. The Egyptians called this sign Serk the Scorpion, the creature that could live only on dry earth. Serk, a name which also signified to disappear, to dry up, etc. Celestially it was a type of breath. Terrestrially it was said first to appear as a mist or cloud, hence it was made to signify exhalation. When Scorpio arose above the horizon, the end of the inundation was over and the earth was being prepared. Seb (later Jupiter), god both of heaven and earth, was placed in the decans of this sign. As Seb-Kronus, the Father God of a later creation, he was the Great Inundator, "Lord of the Ark," for three months, and of the earth for nine months. The Great Ark of Seb-Kronus was the circle made by the Seven Great Stars, belonging to the Mother. Seb, "God of the re-illumined earth," is portrayed with an arrow, symbol of a sunbeam, in one hand and a torch in the other.

Cancer was called the Dark Constellation, as it contained no brilliant star. A place of temptation however was said to be in Scorpio, also a dark sign, but containing the brilliant Antares, and called the "Evil Red Star," one of the first "Crossing Stars."

Sirius, the Dog-star, was consecrated to Serk, the Scorpion goddess. The planet dedicated to Sirius is Mercury, guide of Sirius through the underworld or night, a Messenger at the eighth gate, that of Scorpio. The Eighth Gate, which reflects itself in the universe or macrocosm, together with the Ark of the seven so-called "Fixed Stars," is a center or gate of consciousness. Every gate is an octave lower in rate of vibration than the one anterior to it. Every gate reflects a different color, and the seven colors thus become the circumference of space or aura of the Universe. Scorpio was called the "Great One" of the Sun with the devouring mouth. In one of the paranatellons of Scorpio the Egyptians placed a crocodile (typifying Seb, or Sevekh,) who was also a devourer because of a great mouth. In the Egyptian "Book of the Dead" it is written "Back crocodile of the West, living off those who never rest." The West was the place of the setting Sun, the place of trial, and those who never rest were the endless Watchers in the sky, the setting stars.

"The 'West' was the place of regeneration. The higher forces of generation and regeneration are more potent in the corresponding earth centers, the *Red Life* force of each. The generative force of Red must unite with the yellow of the Christ Love and then it becomes the *Red Gold* or Universal Solvent, the 'Alchahest' when we shall have life more abundant."[1]

Scorpio at this western angle was called the Hornet, the Stinger. Many fables regarding it, pictured the struggle of the soul with the Powers of Darkness and lurking enemies. Both Scorpio and the crocodile were called "The Seizers," one using its claws and the other its mouth. They were types of equal strength, and were made the symbols of ene-

---

[1]Conrow, Edgar.

mies of equal strength and placed at the points of the equinoxes (Equal Power—Balance). Scorpio represented Breath and the crocodile Water, the heaven above and the earth below the two creative elements of life.

Exhalation began when the sun was in the sign of Serk or Scorpio. And a scorpion was placed on the head of the goddess Serk, associated with the original four corners, bearing witness to the antiquity of the Zodiac.

ASTROLOGY

The cusp of the eighth house, Scorpio, is a luni-solar cusp of the house of death, and often of death under distressing circumstances. Benefic aspects at death mean a successful discharge of Karma and continuity of motive power.

There must be a polarity in reincarnation, i. e., in the synthetic relation between lives. In a polarity between synthesized charts the eighth house is transition; so is the eighth gate. It is the going over into another range of consciousness. The figure eight denotes the point of contact of two spheres, and there is a relation between the number Eight and the symbol of infinity, which is two circles combined. The key to the house of life is the eighth, generally considered to have direct bearing upon death. The ancients claimed that the Eighth Gate led to infinity. Direction and laws of reincarnation are positive and negative, receptive, or negative, and ineptic. They may be found in the relation of polarity in lives. The positive and negative signs are in juxtaposition, the sun or life force coursing through first one and then the other.

Scorpio is the world serpent in dual aspect. In its lower aspect it is an unregenerate force. In its higher aspect it is regenerate force, which has been transmuted or regenerated by the Super-Solar Fire. The serpent *is* Scorpio, but Scorpio is not the serpent. Scorpio is the negative polarity of the Serpent, or the world serpent needing its vibration in matter. Capricorn is the higher polarity or manifestation in the Super-Solar Heaven, and is the positive or higher triangulate. Capricorn is the higher polarity of Scorpio, as the serpent, and is positive. Scorpio is negative.

Water signs indicate a strong relation to the Light, and are to be considered as the Light-givers. Cancer, symbol of Water, is the past; Pisces, Water, the present; and Aquarius the future. Aquarius is the water animated by the fire, which becomes steam or air. It is the watery transitor, and Scorpio was the watery sign of the far past, when the water was enveloped in fire and mist and the world serpent was a great being, entity, Deva, which gave the world its conscious life and then sank into oblivion, a crucified God-Man, or Fish-Man. Dagon was his name, and he is seen as a serpent man in Scorpio. That is why Scorpio is the only sign not given by the ancient astrologers as a heliacal or Solar myth, because Scorpio was never Solar in its earthly manifestation until it had been lunar for many cycles and had become identified in the ancient consciousness with the serpent of the world. The floods of the Serpent were the inundations of the unseen Scorpio Power, which has always been regarded as a danger in maps which are either exalted or abased, because it floods the whole native with a power that cannot be kept at bay but can be transmuted. A Venus vibration can be averted by the mind, but the sting of the Scorpion is the fire which dries up the flood and which transmutes the earthly passion or material deflection into a heavenly exaltation and redeems the native through a changed consciousness and makes him susceptible to higher instruction, that is, under Uranian and Neptunian exaltation. Scorpio is the gate of the Super-Solar system, and enables a Scorpio native who is evolving spiritually to gain a powerful polarity and ascendancy and thus to arrive at attainment. The Scorpion is an insect which begets prolifically, and the Scorpion native when once illumined is a great spiritual begetter. Spiritual generation is never confined to Virgo; it is in Scorpio that the generation of spiritual force on earth is generatively polarized, because in Scorpio are the Water, and the Fire, and the Breath, a combination productive of great spiritual radio-activity.

SAGITTARIUS

The Archer—The ninth sign of the Zodiac, follows that of Scorpio, to which sign Sagittarius seems attached. In this sign in an old Zodiac, according to Kircher, a man is seen about to sacrifice an animal, and hovering near is a Dove.[1] After a deluge or period of darkness the people were wont to exclaim "Hail to the Dove, restorer of Light." Sagittarius is the house of Light and a place of regeneration. Generation or evolution was given to Scorpio, to which this sign is joined. Sagittarius is a double sign, in which the human and the divine intermingle. It is a sign of the Centaur, the Archer, whose aim is direct. It is a sign half human and half animal, and is profoundly significant of the truth that matter, or that what is physical, can be transmuted and redeemed until it becomes pure spirit. Scorpio on one side of Sagittarius was the symbol of the negative polarity of the Serpent, and Capricorn on the other side of Sagittarius was the positive, but it is the animal human side that needs the vibration in matter that it may through this house of Light rise to the super-solar heaven just beyond. The Egyptian god Shu, with his bow, from which he shoots his arrows of Light, was placed here, for every arrow tip is a symbol of the light, or a sunbeam, and by repetition makes the Light Waves for the transmutation of the material into the spiritual. The chariot of the Sun, is drawn by the four horses of the Sun, which are the four reflections of its rays as they shoot towards the earth bearing messages

---

[1] In one planisphere a raven is sitting on or near the tail of the Dragon, and not far from it and flying towards the constellation of Argo, the ship, is a dove with a branch in its mouth. It suggests the Hebrew account of Noah's flood. Mythically the legend states that at the termination of all deluges an altar used to make sacrifice to the gods was built marking the place where the fish-man emerged from the flood. In an Akkadian calendar the seventh sign was named "The Altar," and the eighth was named "The Bowing Down."

morning, noon, and night until the last contact with the earth seems to hold them back in a loving embrace, ere the struggle with the dark begins. The Horses of the Book of Revelation were called the Four Spirits of Heaven, her Messengers sent over the entire earth. It was the rider of the white horse who carried the bow and received the crown, for he was the Light Bearer, the Conqueror, of this fiery sign of Light. It is a highly creative spiritual sign.

Both Shu and his sister Tefnut, symbolizing the Two Truths of Egypt, were placed in this sign. They were related to Breath and Water, the first of the creative elements. In the Hermean Zodiac the name given to it is Nepthe, which means breathed, breath, and Shu was god of breath and air. The month Nepthe in Egypt was one of mist, cloud, and vapor, and this month came to be "marked as the Bow in the Clouds." Cloud was an Akkadian name of the month Nephelion, meaning "Heaven born," or "Cloud Born," with power to create true sons of God. In Africa the name of this month was also Neper, the Scorpion, whose tail was joined to Nepthe Sagittarius, and the Assyrians dedicated the month to Nergal, the "Giant King of War," one of the giants who in earlier times constellated in the north as Kepheus, who in one form typified Shu, and in another was the Lion-god, Regulus, of the sign Leo, the Lion. They belong in the decans of Sagittarius, and are represented in planetary form as Jupiter, Mars, and the Sun, while Regulus was the Royal One of the Sun in Leo.

The Pineal Gland is called the "north gate." This, in man, is the central spiritual creative center. Above in the heavens, it is found in the beginning of this sign Sagittarius, and is the point from which spiritual gifts are given. It is called "Vision of God," and is the Light within, a gift to the pure in heart, who verily may "See God," but to the impure or those who abuse this great gift the consequences are very terrible.

"This North Gate, the creative center in man, the most

interior center in the body, has become atrophied, and redemption or regeneration means its restoration to creative ability, by having the electrical or positive and the magnetic or negative forces restored in equal balance in man or woman, and then each thought becomes a creative force, and this creative force radiates from the brain. In the future this unity and harmony in the individual will bring unity and harmony among individuals, and nations and races as such will disappear, for then there will be but one nation."[1]

The 6th degree of Sagittarius is perhaps the most remarkable in the Southern Hemisphere, and of equal importance is this same 6th degree of its opposite sign in the north, which corresponds to the magnetic Pole of the ecliptic of the heaven. Draco is located at 270 degrees as the Pole of the Universe, and 270 degrees represents the beginning of Sagittarius. The earth is passing through this degree of the celestial Pole at about this time, when the changing polarity passes from Pisces into Aquarius, as it ushers in our new era. The magnetic points of earth are found on the equator. Again, we find these first six degrees of Sagittarius represent the temperature of the ether on the centigrade scale. The ether is 273 degrees below the centigrade scale and therefore represents three degrees of Sagittarius.

"Esoterically, meaning by interior information, Argus, or as it is called by some 'Canopus,' is the Fixed Star of the Universe, with Helium as one of its chief elements. It is said to be four hundred thousand times brighter than our Sun. The pole of the ecliptic is in Draco, with Polaris as the pole star now, but as we know, the great cosmic cycle sweeps, moves it onward in its orbit, and in time its place is seemingly filled by another. Each 'fixed star' is a moving center of a greater or lesser system operating on different planes, and each plane is a duality of force. Esoterically considered Argus (Canopus) is the center of the so-called mental-plane of consciousness and as such has four other stars or

---

[1]Conrow, Edgar.

suns, each a center of the other planes of consciousness exterior to it.   They all travel in spirals and never return to exactly the same point in space.   The whole Universe is an aggregate of circles and spirals within spirals, all of different degrees of motion, which give us our seconds, minutes, hours, months, years and other cycles.   Argus is said to radiate radium, which corresponds to our radium."[1]   Canopus was also a type of Sut-Nub, the Golden, the original of Sothis-Canopus, and was represented by a Golden Star.   Canopus as Sut-Nub was the starry son of the Beginnings in stellar phase; in the solar he was the helmsman for the solar God.   Sothis Canopus, and in feminine type, was the Great Mother of the Southern heavens in the pre-solar myth, and belonged to the Kamite beginnings.   Canopus is a first magnitude star in the constellation Argo-Navis, the Ship.

CAPRICORN

The Sea-Goat[2]—The tenth sign of the Zodiac, follows that of Sagittarius.   It has been called the most mysterious sign of the Zodiac, and though familiarly known as the Sea-Goat, has various other names of very great esoteric significance. As Tebet it is related to the water, and means the "Ark City," belonging to the ancient Great Mother, who herself was the primordial Ark of primitive times, and as the constellation the Great Bear was the first ever known to cross the celestial waters.

When the Sun was passing through Cancer, Capricorn was at the opposite point, and Sut-Anubis (Mercury) was

---

[1]Conrow, Edgar.

[2]"Oannes (or Dagon, the Chaldean 'man-fish') divides his Cosmogony and Genesis into two portions.   First the abyss of waters and darkness, wherein resided most hideous beings—men with wings, four and two faced men, human beings with two heads, with the legs and horns of a goat."—Blavatsky, H. P.— "The Secret Doctrine," Vol. ii, p. 54.   The Chinese have a similar tradition, found in a work called Shan-Hai-King, which was compiled by Chung Ku from engravings on nine urns made by the Emperor Yu, B. C. 2255.   An interview is mentioned with men *having two distinct faces on their heads*, before and behind, monsters with bodies of goats and human faces, etc.—Gould, Charles.— "Mythical Monsters," p. 27.

placed in this sign as the announcer of the inundation. Here we find the Bridge on which the departed gathered to cross the mystical waters that led into the Great Beyond. It was Sut-Anubis the Dog-star that led them safely across. Capricorn, Aquarius, and Pisces, the last signs of the last quarter of the Zodiac, were called the "Water Signs of Negation," the Abyss.

Astrological connection between Saturn, ruler of Capricorn, the Moon and Mercury bears very close relationship to the bridging between the material and spiritual worlds. Sut (Saturn) was the original Dog-Star, and was the first form given to Mercury. Taht the Moon-god was also a form of Mercury, and Mercury was placed in the home of Saturn when the Moon was at the full, and was therefore the conductor of the souls over this bridge leading to the higher spheres.

The sign Capricorn was called Makara, loosely translated crocodile, which is of the greatest significance as a spiritual mystery. It begins with the most sacred of all letters, M, and has the meaning of crocodile, because of its connection with water and earth. Many names were given to this sign to convey that it represented a nondescript, amphibious animal. Makaram stands for both the Microcosm, a little world, a man, and the Macrocosm, the great universe, of which man is a copy, and is connected with the birth of the spiritual and the death or dissolution of the physical universe.[1] In the evolution of words it represented the fifth group. A great mystery is connected with the number five. It is symbolized by the Pentagon, the five-pointed star, a symbol of man, and in both India and Egypt the pentagon was connected with the order of the Dhyans, who were gods or

---

[1] "Man is the microcosm or the miniature macrocosm. The idea of the ancients, 'Man, know thyself,' became the key to solve many mysteries. The seven main plexi of the body are the star centers in the body of the seven colors that make up the surrounding aura, and the symbol of the Cross and Circle is the pattern of all else, symbolizing the central microcosm of the macrocosm."—Conrow, Edgar.

co-workers with nature, who bore relation to the crocodile and made their home in Capricorn. This star, with the two horns or points turned heavenward, was used in ceremonial magic and sorcery and has been considered by occultists to be a star of the "Left hand." Esoterically it is a symbol of a Kali-Yuga. Yuga has the meaning of a yoke, yoking, human generation and an age of the world. A Kali-Yuga represents a cycle of 432,000 years. Among lesser yugas there is an astronomical one of five years. The Hindus date their Kali-Yuga from a great periodical conjunction of the planets thirty-one centuries B. C.

The myth states that the Crocodiles of the celestial Egypt are five in number, which in the Egyptian "Book of the Dead" are bidden to come forth in the fifth creation, and that when "The defunct Sun" enters Amenti, they plunge into the Abyss of the primordial waters, and as the Sun of Life rearises, they reemerge from the sacred river. The crocodile has at times been given as a symbol of God. It is both sacred and mysterious.

In ancient Egypt the number Seven as Sevekh, the crocodile, was the supreme one, or the highest soul. In India this animal as it was a personification of Fire came to personify a solar devotee, while the crocodile had its septenary meaning in the constellation of the Lesser Bear, with its seven stars, and Sevekh the manifestor of the seven. The very soul of the ancient cults was celestial law and order, destiny. In India, the Night of Brahma was the period of the negation, or the waters. V. Modelyar very beautifully describes this in the coming of Night: "Strange noises are heard proceeding from every point . . . these are the precursors of the night of Brahma; *dusk rises on the horizon,* and the Sun passes away behind the thirteenth degree of Makara (sign of the Zodiac), and will reach no more the sign of the *Mina* (zodiacal sign Pisces). The gurus of the pagoda appointed to the watch the *râsi-chakra* (zodiac) may now break their circle and instruments, for they are henceforth useless."

The 10th Discourse of the Bhagavad Gita is one of the most recondite, and replete in allusion to the unwritten Mysteries—note verse 20—and in verse 23 "Meru of high mountains am I." The word mountains has the same meaning, "Heights of heaven," as in the Hebrew, "How beautiful upon the mountains are the feet of them that bring good tidings," i. e. super-planetary rays forecasting higher evolutionary progress on earth. In verse 31, "I am Makara of the fishes," is an allusion to the 13th degree of Capricorn and its appulse to Pisces through superplanetary energising at the outset of the Aquarian age—This utterance "I am the Makara of the fishes" is one of the most dynamic in the Gita.

ASTROLOGY

There are thirteen degrees in force on either side of Capricorn, extending into the next sign, provided no planet is in that sign, unless the map is that of an Initiate. Capricorn is the service of the past carried into the present manifestation.

Capricorn, which means "The horns of a Goat," is the most powerful sign in the Zodiac. The Crocodile is covered with horns, and the horns of Capricorn mystically are spirals. It is a sign which involves the synthesis of the Cosmic Powers in their relation to human evolution. The horns of the Sea-Goat were anciently called the Horns of the Centurion, which was the mystical name of The Ancient of Days. The true occult meaning of the sign Capricorn has never been written. There is a new and potent force coming through Capricorn at the present time, which when polarizing the planet Venus, will change personal affection into the impersonal. This force is indicated as the guardian and protector of the unseen world, and is not mentioned by name except in one or two books, but the name is known to the Initiates of the highest degrees.

There is a great deal to be learned about Capricorn, because Capricorn is not a human, but a super-human sign. The

Serpent Power comes through Capricorn at certain times of the Solar Cycle, and particularly in the month of November, the month of the Indian Summer, and is governed by the unseen planet. The unseen planet is in trine to the super-solar period of the Sun behind the Sun, which reflects a heavenly condition in the Western world where the Capricorn influence is felt with power in the month of November. This is not true in all parts of the world. There is something divine about the Indian Summer, which is a Capricorn period and may be likened to the after world of a Solar year, which thereafter descends into Hades, previous to rebirth into a new period of manifestation in the upper Solar system. Capricorn governs the earthly evolution of the higher intelligence, incarnate for the service of humanity.

Capricorn is a very powerful influence in the chart of a recluse, because the power of the unseen planet is reinforced by solitude, and the influence of the major planets are circumscribed thereby. The great mystics of the Seventeenth Century, the Rosicrucians of the Sixteenth and the Seventeenth Centuries in Middle Europe and England, were under the influence of Scorpio, but the mystics of the Age of Justice will be Capricornians. The sign Scorpio is the most powerful next to Capricorn, which is related to the Aquarian Age. Many mystics of the Piscene Age were Aquarian, while the mystics of Aquarius will be Capricornian.

Capricorn is a very unusual force in the horoscope of the Jewish Race. It does not manifest in a personal way, but a group of random Jewish horoscopes will reveal the destiny of the race, which is to manifest the Capricornian Serpent Power with equalizing radiation in the later epoch of the Aquarian era of the new Zodiacal round. The learned Jews are awaiting its ascension in the new age.

The Moon in Capricorn is a great energizer of obstinacy. Capricorn is very benefic to the evolved and very malefic to the unevolved soul, gives a great persistence, but gives selfishness in the obstinate self-willed way, and makes a woman nagging and a man extremely cruel in sex relations. The Moon in Capricorn is a great index of the point of evolution reached; if favorably aspected, it is indicative of easy evolution and a rather sensual nature, but if heavily afflicted it indicates a soul seeking birth into understanding which comes through the Karma of obstinate self-will and results in another life or lives in an upward groping. The Moon in Capricorn is never a good position in any chart which shows either bad quality of soul or bad Karma, and makes anyone difficult to live with unless selflessly protected and loved. Saturn as the sickle belongs to this sign. It has been called the Flying Sickle of Divine Judgment going over the face of the earth, that all who sinned might be adjudged.

AQUARIUS

The Man—The eleventh sign of the Zodiac, following that of Capricorn, was often called The Waterer. This sign is depicted with streams of water (Light) flowing from an Urn held in the arms of a man   In a very ancient Zodiac this sign was represented as Menat called the Wet Nurse, symbolizing the Great Mother, who was the manifold fount or source of the waters, and nourisher of Life. The Waters or Rivers of Light symbolized the Light Bringer, type of the Great Mother of all living, the bounteous, glorified, many-breasted all-conceptive Mother. No river on earth can compare with the River Nile of Egypt, whose original is found in heaven as the Eridanus, the incomparable River above, whose farthest star "points to the Egyptian Akar as the subterranean region or fount of source." This great flowing river, River of Mystery above and below, type of the Mother, the great mysterious source of fertilization, was given to the sign Aquarius, and depicted as the Wet Nurse Menat, who in her lunar form was the great and chief Kamite mother of the Abyss, the first and oldest mother ever known in heaven or on earth.

In a series of twelve legends of creation, based on the

twelve signs of the Zodiac, the eleventh, Aquarius, was named "The Curse of Rain." The Akkadian harvest time was called Se-Ki-Sil, or The Sowing of the Seed, and the cultivation of the land took place after the deluge of Aquarius, the Water-man, at the entry of the sun into Pisces. The Assyrians consecrated their eleventh constellation to Rimmon, the God of Storms and Rains, harmonizing with the eleventh sign of the Zodiac. Their deluges, or destructions by water, became historical in Hebrew writings.

At the present dawning of the Aquarian Era, Light from the Great River is piercing the darkness of the past Piscene manifestation according to precessional law, everywhere seeking out the shadows that it may lighten the travail of the new birth. Aquarius today is the Man whose polarity is the Woman, representing the two extremes belonging to the law of opposites that control everything in the Universe, and expressed in the Woman's Age.

In an Egyptian planisphere by Kircher, Shu, as Kepheus, the Law Giver, fills part of the decans of this sign. In his right hand he holds a rod, and in the left hand a sceptre. On his head are placed the two feathers of Ma-Shu (Truth). He is seen in a marching attitude, which makes him typical of our Aquarian manifestation. He was placed there as a Light Bringer, in his double role as Ma, the woman, and Shu, the Man, liberating that same force which is enveloping the world today. Out of the myth, and out of the great thought of the past, will come a renewal of truth. It is the outpouring of this energy, the coming of a new conscience, which has brought the chaos and complexity of today, but in those who have high imagination, a spiritual understanding of the World-Chaos will develop. Both man and woman as Torch-Bearers of the Light will be instructors on the way toward Brotherhood promised in the Aquarian Era.

PISCES

The Fishes—The twelfth sign of the Zodiac, follows that of Aquarius, and represents the completion of the Zodiacal ring beginning with that of Aries. The number twelve Kabalistically means "Born in Affliction," and no sign was thought to be more unfortunate, probably owing to its being one of darkness. Esoterically it is of great importance. In the backward passage of the signs due to the precessional period, when Pisces is reached, it would represent the point where the final struggle would take place between the dragon of darkness, or the casting out of the dragon, as it were, and the incoming Light of Aquarius. This sign is of special interest, as it ushered in the Christian manifestation.

Anciently the Fish sign represented birth and rebirth from the waters. The original birthplace was from the Waters of the Abyss, Darkness. This fish sign was lastly given as the human birthplace in this sign Pisces, so closely connected with the primal waters. In ancient Zodiacs Fish-goddesses were placed in this sign. In one the goddess holds a Dove in her hand, symbol of the Holy Spirit; in another a child is held in one hand, and a symbol of the four corners in the other; all typical of the gestator. Fish-goddesses belonged to the Great Cycle of Precession that preceded the Piscene or Christian manifestation of two thousand years ago. It would be over twenty-eight thousand years ago that these goddesses were given a fish's head or a fish's tail.

The fish symbol[1] was a favorite one with all ancient peoples. Sometimes when depicting a deluge a fish with the head of a man was employed. In Christian tradition the Gnostics made use of the fish type, which penetrated the history of the New Testament when the twelve Disciples were chiefly chosen among the fishermen. In old astronomical charts

---

[1]Fish cycles were all similar and identifiable as an emblem of the Sun or a Messiah.

the symbol of the month of twenty-eight days was a Fish. The Egyptian Horus was a Fish; Marduk and Bacchus were similarly symbolized. The Fish as a symbol of birth is still found in Japan, and a paper Fish is placed over the door of a house in which childbirth has occurred. The Jewish Passover still preserves the Leviathan as a symbol of darkness which was vanquished by the Sun when the "Crossing" of some two thousand years ago exchanged the Lamb for the Fish. The fish of Horus and Sevekh is the crocodile. Horus is frequently represented crushing the crocodile under foot, he is also depicted standing on the crocodile holding a fish over his head. "When the spring equinox passed into Pisces, the fish which is carried over the head of Horus was not only a zodiacal sign of the Christ (Messiah, or Coming One), but was made eucharistic."[1] Assyrian and Babylonian beginnings were equinoctial when the spring equinox was in the sign of the Fishes, from which we have knowledge of the Fish of Hea and Oannes, and Marduk personating the Fish of Hea.

The Greek Fish *IXΘΥΣ* has the entire Christian teaching symbolically revealed in its letters—

    I—Positive phallic force.

    X—Light descending into upward ascent of matter (a vortex of Light initiates a precessional cycle). It (*X*) is the alphabetical letter of infinity as 8 is the number.

    θ—The cosmic egg polarized (i. e., the fecundated Egg first divides cellularly thus to form the chick).

    Υ—Matrix of Matter.

    Σ—Serpent force.

IXΘΥΣ—Interpreted reveals the positive force of the Sun behind the Sun descending through its garmenting light to fecundate earth (matter) with serpent fire, reascendant.

---

[1] Massey, Gerald—"The Natural Genesis," Vol. ii, pp. 392-393.

The Dove and resurrection are symbols left over from the great past and should be reflected upon by those whose stellar influences proceed from the Piscene sign and can be harmonized with the spiritual force now in manifestation, that Light which is taking the place of the Darkness, and making possible the fulfilment promised in the seed sown by the greatest of Initiates of this past Sidereal Year. The dragon of Darkness can and will be vanquished.

Legends have been written to the effect that a universal resurrection will be heralded by an enormous beast, to arise from the earth and reach up to heaven. In some legends the head only is to reach above. She is to have the eyes of a hog, the ears of the elephant, breasts of a lion, is to be the color of a tiger, with the back of a cat and to have the voice of an ass, and is to appear three different times. This can all be traced back to the Beginnings, in the stellar, lunar and luni-solar periods of time. She is also to bring with her the "Rod of Moses," which was the sceptre of the Egyptian Ma-Shu, who was called the Solsticial divider, and Solomon's Seal, the six-cornered symbol of the four corners, including the Zenith and Nadir. Many variations are given of this myth, with the same mythological astronomical foundation.

Oannes, Vishnu and other manifestors were always born from the water. Oannes was the primordial manifestor of Chaldea as Vishnu was of India, and in ancient drawings can be seen resting on the heavenly Seven-headed Serpent which is identical with the Egyptian Kneph.

Water represented a lunar manifestation, and in the Hindu myth the lunar race of Yadu was identical with the Hebrew tribe of Judah, and in the tribe of Jadu, Vishnu was to be the incarnation of Krishna. There is an ancient prophecy which says, in Luke i, 69, "And hath raised up an horn of salvation for us in the house of his servant David," and in, Zechariah xiii, 1, it is said, "In that day there shall be a fountain opened to the house of David," meaning at the end of a Great Year. And it was foretold in Micah v, 2, "But thou, Bethlehem Ephratah, *though* thou be little among the thousands of Judah, *yet* out of thee shall he come forth unto me *that is* to be ruler in Israel; whose goings forth *have been* from old, from everlasting." These prophecies refer to the return of the cycles. Bethlehem the house of bread, wheat, and Virgo, the Virgin sign, has for its most brilliant star Spica, meaning "Seed of Wheat," therefore it was the place of sowing, and Pisces the opposite sign would represent the "Bringer Forth." Bethlehem-Ephratah has become associated with the Messiah, for in Ruth iv, 11, we read "Do thou worthily in Ephratah and proclaim thy name in Bethlehem" which suggests the sign Virgo as bearing the seed and the opposite sign Pisces as the generator. Anciently this imagery related to Isis who was to conceive, and Nephthys, who was to bring forth.

ASTROLOGY

Pisces representing the twelfth house is the sign of Karma and brings about a new order of things, changes of Karma. It is also the house of spiritual rebirth, and the opposite house, the sixth, is that of transition of force, which would bring a bridging inspiration. But if the planet Mars is in the sixth one cannot afford to indulge in aught that would excite the brain, or create a habit of any kind. The twelfth house is one of reincarnational power. It reveals the Karma setting forth good and evil influences.

The Moon in Pisces is singularly powerful in any chart, is in its element as it were, and makes a very great psychic, and gives unusual flexibility to emotion. The native is under protection, and will be protected even if heavily afflicted. Great protection will flow from unexpected sources, and a new impulse of hope will follow every downfall of fortune or aspiration. It is extremely protecting to the bladder and the kidneys. It protects from diseases of the kidneys. It may make a man effeminate, and a woman intellectual.

The last quarter of the Zodiac, represented by Capricorn, Aquarius and Pisces, was called that of the Three Lunar Water Signs, corresponding to the three upper Solar Signs, which in Egypt were related to the Inundation of the River Nile, counterpart of the celestial River Eridanus. One reflected the other. The three were said to be at the quarters of the Abyss. It was to these signs that the lunar goddesses were wont to go in search of the Fountain of Life. Many legends have arisen from the birth of a mystical god or source of life, who was in reality the Sun. The child of the Sun was the Light in the Moon at night, was the seed, the germ, the point that evolved light or life. In every phase of the birth of the Sun or Lightgiver, opposition came through Darkness, which was typical of night and death. In Egypt previous to the coming of the waters, darkness was preceded by the intense heat of the Sun. Then the mythical errand of the Lunar Goddesses was to go in search of the Waters of the Fountain of Life, found in the night or the Underworld, as it was called, or astronomically in these lower signs Capricorn, Aquarius and Pisces. The Moon was at the full at the "Birth of the River" in the sign Capricorn, opposite Cancer. There they placed the Messenger as the guide for the Goddesses who were going into the dark to seek the life-giving waters. When the Sun was passing through Capricorn in winter, they said that the solar god or soul was "Crossing the Waters of Death." A very, very ancient Mexican myth explains that these three water signs built the bridge across the Abyss in the North.

The ancients created times and seasons for all. Life above and life below were thoroughly understood by them.

There are many far-off glimpses of a divine wisdom, of great beauty, sacrifice and tenderness leading to vast spiritual heights to be found in the interpretations of these three last water signs of the Zodiac. The vision of the ancients reached very far beyond the veil of our present materialistic existence, and as Watchers of the heavens they related every condition above to the earth below, with thoughts of the Eternal always in mind, and gave a reverence to their Creator which is almost unknown in our modern world.

ARIES,

The Ram—Is the first sign of the Zodiac, following that of Pisces in the great wheel "No part of which is more the starting point than any other, or heaven, reminding us of the 'Wheel of Necessity'."

There are Bibical myths of the Sun's receding through the twelve signs of the Zodiac. As Paul says, "which things are allegories" (Gal. iv, 24). Christianity was founded when the Sun was in Pisces, and myths had become extinct when the previous sacrificial sign of Aries the Ram was given to Moses, who even in modern times has been depicted with the Ram's horns upon his head by Michael Angelo. The three decans of the sign Aries represented the first of the twelve gates of the Aah-en-Ru, the Egyptian Elysium, uplifted by the Sun when he sailed forth in his Solar Bark from the sign of darkness, Pisces, into Aries, which became the sign of the rearisen Sun, or the Sun ascending from the preceding sign of Pisces, darkness. When the Sun had passed into Aries, the Ram, it became a type of fulfilment, renewal, and transformation, and appeared as Sebek-Ra, the Egyptian Ram of sacrifice, the Lamb of the Persian Zodiac, and was the type of sacrifice in the cult of the Christians. The Hindus portrayed their Fire-God Agni riding on the Ram (the Sun in Aries) typical of reproduction, and the Egyptians imaged Sebek-Ra in a similar phase. [1]Sebek-Ra was the son of the Great Mother, whose Seven Stars or Spirits of the constellation of the Great Bear, were the Seven Spirits sent forth throughout the earth, of which we are told in the Book of Revelation. Sebek the original Sabean Fire-god

---

[1]When the oldest god Sut was transformed into the youngest Sebek-Ra and two horns were placed upon his head, it brought the celestial into the terrestrial, and with it a religious revolution.

or Star-son was the black god of a primeval black nation. This black god, Son of Darkness, who was Typhonian, was the same that was worshipped in Nubia as Sut-Nahsi; in Syria as Sulika, as Jah in Israel, and as AU the black god of Biben-el-Muluk, for this line of descent is traced from the son of darkness, first son of the Mother, down to the advent of the solar cult. Mythically the ancient child was the dying Sun as a god of darkness, which became the Lamb of Sacrifice in the Christian cult.

In the Book of Hades, found at Biben-el-Muluk in the tomb of Seti I, the sun-god passes through the twelve gates, having the blessed of his keeping on his right hand and the damned on his left. These were the chosen and elect of Ra, of whom the people said, "They hide those which are in the state of the elect. . . . Food is given to them *because of the light which envelopes them in Hades,*" for they were the children of Light passing through Hades, who are recognizable in other myths that come nearer home.

The Lamb, who bore the Tree of Life and stood upon the mount of the four corners, called the Four Rivers that issued from the Mount, or the mythical Garden of Eden, was the Lamb that later became the symbol of the vernal equinox, or crossing.

This Lamb has curiously been transformed into the Lamb that taketh away the sins of the world, and made a symbol of the founder of the Christian Cult. In a similar way the Bull, Apis, was made a symbol of Osiris. The worship of Osiris as Apis, the Bull, ended three thousand years ago, but the worship of the Lamb, still remains. It was not the Bull itself that was worshipped, but the symbol of Osiris. Apis was hemaphrodite therefore cosmic, and this religion was primarily a worship of generative creation, both celestial and cosmic. The Bull was cosmic but the Lamb became terrestrial and human.

The Constellation Triangulum which rises directly above that of Aries, was connected with this sign and became a symbol of the trinity in unity.   This was "Khuti the brilliant Triangle which appears in a shining Place."   When the triangle was placed in the hand of the Egyptian Horus, as Har, he became the Solar symbol or type of this Triangle Constellation.

TAURUS

The Bull—The second sign of the Zodiac, follows that of Aries.   The sign Taurus was symbolized by the "Golden-horned heifer."   This constellation contains the very brilliant star Aldebaran, "Father of all the Fires," "Leading Star of Stars," called the most brilliant among the first four Crossing Stars of the Beginnings.   The Bull as a manifestation of the Sabean time and of the Seven Stars, had the significance of "The Word," and was named "The Interpreter of the Divine Voice."   The Bull was also a symbol of the Sun, and was called "The Great City of God, mother of Revelation."   All the Sun-Gods in some mysterious way became connected with this sign.   These are the gods that later were called Sons of Righteousness.   The God Hu is the Bull, the Mighty Bull, who takes a triadic form as the three Bulls. He was the symbol of the Tongue, emblem of Taste, type of Flame, denoting Word or Utterance, as well as "Mystic Utterances."   He was called the Solar Overseer of the Druids.   The Tongue was painted blue and red, the red interchanging with green, symbolizing heaven and earth, spirit and flesh, or soul and body.   This Bull of the Sun wears the blue woof of heaven for clothing.   In Egypt Hu was a Symbol of Corn, the Seed of Life, and was the good Demon, "the Winged Sun."   The word for Sun in Hebrew is Tur, which would be in Hebrew T R, the same as Taurus.   This constellation has also been called "The Plough."[1]   Ploughing belongs to the month of Taurus,

---

[1]The Constellation of the Seven Stars was called "The Lady of the Lights." In many churches a light was set up before an image called "Plough Light," kept up by husbandmen young and old, who collected money on "Plough Monday." These stars were also called "The Plough."

May, which symbolizes the procreative generative power. Taurus astrologically is physical generation. "The *Bulla* which the Roman children carried around their necks, as an amulet, was succeeded by the Papal *agnus dei*, with the same object; the Pontifical Bull comes from this root, . . . Bal, Lord, Sun, Fire, and Baaltes was a Tsabean name for the Queen of Heaven."[1]

Physically Taurus representing man, the bull, was sacred in every cosmogony. The Pleiades, the group of beautiful stars in the neck of the Bull, is the central group of the Milky Way, and was considered, as was especially the star Alcyone, the centre around which the fixed stars of our universe revolve. The mysterious Pleiades were sometimes called "The Little Ones" of the Milky Way. The early symbologists called the seven Pleiades the wives of the seven Rishis. The latter were the Seven Stars of the Great Bear. Esoterically they were known as the nurses of the "God of War," the "Commander of the Celestial Armies," who was astrologically the planet Mars, to whom they gave the name Karttikeya. Krittikas was the Sanskrit name for the Pleiades. These stars were pictured as a flame, typical of the Fire-god Agni who presided over them. Mars was said to be born or generated from the seed of Siva (the Holy Spirit) dropped by Agni into the sacred river Ganges, and born of water and fire. He was named the "Boy bright as the Sun and beautiful as the Moon."

Great occult significance attaches to the Pleiades and their father Atlas, for the Pleiades contain everything in the cosmos in embryo, forming the male-female principle. They are the conceptive power of the cosmos in embryonic receptivity to the birth of Light. In Atlas we have

A—Beginning, divine creation, super-solar Light.
T—Christ Power.
L—Fire of the Father.

---

[1]Kenealy—The Book of God, p. 194.

A—A reconnection which is necessary with the
higher Cosmic Power so that

S—The Serpent Power can come through. This
descends in times of manifestation. Atlas is
the sustaining force of the four energies of
earth.

The lost Pleiad is the key to the Higher Spiritual Law.
Merope, the lost Pleiad, connected with mortal man, symbolizes the conceptiveness of the Cosmos made manifest on
earth.

The Turtle is a cosmic animal because it has within it the
principle of Cosmic Fire, synthesizing bird, beast, fish and
all animals, in its zoological history. Atlas represents the
earth's polarity. He stands on the Turtle, symbolizing
standing on the elemental fire of all living; up borne as he
bears up. Atlas symbolizes the magnetic polarity on earth
of the cardinal cross. The four different heads or points of
this magnetic polarity are correlative to the pole of the cardinal cross of heaven.

Atlas also represents the supporter of the heavens.
Homer called him the keeper of the pillars that hold heaven
and earth asunder. Many fables have arisen of Atlas, and
his great love for the stars, hence his dwelling on the higher
peaks of mountains.

Associated with the six Pleiades after the seventh had disappeared was the number of the Logos, or Holy Spirit. The
six were named the Doves, and the Dove is a symbol of the
Holy Spirit. It was a bird of Breath and Spirit, and in
the most holy mysteries was welcomed as the Restorer of
Light. In a figure by Didron, No. 125, these six are "portrayed in the Christian iconography in the act of inspiring
a soul into the infant Christ."

Festivals in many lands commemorate the rising of the
Pleiades. The Hindus used them to regulate their year and
month. A Coptic calendar gives the festival of the Ascension, marked by their rising. In the Roman calendar August

sixth is identified as the day of the Transfiguration. The Mexicans used them as a signal for the relighting of the sacred fires which were not allowed to burn during the five days of negation, the intercalary days in their year of 360 days. The relighting took place promptly at the stroke of midnight at the ending of the last day of the year when the Pleiades reached their zenith.

This cluster of stars has had the honor of having great temples oriented to it, and mighty nations have bowed in homage to them. Among the many beautiful legends none are more tenderly spiritual than those of our North American Indians in their quest of the holy mysteries and what the stars had to tell.

> . . . "The Father in Heaven, appointed the stars
> To guide the steps of his wandering children,
> Chaaka, the Pleiades, not only point out the trail for
>   their feet
> They impart wisdom also to the spirits of the people.
> But Chaaka, the still brethren, would guide us all right,
> They would teach the people how we may cleave one to
>   another in the heavenly places.
>
> "They come to us, they rise!
> Over the image of Mother Earth
> Into Father Sky, they rise, they rise,
> Chaaka the silent brethren!
> Ah 'tis a blessed thing to behold them yonder,
> More blessed yet for us to mount with them,
> To shine together each in his place as they!
> They come to us, we rise,
> We as Chaaka mount on high!
> Behold them coming, climbing
> And we are they
> Brethren in unity together."

In the Mithraic mysteries Mithra the Sun-god was depicted slaying the Bull, the Scorpion attacking at the same time. In celestial imagery this is the struggle between darkness and light, the struggle being explained through the sign Taurus the Bull and the sign Scorpio the Scorpion. The Bull was the virile symbol of the Sun, and the struggle began with the Sun's entrance into Scorpio, darkness, or Autumn when it was said to have conquered the earth. Autumn is the time when productiveness is lessened, though potent in the month of May, which represents Taurus, the Bull. This sign is opposed to that of Scorpio and was the real conqueror of the earth in the Spring. The double-headed Bull was called the "Swallower of the earth," swallowing the Sun and Souls (Stars) in the west to reproduce them in the east. In British mythology the solar birthplace and the solar Bull are identified with Taurus, it was their vernal equinox over 6,000 years ago when the Sun had entered Taurus according to the Cycle of Precession and in their mysteries the priests exclaimed, "I am the cell (the matrix), I am the Chasm (equinoctial division), I am the Bull, Baer-Lled."[1] The Egyptians wrote, "I am the Bull of men, the fertilizer of the race, I am the procreator in the image of the Bull," the Bull of the month of May. In this sign in an ancient Zodiac the mother holds a child in one hand, and in the other the Ansated Cross,[2] showing the equinox had occurred in Taurus. In whatever period or sign the vernal equinox occurred, whether in Pisces, Aries, Taurus or another, if a goddess can be seen in that sign holding up a newborn child, or Sun, whether symbolized as a Fish, Lamb or Bull, it was the emblem of the Manifestor or Messiah during that period, typifying birth and rebirth, eternity or immortality.

The root meaning of Tau is Bull, or Cow. They both unite in the ancient hieroglyph, and represent a face with

---

[1] Davie's Mythology.

[2] The Ansated Cross has been found carved on the backs of cyclopean statues, discovered on the peaks of what has been a submerged Continent, known as the Easter Isles in the mid-Pacific Ocean. This Ansated Cross, from which we have the Astronomical Venus, was most sacred in Egypt, but does not belong to that country alone. The first symbol of a circle was made by the Ankh Cross. It was simply a loop and a circle in earliest symbology, an ideograph of a period, an ending, a Time. This Cross also means that the divine had descended into male and female generation.

horns which could belong to either a Cow or a Bull. The Bull has sometimes been given as an emblem of terrestrial illusive life, a "Source of Sorrow."

The Bull, the Cow, the Calf, gave rise to many myths, usually historicized. Venus, Isis and other goddesses were represented with horns, like the cow, symbol of the passive generative power of generation and of Mystic Nature. Venus, as Venus-Lucifer, is connected with the Satan of the Christians, who gave him horns. Venus presided over Taurus, a feminine sign having the symbol of the masculine Bull.[1] "These horns were also sacred to the Jews, who placed near the Altar, horns of Shittim Wood, by seizing which a criminal insured his safety."[2] The Horn is not limited to sex. Placed on the head they were chiefly a feminine symbol. Both Cow and Moon are Horn-bearers, bearers of the Light, as they both carry the solar orb between their horns. Anciently horns represented endurance and supremacy, and they were also emblematic of renewal. An enormous horn was given as a symbol of Typhon, the first Mother, and is today the Unicorn of English Heraldry. The single horn was emblem of phallic power, and a type of unity under male power. The primeval Pillar of Heaven, foundation of all, support of all and at the center of all, was the Horn of the North. Sut-Typhon, the very first Mother, is the originating source of the mythical Unicorn having the single horn in front and the tail of an animal, male, behind. The unicorn was anciently the symbol of the constellation of the Great Bear in its double character, male-female, or Typhon, the Mother, in the North; and Sut, the Dog-Star, in the South.

Venus, ruling planet of Taurus, has the number Six, number of the Word and Procreation. It was on the sixth

---

[1] "Biune beings were often represented as male in front and female behind, as an illustration of the backward way" typical of the Precession of the Equinoxes. Many illustrations were given of this as in the Circle Dance, the Witches Dance, etc.

[2] Kenealy—The Book of God.

day of the Moon, the Moon that is exalted in Taurus, that the six Priests went out together to gather the sacred branch of Mistletoe, as type of renewal, rebirth, and their festivals have come down to us as our May-day rejoicings. Six was the number of the Mother as well as of Venus, ruler of the "Bull of the Solar Splendor." Taht was called the "Mind and the Will of God," and in his symbol of the Moon was given an exalted place in this mysterious and sacred constellation. And amongst the glittering stars of the Pleiades, Venus, as the Egyptian Hathor, the Beautiful, was said to rule.

GEMINI

The Twins—The second sign of the Zodiac, follows that of Taurus. The Dioscuri were the Seven Great Mysterious Gods belonging to the first creative group that circled the Solar region and to the Ship of the North and were mystically surrounded by water. They were the Seven Great Stars, whose regents (or planets) were worshipped by the Sabeans and whose traditions were astrological. In Egypt they were the principal Cosmic Gods. The Greeks limited them to two and called them Castor and Pollux, the two stars that came to represent the Zodiacal sign of Gemini. Through allegory two of the original gods have come down as Seth and Enoch or Hermes. These are generic names for Seers, the true Seer being one who sees things as they are, not as they seem, whether of nature or supernature. Mystical symbolism was always interwoven with the heavens. Seth, Sut, and Hermes were the first and the greatest of all the gods, though exoterically they have become greatly disfigured by the Jews, who either stole or borrowed them from their early Sabean origin. Sabeanism has been said to be the hinge point in nature between good and evil.

An Arabic writer, Soyuti, says the earliest records mention Seth or Typhon as founder of Sabeanism, with Hermes as the son, and states that the pyramids, which embody the planetary system, are their tombs, and that hither the Sabeans went on pilgrimages, "chanting prayers seven times a day as they turned to the north."[1]

The pyramid was oriented to Sirius. Sirius was later represented by the planet Mercury, ruler of the sign Gemini, whose two gods, the Dioscuri, came to represent the poles of heaven and earth, or the spiritual and physical in man.

Another writer, Aba Allatif, says he had read in Sabean Books that one of the pyramids was a tomb of the Agothadaemon, and the other of Hermes, his son, who was his reincarnation.[2] Some have said the Agothadaemon was Seth, Set or Typhon, and Hermes, her son. They are clearly identifiable as the earliest mother and son. Seth and Hermes were identical and as the Bi-une One were finally fixed in the Zodiac as the twins of Gemini, who were primordial in astrology and occultism, and were connected with the two pillars of stone and brick upon which the fundamental principles of astrology were engraved. Sut, Seth Hermes, or Taht, god of wisdom when he sank from being a god, began to be called the Seventh Son instead of the First. Seth was reputed to be the son of Adam, and was the primitive god of the Semites, a semi-divine ancestor of the Jews. He was the reputed progenitor of the Israelites, and thereby a "Jewish travesty on Hermes," who as Set-Typhon was the Great Mother, the original of Jehovah. Her son, El, was the Sun-god of the Syrians, the Egyptians, and Semites, sometimes called Seth (Saturn). And as Hermes he symbolized the planet Mercury of Gemini, of whom it was

---

[1] Operations of the Ancients in and at the Pyramid of Gizeh, Vol. ii, p. 359.

[2] The reincarnation of Hermes Trismegistus is Hermes, counterpart of the serpent. The Agothadaemon was represented by a serpent standing erect on a pole. In the Bacchic Mysteries the *consecrated cup* passed around after supper was called the Cup of the Agothadaemon. Wine was made sacred in the Bacchic mysteries. A communion of bread and wine was used in the worship of almost every important deity, and the initiatory rites were typified by a descent into the underworld (Hades). In the accounts of Bacchus, Heracles, Orpheus and Aesculapius, they all descended into the darkness (Hades), and ascended on the third day.—Blavatsky, H. P.—From "Isis Unveiled," Vol. ii, ch. x.

said "he was the most eloquent of speakers; with chains of gold flowing from his mouth, with which he linked the minds of those who heard him."[1]

After many wanderings among races and peoples, however, the early Seven when reduced to two have remained as Castor and Pollux, the bright stars of the Constellation of Gemini, which are associated with the Caduceus of Mercury and its two interwoven serpents encircling a rod, which is sometimes tipped with a Lotus emblem of the Mother. These two serpents were the gods of wisdom, having knowledge of divine power that guides souls over the bridge of Saturn and the waters of Lethe—the divine power that gives control over immortality and the "Call of Life."

There were two forms of Mercury, Sabean and Lunar. Sut or Sut-Anubis was Sabean, and Taht the Announcer, The Word and the Counsellor was lunar. The god Shu and the goddess Ma or Shu-Ma the Bi-une One as the ancient Nurse were also given to Gemini. The Twins in dual form were the Lion-gods, male and female in their Sabean origin.

The two Lion-gods[2] of Egypt, the two stars that were so recognized before the twelve signs of the Zodiac had been formed, were the Egyptian Dioscuri. They were continued as the male Dioscuri of Gemini, and then Shu and his sister, the male-female twins, were placed in this sign. Shu-Anhar is portrayed wearing the hind quarters of the lioness, representing the male-female. The Sphinx is similarly portrayed, and a figure of Diana of Ephesus is given having her two arms extended crosswise, in which she carries two lions.

______

[1]Kenealy—The Book of God, p. 48.

[2]The Lion, a totemic symbol of Judah, is the Lion-God of Israel, and as the Lion's whelp became the twin Lions, similar to Shu or Shu-Anhar, who as Kepheus, the Law Giver, has two stars, Regulus, called the heart of the Lion in the South and of the Constellation Kepheus in the North. "Shu in his dual character is protrayed in what is termed Bruce's or Harper's tomb at Biban-el-Muluk, in company with the black Sun-God, IU, or AU, who represented Atum in his youthful form," in whom the solar fatherhood was established.—Massey, Gerald—A Book of the Beginnings, Vol. ii, p. 230.

In all mythology the Twins were Bi-une, a completed One. A very interesting illustration is given by Guigniaut in his "Relics of Antiquity," which is copied in Massey's "Natural Genesis," Vol. i, p. 516, of "the Twins, who were Shu and Ma, or Shu and Tefnut, the male and the female *Gemini* in Egypt; the one being of both sexes. The calf below with its tongue thrust out, tells the tale of gesture language, as the type of both sexes. The beard of the male above denotes the third phase, and thus the figure contains the Trinity in Unity."

In the Scriptures the sign Gemini is represented as the Gates and the Pillars of Heaven.

THE FIXED STARS

There was a belief among the ancients that there were seven gates to the seven heavens, and that the eighth led to the heavens of the Fixed Stars, from which all souls descended. The eighth gate of the Fixed Stars was at the North, the abode of the Great Mother. In H. P. Blavatsky's "Secret Doctrine," Vol. ii, p. 700, "we are taught that the highest Dhyân Chohans, or Planetary Spirits (beyond the cognizance of the law of analogy) are in ignorance of what lies beyond visible planetary systems, since their essence cannot assimilate itself to that of worlds beyond our Solar system. When they reach a higher stage of evolution these other universes will be open to them; meanwhile they have complete knowledge of all the worlds within and beneath the limits of our solar system." This knowledge has been acquired by endless generations of Seers and Initiates, and is found in the Secret Books.

The Fixed Stars[1] emit a magnetic energy on our Sun, harmonizing with the energy the Sun gives to the planets, which surrounds and permeates all things within their radius. This

---

[1] "In the Chaldean Mysteries Tops were included among the playthings of the young Bacchus, or Iacchus. They represented the Fixed Stars (humming tops) and the Planets (whipping tops)."—"Chaldean Oracles," Vol. ii, pp. 17-18.

is the energy of light that is needed to bring life into the world, a reflected energy that distributes what it receives. Forces or influences from Star, Sun and Planet are God-given. In the horoscope the Fixed Stars seem to give strength and quality to the planets according as they harmonize with each other, and when in exact parallel of declination or conjunction. The Egyptians understood that astrological influence was due to the chemistry of Light. The Fixed Stars emit light but no rays. The Fixed Star is actually a moving center operating on one of six planes, each plane a duality of force, making the twelve cosmic forces. Corresponding to these we have the Twelve Hierarchies, the twelve signs of the Zodiac, the twelve Temple Gates, the twelve Sons of Jacob, the twelve Disciples, etc.

Diodorus and Berosus both give knowledge of twelve great Gods that presided over both the twelve months and the twelve signs of the Zodiac. Moses honored these signs by dividing the nation into twelve tribes, and by ordering twelve precious stones to be set for the ephod and the breast plate of the Pontiff, the stones represented the twelve signs of the Zodiac. Cruden in his "Concordance" calls the ephod worn by the high priests a richly embroidered robe, "and where the ephod crossed the high priest's breast, was a square ornament, called the breast plate, wherein twelve precious stones were set, with the names of the twelve tribes of Israel engraved on them, one on each stone." There is a magnetic influence thrown off from star and planet upon every metal, plant and human being. Diseases are the result of harmony and disharmony, and are primarily astral before they are physical. A knowledge and understanding of this should belong to all people who are in any way desirous of helping their fellow beings.

Planets are not limited to Seven, but the Seven we use were the primitive primordial houses of the Seven Logoi, and therefore became very sacred.

The first Globe or Chart ever made was Celestial, and the

first mappings out came long before the advent of geography. Stars and constellations were found to influence the civil divisions of the countries and peoples of the world. An apt illustration of this early mapping out of localities is found on an inscription of the Egyptian Khnumhept, who is said to have "established the land mark of the South and sculptured the North, like the heaven. He stretched the Great River on its back. He made the district into two parts, setting up the land marks like the heavens." Kircher has copied a kabalistic figure of the tree of seventy-two branches marking a completed circle. The seventy-two branches are the seventy-two duo-decans of the thirty-six decans of the Egyptian gates of Aah-en-Ru, which preceded the naming of the two Egypts, celestial and terrestrial, and their nomes, which were afterwards adopted geographically by the Egyptians. Primitive geography was first Stellar, then Lunar, and then Solar. Palestine was made to take the place of Aah-en-Ru, when the Typhonian religion passed into Judea and made its home in Jerusalem.

The Burmese called the Constellations "Coasts of Countries," the stars being mapped out or placed in the countries. It all began with the Celestial Mitzraim in the North, the initial birthplace (in the solar adjustment placed in the East) and, with the Constellation of the Great Bear with the Seven Stars. The twelve signs became the Totems of the Hebrews. The Fixed Stars were Totems of many different races. Stellar, Lunar, and Solar periods radiated myths and fables, the origins of which can be penetrated by the earnest seeking student. "Every Ark or tabernacle configurated in the heavens, whether as ark of the seven stars, the seven pillars, the seven horns, the ark of the four corners, the six, eight, nine, ten or twelve divisions, had been founded on the celestial waters, and was thus a symbol of salvation."[1]

The measuring of time and periods originated also in the

---

[1] Vision of Hermas.

North and was then wholly removed from divine revelation or metaphysical problems, since it was founded on the Seven Stars of the Great Bear before the courses of the seven planets were observed. Creations belong to mythological astrology, and are evolved from the recurring courses of the Sun, Moon, and the Fixed Stars. An apt illustration of the founding of mythology in a natural way occurs in the "Nishmath Adam," where the inhabitants of Paradise are called STANDERS, while a select few can go about visiting others. "In Paradise every one has his particular abode, and is not allowed to go out or ascend the dwelling of his neighbor; should he do so he will at once be consumed by his neighbor's great fire. They stand and keep their allotted places. There are indeed some Holy Ones (the holy watchers) who are suffered to ascend or descend. . . . Walk in the quarters of Paradise and pass through all the gates and abodes of the angels." The Standers were the Fixed Stars, and the Movers in the heavens were the Planets, the Egyptian "Gods of the Orbit."

The Secret Wisdom of the Kabala is purely mythical astrology, a doctrine of the stars. Its Hidden Wisdom can be found in the cycles of Time. Later the origins became obscured through being restated as history, and "falsification rings loud, and the ancient meanings are fading in the shadows," but the fixed stars and planets "have a mysterious, unbroken and powerful connection with men and globes. Every heavenly body is the temple of *a* god and these gods themselves are the temples of God, the Unknown."[1]

Today with the changing of the cycle the same elements in nature will build by the same processes in men as in those olden days, but with a greater enlightenment, both spiritual and material. The reflected energy, Light, is awaiting adjustment with man. This God-given blessing as it spreads over the world is life-giving in principle, and will carry us into Eternity, that Eternity which is changeless,

---

[1] Blavatsky, H. P.—The Secret Doctrine, Vol. i, p. 578.

leading neither to the past nor the future, but extisting in the endless present.

There are recurrent cycles in man, ever-changing impulses in human life as well as in the Cosmos, all based on the manifestation of Light. Astronomers are only beginning to measure the great celestial cycles or circles accurately, yet the Egyptians, Chaldeans, Hindus and others did although we have learned of no instruments of measurement used by those peoples of faraway days. Whence their knowledge of the heavens? In the astral publications of the past fifty or seventy-five years we are given great details of the wonderful instruments now in use, as well as of the marvelous observatories, but when we search for that old wisdom of the heavens and all that was found in the constellations with their signs and symbols of thousands of years ago, how little is given. We must go back in research to those ancient Truths ere we can feel at peace, and know that all enlightened faiths were based on the manifestations of Light. All antiquity believed in the universality of life. It is so true that whenever you find a law or force in the universe you will find that same law in yourself. God's law is the Word of God written in the heavens and in man for each one of us. Why so much blindness today? Yet the Light is spreading, and bids us hope that the old Truths that had reached such sublime heights and all the great and truly majestic beliefs of the ancients with which nothing in our civilization of today can compare may return to us. "The subtle and sublime mysticism that would captivate the Egyptian and the Arab intellect would be utterly lost on the dull Hebrew, or the carnal European, whose coarser mind is unable to comprehend those ideas that to the Oriental fancy are the personifications of all that is beautiful."[1]

To the ancients, Life Everlasting was the supreme fact in nature, justified in death. How few of us give thought to the morrow! How few give thought to Eternity, or lift

[1]Kenealy—The Book of God, p. 56.

their eyes above to those celestial Watchers in the Heavens!
"Think in Eternities and the knowledge of Eternity will come
to us." *Think!* There never seems time to think in the
turmoil and chaos and mad rush for gold today. To those
ancient nations and to the Egyptians reverence for God
and His stars was the beginning of wisdom. We know this,
too, but it is down deep hidden somewhere in our hearts.

The Egyptian "Book of the Dead" is the story of the
Zodiac. It is the story of the changing of the cycles, which
represented the changes in life, the basic belief remaining the
same. The changing of the Zodiacal Sign meant merely the
new construction coming. It is quite certain that mystic
relationship with the Zodiac is the foundation of all theologies, wherein are hidden great Truths. Cyrus, at the moment
of his death, gave thanks to gods and heroes for having so
often instructed him about the signs in the Heavens. And
Ptolemy says: "Mortal as I am, I know that I am born for
a day, but when I follow the serried multitude of Stars in
their circular course, my feet no longer touch the earth. I
ascend to Zeus himself, to feast me on ambrosia, the food
of the Gods."

This Mystic Cross or Anchor, type of the Crucifixion, or
Redeemer, was discovered on tombs in the Catacombs of Rome.
The Fishes belong to the Zodiacal sign, Pisces, the Fishes, founda-
tion and symbol of the Piscene Manifestation or Christianity.

CHAPTER XI

"WHAT I TELL YOU IN THE DARK SPEAK IN THE LIGHT"

The cycle of the Piscene Manifestation, with its attendant emanations of Light, which always manifests with the coming of great cycles or periods of time, was the origin of the modern Christian Religion, which combines its spiritual significance with its founder, Jesus. Pisces as the twelfth and last sign completing the circle of the celestial Zodiac was introduced by the Precession of the Equinoxes about two thousand years ago, and though it has represented a period of darkness and limitation, has been of great esoteric significance.

Pisces is a sign that for ages past was called the sign of the fish. Anciently it was represented as one fish, until a time, fully twenty-eight thousand or more years ago, when Fish-goddesses were placed in the sign as gestators giving birth to the fish child. Since then two fishes have been made the symbol of this Zodiacal sign. It is the one from which the sun-gods or ancient Messiahs were said to be born. We call it today the sign of Fishermen, as the followers or disciples of Jesus were chosen from the fishermen. When this cycle began many miracles concerning fish were given by Jesus as symbolical messages of wisdom. Theologically the meaning of fish is phallic, but being metaphysically divine, it was considered a symbol of Spirit. Jesus was called a fish, as were other Messiahs and "Saviours" of mankind. St. Augustine says of Jesus, "For he is a fish that lives in the midst of the waters."

The greatest of all mothers was symbolized as a fish, from

whom all other mothers or goddesses were evolved. She was the Argha, the Ship of the North, mystically and majestically sailing over the great celestial waters for all time, past, present and future.

"The word "Dag," or "THE FISH," is frequently used in the Talmud for the Messiah or regenerative spiritual force. "When man becomes his own Saviour this force passes upward to the brain, where its currents unite for the perfecting of the solar or spiritual body."[1]

The Philistines represented their idol as having a fish's tail, for when speaking of the idol that had fallen on its face, we read in I Samuel, v, 4, "and only the Stump of Dagon was left of him." The symbol of a fish was the sign of Christianity among primitive Christians, sometimes used secretly. Oannes, Vishnu and the Syrian Dagon were all symbols of the Messiah.

Pisces, sign of water, is a symbol of the Great Sea. When a manifestation of Divine Light appears as a cyclic down-pouring, called a Deluge, a new age dawns. This constellation Pisces, which forms a triangular space in the heavens, is in itself a spiritual symbol. The fishes were called "The Leaders of the Celestial Hosts," and swimming in different directions signified mind and body swimming in illusion and fleeing from the bondage of this sign. For Pisces as the twelfth and last house of the Zodiac is called the House of Bondage, ending an Age and the bondage of the Past and acting as agent for that freedom from which spiritual rebirth is attained. It is the house of undoing, or degeneration, prior to regeneration. There is a very subtle magnetism connected with this sign. It is paradoxical and in its highest development gives an impersonal love, silent as the great deep, whose underlying principle is universal love and sympathy. It gives great understanding, though its spiritual symbology has been sadly misinterpreted. But the new down-pouring of Divine Light with its Ray of Justice, will reach out over the

---

[1]Comte de Gabalis—Dudley Edition, p. 276.

world, bringing a true responsibility that will awaken in humanity the higher side of this dark and yet prophetic sign. Its transmutation will come through a great precipitation of the Saturnian individuality, for Saturn is broadcasting his powerful forces for the reconstruction of our world at this period of world history, and as the Planet of Justice will set it free from the trammels of the past. Saturn is a planet of time, and with his scythe will cut, as it were, great rifts in the darkness, letting through the Light, which will enter into the very heart of humanity. A Light from the Central Sun awaits this stroke of the scythe to free the Spark from our Great Father which is sent forth with His imperishable Divine Love.

Gross misrepresentations, and the placing of old spiritual conceptions on a false basis, have contributed very largely to keeping our world the "Dark Star." Jesus recalls to his disciples "Is it not written 'My house shall be called a house of all nations,' the house of prayer? but ye have made it a den of thieves." (Mark xi, 17.) He publicly denounces scholars and those antagonistic to spiritual truths. Hypocrisy and priestcraft are sternly dealt with as perverting religious concepts. "It is in the nature of the religious idea that just in proportion as it was originally penetrated with a divine truth, which has been perverted, does it engender hypocrisy." The religion taught by Jesus contains the most divine truths ever given to the world, and yet they have been so distorted that many of them have been almost lost. Wherein lies the responsibility? It is but right to emphasize the overpowering love of the root of all evil which has been so far reaching in its disastrous results, and so opposed to the teaching of Jesus. But today, with the world at its lowest ebb of manifestation, and when numberless hearts are wrung by need of the common necessities of life, the light is breaking forth from out the darkness. The mind of man, held in ignorance during the Piscene Manifestation, has been literally chained to a rock of false teaching as to the old symbols reverently dedicated to God as well as to man. Pisces is directly related to the mind of man, but when perverted brings an ignorance hard to overcome. Because of the inaccuracy and illusion of the period following the passing of Jesus, no truth under such aspects could be maintained in its integrity.

Singularly blessed are those who have conquered and found their true balance in the neutral center which binds together the symbols of this double sign, representing as it does the positive and the negative poles of existence. Freed from the Wheel of Birth, the Zodiac, and the bondage of the past, they arrive at the understanding of that wisdom which underlies all things.

Every prophecy foretelling the advent of Jesus looked forward to the oncoming after the Piscene Manifestation of the highest spiritual or perfected teaching. Had not the Sun journeyed through all the signs of the Zodiac, a conqueror, while on the earth, the travail of the world seemed nearing its end, for the coming of a great teacher, gave hope for the poor and the downtrodden. Placing spiritual concepts on the wrong basis, however, has resulted in the grossly materialistic world we have today.

There are other solar systems beyond the boundaries of our own and under the dominion of the mysterious Central Sun, governing all things, and very potent at the time of Manifestations. *"Beyond the Sun in the direction of the Dog-Star lies that incorruptible flame or Sun, Principle of All Things, willing obedience from our own Sun which is but a manifestation of its relegated force. The existence of the Sun behind the Sun has been known in all ages,* as well as the fact that its influence is most potent upon earth during that period every two thousand years when it is in conjunction with the Sun of our solar system. Then gathering to itself the power of its own Source and transmitting it through our Sun to this planet, it is said to send the Sons of God into the consciousness of the earth sphere, that a new world of thought and emotion may be born in the minds of men for the stimulation of humanity's spiritual evolution. Such a manifestation marks the beginning or end of an epoch upon earth by the radiation of that divine consciousness known as the Christ Ray or Paraclete."[1]

The Magi, who were astrologers, always knew precisely the time when this configuration in the heavens would occur, when the Sun would be in a direct line with that greatest of all the fixed stars, Sirius the Dog-Star, the well beloved, the harbinger of the dawn.

The birthday of the infant Jesus, being arbitrarily set by the priests, produces a serious discrepancy, as we are told he was born in a manger. The manger is found in the sign of the summer solstice, the constellation Cancer, which was called the Gate of the Sun, through which souls were said to descend from their heavenly home to earth, just as at the winter solstice in December, they were said to return to their heavenly or celestial home, the constellation Capricorn, the other Gate of the Sun. Capricorn was the sign from which Sun-gods were said to be born at the winter solstice and made sacred to the Sons of Light. Connecting the birth of Jesus with this sign has been productive of many doubts in regard to His life and teachings, which have been greatly distorted by the church. The lack of evidence regarding the life of Jesus is, of course, remarkable. We find in the Persian story of the birth of their Sun-god Mithra that he was born at the winter solstice, and the Caves of Mithra were called the "Caves of Light."

In the story of the birth of Jesus as given in the New Testament, an unusual emanation of Light is anticipated. This would manifest through the Sign, Virgo the Virgin, the Great Cosmic Mother. Virgo holds the Seed of Wheat, and coincides with Bethlehem or Beth-lachm, meaning "the House of Bread." The Virgin Mother is made to appear

---

[1]Comte de Gabalis—Dudley Edition, p. 88.

as the gestator in the opposite pole Pisces, where she brings forth her child, the Messiah.

The sacred planets of our solar system, circle, as it were, around the throne of the Sun, one of whose attendants is Gabriel, anciently called the Angel of Announcements. In planetary form he is the planet Mars, ruler of the Zodiacal sign Scorpio, symbol of generation and regeneration. It is Gabriel who announces to the virgin the advent of Jesus, "The Son of the Most High," as a perfected spiritual soul destined to be the expression of the heavenly causation. "The Holy Ghost shall come upon him and the Powers of the Most High will overshadow." This birth, like that of all the other Messiahs, 'was the fulfilment of the promise foretold in celestial configuration. The announcement in Luke poetically emphasises this. The shepherds were the Holy Men upon whom the Great Light was shining, who were said to be watching the rising of the Star in the East, while with Gabriel (Mars) were a multitude of stars, singing praises. In the Book of Job we read of the morning stars singing together, and all the sons of God shouting for joy. These Stars were the Seven Great ones belonging to the ancient mother, and their song was that most ethereal and beautiful "Music of the Spheres," the mystical music that is said to be heard by those who have risen above the sordid influences of the lower plane and to have communed with the stars, those great silent teachers whose secrets become an open book when the kingdom of heaven has been found.

Jesus gives to Peter the keys of Heaven and Earth. Astrologically these represent the keys to the two principal gates of the Zodiac, which are the two solsticial points, the Zodiacal signs Cancer and Capricorn, called the Gates of the Sun. "Through Cancer, or the 'Gate of Man,' the soul descends upon earth, (to unite with the body), which is its spiritual death. Through Capricorn, the 'Gate of the Gods,' it re-ascends up to heaven, its new birth taking place upon its release from the body. . . . The Soul thus descending . . . is furnished with the several faculties which it has to exercise during its probation upon earth, in Saturn it is supplied with reason and intelligence; in Jupiter with the power of action; in Mars, with the irascible principle; in the Sun, with sensation and speculation; in Venus, with the appetites; in Mercury, with the power of declaring and expressing its thoughts; in the Moon, with the faculty of generation and augmenting the body."[1]

In Plato's allegory "Er saw two openings adjoining one another in the earth and exactly opposite them, two openings in the heaven, and he beheld souls on one side taking their departure at one of the openings in the heaven, and the corresponding one in the earth after judgment had been passed upon them, while at the other two openings he saw them arriving squalid and dirty or pure and bright according as they ascended from the earth or descended from heaven."[2]

The path of the soul on its way to be united with the body is said to be along the Milky Way, or from one solsticial point to another. Within the Milky Way, which suggests a circular form, are the same creative elements as in man himself and in the Zodiac. The Milky Way was used allegorically to denote the Great Serpent.

There are three beautiful stars in the belt of the constellation Orion. They were mythically called the "Three Wise Kings." Six thousand years ago, when the vernal equinox was in the constellation Taurus, and this sign rose it was called "The Star of the East." The Three Kings typified the Magi, of whom Giordano Bruno writes, "The Magi were the Holy Men, who, setting themselves apart from everything else on earth, contemplated the divine virtues and understood the divine nature of the gods and spirits more closely, and so initiated others into the same mysteries, which consists in one holding an uninterrupted intercourse with those invisible beings during life."

[1]Taught by the later Alexandrean Platonists, and thus expounded by Macrobius, (Somn. Scrip. I, 12.) From King's The Gnostics.
[2]Republic x, 14.

The Magi were astrologers who had pure unassailable knowledge found in the heavens of the Zodiac and the fixed stars, and an uncorrupted form of worship in all that pertained to the divine. The Magi were said to come from Arabia, but the word Arabia at the time of Jesus' birth meant not only Arabia Felix, but Northern India, i. e., the Himalayas. These Magi were Mahatmas or Masters from India who had calculated astrologically the advent of Jesus and journeyed for two years or more to visit him. Their number, three, is derived from the fact that they offered Three Gifts, but tradition has it that there were twelve or twenty Magi, and that the entire journey from and return to India took nearly five years. "The Magi of Chaldea, their class and their worship were born on the earlier Atlantis,[1] in Sâka-dvîpa, the Sinless." All Orientals agree "that the Magas of Sâka-dvîpa are the forefathers of the fire-worshipping Parsis."[2]

"The esoteric or mystical interpretation of the three Magi and their three gifts will eliminate uncertainties. The Gospels are profoundly mystical. The Three Wise Men represent the Higher Trinity of forces that come to assist the growth and development of the newborn consciousness (positive as symbolized by a man). They would be Wisdom, Love and Mind, and each would bring with it (him) its corresponding negative force represented on the physical plane as Gold, Frankincense and Myrrh. The central or soul force being in Mary, the Mother, and thus the child had the seven necessary qualities for its sustenance and growth."[3]

We are told in King's Gnostics, "The offering to Atergatis were little fish made of gold and silver, thrown into the

---

[1] Atlantis was the Sâka-dvîpa of theogony, "or Atlantis (its earliest portion) in its beginnings. This was when it yet had its Seven Holy Rivers that washed away all sin and its 'seven districts, wherein there was no dereliction of virtue, no contention, no deviation from virtue'."—Blavatsky, H. P.—The Secret Doctrine, Vol. ii p. 322.

[2] Blavatsky, H. P.—The Secret Doctrine, Vol. ii, p. 323.

[3] Conrow, Edgar.

sacred lake. Manilius supplies the reason for such a dedication; his Venus, the Assyrian Urania or Mylitta, took the form of a fish, and hid herself in the Euphrates to escape the pursuit of Typhon. Hence according to his masters, the Magi, came from the sign Pisces."

Great planetary conjunctions are always coincident with critical periods on earth, at which time changes take place on earth that are universal, and are both material and spiritual. It has been maintained that such a conjunction occurred at the incarnation of Jesus. Kepler held to this, claiming positively that all the planets were in conjunction in Pisces at his birth. Every 800 years Jupiter and Saturn are in conjunction, which was thought to be in effect at his birth. The sign Pisces was generally connected with the Messiahs and was called by the Kabalists the "Constellation of the Messiahs."

Sephariel, an English astrologer of the present century, gives as convincing proof a chart for this birth, placing the Moon and Uranus in conjunction in the sign Pisces, with the Sun in the opposite sign Virgo, that of the immaculate Mother. Arbanal, who states that his authority is from ancient reliable sources, in his commentary on the prophet Daniel, claims with others, that the Jews who called their Messiah Dag (the fish) connected him with the conjunction of Jupiter and Saturn in the sign of the Fishes "Which indicated the land of Judea." The Jews, however, knew of the astrological allegory through which the tradition could be interpreted, which accounts for their rejection of Jesus as their Messiah.

The Colure of the Vernal Equinox entered Pisces about the year 255 B. C., but this was not the primal entrance into that sign.

Jesus was the radiator and exponent of the Piscene Manifestation. It is the sign indissolubly connected with Him. And throughout all His teaching we find His allusion to the period of degradation and materialism that would sweep over the world throughout the Piscene cycle of this past two thousand years. Jesus was a great Initiate, who knew and taught the Ancient Wisdom, which is conclusively proven by His many pre-historic and pre-Christian sayings. Hidden Books of Wisdom are found in the Apocrypha, from which Jesus quoted and taught continually. They held the "Sayings" known in the mysteries, and taught orally long before they were ever written down. The Book of Ecclesiasticus contains logia of a pre-Christian Jesus, which were taught to the Initiates. The Apocrypha held the secrets of the stars, their chronology and all relating to them.

In the Jewish Kadish there is a pre-Christian form of the Lord's Prayer which reads, "Our Father which art in heaven, Be gracious to us, O Lord our God, Hallowed be thy name; And let the remembrance of thee be glorified in heaven above, and upon earth here below. Let thy kingdom reign over us, now and for ever. Thy holy men of old said, 'Remit and forgive unto all men whatsoever they have done against me.' And lead us not into temptation, But deliver us from the evil thing. For thine is the kingdom, and thou shalt reign in glory for ever and for evermore." Many other equally beautiful sayings are given.

Jesus began His teaching on the shores of Galilee, choosing His disciples from the fishermen, of whom he was to make "Fishers of Men"—that is to say, He instructed them and made them exponents of the Light, spiritual leaders, so that each finding the Christ Spirit within his own heart would radiate that Light over the darkness that was overshadowing the world.

Jesus performed many miracles of profound mystical significance. The feeding of the 5,000 people with the fish and bread is most mystical. Bread is a symbol of Divine Wisdom, and signified the pouring out of the Light over the multitude, through the significance of the Zodiacal sign Pisces, and was symbolical of the feeding of the world with the "Spirit" which is inexhaustible. There is a mystical parallel rendering in the Egyptian "Book of the Dead," called "Celestial Diet," where Osiris eats under the sycamore tree and has the seven loaves brought to him "to live by," the bread that was the Spirit, of which later he says, "My bread at the heaven was that of Ra (the seven loaves), my bread on earth was that of Seb." Seb has the number Five (a five-rayed star is a hieroglyphic symbol for a God or Divinity). Both these numbers were sacred in the "Book of the Dead," and have great spiritual significance.

Both Jesus and John are asked by the Pharisees for a sign from heaven, and receive the same answer, that "None other should be given them except the sign of the prophet Jonah," which was the sign of Pisces. There is no other in which the Sun symbolical of a Messiah is reborn in the mythical astrology. Jesus further says, "The queen of the south shall rise up in judgment with this generation, and shall condemn it; for she came from the uttermost parts of the earth to hear the wisdom of Solomon; and, behold, a greater than Solomon *is* here." The queen of the south is none other than the star Sirius, which comes in line with the Central Sun every 2,160 years, when a new Era or Age begins. (The name Solomon represents three different names of the Sun.) Sirius has been connected with every religion of antiquity, being in line with the Sun at the close of every great cycle of 2,160 years, and was called the "Keeper of the Celestial Gate" and "Guardian of Heavenly Secrets," and when called Sut-Anubis was "Lord of the Sacred land of the West." Sirius was also called the Bride, who gave birth to a new year.

"Again the kingdom of heaven is like a draw-net let down into the sea, which encloses fish of all sorts. When full, they haul it up on the beach and sit down and collect the good fish in baskets, while the worthless they throw away. So will it be at the 'Close of the Age.' The Angels will go forth and separate the wicked from among the righteous and will throw them into the fiery furnace.—Matthew xiii,

47, 48, 49.   The sea is the great sea of generative life.   When souls have been perfected through conquering of all the lessons of the Zodiac, reincarnation is not a necessity, but those who are still bound to their Wheel of Life, whose gate to those realms remains locked, must be thrown back upon the world and all its suffering.   The Precessional period is now bringing us to the "Close of the Age," and the angels, those upon whom the Light has shone, will help the lowly ones, by pointing out the Ray of Divine Justice which will manifest through the sign Leo, called the Fiery Furnace, being a symbol of Fire and the home of the Sun, where purification can release them from their material existence.

When instructing His disciples Jesus says, "Do you suppose that I came to bring peace on earth, I did not come to bring peace, but a sword!"   The sword was always the symbol of Justice, not sacrifice, and Jesus was the forerunner of the Age of Justice, encompassing the world in its imminent manifestations of Light.   Towards the end of the year 1920 the polarity of the Sun, Earth and the North Pole was in conjunction.   In the year 2000 Polaris, our Pole Star, will be in exact conjunction with the North Pole.   This is very important, Polaris being the highest point in the heavens around which our constellations seem to revolve.   It is The Judgment Seat, and one of pure Justice through which comes the Judgment Ray.   Again, Jesus says, "I came to throw Fire upon the earth and what is my desire?   Oh that it were even now kindled."—Luke xii, 49.   The time now approaches when it shall be kindled, foreshadowed in the new Era.   He foretells that "for us, however, God has drawn aside the veil through the teaching of the Spirit; for the Spirit searches everything, including the depths of the Divine nature—I Cor., xi, 10.[1]

The manifestation of the Sun behind the Sun is the Universal Fire that Jesus came to throw or sow upon the earth, and is the super-solar force, the "Paraclete."   "Knowledge

---

[1]Weymouth, R. F.—The New Testament in Modern Speech.

as to the development of this Force has been sacredly guarded in all ages lest man, through his ignorance, should employ it to his destruction. That soul who will renounce all personal ambition, and will seek by selfless service of his fellow beings to obey the Divine Spirit within may, without external teaching or assistance, evoke the Flame and achieve unaided a knowledge of Nature's secrets and mysteries. But unless governed by the God within and with selfless purpose, this Fire will intensify the lower passions and make of the man a destructive force working contrary to the Law of Nature. He who seeks divine knowledge will surely find it, for the divinity in man ever strives to render unto him his lost birthright. No sincere effort to solve God's mystery passes unheeded by the Silent Watcher within."[1]

In the old days the assimilating of this Force was only accomplished through years of endless prayer, sacrifice and fasting, but today the heavens prophesy a quick knowledge. The Spirit of the Father will speak through those upon whom the Light shines, and the teaching of Jesus will be explained, for "There is nothing veiled which will not be uncovered, nor secret which will not become known. What I tell you in the dark, speak in the light; and what is whispered in your ear, proclaim upon the roofs of the houses."[2] —Matthew x, 26-7.

Jesus as the great Initiate came to earth not for His pleasure, but "to do the will of Him who sent me," (see John vi, 38), shewing that he was freed from the Wheel of Rebirth, the Circle of Necessity. The Zodiac represents the material animal existence of physical life on earth, and every sign must be lived in its symbolical rendering and conquered if the soul is to receive its freedom, and awaken to the reality of a spiritual existence, the lower consciousness becoming merged with the Eternal. "Round and round, like a wheel, no part of which is more the starting point than any other,

---

[1] Comte de Gabalis—Dudley Edition, p. 52.
[2] Weymouth, R. F.—The New Testament in Modern Speech.

this is called the 'Equilibrium of God,' or Heaven reminding us of the Wheel of Necessity."

Spirit or spiritual birth must come from within. From without comes enlightenment, while regeneration is through the baptism by Fire now coming over the world at this period of which Jesus taught.

The entire life of Jesus can be readily followed in the signs of the Zodiac and the Fixed Stars, through symbolical interpretation. The Passover was a passing of the Sun from one sign to another, or the passing of one age into another. At the yearly Spring Festival given in honor of the young God (the Sun), when his suffering, trial, death, burial and resurrection to a new life were symbolically shown, there was an inner (private) and an outer (public) demonstration given. In the Mithraic rites of the mysteries of their Saviour God, this drama was reserved for the Initiates alone.

The Passover of the Gospels was symbolically represented by Jesus and His twelve disciples as the twelve signs of the Zodiac, with Jesus always as the Sun, Light and Life Giver. The two last astrological signs Pisces, water and Aquarius, light are here symbolically portrayed. Water is light and Light is Divine Wisdom. When the Sun has passed the last degree of the sign Pisces and is at the point where the Ecliptic crosses the Equator, forming a cross at this intersection, it is spoken of as being impaled on the cross, before rising in the midst of the glory and splendor of the East.

The teachings in all religions of antiquity, as well as that of Jesus, were fundamentally the same, and were given in parable, myth or allegory. Great truths could only be understood by the few, and these truths were always found in the mysteries of the heavens. Study of these leads one into paths of deep idealization, with an urge to know more and more of the wisdom hidden in the Great Mystery of the heavens.

The message of the Gospels is to the soul, and its mystical teaching has been lost chiefly through lack of intuitive faculty. The spirit of Jesus still remains with us. He represented the Seed of the world Harvest, and the fulfilment of many of His teachings will come to pass. Distance of time matters not, since time is only a concept arising from the consciousness of change in our material world, and the religion of the future will bring a clear knowledge and understanding of the truth. The true spirit is potentially in all peoples, and shall find expression, that it may realize the Divine Law of Nature—God. The outpouring of the Light with which Jesus was empowered will bring At-one-ment in our new cycle. All peoples will be united in its truth, as Jesus taught it, for At-one-ment is the union of man's purified human self with his spiritual and divine self.

To understand the New Testament in all its mystical rendering, one should study and have knowledge of the Serpent Force as it brings a greater realization of the sublimity of the doctrines of Jesus and the Eternal Truths hidden in the miracles and parables.

The bringing through from the past of the religion divinely given through Jesus was reserved for the future, our present day. It was a Gospel of Love, whose interpretations will manifest through our period of reconstruction, when the limitation of matter will be overcome by love and brotherhood, for the stars predict it, and the "Zodiac is the hieroglyph of the Soul."

Great truths are written in the heavens, and not for the especial convenience of theologians, who have too frequently kept man from the true knowledge of his Creator. "The heavens declare the glory of God, and the firmament sheweth his handiwork. Day unto day uttereth speech, and night unto night sheweth knowledge. *There is* no speech nor language, *where* their voice is not heard. Their line is gone out through all the earth, and their words to the end of the world. In them hath he set a tabernacle for the Sun. Which *is* as a bridegroom coming out of his chamber, *and* rejoiceth as a strong man to run a race. His going forth *is* from the end of the heaven, and his circuit unto the ends of it: and there is nothing hid from the heat thereof."—Psalm xix, 1-6.

Jesus was of the tribe of Judah. The tribe of Judah was named after the Zodiacal sign Leo, symbolizing the heart, and the Bible says, "He cometh for the destruction of his enemies (darkness) and the salvation of his people (to give Light.") In the sign Aquarius the circle changes to the spiral, and man's spiritual ascent will begin quickly, not as in the old days, with long preparation to attain the inner Light. Spiritual vision is to come swiftly, and during the changing of the cycle Neptune entering the sign Leo, becomes the Super-luminary bridge, which will guide us over the dark waters of the past. Aquarius represents the man in the heavens polarized by the woman on earth. In the woman's age, when equality between the two sexes becomes balanced, humanity will reach up to the Great Spirit. The submerging of the Piscene in the Aquarian means that "The new Light is now coming forth from the soul, having completed its 'Twelve Labors'."

In the early days of the Christian religion many people accepted John the Baptist as the Saviour of the Nazareans. He was their prophet, and they rejected Jesus. The Mandeans, an old name for Nazareans, were disciples of John. Thirty thousand of their direct descendants are said to reside in Persia. It was through the acceptance of John the Baptist that baptism became a Christian rite. This baptismal rite is one of the very oldest, and was practised by all nations in their sacred mysteries. It was a symbolic purification by water. The Baptizer was an Initiator of the Lesser Mysteries, knowing the Secret Science, which was the wisdom of heaven, and Law of God. Even today, in the Roman Catholic churches, is found the font called Piscina, containing the Holy Water, a very telling connection between the great past and the present.

"It was written of John in Isaiah the Prophet: Behold I

send my messenger before thy face which shall prepare thy way before thee."—Mark ii, 1. See also Mal. i, 111. John announced the coming of Jesus as one far greater than he. John preceded the Light as Darkness, from which Light comes, saying "that He (Jesus) shall baptize you with the Holy Ghost and with fire," Luke iii, 16, and Jesus tells the multitude that John is more than a prophet. Baptism is the drawing near to Divine Consciousness.

Astrologically, John baptizes with the lunar element, water, the lunar self, the Moon, which is both human and divine; but Jesus, who is typical of the Sun, the Spiritual Self, baptizes with the Holy Fire which is wholly divine. John could not impart the highest knowledge to Jesus, for Fire alone could regenerate. Jesus taught that purity of life alone could free man from the bondage of his animal, material existence, and liberate him from the Wheel of Birth, the Zodiac, through the awakening of the Solar Fire that leads to Divine Wisdom.

In ancient times one of the names of the Fish-god was Oannes. This name bears a striking resemblance to Joannes, known as John the Baptist. Christianity spread where Oannes had been worshipped, possibly through the likeness of these two names. The name Oannes, which is connected with On, the Sun, in early times meant a Divine Messenger and was also a symbol of the incarnation of one who was of heaven but fulfilled his mission on earth. Oannes is represented as half fish and half man, the fish acting as a covert disguise of his sacred origin. He comes out of the sea, the "Great Deep," which typifies the Secret Doctrine.

The symbol of the mother of Oannes was a mermaid, who was worshipped as Atergatis, another form of Venus, and by whom was meant the "Holy Spirit," that Great Mother who was the gestator of all the known Messiahs.

Berosus tells us that ancient humanity was civilized by Oannes, the primeval Fish-god of lower Babylonia, called Dag-on, who during the day gave instruction to mankind in everything that would tend to soften manners and humanize mankind, and so universal were his instructions that nothing material has been added by way of improvement since. When the Sun set, it was his custom to plunge again into the sea and abide all night in the deep, as he was amphibious. He is identified with the God Hea of the Chaldean Civilization. "Professor Sayce of Oxford on some cylinders found reference to 'Ea,' the God of Wisdom, as identified with the Oannes of Berosus, half man half fish, who not only taught the Babylonian culture but the art of writing."—From the Secret Doctrine.

The Fish-man An, of Egypt, or the Oan of the Chaldeans, was probably derived from the previous Piscene cycle of twenty-eight thousand years ago. Vishnu taught disguised as a fish. Esoterically this signified the psychic consciousness which had become spiritual.

Fish statues are pre-eminently Assyrian. A cross was the symbol of the Assyrian God Anu, and is typical of an equinoctial crossing that brings forth the child, or a manifestation of the new Sun. Both Assyrian and Babylonian beginning of the year was at the spring equinox when the Sun was in the sign Pisces, the Fish, hence we have the Fish of both Hea and Oannes.

John the Baptist comes under the sign Capricorn. Capricorn is symbolized in the celestial heavens as the Sea-Goat, one of the most mysterious creatures of the Zodiac. Various animals, amphibious in nature, are represented by it, and it is of the greatest occult significance.

Capricorn people are called the Messengers. Their service lies between the highest and the lowest, aiming always towards the highest, in mankind. Their watchword is Service, and they are often ambassadors and priests. They are said to be the forerunners of the activity and expression of Pisces, just as the Piscene Manifestation is the forerunner of our new cycle.

How closely connected are Jesus and John. John, the

Messenger baptizing with water; Jesus, the Redeemer, *baptizing with Fire through which will come the revelation of the Secrets of God.* Matter is but retarded motion, which can be raised and transformed into the Light of Heaven through its baptismal Fire. In those realms of the sky, the Kingdom of Heaven above, are the constellations and the fixed stars, which were mystically called "God's Redeemed Children," and which reflect the Wisdom of God. John was the Servant of the Light, the Moon, and Jesus the Saviour from the Sun. Sun and Moon are called the Secret Planets, and how well they keep their secrets, and how they carry us back to the Fire Mist. Fire, which yields Water; Spirit and Water, this was the primordial baptism.[1] The Fire Mist and the Cardinal Cross of the Zodiac, which is the Path of the Christ and the Sacred River of Life, are indissolubly linked together. The first baptism, even among the Initiates, is lost in the mists of time.

It was at the Council of Ephesus in the year 431 that Mary was declared Mother of God. The goddess Neith was adored under a form of the Virgin Mother at least 7,000 years ago. "Neith is neither more nor less than the Great Mother, and yet the Immaculate Virgin, or female God, from whom all things proceeded. . . . She is the Nerfe of the Etruscans, half a woman and half a fish."[2] Whence the connection of the Virgin Mary with the fish and Pisces; Virgo the sign of the Virgin is its opposite sign or pole. She is also called the "Virgin of the Sea," and the "Lady patroness" of all Roman Catholic seamen, and as Sharp says, "The Feast of Candlemas—in honor of the Goddess Neith—is yet marked in our Almanacks as Candlemas day or the Purification of the Virgin Mary."

Great vistas of truth unfold through the realization that the Bible was written by Occultists and Astrologers,

---

[1] "The great Dragon of Wisdom is born of fire and water, and into fire and water will all be reabsorbed with him."

[2] Bonwick—Egyptian Belief.

learned in all the mysteries of Nature, which originally were astrological or astronomical in character, evolved from the celestial book of God and therefore Divine. Conception of Divine Power came through the study of the stars, and was the origin of the religion first realized by man. May this Divine or Christ Power enter the hearts of all God's children and show them the true way toward the Light. The teaching of the Bible is quite different to that of the Church. The latter teaches of a personal God and of a place called Hell, while the Bible teaches a doctrine of Christ and the supremacy of the Christ Spirit as a Universal Law of God.

The messages of Jesus will live again for "Now is the Judgment of the world; yet a little while is the Light with you. Walk while ye have the Light, lest darkness come upon you; for he that walketh in darkness knoweth not whither he goeth. While ye have the Light, believe in the Light, that ye may be children of the Light," and this is the Light from that Great Judgment Seat penetrating the darkness of today in which all may be baptized anew. It will be revealed to the pure in heart, to the learned and to the unlearned. If one seeks the shadow, in that shadow he must walk; but to those who seek the Light many heavenly secrets will unfold, for "to him that knocketh it shall be opened." And Jesus spake to them, saying "I am the LIGHT of the world: he that followeth me shall not walk in darkness, but shall have the light of life."

We are on the threshold of the new Aquarian Era—Aquarius, the man in whose arms is the Urn, symbol of the Heart, from which he pours the Light that will bring into harmonious coordination the Divine Plan of the balance of Justice signified by the sword brought by Jesus. Aquarius is the Waterman representing spiritual baptism. Water is the living spirit. "He shall pour the water out of his buckets, and his seed *shall be* in many waters.—Numbers xxiv, 7. From the urn in the arms of Aquarius rivers of Light pour toward the Royal Star Fomalhaut, in the Constellation of the Southern Fish, belonging to Aquarius, and along this river is reflected Divine Love.

At the beginning of all Ages, or great Eras, the Cardinal Cross is tenanted in the heavens, which is said to be an infalliable mark of a world teacher or Saviour. Its influence is potent in raising the material to the spiritual, and is always most forceful in its manifestation. The Justice Ray of this Aquarian Cycle will unfold through Leo, the Heart. The adjustment will become complete when the Pole Star and the North Pole will be in exact conjunction about the year 2000.

GLOSSARY

The following Glossary is added for the purpose of elucidating many names and terms used in this work. These definitions or interpretations in their astrological, esoteric and mystical meaning are taken principally from the works of H. P. Blavatsky, Gerald Massey, Dr. Kenealy, and others whose authority is unquestionable.

Aah-en-Ru—The Elysian fields of the Egyptians, their place of illumination. "A place of plenty, a field of rest, also the heaven of the Gates or Divisions, belonging to mythical astronomy, whether Sabean, Lunar, or Solar; the Egyptian Elysium was like.the latest Heaven of the Book of Revelation, which has twelve gates. The Sabean heaven had seven gates, the Lunar, twenty-eight; and the Solar twelve, thirty-six or seventy-two according to the divisions of the Zodiac."—Gerald Massey. The "fields" were the Zodiacal circle with its gates.

Abyss—The bottomless infinite space, darkness. It was the source, the void, sometimes called the hole of the serpent, habitat of the dragon. It was the matrix of birth and the place preceding personification.

Abt—The crib or ark of the divine child; also Teb.

Ad-Ad—The deity of the Syrians. The name signifies King of Kings, the Sun-Father. Ad, the first, the only one.

Adept—One who, through spiritual development has attained to transcendental power or knowledge. In occultism, one who has passed the stage of initiation.

Adonai—The Hebrew word means Lord. It was used in reading the sacred scrolls as a substitute for the unutterable name J H V H Jod-he-vau-he, which is androgyne, or male-female. Adonai, the Lord is astronomically the Sun.

Aeon—An indefinite period of time, a cycle. Among the Gnostics the Aeons were emanations proceeding from the divine essence, celestial beings, genii and angels. Owing to a false translation of the Hebrew word, Asdt. it was given as "Angels" in the Septuagint, when its true meaning was Emanation, Aeon. (See Emanation).

Af-Ra—A god of solar fire whose furnace was the Ament out of which flew the starry sparks. Originally the idea of fire or heat was derived from the Sun, and the Sun below the horizon where the fire that had burned all night would be reproduced at dawn, was called the "furnace of the Sun."

Agathodaemon—The beneficent daemon, the good spirit, and was of great antiquity. Among the Ophites he is later found under the appelation of the Logos, or divine wisdom. In the Bacchic mysteries he is represented by a serpent standing erect upon a pole. He was also the Egyptian Kneph, who mythologically was the Eternal Unrevealed God. He is also represented as a huge serpent, having the head of a lion surrounded by seven and twelve rays, and on each of the points of seven rays of his crown stands a vowel of the Greek alphabet, expressing the seven heavens. On a Gnostic amulet this serpent is called Chnuphis. His head raised with the seven rays, and as a Kabalistic symbol signified the "Gift of Speech to Man." "The seven vowels are represented by the Gnostic signs on the crowns of the seven heads of the Serpent of Eternity, in India, and among esoteric Buddhists in Egypt and in Chaldea and among Initiates of the country."

Agni—In the Veda, a god of Fire. The oldest and one of the most revered gods of India, who represented Fire, especially fire from heaven.

Agnostic—A word used to indicate one who believes nothing which cannot be demonstrated by the senses.

Ahura-Mazda—The Persian god who gave to Zarathustra the magnetized water that induced clairvoyance.

Akh—Spirit was the creative virile spirit to the Egyptians, Assyrians and Hebrews, but the evil spirit to the Japanese.

Akkadian—As a language was an ancient form of speech, now dead. It was spoken by the inhabitants of countries situated along the Euphrates, near its mouth.

Akhekh Gryphon—The dragon with wings. The latest solar bird with wings and feathers furnished a type of fire, but long before there was the winged lightning, which had suggested this winged dragon or the "bird of Thunder."

Al (or El)—The presiding deity in Saturn. Al was the earlier Egyptian Ar (Har), son. Al Shadai was son of the mother the Great Mother. (See El.) A name of the Sun.

Alcahest—"An element which dissolves all metals and by which all terrestrial bodies may be reduced into the original material of which they were formed."

Alphabet—The most ancient tradition attributed the discovery of the alphabet to some great Initiate, hero or priest—Cadmus, Enoch, Taht—who derived it from the stars, i. e., from setting down their configurations, or so the exoteric story runs; but the holy import and significance attached to letters in the antique world betrays to us the truth that in their essence primarily letters were symbols of the emanations which are the star forces made manifest in, to and through man. "Emanation" means that which remains forth, being sustained without from within.

Aliem—The astrologers, the Magi. The Garden of Eden on the Euphrates became the college of the Astrologers, the Aliem, and was not the property of the Jews. The four cardinal points or four corners of the mount, the pole, or Eden, belong to the myths of the world, and the cardinal points were Powers, Winds, Waters, Spirits, etc.

Amenti—The name given by the ancient Egyptians to their abode after death. It was the hidden land where judgment was given on the way towards Light and Blessedness. Habitation of the heaven God; place of union with the unseen father.

Amen—Is a later creation. He had nothing to do with the "Book of the Dead," but is identified with Atum, and like Atum was said to be born out of the cycles as god of Time. He was the hidden sun, the mystery god, and when rising on the horizon was the Sun of the Resurrection. As Amen he was the god of Thebes from the Twelfth to the Seventeenth Dynasty, when the solar reckoning appeared. During the Thirteenth Dynasty when all older gods were merged into the image of one God, his name was changed to Amen-Ra, "Lord of the Throne of Egypt," and all the attributes of older gods were ascribed to him as the creator of things celestial and terrestrial and the illuminator of the Universe. Hymns of great praise and adoration were given him. He was called the "One One" who "had no second." This was the origin of the one god. During the Twelfth Dynasty Amen-hept I, 2466 B. C., founded the temple of Amen at Thebes, shrine of the ram-headed god.

Ancient of Days—Called the Eternal Keeper of Time, in the Book of Enoch. The Eternal Keeper of Time is the Great Mother.

Ancestor Worship—"According to the system of thought and theory of things unfolded in mythology and symbolism, and enforced in the imagery of the Egyptian Ritual, the Sun as father, he who descended into the grave or lower heaven every year, and was renewed in the person of the son, was the first ancestor whose death had any sacred significance. The worship of the dead ancestor began with, and was associated with and determined by, the mummy figure. The first of the fifty claimed by Thotmes III in his ancestral chamber was Ra, the Sun-god. Long before fatherhood had been established, the bones of the mummy were covered with red ochre as a preservative, and the embalmed body represented the ancestor of the soul in the primitive cult." The thought has been advanced that religion began with the worship of the dead ancestor.

Androgonous—Man-woman, one having the characteristics of both sexes, hermaphrodite.

Angels—Winged celestials of the Hebrew writings, in which the word used is Asdt, falsely translated "angel." They were the time-cycles, the Aeons, called genii of the Gnostics.

Anima Mundi—The Soul of the World.

Ankh-Cross—Emblem of Eternal Life, continuity. It was also a phallic sign for the generative forces of nature. Symbol of an oath, covenant. (See Crosses.)

Anu—Abode of the blessed in heaven. It was the capitol of the mythological world, the abode of the gods, the center and source of divine instruction. It had no geographical position. Anu as god of heaven was a Babylonian divinity. He belonged to the Chaldean trinity, was double sexed, and was closely related to Jehovah.

Anubis—A dog-headed god, one of the oldest of the Egyptian deities. He was the "embalmer" and the "Guardian of the Dead." He represented Sirius the Dog-Star.

Apap—The great monster of darkness, the eternal enemy of the Sun, and the first form of the devil.

Apis—Osiris incarnate in the sacred white bull, the Bull-god. The bull was worshipped as the symbol of Osiris, who was the greatest god of Egypt, a self-created god identical with all "First Causes."

Apocrypha—Collection of the Books of Wisdom. Jesus taught the ancient wisdom with which these Books are filled, many of his sayings being pre-Christian. The Rabbins borrowing everything possible from the heathen (?) philosophers, secreting them in allegories, fables, and "dark sayings." Traditions, statutes, mysteries, etc., were said to be kept or written on scrolls of parchment by the Israelites, taught to them by their Masters, and these were the "Secret Sayings" which Jesus declares were known to the Scribes and Pharisees, who had the Key of Knowledge, which they denied to others. (Matt. xxiii, 13, and Luke xi, 52.) "When the council of Nice was convened to decide what books of the Jews were and were not canonical, we are informed that the bishops there assembled were by a very extraordinary miracle convinced which were inspired and which were apocryphal books after this manner. Having put all the books that laid claim to inspiration under the communion table in a church, they prayed to God that those which were not apocryphal might be found above or upon the table, and those whch were apocryphal might be found under, and accordingly as they prayed it came to pass ! ! !" —Kenealy, "Book of God," Note 33, p. 79.

Apocalypse—The word Apocalypse means unveiling. A profoundly esoteric work replete with the mystery language of the Zodiac. Its divinities were gods and goddesses, with the Sun the central figure. The hidden wisdom of the Apocalypse is entrenched behind allegory and symbolism and was not written to be understood by the masses. The Apocalypse, the Sepher Yetzirah and the Zohar are masterpieces of occultism. The Apocalypse surmises, completes and surpasses all the science of Abraham or Solomon. The Zohar is the genesis of Light, absolute Truth. The Sepher Yetzirah is called the Ladder of Truth, because of its method of discernment and application.

Apophis—The monster of darkness, "Dweller in the deep," which lives on the blood of the condemned and executes vengeance on the wicked. The crooked serpent set with sword blades and typical of destruction.

Arabia-Felix—Till the time of the Emperor Justinian, a part of Abyssinia. It was inhabited, like that country, by the Sabeans and by the Jews. Sabeanism, the most ancient religion of the world, was from the beginning mixed with Judaism. (Bruce, on the Book of Enoch.)

Argha—Ark, was the navi-formed Argha of the mysteries and a mystic name for the Holy Spirit. The Argha of the mysteries was always oval or boat-shaped. It was the Ship of the North holding the seed of all life, symbol of the matrix.

Ascendant—The eastern horizon, cusp of the ascendant or first house of the horoscope. It includes the space below the cusp of the first house.

Astral body—Counterpart in finer matter or double of any physical body.

Astral Light—Light derived from the stars, only perceived psychically.

Astrology—"The science which defines the action of the celestial bodies upon mundane affairs, and claims to foretell future events from the position of the stars. Its antiquity is such as to place it among the very earliest records of human learning. It remained for long ages a secret science in the East. . . . The Egyptians and the Chaldeans were among its most ancient votaries, though their methods differ" greatly from those of the present day. As to the origin of Astrology, Thebes claimed the honor of its invention, on the other hand it has been claimed that Chaldee gave it origin. "Thebes antedates considerably not only 'Ur of the Chaldees,' but also Nipur, where Bel was first worshipped, Sin his son (the Moon), being the presiding deity of Ur and the land of the nativity of Terah, the Sabean and astrolater, and of Abraham, his son, the great astrologer of Biblical tradition." Astrology originated in Egypt. It fell into disrepute in Rome as it had become a money-making project beyond the pale of the Sacred Science of the Mysteries, which the ignorant did not understand. Adherents to astrology are found among the most intellectual and scientific minds. Later votaries need not blush for even in its present distorted and imperfect form it is very great. To quote from Isis Unveiled (Vol. i, p. 259): "Astrology is to exact astronomy what psychology is to exact physiology. In astrology and psychology one has to step beyond the visible world of matter and enter the domain of transcendent spirit."

Asuramaya—See Narada.

Atef-Crown—Crown of Illumination, patterned after the Zodiacal light that was called the Glory of the Supreme Heaven. The Atef-Crown of Upper Egypt or the southern heaven consisted of a white crown with double feathers placed on the solar disk. The wearer of this crown symbolized the hidden Sun.

Aten—The child-god, son of the spirit of the hidden deep, Atum, said to be born in the Moon as the solar light by night. He appears on the horizon as his own son. As the Sun-god he was the Light-Born, born in the cycle of the Sun. He was the "Eternal Child," the youthful solar god, and as the divine son was solely the offspring of the Mother, not the Father. The Aten-Disk was his symbol. He was named the "Unbegotten son of the Mother," the woman who in the Book of Enoch is called the Messiah. Aten as the circle-maker was the Sun of the Disk Worshippers. The Aten Disk was an especial symbol of the Ethiopians. The Aten Disk worship began with Amenhept III and was Sun worship under another form. Aten-Nefru and Aten-Ra were identical with Adonai of the Jews, the "Lord of Heaven," or the Sun. The winged disk was at once emblem of the soul, and of the Sun and symbol of Universal Deity shining on the whole world and all its creatures. Aten, was the earlier form of the solar Baal, Adon, Adonai, and El-Shadai each a personification of the Mother, and belonged to the cult of Sut-Typhon. Their worship is identical with that of the Roman Catholic Virgin Mother and Child.

Atheism—Disbelief in the existence of a God.

Atum, or Tum—Colloquial form of Ra, who was the divine father of the Egyptian Genesis, and became the Adam of the Hebrew Genesis, progenitor of human beings and the first hearer in heaven among Egyptian gods. The first Atum or Adam in the Ethiopian portion of the "Book of the Dead" is called "The Mother-Goddess of Time." He represented Ra in the reckoning of solar time that followed the Lunar and Sabean periods. The solar fatherhood was established in Atum.

Aura—A subtle, invisible essence or fluid that emanates from human, animal, and other bodies. It is a psychic effluvium partaking of both the mind and the body, as there is both an electro-vital and an electro-mental aura, called in Theosophy the akashic or magnetic aura.

Avatar—A divine incarnation. The appearance of a deity on earth. The descent of a god, or some exalted being who has progressed beyond the necessity of human rebirth.

Avaris—Typhonian city, refuge of the expelled shepherds, City of the Leg, or Thigh, identified with the constellation of the Thigh in the Northern heaven, which is pictured in the Denderah planisphere as the Leg.

Axieros—A distinctive appellation given by the ancients to the two Poles. Axieros, Axiokeros, Axiokersa and Kadmus or Kadmillos were names of the Kabiri. Dr. Kenealy in his "Book of God" states: "The Samothracian, Axieros (or the Almighty) Axiokerses-Axiokersa (God in union with the Holy Spirit, the Great Fecundator, the Great Fecundatrix), and Casmilus, or he who stands before the face of Deity," represented the Trinity which shines through the whole Universe, the Creator, the Created and the Dispenser of Blessings, the Messenger.

Baal—A fire or sun-god and type of Sirius, the Dog-Star. Saturn, Bacchus, Mithra, Apollo, Jehovah, Brahma, Horus, Hercules, Adonis and others were all types of the same star, Sirius. The worship of Baal and Ashtaroth was that of the sun and the moon, which they represented, belonging to the Egyptians, the Persians, the Hindus, the Greeks, the Greek-Romans, the Druids, the Peruvians, Mexicans and Christians, as well as others, and under various names, which have descended to the present time. His worship was found in Palestine on the arrival of the "Children of Israel" from Egypt, when they were said to forsake their Lord and serve Baal and Ashtaroth. (Judges ii, 13.) His ritualistic worship was said to be in sacred groves, showing its ancient origin. The passing of the children through the Baal-fires at the festival of the summer solstice in Great Britain was a survival of the past. The sacrificing of children in the fires at the feet of Baal and Moloch occurred in a period of degeneracy.

Baptism—Symbolical of rebirth from the water into a new life and belonging to the religious mystery. When the Egyptian Neophite emerged from the baptismal font he was "born again," and became an Adept. As an ancient rite sacred ablution was performed by all nations in their mysteries. Water used for purification was "the greatest purifier of men and gods." Every sacred place of worship had its fountain or basin for lustration. Water was a symbol of the Holy Ghost. Baptism is a rite of regeneration. The Christ was baptised by the Holy Ghost in the form of a dove (emblem of soul), and with Fire (another type of soul), and with a Fan (type of the regenerator) borne in His hand. Matt. iii, 11. A beautiful allusion to the esoteric significance of baptism occurs in the Vision of Hermas. "The Holy Spirit, or the 'old woman' who was the first of all creation, shows him a tower that was built upon a square by six young men, which tower stands upon the water as its foundation. Then said Hermas, *'Lady, why is the tower built upon water?'* She replies that it is because his life is and shall be saved by water."

"Every ark or tabernacle configurated in the heavens, whether as the Seven Stars, seven pillars, the ark of the four corners, the six, eight, nine, ten or twelve divisions, had been founded on the celestial waters and thus was a symbol of salvation."—Gerald Massey.

Berosus—A priest of the temple of Belus, at Babylon. About 261-246 B. C. he wrote a history of Chaldea, some fragments of which are preserved by Josephus.

Bi-Une—Male-female, two combined as one.

Boehme, Jacob—A German mystic and great philosopher, as well as a natural clairvoyant of the most wonderful powers, born 1575—died 1624. He had no education except a knowledge of reading and writing, yet his books are filled with scientific truths. Speaking of what he wrote, he says he "saw as in a deep well in the eternal."

Book of Enoch—The Book of Enoch, which is far anterior to the Books of Moses, has been called the inspired writing of an antediluvian patriarch. It contains most ancient matter and was not included in the sacred writings of the Jews. It is copiously quoted in the Pistis Sophia and the Zohar, and much in the New Testament is borrowed from it. It calls itself "The Book of the revolutions of the luminaries of heaven," is a treatise on astronomical mythology. It was a Book of Parables and Allegories concerning the heavens and has no earthly relation to human history into which it was later converted. It begins with the myths of the Old Testament and concludes as does the Book of Revelation with the fulfilment of the New by foretelling the ending of a great Precessional Period and the "going forth" of the Messiah, son of the "Ancient of Days," as the "Word." Some say that Enoch was a Great Saint, beloved of God and taken to heaven; which needs esoteric interpretation. He represented a type of the dual nature in man, the spiritual and the physical. It was the spiritual Enoch who walked with God and did not die. He typified humanity as eternal in spirit.

Brahma—"Is the impersonal, supreme, and unrecognizable soul of the universe, from the essence of which all emanates, and into which all returns; . . . beginningless and endless. Brahmâ, on the other hand, the male and the alleged 'creator,' exists in his manifestation periodically only, and passes into *pralaya*—i. e., disappears and is *annihilated*—periodically.—H. P. Blavatsky.

Bull Worship—The worship of the Bull—Apis—was celestial and cosmic and ceased 3,000 years ago in Egypt. The Apis was hermaphrodite showing its cosmic character.

Caduceus—The wand of Hermes with two serpents twined about it. "It is a cosmic, sidereal as well as spiritual and even physiological symbol, its significance changing with its application. Metaphysically, the Caduceus represents the fall of primeval and primordial matter into gross terrestrial matter, the one Reality becoming Illusion. Astronomically, the head and tail represent the points of the ecliptic where the planets and even the sun and moon meet in close embrace. Physiologically, it is the symbol of the restoration of the equilibrium lost between Life, as a unit, and the currents of life performing various functions in the human body."—Alan Leo.

Cardinal Points—The North, East, South and West points of heaven.

Central Spiritual Sun—The Sun behind the Sun. "The Central Sun is simply the center of Universal Life-Electricity! The reservoir within which that divine radiance, already differentiated at the beginning of every *Creation* is focused."—Blavatsky, H. P.—The Secret Doctrine, Vol. ii, p. 240.

Chaos—"Storehouse of future worlds, and when once awakened stirs up and fructifies the latent forces, which are the ever present eternal potencies in it." The Pythagoreans called Chaos the "Soul of the World" after its impregnation by the Spirit of *that* which broods over the Primeval Waters. Chaos and Space are synonymous, and by the Egyptians Chaos was called Am-Smen, Place of Preparation.

Champollion—A Frenchman, born 1790; died 1832, was a great archaeologist who spent most of his life in exploring archaeological remains. The Rosetta Stone was found in Egypt by a Frenchman by the name of Boussard, in 1799. It bore a trilingual inscription, which afforded a key to the hieroglyphics of ancient Egypt. This key was discovered by Champollion in the year 1822. He was the first to interpret and read the pictured and weird writings of the Egyptians.

Chela—A pupil, a disciple.

Cherubs—Likenesses of the celestial constellations. The word cherub has the meaning of a serpent in a circle. Kr is circle, and Aub serpent.

Chess—The earliest division of Light and Shade is found figured on the chess board. Playing cards were based on the four quarters, and the dice upon the cube of the Egyptian god Ptah. (See Tat Cross.)

Christ—Greek work meaning anointed with the Light.

Christos—Early Gnostic name for Christ, the Higher Self. In the New Testament the word Christos has often been substituted for Chrestos, a term applied to a worthy candidate for initiation. Justin, the earliest Christian writer, calls his co-religionists Chrestians, and Lactantius (lib. iv, cap. vii) says: "It is only through ignorance that men call themselves Christians instead of Chrestians." "These terms, Christ and Christians, spelled originally Chrest and Chrestians, were borrowed from the temple vocabulary of the pagans. Chrestos meant, in that vocabulary, 'a disciple on probation,' a candidate for hierophantship; who when he had attained it, through initiation, long trials and suffering, and had been anointed (i. e., 'rubbed with oil' as Initiates and even idols of the gods were, as the last touch of ritualistic observance), was changed into Christos—the 'Purified' in esoteric or mystery language. . . . At the end of the 'way' stands the Chrestos, the 'purifier:' and the union once accomplished, the Chrestos, the 'man of sorrows,' became the Christos himself. Each can find the Christ within himself, and as Paul says (Eph. iii, 16, 17) 'that he would grant you, according to the riches of his glory, to be strengthened with might by his Spirit in the inner man; that Christ may dwell in your heart by faith."—H. P. Blavatsky.

Clairaudience—The faculty— whether innate or acquired by occult training—or hearing things beyond the range of physical audition and at whatever distance.

Clairvoyance—Spiritual Sight, the faculty of seeing with the inner eye, or the pineal gland.

Colure—One of two circles intersecting at right angles in the poles of the equator. One of them passes through the equinoctial points and hence is denominated the equatorial colure. The other colure intersects the equator at a distance of 90 degrees from the former, and is called the solstitial.

Constellations—Groups of stars prominent in the heavens bearing names from the most ancient times, as the Great Bear, the Phoenix, the Pleiades.

Cosmic—Pertaining to the universe, and having an especial reference to universal law and order. Pertaining to the solar system as a whole.

Cosmogony—Science of the formation of the worlds, the doctrine or science of generation, origin or creation of the world or universe.

Cosmos—The Universe as distinguished from the worlds, such as our globe or earth. The Universe as an orderly system.

Crown Double—The double crown of Egyptian kings and Pharoahs which was two-fold representing upper and lower heaven, or upper and lower Egypt. The upper crown was white, the lower one red. They were placed one within the other to represent the two heavens. Of the Deities Atum is the only one who wears the double crown.

Cross and Circle—The first circle was made in heaven by the Seven Stars of the Great Bear, which marked the four cardinal points and established the four corners of the Cross, which was assigned to the old Typhonian mother. Thus the circle and the cross became inseparable. The Ankh Cross in early days was a sign of human procreation, a hieroglyphic sign of life and reproduction, ideograph of periodicity. The Great Mother was a type of the Ankh Cross of Life, from which we have the symbol of the planet Venus which is the circle above the cross. "The most sacred cross of Egypt carried in the hands of the gods, the Pharaohs, and the mummied dead, was the *Ankh*, the sign of life, the living, an oath, a covenant. . . . The top of this cross is the hieroglyphic Ru, set upright on the Tau-cross. The Ru is the door, gate, mouth, the place of outlet, which denoted the *birthplace* in the northern quarter of the heavens, from which the sun is reborn. Hence the Ru of the *Ankh sign is the feminine type of the birth-place representing the north.* It was in the NORTHERN QUARTER THAT THE GODDESS OF THE SEVEN STARS, called the 'Mother of the Revolutions,' gave birth to time in the earliest cycle of the year. The first sign of the primordial circle and cycle made in heaven is the earliest shape of the Ankh-cross, a mere loop which contains both a circle and the cross in one image. This loop or noose is carried in front of the oldest genitrix, *Typhon of the Great Bear, as* her *Ark,* the ideograph *of a period, an ending, a time,* shown to mean one revolution."—Gerald Massey, whose chapter on The Typology of the Cross contains marvelous information about the cross and its origin, as well as its connection with the circle.

The Ankh Loop, tie, or knot, was a sign of one turn around consisting of a circle and a cross or crossing at the end. Originally this was not the circle and cross of the four corners. The tie, loop, or knot was a sign of the covenant but did not originate as a symbol of the marriage ceremony. It was carried by the enceinte mother as her emblem, an ideograph of periodicity, and applied to the woman at puberty. It is in existence today among the leaf-wearers and became a sign of reproduction.

The Tat Cross was equivalent to the mount of the four corners, or the tree or cross with four arms. It was an especial type of the god Ptah, the establisher of the four corners of the solar Zodiac in the solar myth, but existed as a lunar emblem of the Moon god Taht, from which we have the four quarters of the Moon. Tat has the number 9 and represents a cross of three quarters instead of the four and so becomes a figure of the nine months or nine divisions of the twelve that were completed in the three water signs of the abyss of the north, which was represented by the Ru, the circle on the cross.

Crucifixion—Symbolized the Cross of the Equinox, by which the cycle was fulfilled when the Sun had passed the last degree of a sign at the point where the ecliptic crosses the equator, forming a cross at this intersection. Thus the Sun was spoken of as being impaled upon the cross before rising in the midst of the glory and the splendor of the East.

Cusp—The point of beginning or boundary between one house and the next of any one of the twelve divisions of the Zodiac.

Cycle, or Circle—"The ancients divided time into endless cycles, wheels within wheels, all such periods being of various durations, and each marking the beginning or end of some event, either cosmic, mundane, physical or metaphysical. There were cycles of only a few years, and cycles of immense duration. The great Orphic cycle, referring to the ethnological change of races, lasted 120,000 years, and the cycle of Cassandrus of 136,000 which brought about a complete change in planetary influences and the correlation between men and gods—a fact entirely lost sight of by modern astrologers." A cycle or a circle symbolized the everlasting, and the ever-repeating. "Limitless Time in Eternity" and was founded on the circle and continued cyclic repetition. This subject of cycles is of the greatest importance, as it includes all history and all evolution.

Cynocephalus—Baboon. Egyptian God-headed Ape. As a reckoner of time with the Moon became one of the sacred animals of the temples. The Cynocephalus of all animals bears closest resemblance to humanity.

Dagon—The Fish-god. Same as Oannes. See Oannes.

Daimon—A God, spirit or ghost.

Decan—The third part of each Zodiacal sign consisting of ten degrees, governed by a special star and associated with the thirty-six paranatellons.

Deva—A "resplendant" deity—Deve (Deus) from the root div, to shine. A Deva is a celestial being, whether good, bad, or indifferent, which inhabits the three "worlds" or the three planes above us. The word DEITY is derived from the Sanscrit word *Deva*, and the word Devil from the Persian

Daeva. These words are practically the same." (The gods were said to be below God but of a divine nature.)—Blavatsky, H. P. —Isis Unveiled ii, p. 512.

Dhyan-Chohans—Literally the "Lords of Contemplation," the highest gods, answering to the archangels of the Romish Church. Divine intelligences charged with supervision of the Kosmos. They are the souls who became gods, co-workers with nature.

Diordorus—Surnamed Siculus. A Sicilian, who wrote a Universal History, of the forty books into which his work was divided only fifteen have come down to us entire, of the rest only a few fragments have been preserved. He flourished about 44 B. C.

Disk Worship—Re-began with Amenhept III, and was Sun-worship under another form. The winged disk was an emblem of the soul, and of the Lord in heaven, giver of Light. It was also an emblem of the divine and only son of the mother, who was the young child-god.

Dove—A name of the Holy Spirit, the Great Mother. The Seven Stars of the constellation of the Great Bear were originally called the Doves, long before the seven of the Pleiades received this honor. To Christians the Dove is a symbol of the Holy Ghost. Dove was an emblem of the soul and of the Great Mother who was "The Soul of the World."

Dvîpa—An island or land surrounded by water; any continent on which a root-race is evolved. The Dvipas are mentioned in the Surya Seddhanta, the oldest astronomical work in the whole world.

Dynasty—An especial line, race of kings of the same family, who govern a particular country. There were divine and human dynasties in Egypt and Chaldea, also Persian dynasties of gods and men.

Ecliptic—Celestially the Earth's orbit around the Sun. A great circle or sphere in which the Sun appears to move. It is called the Ecliptic because all Eclipses happen therein.

Eclipse—An obscuration of the light of the sun, moon, or other luminous bodies by the intervention of some other body, as of the moon, by passing through the earth's shadow, or of the sun, by the moon coming between it and the observer; or of a satellite, by entering the shadow of its primary.

El—Originally Al, the God Mithra, the Sun, preserver and savior, Beth-El is house of the Sun, El signified Sol and is an ancient word for the Sun behind the Sun.

Elementals—Nature Spirits presiding over the elements, earth, air, fire, water. Called by the Kabalists gnomes (of the earth), sylphs (of the air), salamanders (of the fire), and undines (of the water).

Elementaries—The phychic remnants left in the astral sphere after death, where it eventually becomes dissipated. A name given to the astral shells of defunct human beings, which often take part in spiritualistic communications, and materializations.

Eleusinian Mysteries—The ancient Greek mysteries performed near the hamlet of Eleusis, not far from Athens. Epiphanius traces them to 1800 B. C. They were held in honor of the goddess Demeter, the great Ceres, and the Egyptian Isis. The last act of the performance referred to a sacrificial victim of atonement and a resurrection, when the Initiate was admitted to the highest degree of the Epopt (Seer). The Mysteries began at the time of grape-gathering (September) and lasted from the 15th until the 22nd. The Hebrew Feast of the Tabernacle also began on the 15th and ended on the 22nd of the month. The sacrifice of "bread and wine" was performed both at Elensis and during the Feast of the Tabernacle.

Elohim—The "Sons of God" and creators of the world, or rather fashioners of it, in six days, resting on the seventh, were but the euphemerizing powers of nature, the faithful manifested servants, the Laws of Him who is the immutable law, and harmony Himself. The earthly Elohim, tradition tells us, lived on an island which for unparallelled beauty had no rival in the world. They were the remnants of a race that preceded ours, the race that could live with equal ease in water, air, or fire, for it had unlimited control over the elements. It was they who imparted nature's secrets to man, and revealed to him the now "Lost Word," which lingers as a far-off dying echo in the hearts of some today. Hierophants of all the sacredotal colleges had knowledge of this island, but the "word" was only known to the Java Aliem, who was the chief Lord of every college and who at the moment of his death passed it on to his successor. There were many of these colleges, of which old classic authors speak. The Great Mother was known as the "Living Word," whose Seven Great Stars were the Elohim.

Emanation—The doctrine of emanation was at one time universal. In its metaphysical meaning it is opposed to evolution, yet one with it. "The evolutionist stops all inquiry at the borders of the unknowable; the emanationist believes that nothing can be evolved—or as the word means, unwombed or born—except it has first been involved, thus indicating that life is from spiritual potency above the whole." This doctrine was taught by the Alexandrians as well as the Indian philosophers, by the Egyptian, the Chaldean and Hellenic hierophants, and also by the Hebrews (in their Kabala, and even in Genesis). For it is only owing to deliberate mistranslation that the Hebrew word Asdt, from the Septuagint, was translated "angel," when it means "emanations," "eons," just as it did to the Gnostics.

Epiphanius—A Father of the church, and of Jewish extraction. His "Panarion" is a connected history of the Gnosis in all its developments during the first three centuries. He displayed great zeal against the writings of Origen. He has been called a Gnostic renegade, who turned state's evidence and betrayed his associates.

Esoteric—Hidden, secret, concealed. Known to the initiated.

Ethiopia—Country formerly extending as far as the equator into the very heart of Africa, and at one time subject to Egypt.

Exodus, Book of—"The beginning of Exodus, and the story of Moses, is that of the Babylonian Sargon, who having flourished 3,750 B. C., preceded the Jewish lawgiver by almost 2,300 years." —Alan Leo. The "Coming out of Egypt" typifies the transit of the vernal equinox, and was the festival of the Passover, before the migration of the Jews.

Exoteric—Outward, public. Known to the uninitiated.

Fan—Symbol of breath, one of its names in Egypt was Neft; Mes-Neft is Egyptian for the fan which was worn as a crown. The fan-bearers of the Pharoahs or kings bore the crown on a tray, with the fan above it. Fan as breath, wind, or conception, also represented rebirth or regeneration.

Feather—Symbolized Breath and was an early type of Fire. In the Quichi legend the Feathered Serpent was a symbol of primordial power.

Genesis—The Book of Genesis is an almost unaltered version of the cosmogony of the Chaldeans, repeatedly proven from the Assyrian tiles. "The first three chapters are transcribed from the allegorical narratives of the beginnings common to all nations. . . . Chapter six is an astronomical narrative of the solar year and the seven cosmocratores from the original of the Pymander and the symbolical visions of a series of *Enoichoi* (Seers)—from whom also came the 'Book of Enoch'."—Alan Leo. It neither borrowed nor disfigured universal symbols, but adapted the eternal truths to its own national spirit and clothed them in cunning allegories understood by the Kabalists and Initiates. The key to Genesis is found in esoteric rendering.

Gnosis—Knowledge, wisdom. It was a technical term used by schools of philosophy before and during the first years of Christianity. "It existed long before Christianity was formulated by the exoterist priests who fabricated the Gospels probably not earlier than the latter part of the First Century."

Gnostics—Revealers of the Gnosis or "knowledge." They flourished during three centuries of the early Christian era. Their teaching is similar to the doctrine of the present day Theosophy. They taught the ancient wisdom of Egypt and Chaldea, which they had inherited. The Gnosis, an unwritten science and taught previously from mouth to ear, had been kept concealed. Its foundation was astronomical. The early fathers seemed to know nothing about evolution and the survival of types or else refused to make use of their knowledge. The new beginning was to obliterate all else, save when the myth was made the miracle that proved divinity, and Gnosticism "was the voice of the older cult, growing more and more audible, protesting against the superstition and the debasing or falseness being replaced by the old, that made the Gnostics bitter enemies of the new Christianity."

God—Called by Egyptians "The Light." Mystically "when the gods forsook the earth, it included the minor gods who were the regent of the Zodiacal signs. These are the angels of the Christians and are the seven planets of every religion, the

sacred seven. Every early religious scripture gives evidence
of a time when the gods as Entities actually existing gave birth
to and nursed and instructed mankind in its beginning or early
period."

Hades—A place of complete darkness. During the seventeenth or
eighteenth Egyptian dynasty, when Typhon was transformed
from a god into a devil, Hades or Hell became a place of punishment by fire. Hades was the Egyptian Amenti which could
only be reached by crossing the river to the "other shore."

Har—Earlier name for Ra the Sun. Har-Ma-Keru means "The
Word Made True." Keru is voice, word, logos—Ma, true.

Hawk and Serpent—Combined, was a dual type of primordial divinity. The Hawk and Eagle interchange, as types of soaring,
and were the birds of fire or light.

Hea—The Akkadian God of Wisdom, is represented by the serpent.
Hea the great Babylonian deity was also represented by the
serpent of fire.

Heh—Hebrew Eve, the serpent woman, the female Jehovah. HEH,
Egyptian, meant Eternal, an age, an aeon or cycle of time, and as
the serpent-goddess was called "the maker of invisible existence
apparent," characterizing the serpent as the revealer of the
unseen world.

Heliacal—Rising of a star is its first appearance after being
merged in the rays of the sun. Heliacal setting of a star means
its approach so near to the sun that it is hidden by its rays.

Heliocentric—Having the sun for the center. It is the situation
the earth and planets exhibit if viewed from the sun in respect
to their latitudes and longitudes.

Hell—There was a cold hell as well as the hot one of the Christians and other exoteric religions. The only difference was
found in the temperatures. "A hot hell is an afterthought, the
distortion of an astronomical allegory." It began to be a place
of punishment about the seventeenth or eighteenth dynasty, at
the time that Typhon was transformed from a god to a devil,
male exalted above the female. Its origin seems to have been
Egyptian. Ra (the sun) became Lord of the furnace in *Karr*,
the Hell of the Pharoahs and the sinner was threatened with
misery "in the heat of infernal fires." "The Hebrew word gai-
hinnom (gehenna) never really had the significance given to it
in Christian orthodoxy." It has been made quite a unique place.

Hermas—An ancient Greek writer, of whose works only a few
fragments are extant.

Hermes—The shepherd god, was patron of all arts and sciences and
especially of occult wisdom and magic. Symbolized as the serpent he represented divine creative wisdom. He was called
guardian of the Zodiacal sign Cancer, and regent of the planet
Mercury. As Taht the Moon-god Hermes was the bright side
of the Moon containing the essence of all wisdom. He was a
mythical personage after whom the Hermetic Philosophy was
named, and on his tablets can be found the mysteries of the

ages. Hermes is a generic name. As Hermes Trismegistus, the "Thrice Great Hermes," the Egyptian, he was called the "founder" of the Hermetic Philosophy. Trismegistus was the Greek name given him. Many Greek writers of philosophy and alchemy appropriated his name.

Hermaphrodite—Male-female in one. Dual-sexed, whether man or animal.

Hieroglyphs—Characters or figures supposed to be of a hidden or mysterious significance. Specifically, the picture writing of the ancient Egyptian priests, of which there are two classes of characters, symbols representing ideas, not sounds, as the feather was the symbol of truth; and symbols (called phonetic) employed as syllables of a word, or as letters of the alphabet, and with sound, as a hawk represented the vowel a.

Hierophant—An instructor of the mysteries, one "who explains secret things." A title belonging to the highest Adepts in the temples of antiquity, and the Initiators into the final great mysteries; a High Priest.

Holy Spirit—The second Great Being of the Universe. The Great Mother, Nature.

Hohgates—The coast peoples of California preserve a tradition of an ancient race, called Hohgates, who once lived in that country and are credited with building vast mounds of mussel shells and bones. These can still be seen on the tableland of Point St. George near Crescent City. Their origin is usually connected with water, from which in some mythical way they were miraculously saved, and became transformed into, or related to, the stars. They are identical with the Kabiri, the Giants, and endless other Sevens belonging to the constellation of the Great Bear, with its Seven Great Stars.

Hor Apollo—A grammarian of Panoplus, in Egypt, in the Fourth Century. He taught first at Alexandria, and next at Constantinople. There are two books of his extant concerning the hieroglyphics of the Egyptians, printed in Greek by Aldus, in 1505.

Horoscope—A term used for the figure of the heavens, used by astrologers for giving judgment of nativities.

Horus—Son of Iris and Osiris. He was the "Mystic Child of the Ark," from which the whole universe grows or becomes. He was the "beloved of heaven," beloved of the Sun, the offspring of the gods, and was said to have come from the womb of the world. He was the greatest of all heroes because celestial, and therefore divine. The name Horus denotes one who ascends as a spirit. In astronomical allegory the child Horus was called Ma-Kheru, the True Word, or the Word made the Truth. The elder Horus was portrayed with his finger to his mouth, as the Silent One who becomes united to the True Voice or Word.

Houses—Of the horoscope. The twelve divisions into which the circle of the heavens is divided, which are noted in the chart of the horoscope as an aid to its delineation. A sign in which any planet is posited is said to be its house, e. g., Aries is said to be the house of Mars.

Hu, or Hut—The good demon of the Egyptians, double-winged disk, which was the sign of the Great God, Lord of Heaven and giver of life. The winged Hut was a symbol of the Sun and the horse Hutr a type of the swift goer. "The horse was substituted for the Ass of Sut which was condemned at a very early period in Egypt, so early as to be almost absent from the monuments except as a symbol of Typhon." The Horse-head was typical of Hut and the constellation of Pegasus, the winged horse, symbol of the Sun, who was the good demon overcoming the powers of darkness.

Ichthus—Greek word for a fish; name of the young Fish-god or Messiah. The symbol of a fish has been frequently referred to Jesus, hence early Christians were called Fishes, and drawings of fish were often found in the Catacombs. Ichthus, the fish-child, belonged to the early fish-goddesses. The sign of the Fishes in the Hermean Zodiac is called Ichthon. "'Ichthus is identified with Iu-em-Hept, who was born or incarnated for the last time when the equinox entered the sign of the Fishes 225 B. C., from which time Ichthus became the sign of salutation of the equinoctial Christolators, who were called Pisciculi."

Ideograph—A representation of a notion or an idea without reference to the name given it, as by means of figures, symbols, or hieroglyphics.

Ilda-Baoth—"Son of Darkness" and tyrant of the lower world. He was identified with Johovah, the God of the Jews. "Ilda-Baoth is the genius of Saturn, the planet; or rather the evil spirit of its ruler."

Immaculate Conception—Divine incarnation, or the Avatar doctrine constituted the grandest mystery of every old religious system, and is as preeminently Egyptian as Indian in origin. "It is not the vulgar, coarse and sensual story of the Greek mythology, but refined, moral and spiritual."—Bonwick—"Egyptian Beliefs." From the divine it has descended into the mortal inviting the scepticism it deserves through being clothed upon with flesh.

Incarnation—The descent into matter, or the contracting of the Soul with physical existence through embodiment.

Initiate—"The designation of anyone who was received into and had revealed to him the mysteries and secrets of either Masonry or Occultism. In ancient times those were called Initiates who had been admitted into arcane knowledge taught by the Hierophants of the Mysteries.

Intercalary Days—Were the five days called negative, or no-time, and as such they were finally placed at the end of the Egyptian year of 360 days. They were called Nahsi, the *black* days, days of negation. At the end and the re-beginning of the Egyptian year the Egyptians celebrated the renewal on two particular Days—the night of the last day of the old year, and at the evening meal of the first day of the new year. Between these two dates the five black or negative days, "The Birthdays of the Gods," called the Epagemenae, were intercalated.

Irenaeus—Bishop of Lyons, France, born in the early part of the Second Century. Irenaeus was the one who insisted that Jesus "Passed through every age and lived on to be an oldish man!"

Isis—Issa in Egyptian, the goddess Virgin-Mother; personified nature. She is the "Woman clothed with the Sun" of the land of Cheni.

Iu-em-Hept—The mythical divine Son, the peace-bringer. As Ecclesiasticus he was the Preacher, and in the Hebrew writings is identified with Jesus. He wore the long garment symbol of the hermaphrodite. He was the Egyptian Jesus and in the "Book of the Dead" was called the "Eternal Word."

Ixisthrus—Chaldean Noah.

Je-shu-run—Is identified with the first circle made in heaven by the revolution of the Seven Stars of the constellation of the Great Bear, and the celestial four quarters which were represented by the four sacred animals—The Bull, the Lion, the Eagle, and the Man.

Josephus, Flavius—An historian of the First Century; a Hellenized Jew who lived in Alexandria and died at Rome. His writings, in which he acknowledged the Messiahship and divine origin of Jesus, have been declared spurious by most of the Christian Bishops, but were for centuries one of the weightiest proofs of the real existence of Jesus, the Christ.

Kabala—Book of the hidden wisdom and traditions of the Hebrew Rabbis of the Middle Ages, derived from the older Secret Doctrine concerning divine things and cosmogony, and combined into a theology after the time of the captivity of the Jews in Babylon.

Kabiri—First seven sailors to sail annually over the waters of the celestial sea, in the earliest cycle of time. They were the Seven Great Stars of the Great Bear, children of the Great Mother. Kebeiros means "Powerful through Fire." They were called "The Mighty Ones" and the "Great Beneficent and Powerful Gods." Astronomically Kabirim means "The Measures of the Stars."

Kam—Name for Egypt and the dark people. Kam signifies black, and Egypt is often called Kam the Black Land. It was a name applied to the earliest inhabitants, and also means, to create. Kam is extant in Egypt as Khebma, the Mother of the Waters. It is maintained, and with considerable authority, that "The oldest mythology, religion, symbols and language had their birth place in Africa, while the primitive race of Kam came from thence, the civilization attained in Egypt emanated from that country and spread over the world. Africa with its background of Blackness, the land of Ham, whose Source was fed in secret by tributaries that flowed as stealthily as the hidden fountains of the Nile."—Gerald Massey.

Karast or Christ—Embalmed mummy, or spiritualized other self, placed in the tomb to await its rebirth into spirit life. As a type of immortality it was the anointed, the Messiah, the Christ. The root of Messiah, mes, in Egyptian, means to anoint, to generate, as well as to give birth. The erect mummy was a type of the risen dead, image of the resurrection.

Karma—Physically, action, metaphysically the Law of Retribution, Law of Cause and Effect. "As ye sow, so also must ye reap." Law of universal harmony or of the self-adjusting forces of nature, restoring harmony disturbed by action.

Kar-tek—Spark-holder or Fire-keeper, a name given to the ancient Mother of the Seven.

Karttikeya—Skanda, God of War, so called because he was nourished by the Pleiades or Karttikas. The planet Mars.

Kepheus—An ancient star-god, who was represented by the constellation of that name and by the star Regulus, also by the two lion-gods of Egypt, Shu and Anhar, the Moses and Joshua of the Jews. The Kephenes were synonymous with the Ethiopians and Kephene is identified with Kush, called the Begetter of Nimrod, Gen. x, 8. Kush is the Egyptian Khepsh, the north, the birth-place. In the planisphere Kepheus is the King of Kush. Kush is not a person but a quarter of the Egyptian planisphere, Kepheus as Regulus was the Shepherd King of the heavenly flock.

Khepr—Egyptian Beetle was called the creator, the transformer. An early form of Khepr was Ptah, the Opener, the Circle Maker, and Khepr-Ptah symbolized the Potter at his Wheel as he shaped the Egg of the Sun and the Moon and the Vase of Matter that contained the Seed of Life. He was the fashioner and builder of heaven, father of Atum, the Red One. Khepr-Ra symbolized the "Boat of the Sun," the circle of Khepr-Ra was the solar Zodiac.

Khepsh—The especial ideograph of Typhon of the Great Bear Constellation. Typified the Genitrix, the crooked sword of Egypt called the Thigh.

Kneph—The Eternal unrevealed God in Egyptian mythology. A snake emblem of Eternity. Kneph encircles a water urn its head hovering over the water which Kneph incubates with its breath. Nephesh (Hebrew) is soul, breath of life, and Nef in Egyptian is breath or spirit personated by Kneph the breath of souls, or breathing Life in the firmament. Kneph became the sailor on the water, hence the Hebrew Spirit moving on the face of the waters.

Kriya-shakti—Potency of thought, occult creation. The power of thought which, through knowledge, produces results on the objective plane.

Krishna—The "savior" of the Hindus, and their most popular God. The story of Krishna's conception, birth and childhood is the exact prototype of the New Testament story of Jesus. Krishna was the personification of the Supreme Spirit; a divine Avatar who remained in mortal form 125 years and died 3001 B. C.

Krittikas—Sanscrit name of the Pleiades.

Kronus—Time, Seb-Kronus was the repeater of time, regent of the planet Saturn, and Sun-god of the Golden Age. Israel was the Phoenician name of Kronus.

Kundalini—The power that moves in a serpentine path, the basic force of life. A force which can as easily kill as create. The Serpent Force.

Labyrinth—(Egyptian) Herodotus regarded the Labyrinth as far more marvellous than the pyramids themselves, and as an eye witness, minutely described it. His account has been confirmed by French and Prussian savants as well as other Egyptologists.

Herodotus says that he found therein 3,000 chambers; half subterranean and the other half above ground. "The upper chambers," he says, "I myself passed through and examined in detail. Into the underground ones, the keepers of the building would not let me go, for they contain the sepulchres of the kings who built the Labyrinth, and also those of the sacred crocodiles. The upper chambers . . . I found to excel all other human productions. The passages through the houses and other varied windings of the paths across the courts, excited in me infinite admiration as I passed from the courts into the chambers, and from thence into colonnades, and from colonnades into other houses, and again into courts unseen before. The roofs were throughout of stone like the walls, and both were exquisitely carved all over with figures. Every court was surrounded with a colonnade, which was built of white stone, sculptured most exquisitely. At the corner of the Labryinth stands a pyramid forty fathoms high, with large figures engraved upon it, and it is entered by a vast subterranean passage."—Blavatsky, H. P.—Isis Unveiled, Vo. i, pp. 522-3.

According to Mr. S. A. Mackey, These winding Allies "Ascending and winding from the surface of the earth; forming a spiral line from the middle upwards; and descending and winding, forming a spiral line from the middle downwards. Which is precisely the figure described by the North and South Pole of the Earth, in passing from the Ecliptic, till they coincide with the North and South Pole of the Heavens—describing at once, the precession of the Equinoxes, and the diminution of the angles of the Poles."

Latitude—Perpendicular distance of any star or planet north or south of the equator.

Lemuria—A continent supposed to have existed at one time, now hidden under the waters. According to the Secret Doctrine it was a land inhabited by the Third Race, extending between India and Africa.

Light—First demonstration of the Infinite, the First Begotten. "The true Universal Light, which means Darkness, is ever existent." (Chaldean Book of Numbers.)

Logos—The Word, the First Cause, the Logos was pre-Christian and in its first form was feminine. The Logos was passive wisdom in heaven and conscious self-active wisdom on earth.

"Logos is a word with three meanings. First the Holy Spirit, the first Word that God spoke, and consequently the first of His created Essences. Second, the Universe, which He next formed. Third, the Messenger from God to Man, who proclaims the celestial Word or Revelation."—Dr. Kenealy.

Longitude—Distance east or west of Greenwich.

Lotus—Sacred water lily plant of oriental nations—Egypt, India, etc. At one time a universal symbol of the Universe, and in a narrower sense of the Earth. A reverenced symbol of the Great Mother.

Lucifer—Venus, the morning star. Venus was the representative of the ancient Typhon, and Satan was her son Sut, or Satan, whose home was "upon the mount of the congregation." (Isa., xiv, 13.) Venus is also a symbol of the "Creative Word" and is metaphorically spoken of as the instructor of the giants, energizing the creative work of the geniuses when placed in her own powerful and virile sign of Taurus, the Bull. Theology extinguished the radiance of Lucifer, who was both divine and terrestrial light, the Holy Spirit and Satan, whose deep scientific meaning is found in astronomical truths.

The ancient tradition of Lucifer, the Light-bearer, may have referred to the planetary spirit of earth itself, cast down into darkness but ever vibrating heavenward in ceaseless inspiration of celestial emanations.

Luminaries—The Sun and the Moon.

Macrocosm—The great Universe or Kosmos.

Magi—Fire worshippers. The great magicians or wisdom-philosophers of old. Astrologers.

Magic—Divine Science. "It unveils the operations of Nature and leads to the contemplation of celestial powers," says Philo Judaeus. A practical knowledge of the hidden mysteries of nature known only to the few. "The cornerstone of magic is an intimate practical knowledge of magnetism and electricity and their qualities, correlation, and potencies. Magic is spiritual wisdom; Nature is the material ally, pupil and servant of the magician." Magnetism is called the Alphabet of Magic. Magic is not supernatural. What is called White Magic is wholly devoid of selfishness, bent only upon doing good to the world at large and its people, while Black Magic is the use of abnormal powers for the gratification of self and for sorcery. "If the ancients knew but little of our mode of investigation into the secrets of Nature we know still less of their mode of research," remarks Mr. Bonwick.

Mama—Egyptian word for mother. "Ideographically it is written with the type of the mother bearing seed; phonetically, with the double boat-stand. The Mamuti or Mam-kuti is the cabin or a boat (cabin was the birthplace), and doubly identifies the Mama as the bearer."—Gerald Massey.

Manna—Celestial Wisdom. We read in Hebrew ix, 3, 4, that there was after the second veil, the tabernacle which is called the Holiest of all; which had a golden censer, and the ark of the covenant overlaid round about with gold, wherein *was* the golden pot that had the manna, and Aaron's rod that budded, and the table of the covenant." Also in Revelation ii, 17, it says, "To him that overcometh will be given to eat of the hidden manna." The rod or staff was a male image, and the pot of Manna feminine, thus the mother and the male child are signified by the pot of Manna and the rod that budded. The "Ark of Testimony" contained the pot of Manna. During the entire sojourn in the wilderness of the Children of Israel they were fed on Manna, meaning they were nourished by Menat, the Wetnurse, Shadai, or the Great Mother. Manna was emblematic of the feminine reckoning and rule and the Manna of the desert related to the reckoning by the Moon. Manna was gathered during six days, but on the seventh there was none. The Manna ceased when the masculine cult became dominant at the time of the circumcision in Gilgol.—Joshua v, 12. Manna as the Angel's Food was Bread of the Mighty, i. e., Celestial Knowledge.

Manu—The first legislator—almost a divine being—who was the lawgiver of India.

Manvantara—A period of evolution. A term applied to various cycles. The period of creative, formative and re-constructive activity on the objective planes of the universe, intervening between two pralayas of dissolution or rest. Pralaya—The period of cosmic rest.

Mâyâ—"Illusion; the cosmic power which renders phenomenal existence and the perceptions thereof possible. In Hindu philosophy that alone which is changeless and eternal is called *Reality;* all that which is subject to change through decay and differentiation, and which has, therefore, a beginning and an end, is regarded as Mâyâ, illusion."—H. P. Blavatsy.

Meridian—The place of the Sun at noon, the mid-heaven, the cusp of the tenth house of the horoscope.

Merkabah—The chariot in the vision of Ezekiel, is the chariot of the Sun, emblem of the solar worship, and of the Cherubim, "and gold for the pattern of the chariot of the cherubim, that spread out *their wings* and covered the ark of the covenant of the Lord." I Chronicles xxviii, 18. The Chariot was a symbol of the Great Mother, the "Bearer." Mer is a circle and Kab is the circle made by the Seven Stars of the Great Bear as they move about the pole.

Meru—Garden of the Tree of Life, the Pole or Polar region, said to be "like the Seed-Cup of the Lotus," the "Lotus of Immensity." Meru was called the "Great World's Altar Stairs," by which men could climb heavenward. At each step a planetary heaven was established in their different cycles of time. Meru was also a name for the Thigh, the Matrix, or the Mother. Occultists have described it as "The exalted mass of glory, the veritable haunts of the Gods and heavenly choristers . . .

not to be reached by sinful men . . . because guarded by the
Serpents." These were the Fiery Serpents, the "Winged
Wheels." (See Seraphim.) Its four rivers, or cardinal points
of the world, were symbolized in the four sacred animals, the
protectors of mankind, who were the watchers over Karma on
Earth. Meru was the celestial mountain where the gods and
the highest celestial beings dwell, as well as the mythical birthplace, astronomically the celestial pole, the throne of Jehovah.
Ru is the mouth, the outlet. Meru is also imaged as an Island,
a Lotus, and Tree, co-types of emanations from the water. It
was celestial.

Mes-ken-Mishkan-Meska—The Holy or "Hidden Shrine," the place
of transformation, interior birthplace, habitation of the child,
place of the new birth of the Sun in heaven and the burial
place for rebirth of Sun, Moon and Stars in the region of the
underworld. Mishkan was the place of purgatory and spiritual
rebirth, and Meska, founded on the tomb, was the eschatological
place of the rebirth of the mummied dead. Mes-ken, Mishkan,
Meska have the same meaning (the root of both Mes-khen and
Shekinah may be found in the Egyptian Khen, or Sken).

Messiah—The Christos, the Anointed, a divinely sent teacher or
spirit, a messenger of God. The true root of this word is the
Egyptian Mes, Meska, place of birth and rebirth, whence the generation and rebirth of a Mes-iah. The Messiahs who were
the incarnations of the Sun, were concealed, buried and arose
from the dead, and were symbolized in the rising and the setting
of the Sun. Messiahship represented a cycle, and was wholly
dependent upon the fulfilment of the cycles of time. When the
Sun was elevated above the female or the Moon, and the child
El, Aden, Aten, Adonai, Iu-em-Hept and other Sun-gods personated a Messiah, they became known as the son of the father
instead of the mother.

Metatron—King of Angels, or the Angel of the Name, so called
because he is the messenger, the revealer, or the manifestor. In
Hebrew the mystery of the Metatron was caused by his being
the Son of the Mother. The first Name came from Motherhood.
Fatherhood was secondary. Name was a word of magic power
in ancient Egyptian religion, as it is now.

Metonic cycle—A period of nineteen years, the period of eclipses.

Microcosm—The little Universe, meaning man in the image of his
creator, the macrocosm. Term used in occultism and theosophy.

Mithra—Persian Sun-God, a kind of Messiah who is expected
to return as the judge of men, and a *sin-bearing* god who atones
for the iniquities of mankind. He is represented as having a
Lion's head symbol of the sun.

Mother—A word derived from the Egyptian name of mother, Mit,
meaning the Emanator, the mouth. She was the mystical
mouth of the breath of being.

Mut-Ar—The gestator, emanator of the child.

Mysteries—"The secret ceremonies which took place during ancient
Initiations, in which the candidates were taught the origin of

things, the nature of the Soul and shown the births of worlds and systems of dramatic representations." The most solemn and occult were those which were performed in Egypt by their Hierophants. "The mysteries of cosmogony and Nature in general were personified by the priests and neophites, who enacted the parts of various gods and goddesses, repeating supposed scenes (allegories) from their respective lives. These were explained in their hidden meaning to the candidates for initiation, and incorporated into philosophical doctrine."

Mythology—Sacred truths told under the guise of fable, symbol and parable.

Nadir—Point of heaven opposite the zenith, cusp of the fourth house of the horoscope.

Nahsi—Negroes. Na is black. Su is the person, or birth. The Nahsu is one who is black born, or, in Egyptian phrase, black from the egg. "The Africans in Nubia at times attained a type of face and a sculpture of form as noble and refined as any of the white skins of all the vaunted Caucasian and Aryan races," says Gerald Massey, who continues that "the greatest difficulty in creation is the beginning, not the finishing, and to the despised black race we have at length to turn for the birth of language and the beginning of all human creations."

Narada and Asuramaya—Were two ancient mysterious figures connected with mystic astronomy, chronology and their cycles. Narada had charge of all progress and national affairs, wars and endings of wars, and bears a great resemblance to Jehovah. Dr. Kenealy compares him to Hermes, or Mercury, a prophet forever wandering around the earth, giving good counsel—an eloquent Messenger of the Gods. Asuramaya was an Atlantean, called the greatest of all astronomers. He was a mighty magician as well, and his "Atlantean Zodiacal records . . . are due to the guidance of those who first taught astronomy to mankind."

Nephilim—Giants, "Fallen Ones." Giants begotten by the sons of God and the daughters of men. Gen. vi, 1, 4. The Scriptures claim they lived before the flood. They were the celestial Giant timekeepers, the "Mighty Ones" of old, who became the "Fallen Ones" only because their timekeeping cycles were not quite true when compared with later reckonings. They were the Seven Stars of the Constellation of the Great Bear.

Nirvana—According to esoteric explanation it is the stage of absolute existence and absolute consciousness, into which the ego of a man who has reached the highest degree of perfection and holiness during life passes after the body dies. The Kingdom of ineffable peace.

Noumenon—Greek word signifying the true essential nature of Being as distinguished from illusive objects of the senses.

Nu—The celestial waters, primeval, fathomless, and boundless.

Oannes—A primeval Fish-god "Man Fish." A generic name for the Initiates of Chaldea. "The man-fish Oannes is the great

Fish, Leviathan, on which according to the Rabbins, the faithful are to sup at the day of Judgment."

Occultism—Special science of the secrets of nature and the development of psychic powers latent in man.

Occultist—An Adept in the secret sciences, but the name is very often applied to a mere student. Occultism embraces the whole range of psychological, physiological, cosmical, physical, and spiritual phenomena. It applies to a study of the Kabala, Astrology, Alchemy, and all arcane sciences.

On—City of the Sun. Heliopolis.

Ophiuchus—Constellation called the "Serpent Bearer." It is situated almost in the mid-heaven and is identical in its symbolical meaning with Hercules' triumph over the serpent, representing evil powers of darkness. The Sun passes through this constellation for a number of days at the time of its passage through Scorpio. A star of the second magnitude in Opiuchus was called by the Arabs Ras-al-Hawwa, or Ras-Alhague, the head of the serpent charmer.

Orb—Similar to aura, the distance around the planet in which its influence particularly extends.

Osiris—Greatest god of the Egyptians, Son of Celestial Fire, Primordial Matter and Infinite Space, self-existent and self-created, and a personification of the Universe. He was the "All Seeing," and the "Many Eyed." Osiris represented the Sun behind the Sun, and Isis the Moon, while their youthful son Horus was the Messiah of the Egyptians.

Ouranus—Celestial Ocean. The expanse of heaven was called the "Waters of Space." Ouranus (or Uranus) is one of the oldest of the gods, as well as a planet.

Pantheism—The doctrine that the Universe is God.

Paraclete—"Universal Fire. . . . The Paraclete or Super Solar Force (The Force of the Sun behind the Sun), Solar Force (the Force of the Sun), and Lunar Force (the Force of the Moon)."—S. E. Dudley. It is "the light of the Logos, which in energizing becomes what may be described as living, conscious electricity, of incredible voltage and hardly comparable to the form of electricity known to the physicist."—James Pryse. This is what Jesus promises that the Father will send to the Disciples in His name. "But the Advocate, the Holy Spirit whom the Father will send at my request, will teach you everything, and will bring to your memories all that I have said to you."—John xiv, 26. New Testament in Modern Speech.

Parallel—In the Zodiac, stars and planets at an equal distance from the equator (i. e., having the same degree of declination—whether north or south does not signify) are said to be in parallel of declination.

Paranatellon—A constellation lying north or south of the Zodiac, and given to one of the decans. In ancient astronomy the Paranatellons were thirty-six in number.

Pasht—Cat-mother, who in this form kept watch for the Sun, which she holds down with her paw as she bruises the head of the Serpent of Darkness. Pasht was also the She-lion and Leopard, the Lion-Leoparded of Heraldry. In Egyptian mythology she was the shorn and maneless Sun of the lower region. The Chickasaw Indians called the Panther their emblem of the Sun the Cat of God. The "name of this cat-headed goddess is Pash, and Pekh. She who gives the name to our 'Pasch, Passag, or Easter Festival'." There is a vignette of the Ritual representing the resurrection of Osiris as taking place in the presence of the Egyptian Trinity. The human form being the highest available, is required by the supreme three; and in order to represent the lower nature, or divine humanity, it is necessary to take the lower creature, whose characteristics should indicate that of the divine person represented. Of such a nature was the cat, whose eyes, varying in form like the sun with the period of the day, imaged to the Egyptians the splendor of the light. And we thus have the cat cutting off the head of the serpent of darkness in the presence of the sacred three."—M. Adams, The Book of the Master, p. 90.

Passover—Easter festival celebrated at the Vernal Equinox when the Sun crosses over into another sign of the Zodiac.

Peniel—Place where Jacob wrested with the angel. Celestially speaking it is located in the constellation Scutum Sobieski at the beginning of Sagittarius, and if this degree is well aspected in a horoscope spiritual vision or gifts develop in the native.

Pericyclosical—Polar motion.

Philo Judaeus—Famous historian and philosopher of the First Century, called the most learned Jew and surnamed The Jew. He was a descendant of the Tribe of Levi, the holy caste and an Initiate in the mysteries.

Phoenicians—Identical with the Hek-Shus, the Shepherds of Egypt, The Typhonian servants and followers of Horus. The Israelites and Phoenicians were one and the same. The Egyptian name of Phoenicia is Kefa (Khept), the North, the home of Typhon, the Great Bear, "Who came out of the North," Kefa or Phoenicia. The Phoenicians changed the language from Hamitic to Semitic.

Pistis Sophia—Oldest and best "preserved gospel of the Gnostics, an extraordinary piece of religious literature, a Gnostic fossil" belonging to the same school as the Revelation of St. John. It is called "A literary curiosity of our age." "It is genuine and ought to be as canonical as any other gospel, unfortunately it remains to this day untranslated."—H. P. Blavatsky.

Planetary spirits—Regents of planets. Primarily the rulers or governors of the planets. In Occultism the term "planetary spirit" is generally applied only to the seven highest hierarchies corresponding to the Christian archangels.

Plato—Philosopher and poet, born in Greece about 428-9 B. C. He studied thirteen years in Egypt and had the distinction of converting the "hidden mysteries into metaphysical mists."

Pleroma—"Fullness," a Gnostic term used also by St. Paul. The Divine world or the abode of the gods. Universal space divided into metaphysical *aeons*. Akasa, Sky.

Pralaya—Period of rest. Dissolution in contradistinction to Manvantara period of full activity of a planet, or the whole universe.

Precession of Equinoxes—The Equinoxes, nights equalling days in their duration are created at the places where the ecliptic and equator intersect or cross. It takes the equator 25,920 years to pass through all the signs of the Zodiac, or the pole of the equator to pass around the pole of the ecliptic. Each of these rounds measures out four degrees from the equatorial point in its ascent or descent from the pole, making an imaginary spiral winding, or every siderial year the tropics recede from the pole four degrees in each revolution from the equatorial point as the equator rounds through the Zodiacal constellations. "So ancient was this knowledge that the legends of many lands try to talk with us in that scale of knowledge and we do not understand their language—it is too large for our limit. . . . It is a science so ancient that its most hidden secrets live on in legends alone. Even those who were unable to follow the cycle to the end preserved traditions of the beginning."—Gerald Massey.

Primordial Light—The light that is born in, and through preternatural darkness or chaos, which contains the "all in all," the seven rays that become later the seven Principles in Nature.

Ptah—Father of the Fathers of the Gods. Spiritual creator of divine force. The Potter who sits at his wheel, and maker of the solar Zodiac.

Pymander, The Divine—In the Books of Hermes, that of Pymander is the most ancient, and contains an account of the Mitzraim philosophy. Pymander is called by H. P. Blavatsky "the oldest and most spiritual of the Logoi of the Western Continent, who appears to Hermes in the shape of a Fiery Dragon of 'Light, Fire and Flame'," and is called the "Thought Divine." "The name Pymander is from poimēn, a Shepherd, and anēr, genitive plural, andrōn, the Guide of Man," almost a Messiah. The Divine Pymander of Hermes is filled with information concerning the ancient mysteries of Egypt, and their initiations, giving knowledge of divine powers, man's connection with the Divine Source. The original has been greatly disfigured by Christians, Neo Platonists and the Alexandrian School, but still has enshrined within it the old Egyptian ideas and wisdom of the Hierophants. Hermes was looked upon as the embodiment of the Logos, or Manifestation of the Divine Spirit, and was said to possess "three parts of the divine philosophy of the world." He was an inspired teacher of the priests and rulers of Egypt, the Shepherd of men.

Pyramid—The Egyptian idea of a pyramid was that of a structure on a square base, with four inclining sides, each one of which should be an equilateral triangle, all meeting in a point at the top. The Egyptian pyramid eternally symbolized the creative principle of nature, illustrating also the principles of geometry, mathematics, astrology and astronomy. "Internally it was a mystic fane, in whose sombre recesses the mysteries were performed." The builders showed their astronomical knowledge, which is displayed in perfect orientation, and on this knowledge "the program of the *Mysteries* and Initiations was based: thence, the construction of the pyramids, the everlasting record and the indestructible symbol of these Mysteries and Initiations on Earth, as the courses of the stars in heaven."

Ra—Name given to the Sun in Egypt, especially signifying the sustainer of all that exists on earth, the life-giver, the "Eternal Truth," called the "Divine Essence."

Ram or Lamb Worship—The ancient worship of the Ram or Lamb became terrestrial and human and continues to this day. "It is only the lunar god and the rams and the lambs which are priapic, and it little becomes a (Christian) religion which, however unconsciously, has still adopted for its worship a god pre-eminently *Lunar*, and accentuated its choice by the selection of a lamb, whose sire is the ram, a glyph as preeminently phallic, for its most sacred symbol—to vilify the older religions for using the same symbolism."—Blavatsky, H. P.

Reincarnation—Rebirth of the soul into human body. One of the oldest beliefs in the world, taught by Jesus, but now denied by the Christians.

Rephraims—In the Scriptures were called the Giants of old who had deviated from the ways of wisdom and were therefore called rebellious. The true meaning of this is they were the Seven Great Stars of the constellation of the Great Bear that had been unable to maintain the truer time-keeping of a later period. These are the same Giants who supported the world on their backs, or built the tower that was intended to reach heaven. They were the Kabiri, the Hohgates and all other Sevens that belonged to the celestial waters.

Ruach—The spiritual soul, was represented as a descending dove, and called "The Spirit of God" or the Breath of Life of God. Earliest anointing was a consecration of puberty.

Sabean—Stellar. Sabean worship was the oldest known, beginning with the Great Mother and her Son. The mythical migration was from the Sabean to the Lunar and thence to the Solar, or from the Star and Lunar time, to the corrected Solar time.

Sanctum Sanctorum—The Holy of Holies, a symbol of the matrix of nature and of resurrection.

Scarabaeus—A lunar astrological symbol of immortality, in Egypt called Khepr, the Beetle, and made an image of a cycle of time, creating, becoming and transforming. Khepr means to become. The beetle deposits its egg in a lump of mud, which it rolls into a ball, and anciently was thought to have divine power of resurrection and self-creation. Portrayed with wings closed it was held in deep reverence as an emblem of human and universal life, resurrection transformation and metempsycho-

sis, the translating of the soul from one incarnation to another,
or the reembodiment of the soul in a human body. This term
metempsychosis seems to be generally misunderstood, or vulgarly
believed to be the rebirth into animal bodies. It is readily
explained in the Kabalistic axiom, as "A stone becomes a plant,
a plant an animal, an animal a man, a man a spirit, and a spirit
a god." The Scarab was held sacred among early Christians.
St. Ambrose, Archbishop of Milan, called Jesus "The Good
Scarab, who rolls up before him the hitherto unshapen mud of
our bodies." (Works, Paris, 1686. Authority, Samuel Sharpe.)
Also Epiphanius says of Christ, "He is a Scarabaeus of God."
The Egyptian Scarab is very familiar as an amulet. The back
of the beetle is in imitation of nature, but underneath it is
engraved to represent many different ideas.

Scutum Sobieski—Constellation near Sagittarius, sometimes called
"Coal Sack" because it is a dark space in the heavens. In this
part of the heavens shooting stars appear in the month of
November, birth-giving elements preparing new worlds.

Secret Doctrine—Esoteric teaching of antiquity.

Sekhem—The Holy Shrine, always found as the inmost room
of the temples. It was expressly connected with the Great
Mother.

Senzar—Mystery language of ancient initiated Adepts, known to
all schools throughout the world.

Sepher Jetzirah—The Book of Creation, which some Jews ascribe
to Abraham. Most famous of the Kabalistic Writings.

Seraphim—Serpent images, in the likeness of the heavenly
constellations. They are identified with the Teraphim, both
being symbols of immortality. The four sacred animals found
in the Bible, as well as in the Kabala, have profound significance
relating to the Seraphim. "In the Sepher Jetzirah it is stated,
'God engraved in the Holy Four the throne of his glory, the
Ophanim (Wheels or the World Sphere), the Seraphim, the
Sacred Animals, and the ministering angels, and from these
three (the Air, Water, and Fire or Ether) he formed his habitation.' Thus was the world made 'through three Seraphim—
Sepher, Sapher and Sipur' or 'through Number, Numbers and
Numbered.' With the astronomical key the 'sacred animals'
become the signs of the Zodiac." Blavatsky, H. P.—Secret
Doctrine, Vol. i, p. 92.

Seraphs—"Burning fiery" messengers, or the serpent gods.

Serapis—Serapis was identified with Iu-em-Hept and Aesculapius
who were represented in astrology by the planet Mercury,
and originally by Sut, or Sirius the Dog-Star. Iu-em-Hept was
thought to be a form of Serapis, the epicene or dual type of
Apis. Although called a Graeco-Egyptian God Serapis does not
belong to primitive Egyptian mythology. This worship was a
widely diffused one belonging to Christian, Jew and Gentile.
Seraph was considered by some as a compound of Sirius and
the solar Apis, type of the Sun and Sirius. Serapis, or Sarpa,
means serpent, and statues of Jesus and Serapis were repre-

sented by serpents, symbolizing divine wisdom. An enormous statue of Serapis formed from plates of different metals artificially joined together, was placed in a shrine or temple and held in great reverence. "The statue probably suggested to the Alexandrian Jew who wrote the Book of David the idea of the similarly composed image of Nebuchadnezzar's Dream."—King, The Gnostics, p. 69.

Serpent—Symbol of Spirit and emblem of Eternity. From remotest antiquity was held in veneration by every people as the embodiment of divine wisdom. The Serpent in its sloughing was an emblem of transformation, resurrection and immortality. With its tail in its mouth it represented infinitude, and with the egg in its mouth immortality and eternity. It was emblem of the Logoi, the self-born. Serapis and Jesus were both represented as a great serpent. Serpent or Solar Force is Cosmic Fire, the blind refractive force of nature, the generator or destroyer, which when understood and conquered leads to the highest spiritual development. Called the great **SNAKE** of Creative Power. See Kundalini.

Seth—Set, Sut or Typhon, asinine deity of the Syrian tribes. He was the primitive god of the Semites, and as Set-Typhon was the founder of Sabeanism.

Seven Early Gods, The—Elementary powers. "The Seven were all correlated, the seven elemental powers, with the seven elements in man; and these seven souls, or elemental parts of man, were assigned to seven creators, or gods, as considered as seven creations in mythology, each of which had its zootype, such as the red mouse, the hawk, the ape, jackal, serpent, beetle, and crocodile. Seven zootypes having been adopted to represent seven elements in external nature, these or their *equivalents* were continued to express the seven elements or souls in man."—Massey, Gerald—"Seven Souls of Man." The Seven Great Stars.

Shebti—Duplicate figure of the Egyptian dead before its transformation. It was called the second breath. The Shebti and the Ka, the image or genius, were two images placed with the dead in the Egyptian tomb.

Shiloh—"The Returning One," was called Serah, the Revealer, the Sun reborn at the equinox. The Egyptian Shiloh or Sherau was the second Horus, the adult son, the one who came with peace. In Hebrew Shiloh was called the afterbirth, typifying the adult youth. The Law-giver was to remain until Shiloh came. The ancient star-god Shu was the supporter and Law-giver of heaven until the Sun-god was reborn from the Abyss. Shiloh was the Sun-symbol of a divine messenger.

Shus-en-Har—(Hek-Shus)—Followers of Horus, belonging to the ancient Typhonian religion which embraced the entire ancient world and is perpetuated today in the worship of the Mother and the Son.

Sibylline Books—Sacred Books of the Sibyls. The original Sibylline Books were kept concealed in the Capitol at Rome, and were lost when it was destroyed by fire in 405 A. D. They were held in profound veneration and were consulted only by decree of the Senate. Cicero bears witness to their worth saying, "How often has our Senate enjoined the decemvirs to consult the books of the Sibyls," when "portentous events announced to the Romans terrible wars and disastrous sedition. On all these occasions the diviners and their auspices were in perfect accordance with the prophetic verses of the first Sibyl." —Comte de Gabalis, Dudley Edition. Dr. Kenealy considers these books were the original Apocalypse. They told of ten ages or generations of the world. The Sibyl was to live these ten generations, the number of the Sibyl was ten and there were ten keepers of the books. The Sibyl was a lunar form of the feminine Logos, which accounts for her reckoning by ten, the ten lunar months of gestation.

Siderial—Relates to the stars; measured by the apparent motion of the stars; pertaining to, designated, marked out or accompanied by a return to the same position in respect to the stars; as the Siderial revolution of a planet; a Siderial day. A Siderial year is the time which the sun takes in passing apparently from any fixed star around to the same star again, or one complete revolution of the earth in respect to a fixed point in space.

Sin—"The unatonable and unpardonable sin, for which there is neither punishment nor purification; it is inexpiable forever" is the sin against the Spirit—against the Holy Ghost. "The Persian teaching respecting the seminal soul, and the sins against it, was continued in the Gospel according to Matthew xii, 31, 32. This doctrine was adopted by the Christians with no knowledge whatever of its real foundation, nor can they explain it. No theologian has ever been able to tell the world what constitutes the sin against the Holy Ghost, 'the ghost which in the Christian scheme is identified with procreation and Begettal. · Mary was with child of the Holy Ghost.' Matthew i, 18. "Breath was the first representation of Soul or Spirit, the Seminal Source was another, and the sin against this . . . was not only unpardonable, it was destructive for eternity—the eschatological reflex of the human phase . . . which alone explains *how* the sin was unforgiven in the next world by non-restoration to life." In other words, the destroyers of the seminal soul, source of procreative power, were threatened with death by non-production hereafter, "The sin against the Spirit was *non-fructification* through corrupt manners," this was also taught by Paul, Gal. v, 21.—Authority, Gerald Massey.

Sinai—Sheni signified the region beyond the tomb and Mount Sinai was the steps of the ascent into that region attained by the gods and the souls after their resurrection from Hades. Sheni is the place where the divinity appeared on the horizon." Mount Zion (Heb.) and Shena (Eg) represented the same region beyond the tomb when the circuit in heaven had been completed. Shenah (Heb.) Shena (Eg.) denotes the place of repetition or transforming from one into another. Shennu, Hebrew Sinai, is a circle, orbit, and in Egyptian means crowds, millions, etc., typical of time, periods, and angels. It is the region of the time cycles.

Siriadic Land—Where the primeval stelae, or columns of Seth were found on which the lore and wisdom of the primeval world was transmitted by it to Hermes.

Sirius—Dog-Star. The Egyptian Sothis. Worshipped in Egypt and reverenced by occultists. It is mysteriously associated with Taht-Hermes, god of wisdom, and Mercury in another form. "Thus Sothis-Sirius had, and still has, a mystic and direct influence over the whole *living* heaven, and is connected with almost every god and goddess. It was 'Isis in the heaven' and called *Isis-Sothis*, for Isis was 'in the constellation of the dog,' as is declared on her monuments. Sirius is also Anubis, and is directly connected with the 'Pass me not;' it is moreover identical with Mithra, the Persian Mystery God, and with Horus and even Hathor called sometimes the goddess Sothis."—Alan, Leo. Sirius is connected with the Pyramid and the Initiations that took place there. A temple to Sothis-Sirius once existed within the temple of Denderah, and Sirius-Sothis is connected with almost every religion of antiquity. Sirius as Sut was the first son of the primeval Mother of the Immaculate Conception, Typhon.

Sistrum—Rattle used in the worship of Isis. The wires of the sistrum made a peculiar sound, sometimes employed in the choruses, when it was supposed to be efficacious in driving away fiends from the sanctuary. The sistrum or Seshsh, was a figure of 6, with its three wires and six ends. Seshsh represented motion and generation in its relation to the six-day period. It was sometimes ornamented with a mirror of reproduction in place of the wires. Ses, in Egyptian, is a number six and a name of breath.

Smen—Place of preparation, change and petition, home of the eight great gods, the Seven of the Great Bear and their Manifestor. The earliest deities found on the monuments were the Smen, the great gods or spirits of many races. Gods of chaos, night, darkness. "All the earliest human transactions in the world related in myth and tradition, belong to the time of the Goddess of the Seven Stars whose manifestor she was. Am-Smen was the paradise of the eight. The number eight has the numerical value of the place of Beginning out of which all came. It is a type of Infinity.

Stellium—A crowd of planets in an angle or house in a nativity. It causes stirring events according to the nature of the combination and influence.

Terrestrial—"The Sphere of Matter."—Dr. Kenealy.

Sut—Son of the primeval Mother of the first Immaculate Conception. He was a first type of Sirius the Dog-Star, and afterwards affiliated with many other gods as sons. As Sut-Har or Horus, Sut was a double manifestation of light and darkness. As Sut-Nub he was connected with the Golden Age. As Sut-

Nahsi he was the black negro god in his earliest image, the black Christ. Types of Sut followed through the Sabean period down to the Christian times, although first known as the Son of the Mother, Sut in his latest manifestation became known as the Son of the Father. In his double type he was the planet Saturn, the El of the Hebrews; and, the planet Mercury, the Messenger, both symbolizing the Divine Son.

Swastica—"Most sacred and mystic symbol of India. It is a summary in a few lines of the whole work of *creation*, or evolution. . . . Whose *genesis is as unknown* to that science (materialistic) as is that of the All-Deity itself. . . . The Swastica is found heading the religious symbols of every old nation. It is the 'Worker's Hammer' in the Chaldean *Book of Numbers*, 'the Hammer which striketh sparks from the flint' (space), those sparks becoming worlds. It is 'Thor's Hammer.' In the *Macrocosmic* work, the 'HAMMER OF CREATION,' its four arms bent at right angles, refer to the continual *motion* and revolution of the invisible Kosmos of Forces. When represented with arms turning to the left the Swastica is said to be feminine in polarity, in converse position, with arms rotating to the right the Swastica is said to be masculine. The Swastica points to the rotation of the world's axis and the equatorial belts in the cycles of Time. The two lines forming the Swastica mean spirit and Matter, the four hooks suggest the motion in the revolving cycles. Applied to the Microcosm, Man, it shews him to be a link between heaven and earth. . . . It is at one and the same time an Alchemical, Cosmogonical, Anthropological and Magical sign, with seven keys to its inner meaning. . . . It is the *Alpha* and the *Omega* of universal creative Force, evolving from pure Spirit and ending in gross Matter. It is also the key to the cycle of science, divine and human; and he who comprehends its full meaning is forever liberated from the toils of the great Illusion and Deceiver. The Light that shines from under the divine hammer, is sufficient to dissipate the darkness of any human schemes or fiction."—Blavatsky, H. P.—Secret Doctrine. So ancient and so sacred is this symbol that it is to be found everywhere. It was the sacred sign and instrument for kindling the *sacred* fires. The cross when separated from the circle becomes phallic. The "Swastica is a cross supposed to be whirling round rapidly and leaving a trail behind from the end of each of the four arms." (These ends should be circular, not straight lines.) "It indicates the spiral movement of electricity around a magnetic axis; the serpentine motion of the fiery electric life power, called Kundalini," (the serpent-fire), as it "indicates some sort of spirally moving force working in matter, moulding matter setting it in motion. Depicted as rotating from right to left, it stands for the direction of revolution of the earth in its orbit round the sun, and also for its direction of axial rotation." (Turning in the opposite direction) "it indicates the apparent direction of the Sun, Moon, and planets in their rising and setting, as seen from the earth." Alan Leo. It is looked upon as a lucky or auspicious object.

Syria—Country of the Holy Land, called "ass land" Imiri-su, in the cuneiform inscriptions; where Set, Seth, or Typhon was worshipped.

Tabu—Law respecting chastity during feminine periodicity and the sabbath of the Fast Days before appearance of the New Moon.

Taht—Egyptian Moon-god or the planet Mercury. He was the celestial scribe and the Sweet Singer of the "Book of the Dead" and symbolized the bright side of the Moon which was said to contain the essence of creative wisdom. When he was portrayed as Ibis-headed he represented the scribe of the gods and priests. As the serpent, Taht represented the first divine creative wisdom. He was the lunar Word or Logos, the "Revealer of the secret wisdom giving Truth its Splendor," the "Eternal Divine Wisdom" and the "Divine Recorder." He was lord of the Moon, reckoner of the Universe, and the Mind and Will of God. The Tat cross, sacred lunar emblem of Tat, was regarded as the highest expression of sanctity and was the final ornament placed upon the holy dead." "Tut in Egyptian means speech, utter, to be the tongue or mouth of utterance, what Taht was as the lunar Word or Logos of the gods."

Talmud—A Hebrew work in which the oral traditions are committed to writing. It was divided into two parts, the Mishna and the Gemara, the written and the unwritten law, the one open and the other hidden. It represented the two stone tablets of Testimony of Sinai. It was the oral in relation to the written law of the Pentateuch. The Jews have always insisted that two laws were delivered to Moses on Mount Sinai. One was written and the other transmitted orally to pass from generation to generation. The oral law was the key to all hidden wisdom, the written law was intended for the ignorant outsider. The interpretation was for the Initiates. The Gemara has been termed a critical expansion of the Mishna.

Targum—A translation of the sacred Scriptures in the Chaldean language. A writing in which the doctrine was hermetically concealed and transposed into an alphabet for common use and serving as an intermediate between the secret law and the general public.

Teraphim—Images made by the astrologers or diviners, called Images or Tellers of Time. They were the Jewish oracles or types of Time, and as such were used and consulted in Israel for oracular answers. They were symbols of immortality. Ancient writers assert they were "made by Astrologers under certain constellations, capable of heavenly influences whereby they were enabled to speak." They were called the tutelary gods. See Seraphim and Cherubs.

Theogony—Genesis of the gods, a branch of all non-Christian theologies which teaches the genealogy of the various deities. It is an ancient Greek word translated later as the "genealogy of the generation of Adam and the Patriarchs," the latter being all "gods and planets and Zodiacal signs."

Thigh—Constellation of the Great Bear, Thigh of the northern heavens, the Meshkin, the birthplace in heaven.

Tomb, The—Dwelling house of the dead, planned according to the Egyptian idea of life after death, was their Eternal Home. Certain rooms were sacred and therefore sealed, these were for the soul of the dead and there were reception rooms and gathering places for priests, friends and offerings. There was also a chapel with a passage and vault leading to it. The vault and the mummy passage were on one plane, and the place of prayer on another. "In the Egyptian tomb a small aperture was made opening towards the north. It was the African idea that from the north came the Breath of Life, which created the rebirth or rebegetting of the god or soul in the matrix of the tomb for its next life."—Gerald Massey. The north typified the Mother, the Genitrix, considered by men of early times as the sole progenitor.

Mummy—Memorial images of the dead; i. e. Physical body after death anointed, preserved and wrapped according to the Egyptian ritual. Placed in the tomb was the type of preservation and for transformation. Many entities were supposed to comprise man, each functioning in a separate life in the tomb with the mummy.

Khat—Physical or mummified body. The process of embalmment prevented decomposition taking place, while prayers and offerings saved the entities from a second death. Man was thought to consist of the Sahu, the Ka, the Ba, the Khoo, the Khaibit, the Sekhem and the Ren.

Sahu—Spirit-body, which was lasting and incorruptible. Man's body through prayer and ceremony was thought to be endowed with power to change it into a Sahu. Souls were said to enter into their Sahu.

Ka.—The Ka was said to come into being when the body to which it belonged was born, and it lived in the body until it died. It was the ethereal projection, the divine image or double of Eternal Being, image of the Spiritual Ego, the glorified second self as a type of the higher mortal self, the genius, depicted as being born with the mortal into this life. It was in a perfect likeness, whether as the child, the man or the woman. The Ka separated and united with the body at will, and when uniting or coming to the body says, "Thou hast let my Eternal Soul see my body." There was a special chamber for the Ka.

Ba—The Heart-Soul, most refined and ethereal in substance. The Ba could enter heaven at will. It would revisit the body in the tomb and reanimate it, and like the other entities was thought to decay if not well nourished, so food was supplied it by man or the gods. The Ba could transpose itself.

Khoo—The Khoo was the Spark of divine Fire, the Luminous Spark and dwelt in heaven as well as in man's body. It was the translucent Spirit Soul that ascended to heaven.

Khaibit—The Shadow, and regarded as a part of the human economy. It held an independent existence, and could separate from the body, visiting it at will. It was thought to be always near to or with the soul.

Sekhem—"Vital Power" usually mentioned with the Khoo and the Soul. It also had its existence in heaven.

Ren—Name, had its existence and thought to be in heaven, a parallel is found in the Christian Scriptures, I "will give him a white stone, and on the stone a new name, which no man knoweth save he that received it." Rev. ii, 17.

All these were said to be indissolubly bound together, although in primeval times they were thought to be separate and independent parts in man's mortal nature. The natural body needed to be kept from decay, for the well-being of the spiritual.

The Osiris—Assembling of the spiritual parts of man. The Osiris of a man attained spiritual bliss after the ceremonies for the dead. These spiritual parts when gathered together resembled him exactly. All offerings were accepted by the Osiris, and amulets laid upon the mummified body were accepted and made use of by the Osiris for its protection. The deceased was called the Osiris and continued to be so called until the Roman period.

Torah—The law of Moses, also a Teru, a roll of papyrus. In Egypt the Torah was the doctrine of the religion of the Ritual written in hieroglyphics and equivalent to the Hebrew Torah, the sacred scroll of the law.

Tortoise—Symbolized the base and support of celestial beings, but as with other Typhonian figures in monumental times, sank from the highest place in heaven to the lowest called Hades, or darkness, the opponent of light. The Tortoise was fabled to support the earth and sustain the Universe. Atlas stands on the back of a Tortoise as he supports the world. The Chinese looked upon the Tortoise as a symbol of longevity, "this word in Chinese meaning, is 'old age, years, a long and prosperous life, birthday, to endure forever'." Used euphemistically for "death" it represented immortality. The Chinese reason that the original hieroglyphics were invented from the figures marked on the Tortoise, that came from the celestial waters. The Tortoise was said to be mysteriously connected with writing. It was their way of establishing the fact that the Tortoise was a type of Typhon, who was the primordial type of the hieroglyph and ideograph in the heavens. The origin of music is traceable to Hermes, who slew the tortoise which supplied the shell for the first lute, whilst its muscles were cut out and made into the seven strings. The first lute is thus seen to be Typhon and its seven strings were the seven stars of the Great Bear. Tradition says that Taht, God of Night, cut out the muscles of Typhon and made them into lute strings, but Typhon cut out the eye of Taht and swallowed it. Interpreted the eye is the eye of night which the Sun swallows up and restores to light at the time of the renewal of the Moon. The lute is the constellation of the Lyre and its star Gamma, in Arabic, Sulhifat, means the Tortoise. This constellation of the Lyre, because of its slow motion around the pole, typified the tortoise. The four animals endowed with spirituality are the Tortoise, the Unicorn, the Phoenix, and the Dragon.

Trinity—The three in one in every religion and philosophy. Fire, Water and Air are the primordial cosmic trinity, as are also the "Circle, the Word, and Life. The Circle is the Thought; the diameter is the Word; and their union is Life." Mythologically and celestially the original Trinity consisted of Typhon, Sut, and Har or Horus, types repeated in the important Trinity of about 2,000 years ago. A triune God belonged to Egypt invoked by many names but ever consistent and worshipped as the Supreme. In the Ritual the Creator says, "I am Tum in the morning, Ra at noon, and Harmachi in the evening," representing dawn, noon, and sunset, "three distinct forms co-existing perpetually and co-equally in the substance of the Sun, so also did the three divine persons co-exist perpetually and co-equally in the substance of the Uncreated Light." Marsham Adams.

Typhon—Dragon of Chaos and the Abyss, imaged as the ancient Mother who gave birth to the Seven Primal Powers, Elementals, Energies, or Demons who were first heard of as warring in Chaos, and who were later changed into children of inertness for being too slow in their revolutions compared with the later Time Keepers used in the registration of Time. Typhon was the Universal Mother of Beginnings, on earth as well as heaven. She was the first form remarked in space and the first to be observed and honored when time and space were reckoned. She was the original of all the Immaculate Conceptions, Virgin and Gestator, and Goddess Mother of the constellation of the Great Bear and the Seven Stars. that were the originals of all the endless Sevens of importance of which the world is aware. She was the creator of the First Cross and Circle made in heaven and symbolized sacredly on earth. She represented Boundlessness, Infinity, and Eternity, and was called "The Living Word" and Shadai the "Almighty One." The Seven Gifts of the Holy Ghost are from her, for the Holy Ghost was the Holy Spirit, the first created by the Creator. She was the great nourisher of life, the all-conceptive, many-breasted, and the "Bringer Forth." The Dove, bird of Breath and Soul, was one of her symbols. Breath and Water as symbols were the first assigned to and perceived in Motherhood. During the sixth dynasty Typhon was known as the "Old Great One" and the "Nurse of the Gods." As the mythical Mother she was always divine, but theology degraded Typhon and brought her downfall, causing her to sink from the highest place celestially to the lowest terrestrially, called Hades, a place of evil and death. Our Bible has called her a harlot and a demon while worshipping her under other names.

Unicorn—Express symbol of Typhon, the Genitrix. The Lion and Unicorn are not only traceable to the ancient Sut-Typhon, Unicorn in front and Lion behind, but are the extant forms of the twin lions of Egypt. The single horn is the emblem of Sut-Typhon, not as the type of the Moon but of phallic power. The twin lion-gods in their lunar phase were the children of the Mother Moon who was horned in the fore part and lion-tailed behind, to symbolize the waxing and waning Moon. In heraldry the Unicorn still retains the Lion's tail.

Uraeus—Serpent emblem of Cosmic Fire worn on the forehead of the Egyptian Kings. "The soul was said to pass into the form of the Uraeus, 'the soul of the earth,' the serpentine curve traced, year by year, upon the earth along the path immediately irradiated by the vertical Sun as the senses are radiated by the supreme illumination of the soul."—Marsham Adams. Uraei—The sacred serpents, the insignia of the Royal Power.

Urim and Thummim—Two small images, one of which was emblematic of Revelation, and the other of Truth, according to Philo. To the Hebrews they were also symbolical of Light and Darkness or the rising of the Sun and the ending of the day. They are a survival from the sacerdotal worship of the Egyptians The breastplates of their priests bore the images of Truth and Justice. The solar disk was on one of these breastplates, a symbol of Atum or Ra, the Sun-god of Light and on another was the Feather, emblem of Ma, which being feminine symbolized Darkness The two Feathers of Ma are Truth and Justice. The breastplate denoted the symbolic Eye, a form of Ma, meaning speech, giving forth, a voice. The Great Judge was the Sun in Hades (Darkness) and the breastplate was the Judgment. The Thummim was an ornament in the breastplate of the ancient priests of Judaism, and both the Urim and Thummim were used as modes of divination, instruments of *Magic* and oracular communication, theurgic as well as astronomical. When the oracle answered it was said to be the Voice, which was considered the Voice of God. Josephus identifies the Urim and Thummim with the twelve jewels worn on the breastplate of the high priests, and in every jewel was a name of one of the twelve sons of Jacob, whose sons were personifications of the twelve signs of the Zodiac. The Chosen was a four-cornered gorget set in gold with twelve precious stones, symbolizing the four corners, or quarters, of heaven and the Zodiac and worn as a breastplate by the high priests of Israel. The Ephod, mentioned in close connection with the Urim and Thummim, and "the piece inserted in the void of the Ephod," was the Essen, the oracle, circle of divination, and the Essen modifies into the Chosen. The inward of the Essen is the place of the king, child of the divine house, the Ark, of a most mystical and hallowed nature, imaged in one figure, as the womb and the tomb, birth and rebirth. Paul Carus concludes that the Ephod was a pouch worn by the diviner, who hung it around his loins using a string as a girdle, which later was suspended from the shoulders and hung upon the breast. It has since been made of gold and placed upon altars, as a receptacle for the Urim and Thummim (male-female) which were regarded as objects of worship. Kabalists and occultists well know the first purpose of the Urim and Thummim, though modern Rabbins make a pretense of not knowing. They were not original with the Hebrews, only borrowed, like most of their religious rites, from the Egyptians.

"Astronomically Urim is the plural of Ur, a word for heaven. Thummim is an abbreviation of Aith, fire, and om, all; and Im, the plural termination. 'Urim Aithomim' means 'all the fires of heaven;' all the stars in the twelve signs of the Zodiac."—S. A. Mackey. In the ancient days the priests placed six of the gems on the right shoulder and six on the left shoulder, symbolizing the summer and the winter signs, Light and Darkness.

War in Heaven—"The final war in heaven was described (in the Book of Revelation and in the Bahman Yasht) between the new-born Sun and the ancient Dragon, and has been identified with the apostate dragon that fell away from the pole so far as to cease being a true guiding-star, about the time the equinoctial colure entered the sign Aries, the Lamb.

Whydah—City in Equatorial Africa, whose chief and sacred river was the Euphrates. It had its temple and "if one of the snakes, which are kept in the temple called the Serpent House and permitted to leave at will, should in its wanderings chance to touch a child, the priests immediately demanded the child of the parents to be brought up as an Initiate in the mysteries."—Sketcherley, Dahomey, p. 56. The serpent was an ideograph of Hermes or Taht. But in Whydah the Tet, as teller and fore-teller, was the snake itself, the living ideograph which was afterwards drawn as a pictograph to express the same idea.—Gerald Massey.

Word, Lost—"The word that is no word." "This word, composed of seven letters in each tongue, is found embodied in the architectural remains of every grand building in the world; from the Cyclopean remains on Easter Island (part of a continent buried under the seas nearer four million years ago than twenty thousand) down to the earliest Egyptian pyramid."—Blavatsky, H. P.—The Secret Doctrine, Vol. i, p. 439. It is found in the secret Scriptures of all great nations.

Zodiac—(Gr). Zodiac. From the word *zodion*, a diminutive of *zoon*, animal. "This word is used in a dual meaning; it may refer to the fixed and intellectual Zodiac, or to the movable and natural Zodiac. 'In astronomy,' says Science, 'it is an imaginary belt in the heavens sixteen or eighteen degrees broad, through the middle of which passes the sun's path (the ecliptic).' It contains the twelve constellations which constitute the twelve signs of the Zodiac, and from which they are named. . . . The Astrological Zodiac proper, however, is an imaginary circle passing round the earth in the plane of the ecliptic, its first point being called Aries, 0 degrees; it is divided into twelve equal parts called 'Signs of the Zodiac,' each containing thirty degrees of space, and on it is measured the right ascension of the celestial bodies. The movable or natural Zodiac is a succession of constellations forming a belt of forty-seven degrees in width, lying north and south of the ecliptic." Alan Leo. Every sign of the astrological Zodiac is an ideograph, a hieroglyph, especially important in its esoteric interpretation, which combined with the symbolism of the planets affords a key to the inner laws of nature. Esoteric astrology is deeply concerned with causation and through its symbols knowledge and understanding of the principles governing humanity in its relation to the heavens can be obtained. Briefly the signs are:

♈	Aries, the Ram.	♎	Libra, the Balance.
♉	Taurus, the Bull.	♏	Scorpio, the Scorpion.
♊	Gemini, the Twins.	♐	Sagittarius, the Archer.
♋	Cancer, the Crab.	♑	Capricorn, the Sea-goat.
♌	Leo, the Lion.	♒	Aquarius, the Man.
♍	Virgo, the Virgin.	♓	Pisces, the Fishes.

The Planets are:

♂	Mars.	♀	Venus.	☿	Mercury.
☽	The Moon.	☉	The Sun	♃	Jupiter.
♄	Saturn.	♅	Uranus.	♆	Neptune.

(☊ North Node; ☋ South Node; ⊕ Pars Fortuna.)

Mars rules Aries and Scorpio. Venus rules Taurus and Libra. Mercury rules Gemini and Virgo. The Moon rules Cancer. The Sun rules Leo. Jupiter rules Sagittarius. Saturn rules Capricorn. Uranus rules Aquarius, and Neptune rules Pisces.

	Metals	*Day*	*Color*	*Musical Notes*
Mars	Iron	Tuesday	Red	do
Venus	Copper	Friday	Indigo	la
Mercury	Mercury	Wednesday	Yellow	mi
Moon	Silver	Monday	Violet	si
Sun	Gold	Sunday	Orange	ra
Jupiter	Tin	Thursday	Blue-white	sol
Saturn	Lead	Saturday	Green	fa
Uranus	Radium	Super-solar	Electric blue	(?)
Neptune	Aluminum	Super-lunar	Deep-sea blue Aquamarine	(?)

Identifiable with these in astrological mythology are—
Aries, the Ram, with Amen-Ra, Num-Ra, and Sebek-Ra.
Taurus, the Bull, with Shu, Osiris, Khem and Ser-Apis.
Gemini, the Twins, with Sut-Horus, or Shu, and Tefnut.
Cancer, the Crab, with Khepr (Ptah), and Taht as Hermanubis.
Leo, the Lion, with the Great Mother, and the Lion-gods.
Virgo, the Virgin, with Isis.
Libra, the Scales, with Har-Makku, or Har-pi-Khart, and **the** Tortoise-God.
Scorpio, the Scorpion, with Serk, Seb and Sevekh.
Sagittarius, the Archer, with Shu and Tefnut.

Capricorn, the Sea-goat, with Sut-Anubis.
Aquarius, the Waterer, with Hapi-Mu and Menat.
Pisces, the Fishes, with Hathor, or Iusâas, and Son, and Khunsu.

Typhon can be identified with the Great Bear.
Sevekh can be identified with Draconis and Lesser Bear.
Shu   : : : : : : :—Regulus.
Horus   : : : : : :—Triangle or Pyramid.
Ra   : : : : : : :—Sun.
Sut, Taht, Aan and Aahti—Moon.
Shu   : : : : : : :—Mars.
Sut-Anup   : : : : :—Mercury.
Seb   : : : : : : :—Jupiter.
Hathor   : : : : : :—Venus.
Sevekh   : : : : : :—Saturn.
                Massey, Gerald—The Natural Genesis, ii, p. 218.

The Sun is in Aries between March 21 and April 19.
The Sun is in Taurus between April 20 and May 20.
The Sun is in Gemini between May 21 and June 20.
The Sun is in Cancer between June 21 and July 22.
The Sun is in Leo between July 23 and August 22.
The Sun is in Virgo between August 23 and September 22.
The Sun is in Libra between September 23 and October 22.
The Sun is in Scorpio between October 23 and November 21.
The Sun is in Sagittarius between November 22 and December 21.
The Sun is in Capricorn between December 22 and January 19.
The Sun is in Aquarius between January 20 and February 18.
The Sun is in Pisces between February 19 and March 20.

The Hebrew Zodiac of ten signs has a parallel in the Chinese
ten Ki or the ten celestial signs. "Ten celestial signs belonging
to the cycle of ten, called Kea, Yich, Ping, Ting, Woo, Ke, Kang,
Sin, Yin, and Kwey, are a series of characters kept quite distinct
from the twelve signs called terrestrial. The ten, however,
involved the same mythological history of prediluvian times as
the ten kings of the Chaldeans, the ten Hebrew patriarchs, the
ten in lost Atlantis, and the ten Lost Tribes. Also there was a
tenfold division of time corresponding to the nine solar months."

Zohar—The Book of "Splendor;" a Kabalistic work attributed to
Simeon Ben Iochai, in the first century of our era.

Zoroaster—Prophet of the Parsis, and sun and fire worship. "'The
sun is sometimes called in Persian *Zartushti* or *tasht-i-zer*, the
golden orb (zer, gold; tasht, a disk). And in honor of the sun,
I conceive, was named the celebrated philosopher Zerdusht,
whom the Greeks have called Zoroaster, retaining the first part
of his name, but altering the second into 'Ασγρου, equivalent in
their language to the Persian *tasht*, an orb or disk.' It may be
added, that the first Zoroaster was evidently mythical (probably
a mere name for the sun himself." The Journal of the Royal
Asiatic Society of Great Britain and Ireland. New Series,
Vol. iii, Part 1, 1867, pages 10, 11. Zoroastrian Scriptures are
of great antiquity.

INDEX